Words in Reflection

Allen Thiher

Words in Reflection

Modern Language Theory and Postmodern Fiction

The University of Chicago Press
Chicago and London

ALLEN THIHER is professor of French at the
University of Missouri. He is the author of *Céline*
and *The Cinematic Muse.*

The University of Chicago Press, Chicago 60637
The University of Chicago Press, Ltd., London

© 1984 by The University of Chicago
All rights reserved. Published 1984
Printed in the United States of America
93 92 91 90 89 88 87 86 85 84   54321

Library of Congress Cataloging in Publication Data

Thiher, Allen, 1941-
    Words in reflection.

    Includes bibliographical references and index.
    1. Fiction—20th century—History and criticism.
2. Postmodernism. 3. Languages—Philosophy. I. Title.
PN3503.T5   1984   809.3'04   84-65
ISBN 0-226-79491-1

Contents

Acknowledgments   vii

Introduction   1

1. Ludwig Wittgenstein   8
2. Martin Heidegger   35
3. Ferdinand de Saussure and Jacques Derrida   63
4. Representation   91
5. Voices   120
6. Play   156
7. Reference   188

Afterword   224

Notes   229

Index   243

For Ott and Gary

Acknowledgments

First I should like to give thanks to the Guggenheim Foundation for the generous gift of a year of time during which I began to pursue in a more organized way an inquiry that had previously been the subject of isolated and uncollected thoughts. This foundation's truly aristocratic sense of the intellectual mission is a model of its kind. And I hope that this work does justice to the confidence that the foundation and its representatives placed in me. Secondly, I acknowledge with pleasure the frequent support given to me in the intervening several years by the Research Council of the University of Missouri in Columbia. With its contribution of travel grants, a summer research fellowship, and secretarial support, the university greatly deserves thanks for making possible this kind of a long-term project. The medieval scholar had his church, the Renaissance savant depended on his prince, and we rely on their modern equivalents that continue to make possible the pursuit of knowledge.

With regard to personal acknowledgments my task is much more difficult; I am indebted to so many friends, writers, scholars, and thinkers that a listing would be nearly impossible. Rather than run the risk of committing the injustice of an omission, I prefer to offer here general thanks to all who have helped and guided me in this study by their counsel, their example, or their work. The one exception I must make is for Catherine Parke, whose patience and good advice, not to mention good humor, have contributed to the writing of this book.

Finally, as concerns scholarly acknowledgments, I recognize a certain injustice in my decision to economize on the footnotes and scholarly apparatus. But all scholars incur an intertextual indebtedness that it would be unreasonable to express. I have used hundreds of sources for this book, and it would be impossible for me to note every case where my thought coincides with or differs from that of all the scholars who have written about the various areas involved in this study. I have acknowledged the major influences on my thought in the text or in the notes. But in order to keep this work as readable as possible, I must content myself here with offering another general expression of thanks to those many scholars in many countries whose work has helped me shape and formulate my thought. I hope that this book is a testimony to the fact that scholarship is still an international undertaking and that we who participate in it are all members of a true community, without borders, dedicated to a generous intellectual and creative mission that depends on the work of many thinkers undertaking many tasks.

Introduction

I begin this study with a question brought up by the French writer Roland
Barthes:

> . . . by an initial rite the writer must first transform the "real" into a painted
> object (a framed one); after which he can unhook this object, pull it out
> of his painting, in a word, de-pict it. . . . All of this opens up a double
> problem. First of all, whence and when began this preeminence of the pic-
> torial code in literary mimesis? Why has it disappeared? Why did writers'
> dream of painting die? (*S/Z*)

Barthes's question opens up a path of inquiry into understanding the nature
of contemporary fiction and the historical changes that have accompanied its
development. In one sense the entire work that follows suggests some answers
to his question. Before turning to thought about language in the twentieth century,
and to contemporary fiction, I should like, in this introduction, to make a few
comments about the primacy of the visual in earlier thought about language and
literature. How was it, as Barthes asks, that writers once believed that their task
was to transform the real object into a painted one? Or, more precisely, how
was it that writers, throughout much of the history of Western literature, thought
in terms of a preeminently pictorial code? How did writers—neoclassical, romantic, or modernist—-come by the strange notion that they were to de-pict
something? If not from Plato, perhaps from an Enlightenment philosopher. If
they read David Hume, for example, they would have learned the following
about their craft:

> *First,* all poetry being a species of painting, approaches us nearer to the
> objects than any other species of narration, throws a stronger light on them,
> and delineates more distinctly those minute circumstances, which though
> to the historian they may seem superfluous, serve mightily to enliven
> the imagery and gratify the fancy.

In his updating of the Horatian doctrine of *ut pictura poesis,* Hume is making
literature a form of visual presence. Like Locke, like Addison, he is assuming
that the visual world is somehow translated through language into an inner visual
world. Poetry throws light upon the objects it illuminates—much as the sun
illuminates objects in the world that are in turn seized by the eye for their

1

appropriation as knowledge. Poetry is painting, much as seeing is knowledge when ideas are organized on the canvas of the mind. And both are allegorical transpositions of the world.

The neoclassical consensus, and it was a remarkable consensus, about the primacy of the visual began to have its moments of doubt as the eighteenth century progressed. I mention, as an example, Lessing's critique of the thought that would ascribe the same characteristics to the ontology of a plastic artwork and the ontology of a verbal artwork. (Or Hamann's revision to the Renaissance belief in a Golden Age when man *spoke* in images). For our purposes of exemplary moments let me invoke the figure of Goethe. Goethe, it seems to me, is the kind of exemplary figure who displaces a tradition while essentially maintaining it. For if Goethe rejected the allegorical basis of the primacy of the visual, he reformulated its primacy in terms that would underwrite romanticism and modernism, and which only today seem exhausted. Goethe's rejection of *ut pictura poesis* and its concomitant doctrine of allegory in no way rejects the primacy of the visual as the foundation for the true or essential appropriation of being. For Goethe desires to maintain the motivated, visual relationship between language and some kind of image or *Bild* that underwrites the belief in pictorial mimesis. Goethe's symbolism thus retains the neoclassical idea that art is a making visible, though Goethe construes it as a form of revelation, an *Offenbarung*, that presents an image or *Bild* of an otherwise ineffable idea (*Idee*). The image found in writing is now a unique form of expression, not one of an indefinite number of visualizations that could express allegorical concepts; but the *Bild* the writer seeks is nevertheless an iconic expression of what would be ineffable without that image.

Goethe's aphorisms have been privileged by literary history as the locus where neoclassical views of allegory are replaced by modernist views of symbol:

> Symbolism transforms appearance into an idea, the idea into an image, so that the concept in the image remains unendingly effective and unattainable and, when pronounced in all languages, remains ineffable. [749 in the Hamburg edition] Allegory transforms appearance into a concept, the concept into an image, so that the concept in the image is always limited, can be completely grasped and laid hold of and in the same movement can be spoken forth. [750 in the Hamburg edition]

It is more than a little revealing that literary history has privileged these two aphorisms in which Goethe is probably speaking about painting. One can note how easily the discussion of symbol and allegory, reduced to variant expressions of the image, can be unquestioningly applied to painting or literature—for the fundamental axiom here is again the primacy of the visual as the center of knowledge, hence for the appropriation of being that art aims for, whether this appropriation is understood as the depiction of the neoclassical universal concept or the unique expression of the romantic idea.

Goethe's form of the primacy of the visual finds direct ramifications not only in the development of poetry but also in the development of realist and modernist fiction. Iconic revelation becomes, it seems to me, the goal of most serious fiction for at least a century after Goethe; the novel becomes a search for forms of realism in which, as Goethe phrased it, "the particular represents the general, not as dream and shadows, but as the living-instantaneous disclosure of the unfathomable." Whatever scriptural form it may assume, writing becomes a search for those moments of visual revelation in which, as Goethe put it in a letter to Schiller, "symbolic objects" allow one to read the world as a great book of pictures, or perhaps as an illuminated manuscript that the genius, by his special reading ability, can bring to full vision. There is such a seductive naturalness in this use of iconic terms that we hardly stop to ask ourselves how can it be that a scriptural form could take on an iconic dimension. How can writing be literally an image? Perhaps it is only after the epistemological displacements brought about by Wittgenstein, a certain structuralism, and post-structuralism that we can see the metaphysical axioms which declare that, since language clearly does offer knowledge, and since knowledge is ultimately vision, then language must be iconic in some way.

Let me turn now to two specific examples of the kind of writing I have in mind as scriptural forms that are determined in their practice by this belief in the iconicity of language: Flaubert's *Madame Bovary,* then Virginia Woolf's *To the Lighthouse,* which for our purposes can stand metonymically for the high points of romantic as well as realist and modernist fictions. The cultural consensus at issue here is to be found in the correspondence between Goethe's formulation of symbolism as the search for image and Flaubert's belief that fiction is justified by its quest for the iconic *idée.* In this perspective one can see that it is the Goethean quest for the visual that informs the rhetorical techniques in Flaubert's novel, a work which is the point of departure for an understanding of fiction for the next two or three generations. Flaubert works logically from the visual status ascribed to writing, for if the text is to exist as image there must be a viewer who sees that image. The autonomy of the artwork demands that a viewer be permanently inscribed within the text, one who, like Berkeley's God, is always watching the image, even when the book is closed. In *Madame Bovary,* for example, at the beginning of the famous agricultural fair, the *comices agricoles,* Flaubert presents a crowded "canvas" thronged with notables, bourgeois, and peasants who have gathered for the event. The rhetoric of presentation turns on a constant attempt to add indices of explicit visualization to the description. The passage is punctuated with a series of "on voyait . . . ," "on admirait . . . ," or "on lisait . . . ," the net effect of which is to suggest a constant act of viewing. The "one" of "one could see. . ." could be taken to be the third person of objective consciousness, though such an interpretation is a quite circular way of justifying the primacy of the visual. The third person is encoded as an "objective" God-like point of view because "objective" is defined as the third person singular.

Of course, consciousness is always consciousness of someone, even if of God. Or, the "one" who constantly sees, notes, or observes in *Madame Bovary* is more like any gallery viewer, ideal or virtual, who might place himself in the viewing perspective inscribed in the text. As in certain Renaissance paintings, the viewer is inscribed within his own field of vision.

The chapter in *Madame Bovary* presenting the juxtaposition of oration and Rodolphe's first seduction of Emma is a bravura attempt to achieve what Joseph Frank called spatialized form. The spatialization of form is another aspect of the writer's attempt to transform linguistic signifiers into iconic emblems. At this macro-level of textual organization Flaubert attempts through the practice of juxtaposition to achieve the kind of iconicity that complements the rhetoric of iconicity he seeks in the use of third-person pronouns. If the sequence making up the *comices agricoles* reads like a shooting script for a film, it is not because there is anything inherently cinematic in narration. Rather this impression results from the way the text is thought out visually in terms of a perceptual field that might correspond to a visual seizure of the events. This is true not only of the vision that might be attributed to the third-person *on-*—the pronoun coded to read as a viewing presence. Flaubert also feels compelled repeatedly, to describe what his characters are seeing at any given moment before allowing them to speak or act. The Flaubertian text is in this way crissed-crossed with a network of observation posts from which "one" looks at characters looking at characters who in turn become observation points from which the world is viewed. The Flaubertian world exists only insofar as it is viewed—which brings us back to Berkeley's God and the Western metaphysics that gives ontological primacy to visual perception.

Modernists from Henry James to early Joyce took the Goethean quest for the essential image, as refracted through Flaubert's example, to be the essential goal of fiction, and in their self-consciousness they made the central theme of the great modernist works to be the epiphanic revelation of that image. Virginia Woolf's *To the Lighthouse,* for example, unfolds as the quest for the image that, in its fullness, might offer some form of plenitude in a world otherwise given over to the absurd. Woolf's novel is divided into three parts, each of which presents a different moment in the process leading to that revelation. In the first part, "The Window," Woolf presents a single day in the life of a middle-class English family on holiday, the day before a planned outing that would take them to the lighthouse. As the title of this first section, "The Window," suggests, this day is a moment of fullness, illuminated by the light that passes through the glass. The day is the luminous paradise of planned childhood excursions. The second part's title, "Time Passes," underscores a generalized fall into time. This fall is marked by the decay of the family house and by deaths recorded by an omniscient narrative voice. And finally, the third part, "The Lighthouse," offers the illumination that art grants in the form of the vision that overcomes time. Not only does the protagonist, once a boy, now the man James Ramsay, sail, after the passage of many years, to the lighthouse and complete the projected excursion; but the artist Lily Briscoe finishes at last the painting begun long ago. This painting offers the novel's final image of permanence. The pictorial revelation completes the book's iconic vision.

Reduced to this outline Woolf's *To the Lighthouse* stands forth as an exemplary modernist solution for the problem of salvation in a world bereft of either a transcendent or an immanent domain of values (the latter as found in Goethe's pantheism). Much as in the case of Proust's chance revelations of essence, Lily's completion of the painting is a kind of fortuituous iconic revelation that may or may not occur to all. As Woolf phrases it, it is one of the "little daily miracles, illuminations, matches struck unexpectedly in the dark." The visual is, as in Goethe, still the only way to appropriate true being. In Woolf's work, however, the visual gives access to the mind mirroring its own desire, not to the mind mirroring the image or essence of nature as in Goethe and most of the romantics. Nature, as Woolf puts it quite explicitly, is a broken mirror that can no longer offer an essential image.

With the Goethean mirror of nature broken, the minds of men—those other "mirrors"—must create their own vision of permanence. The idea of creation, whatever its theological sources, would seemingly suggest that "vision" is an inappropriate metaphor for writing. But the primacy of the visual is so determining that Woolf cannot abandon her metaphor, even when her rejection of the mirroring relation of essence and mind should lead her in that direction. Lily's vision comes to her from different origins, from fortuitous encounters in railway carriages and omnibuses, but it must be "perpetually remade." For collecting and "reading" the visual essences of the world is a potentially infinite task.

In terms of narrative technique Woolf's use of a multiplicity of narrative perspectives to convey a sense of multiple viewpoints is another and perhaps final step in the visualizing of narrative space. After Goethe, we can trace this visualizing in a development of the rhetoric of fiction that runs from Flaubert through Henry James and culminates in the so-called stream of consciousness technique. Flaubert's indirect discourse had already suggested a sense of a world inhabited by the atomistic self, a world that could only exist as a function of the isolated vision of the solitary subject. I would suggest that the primacy of the visual again dictated this development of narrative technique, for novelists felt increasingly obliged, in the interest of "organic totality," to find rhetorical techniques that would suggest the unity of visual perception. Increasingly language served to report a series of images as supposedly observed by a single subject. In terms of the ontological aspirations of the modernist novelist, this psychologizing created problems. For example, was the locus of iconic revelation to coincide with a character's vision or with the work taken in its totality? Were images to have an "objective" ontological status, or were they merely privileged sense data?

Proust solves some of these problems by using a first-person narrator who is ultimately not in the work but represents a transcendent point of view that allows for a coincidence between the work's revelation of essence as image and the inner space of the narrating self. Woolf, however, attempts to get around these problems by metaphorically equating the novel *To the Lighthouse* with the painting or work of vision that Lily achieves at the novel's end. Book and painting are joined as a common approach to vision. Mr. Ramsay reads his book ever more quickly as the boat approaches the lighthouse: the book must end with the arrival at the source of luminosity. The novel's final words belong, however, to the painter, to Lily, the artist who is a double for the writer within the novel and, I think, for the novelist Woolf outside the novel. Lily announces she has had her vision, and the novel ends. The novel has completed its vision in a modernist version of *ut pictura poesis*.

It is at this point in the history of literature that my study begins. In the following pages I wish to examine some of the philosophical thought about language that has made problematic our belief in the primacy of the visual; and then to consider the kinds of fiction that writers have created since modernism reached its high point in the works of Woolf and Proust. In the first three chapters I shall examine the thought of Wittgenstein, Heidegger, Saussure, and Derrida, for these thinkers strike me as the most important for an understanding of how thought about language has changed our expectations about literature. These chapters are embedded in an unfolding history of literature and, I hope, will take us from modernism to a better understanding of contemporary fiction, or what many critics now call postmodern literature.

After explicating Wittgenstein, Heidegger, Saussure, and Derrida, I discuss postmodern fiction in four chapters, each centered on an area of inquiry that the preceding chapters on language theory have suggested: representation, voice, play, and reference (the latter construed as reference to the order of the real or to history). My central proposition in this part of the study is that the writings of contemporary authors offer numerous homologies with the thought of theorists about language. An understanding of these homologies illuminates not only the practice of fiction but also the uses and limits of theory, for fiction often puts language theory to a kind of experiential test, the results of which at times threaten as much to destroy our acceptance of theory as to confirm it. The exposition of philosophical and linguistic thought that I undertake in the first three chapters finds its full justification in the way this thought is not only useful but often presupposed for an adequate reading of much contemporary fiction.

As for my choice of writers, I have necessarily been limited by my own capacities, both physical and critical. I would propose that the writers I discuss are among the most important of our time, though they are hardly all the important writers of our time. I beg the reader to bear this distinction in mind if he or she finds that some important writer seems to have been neglected. And I should hope that one of the pleasures of reading a critical study is to contribute one's own examples and to continue the experiment that the author has proposed. I might add that limits of space and time have even obliged me to omit a few of my own favorites. This study aims at a certain exemplarity, not in order to find the "essence" of postmodern fiction but to identify a number of common traits that can be called, in Wittgenstein's phrase, "family resemblances." With a sufficient number of these resemblances in hand one can then sketch out an adequate definition of what we mean today by postmodern fiction. Such a definition hardly need be all inclusive to justify its usefulness.

More than one reader is probably asking at this point why I think that postmodern literature even exists. I defer the answer provisionally, trusting that the strength of demonstration in the following pages will convince him or her that this critical and historical notion is useful; that it proposes an economical way of making some necessary distinctions between earlier and later fiction in this century; that without it we risk not understanding much of what is going on in fiction written in the past two or three decades. One can define postmodernism as tightly or as loosely as one needs for one's particular purposes. My use is rather broad, and I intend to stretch the term back to include some works written in the 1930s. Postmodern is not an attractive term, and I have looked for a better one. But all recent competitors strike me as either misleading in their connotations or really rather silly. "Late modern," as art critics are wont to say about the plastic arts, strikes me as a good compromise, and, were I writing a book stressing continuities, I might have used that term. I am, however, more concerned wi'' differences, since I think we have come to live, since approximately World ' ar II, in a different world from from the one that the modernist inhabited. Howe 'er, the reader may let Lewis Carroll be his guide to terminology in this study about language and literature: post, late, or not modernism at all, contemporary literature is on our bookshelves—at least a few bookshelves—with its challenge to understand the language we use to write it.

1. Ludwig Wittgenstein

I prefer to begin, in this first of three chapters on thinkers who have shaped our thinking about the nature of language, by considering the work of Ludwig Wittgenstein. This beginning does not precisely correspond to a chronology of the works I shall consider. Saussure's work was completed before Wittgenstein began writing, and Heidegger died some twenty years after Wittgenstein. But this study is not a history of recent theories about the nature of language. And, if the work of all three of these men is in many ways rooted in, as well as a response to, ideas about language that developed in the nineteenth century, it seems to me that Wittgenstein's first work, the *Tractatus,* can be immediately situated in the context of the development of modernism that I have outlined in the preceding introduction. In many ways Saussure's earlier founding of structural linguistics seems to be a much more contemporary undertaking, especially in its break with earlier thought about language. History is not composed merely of dates; the way in which works of thought come to create their own history can be a complex process of overlappings and regressions that constitute orderings other than mere chronology.

Wittgenstein's *Tractatus,* apparently written at least in part while its young Austrian author was in the trenches during World War I, has been one of the most influential philosophical works of the twentieth century. This influence was initially due to the reception given to the work by Austrian and English positivists after the war. Today it is also due to the kind of antilanguage mysticism that, paradoxically enough, many writers have taken from the book. But, perhaps even more paradoxically, the work's influence lies in the fact that one must understand the *Tractatus* before one can fully understand what Wittgenstein is attacking in his later writings. For Wittgenstein is unique in the history of philosophy in that his later work is a repudiation of his first work. Thus one turns to the *Tractatus Logico-Philosophicus* not only for its intrinsic interest as a seminal work in language theory—one that continues to haunt the contemporary mind— but also for a negative introduction to the later Wittgenstein of the *Philosophical Investigations.* In many respects what one might define as the transition from modernism to a postmodern style of thought can be defined as the passage from the *Tractatus* to the *Philosophical Investigations.*

Published in 1922 in German and quickly translated into English, the *Tractatus* and its representational theory of language should be viewed in large measure as a response to the nineteenth-century crisis about the status of language that was felt with particular acuity in Vienna. The Viennese intellectual circles at the turn of the century saw a revival in empiricist thought about language and undertook the development of several types of critiques of the limits of language. The *Tractatus* is an expression of both of these developments. In a postmodern perspective it represents a magnificent dead end to the development of thought about language that, using a radically empiricist metaphysics, gives total primacy to the visual. As such, the representational theory of language Wittgenstein proposes in the *Tractatus* appears as the last serious attempt to view language in much the same way that classical metaphysics did, as a mirror of the world. In the *Tractatus*, however, Wittgenstein intends, like Nietzsche before him and the Viennese positivists after him, to put an end to metaphysics. It is not one of the smaller ironies in the history of thought that this brash young man should have accomplished his goal, but almost in spite of his intention, by demonstrating the impossibility of defending the metaphysics upon which a representational view of language is based. As Virginia Woolf lamented in *To the Lighthouse*, the mirror of nature had cracked. The *Tractatus* was in one sense an attempt to patch together enough of that mirror so that we could again see the world reflected in language.

To accomplish that task, as well as to put an end to metaphysical discussion that allows language to mirror too much, Wittgenstein proposes in the introduction to the *Tractatus* that his work will demonstrate the limits of thought, or, more precisely, of language and the expression of thought:

> for in order to be able to set a limit to thought, we should have to find both sides of the limit of the thinkable (i.e. we should have to be able to think what cannot be thought). It will therefore only be in language that the limit can be set, and what lies on the other side of the limit will simply be nonsense [*Unsinn*].[1]

This introduction to the *Tractatus* already suggests a paradox about its central project, for if the task of setting a limit to thought would require that we think the unthinkable, then by analogy the task of setting a limit to what can be said requires that we say the unsayable. In short, the *Tractatus* sets out to say the ineffable, which is not the least of the charms of this antimetaphysical work of metaphysics. The desire to use language to say the ineffable suggests a kind of structural analogy with the aesthetic projects of modernist literature. This modernist side to the *Tractatus* illuminates its contradictory desire. Just as the modernist verbal artefact strives to abolish itself in favor of the ineffable image, so the *Tractatus* offers metaphysical language that will be discarded once it has led to an encounter with the limits of language: the limited mirror-image of the world.

The *Tractatus* has, of course, generated a variety of interpretations both as to its essential purport and to the particulars of its view of language. The work's cryptic style and nearly hieratic way of proffering its truths are often responsible for interpretative doubt. There is a modernist side to this style. The *Tractatus* resembles, as befits a work that intends to put an end to the history of philosophy, an eschatological form of revelation. It is a table of the laws setting forth the atemporal conditions prerequisite for language's functioning if language is to be meaningful. With appropriate Kafkaesque irony about the law, one may note that all revelations must be interpreted and that it is already an interpretation to state that Wittgenstein's book is legislatively about how, in a priori terms, language must function. This interpretation is at odds with the one Bertrand Russell formulated in his introduction to the English translation. Russell stated there that Wittgenstein "is concerned with the conditions which would have to be fulfilled by a logically perfect language."[2] That Wittgenstein himself did not agree with this interpretation was made clear when he refused to allow Russell's introduction to accompany the German edition of the *Tractatus*. Historical distance enables one today to say that it is plausible to ascribe to these oracular axioms the intention of offering an a priori description of how language—real language—*must* function if it is to mirror the world. This interpretation does not exclude a recognition that confusion about whether the book offers juridical or empirical description of language has been a rich source of the book's suggestiveness.

The *Tractatus* is concerned as much with what language cannot do as with what it can do. Wittgenstein offers not only a description of the realm of the sayable but also posits a realm for that which cannot be said. This is the realm of silence, wherein dwell art, ethics, and the mystical. And it is also plausible to claim that Wittgenstein was as much or more interested in this realm of silence as he was in determining the status of logic. In the English-speaking world he is perhaps best known for having made of logic a propositional calculus; this leads many to suppose that he was some sort of unfeeling thinker without "human" concerns. But a better knowledge of Wittgenstein makes clear that the project of defining the status of the ineffable was proposed as a defense of it, hardly as an attack on such human concerns as religion and values, about which one cannot speak.

Wittgenstein's passionate interest in art and ethics shows what a curious cultural misunderstanding it was for the *Tractatus* to be taken primarily as a work of logical positivism. There is, to be sure, a positivistic thrust to the work's claim that only statements capable of empirical verification—statements that can be *seen* to correspond to a state of affairs in the world—have meaning. It does not seem to me, however, that he ever claims, in positivistic fashion, that the process of verification is a proposition's meaning.[3] As Allan Janik and Stephen Toulmin have shown, these positivistic inclinations were characteristic of the Viennese milieu in which Wittgenstein grew up.[4] Positivism was a specifically Viennese reaction to the more general crisis about modernism that was lived with particular intensity in the last years of the Hapsburg empire. From this background, I would say that Wittgenstein shared the positivist's desire to find some form of language that was reliable, but that he did not share the positivist's faith in scientific language in this respect. Rather than a faith in logic or scientific statements, the starting point of the *Tractatus* was the anguish that Wittgenstein, like other doubtful modernists, felt before the opacity of language, before the impurity and ambiguity that language introduced into attempts to express the essential. Russell's misinterpretation of the *Tractatus* is quite understandable, since the work is very suspicious of real language. It does distrust any language that does not have the formal purity of logic. Nevertheless, in the *Tractatus* Wittgenstein wants to bring order to real language by finding a kind of minimum security: this minimum is to be secured by the limits of what language can say.[5]

In this perspective the *Tractatus* is an a priori *summa* that attempts to reduce the realm of the meaningful to a series of axioms. The title and the axiomatic presentation recall Spinoza, but I can think of another and perhaps equally apt comparison. By reducing the world to a single book, Wittgenstein has achieved the book that Mallarmé dreamed of—a single work of pure, essential language that would be an Orphic explanation of the earth. The impossible beauty of the *Tractatus* lies in the way Wittgenstein's book has in a sense realized Mallarmé's dream, for the *Tractatus* describes the essential unity of being, thought, and language in seven pure axioms that never descend to examine the practical and transitory world of real experience and real language, the world of Mallarmé's *parole brute*.[6] And Mallarmé's dream of a poetic language of pure symbolism, of pure revelation untouched by language's contingent being, unsullied by the necessities of daily usage, is another side, I think, of the same kind of reaction that led Wittgenstein to seek in logical symbolism the transparent forms of pure thought.

Mallarmé's despair over the impurity of language and Russell's distinction between a proposition's verbal form and its logical form are two sides to a crisis about language that gives full resonance to the problems Wittgenstein wished to solve in writing the *Tractatus*. The uninitiated reader who first opens the work is most likely to be struck, however, by Wittgenstein's intent to elaborate the mathematical logic that Frege and Russell, among others, had developed. It is not easy to evaluate Wittgenstein's attitude toward logic. At the outset of his *Notebooks,* written while he was working on the *Tractatus,* he declares that logic must take care of itself. In the *Tractatus* he insists that the propositions of logic are mere tautologies that say nothing about the world of empirical, contingent facts. But if these timeless, necessary propositions can say nothing, they can seemingly show much: "The fact that the propositions of logic are tautologies *shows* the formal—logical—properties of language and the world [Eigenschaften der Sprache, der Welt]" (6.12). In a world of contingent facts Wittgenstein proposes logic as a kind of visual necessity that illuminates "the scaffolding of the world" (6.12).

Wittgenstein's attitude toward logic is nonetheless ambivalent. On the one hand he seems possessed by a nearly mystical belief in the power of formal propositions to determine the formal conditions of language—and hence the world. On the other hand he denigrates logic for its incapacity to "say" anything. But perhaps the denigration here is really directed against the notion that "saying" could ever produce anything of interest. Wittgenstein himself recognized his contempt for real language and what it might say when, in the *Philosophical Investigations,* he offers the following description of what had been his attitude toward logic in the *Tractatus:*

> Thought is surrounded by a halo.—Its essence, logic, presents an order, in fact the a priori order of the world: that is, the order of *possibilities,* which must be common to both world and thought. But this order, it seems, must be *utterly simple.* It is *prior* to all experience, must run through all experience; no empirical cloudiness of uncertainty can be allowed to affect it—It must rather be of the purest crystal. But this crystal does not appear as an abstraction; but as something concrete, indeed, as the most concrete, as it were the *hardest* thing there is (*Tractatus Logico Philosophicus,* no. 5.5563).[7]

"Saying," in contrast to formal logic, can only produce empirical cloudiness, an image that again recalls Mallarmé's attitude toward the impurity of everyday language. Logic can show pure form in crystalline purity, in all its adamantine hardness, as that which will never be subject to the sullying flux of the contingent world. And whatever be the uncontested ingenuity Wittgenstein displayed in developing mathematical logic, it seems clear that underlying this development is an attitude akin to the Platonic mysticism that placed mathematics outside the realm of temporal flow and ordinary language.

Within the limits of Wittgenstein's vision of logic, his theory of language is actually quite simple. It is essentially a revised version of a theory of representation that finds its classical source in Aristotle. It is not unlikely that the final significance of the *Tractatus* will be that, by its very self-conscious impossibility, it marks the closure of the Greek metaphysics of language that has dominated Western thought. Like Aristotle's, Wittgenstein's theory of language is based on the view that language represents the order of thought, which in turn represents the order of the constituent parts of the world. In propositional terms, elementary facts, made up of simple objects in the world, are mirrored by elementary propositions in language that are made up of names. According to the visual metaphor behind the mirroring relationship, language should be transparent. Yet, "empirical cloudiness" does steal into language, and one of Wittgenstein's central tasks is to explain how opacity can find a way into language. His problem is perhaps analogous to that of the theologian who must explain how sin comes to exist in a perfect creation. Wittgenstein must also explain how language can be a deceiver and allow the existence of such aberrations as the propositions of metaphysics. One solution to this problem is simply to declare in an appropriately draconian fashion that, aside from the empty but necessary tautologies of logic, no proposition has meaning that cannot be empirically verified. Such a legislative decision does singularly reduce the scope of the problem. But like the theologian's explanation that evil is mere negation or illusion, it does little more than solve the problem by denying it.

This positivist thrust to Wittgenstein's thought should not cause one to lose sight of the way Wittgenstein fundamentally distrusted the messy stuff of language itself, especially when contrasted with the purity of logic or, perhaps more importantly, the transcendence of silence. Wittgenstein's attitude toward science is revealing in this respect: if the propositions of science seem to provide a model for meaningful discourse, if they offer a supposed example of a language without opacity, it is because they, too, have a circular, a priori purity and do not speak directly about the world. Such is the sense, for example, of Wittgenstein's way of describing Newtonian mechanics: "Thus it says nothing about the world that it allows itself to be described by Newtonian mechanics: except indeed that it does allow itself to be so described, as indeed is the case" (6.342). Opposed to the a priori rigor of scientific propositions stands ordinary language—*Umgangssprache*. It can deceive because it is subject to ambiguity: "In everyday language it very frequently happens that the same word has different modes of signification, and so belongs to different symbols—or two words that have different modes of signification are employed in propositions in what is superficially the same way" (3.323). Confusion arises because we do not note that the same sign *(Zeichen)* can refer to different symbols.

For example, in the sentence "Green is green," the meaning changes according to whether "green" is a proper noun or an adjective. This determination in turn changes the meaning of "is": the verb can be either an expression of identity or an expression of existence. This example is, I think, a rather lame choice to show how philosophical confusion might come about, but it suffices for Wittgenstein's purposes in the *Tractatus*. By establishing an opposition between sign and symbol, he can dismiss the sign—the signifier of ordinary language—and postulate the existence of an ideal-language realm in which the symbol or idealized concept would function in purely univocal terms. This postulate explains why Russell saw in the *Tractatus* only a concern for a "logically perfect language." To get around the errors caused by the polysemantic nature of real language and signs, Wittgenstein claims he needs to invent a *Zeichensprache*— a sign language governed by logical grammar—that would avoid all ambiguity (3.325). Hence the recourse to the formalization of symbolic logic: if logic forms the scaffolding of the world, logic as grammar might describe how to use a language purged of ambiguity. Such a language would be a transcription of what must be.

This project demands, however, more than the mere formalization of the rules of logical operations. It also demands that one show the conditions of possibility that would allow the reduction of language to a system of univocal symbols that would correspond to the simple constituents of the world. That the world is composed of simple constituents is of course a metaphysical assumption. This assumption justifies, in a circular way, all the theoretical considerations that demonstrate what are the conditions of possibility for language to be conceived as a univocal system of signs. If signs are to refer to only one "object," then there perforce must be simple objects to which they might refer; and if there are simple objects, then they must perforce be named by univocal signs. Wittgenstein's metaphysics and his representational theory of language are joined in an attempt to show that language must be unambiguously anchored in the world. For only if language is anchored in a transparent manner can words have single, simple meanings.

Ambiguity is one of language's sins, one aspect of a kind of ontological lack. Another aspect of this lack is the perverse way in which language often seems to refer only to language. Meanings can be expressed only in terms of other meanings; definitions can be derived only from other definitions, ad infinitum. From this viewpoint language seems to have a dubious autonomy, cut off from the world. It seems almost to hover above the world. To counter this autonomy, to anchor language solidly in the world and to offer a guarantee that meaning is more than mere verbal play, Wittgenstein declares that the world "divides into facts" (1.2). Moreover, these facts are made up of the relationships of simple objects—metaphysically necessary simple constituents that one might find analogous to Leibniz's monads. Mind must not be viewed as an arbitrary producer of meanings, since it is the world's facts that are reproduced as an image in thought: "A logical picture of facts is a thought" (3). Thought, in turn, is represented by language. Meaningful language is a representation of objects whose relations are given in *Sachverhalten*—atomistic facts—the totality of which constitute the world.

That one can give no example of these simple objects is beside the point from a logical point of view. If language is to be anchored in the world, then these simple objects must exist. They are the metaphysically simple or indissoluble objects that are not subject to further definition. To them correspond the univocal, simple names of language. With this one-to-one correspondence of names with things definitions come to an end. The dictionary may be closed forever.

Accompanying this view of language is a correspondence theory of truth. The visual still rules supreme in this theory, since the truth or falsity of elementary propositions—or the expression of the relationship of simple objects in elementary facts—can be *seen* by comparing the proposition with the world. Even the truth of complex propositions, those propositions mirroring a combination of elementary facts, is ultimately grounded in the visual, since their truth value is a function of the truth of elementary propositions. The truth tables Wittgenstein developed in the *Tractatus* give us the truth and falsity of complex propositions, but only when once we know the truth values of the elementary propositions that make them up. All in all, in the *Tractatus* Wittgenstein provides a powerful metaphysical vision of how a world without ambiguity might exist in mythic purity. Reality, thought, and language are open to common inspection. All problems of meaning have disappeared—in part by being relegated to the realm of the ineffable.

Central to the theory of language in the *Tractatus* is Wittgenstein's view of language as nomenclature. Since he (as well as Saussure) later rejects the view, it is worth stressing that this biblical perspective on language underwrites the effort Wittgenstein made in the *Tractatus* to guarantee the determinacy of being. Language must be made up of simple names, since "The requirement that simple signs be possible is the requirement that sense be determinate" (3.23). The a priori demand for a univocal correspondence between language and the constituents of reality brings up in addition the problem of how words can represent these postulated constituents. To answer this question, which is a query about the ontological status of language as well as a demand for an explanation of how language functions, Wittgenstein offers us another variation of the notion that language functions visually, that language is a kind of image. (At this point I might also add that Wittgenstein's view of language as *Bild* seems more than a little homologous to the modernist vision of language as a form of partially motivated image.)

Like Locke, Wittgenstein knows that the relation between what he calls sign and symbol is arbitrary, but this relationship is not the locus of the picturing relation. For Wittgenstein the proposition is the picture, a *Bild* representing a state of affairs. A proposition is a picture by virtue of possessing the same logical form as the atomistic fact (2.18). Representation is thus achieved by a formal iconicity whereby language takes on the form of what is represented in the world. However, Wittgenstein's use of the term "representation" is not always clear, and in other passages *Bild* really seems to mean a form of pictorial representation. In any case it is clear that any theory that attributes visual and/or spatial qualities to language raises serious interpretive difficulties. Various interpreters have offered a range of possibilities about what Wittgenstein meant by "image," ranging from analogies with models used by physics to a quite literal iconic interpretation. The variety of analogies Wittgenstein offers in his *Notebooks* does not simplify the issue; there he was intrigued by courtroom maquettes for representing automobile accidents, hieroglyphs, and Maxwell's projective models. All these possibilities probably point to the simple fact that Wittgenstein was not fully certain what he meant when he said language could offer an *abbildende Beziehung*, literally a copying relationship (2.1514). These possibilities also underscore the difficulties any theory faces when it attempts to put representation at the heart of its ontology of language. Representation seems to carry with it a range of visual analogies that inevitably reduces language to a kind of colorless painting.

To return to an earlier remark, however, I should like to stress how much Wittgenstein's metaphysics overlaps the modernist view of language; both wish in some sense to spatialize language and thus make it apprehensible in visual terms. Whatever be the exact purport of the notion of *Bild,* in Wittgenstein or Goethe, this choice of terminology, even if taken metaphorically, reveals a nostalgia for the directness of revelation that vision can supposedly grant. Wittgenstein's theory of truth again appeals to the primacy of the visual, for truth is a kind of pictorial revelation in which one sees if a proposition's *Bild* exists in a state of analogy wth the world. This kind of iconic theory of truth also comes into play, as we shall see, when a Heidegger attempts to revise the correspondence theory of truth by making it subordinate to the idea of truth being a form of unconcealment. Heidegger accepts, in part at least, the implications underlying such a visual theory and attempts to think them through to their full conclusion: truth is simply a making seen.

Whatever the basic problems involved in the theory of language the *Tractatus* proposes, one should not underestimate the work's continuing appeal, anymore than one should suppose that modernist aesthetics no longer works a continuous seduction on our imagination. Since the metaphysics of representation and the primacy of the visual have hardly disappeared from the cultural repository of our imaginative possibilities, what could be more alluring than a work like the *Tractatus* that both eliminates opacity from language and promises us, at least theoretically, the possibility of an exhaustive knowledge of the world. And which, moreover, in a way that can be both a cause for elation and despair, vouchsafes a transcendent realm of silence for art, ethics, and the mystical.

The realm of silence found in the *Tractatus* has a resolutely contemporary aspect to it, for silence has become one of the more recurrent postmodern metaphors. Related to this seemingly transcendental realm is Wittgenstein's exclusion of the knowing self from the world. No self need be presupposed for propositions to function:

> It is clear, however, that "*A* believes that *p,*" "*A* has the thought *p,*" and "*A* says *p*" are of the form "*p* says *p*": and this does not involve a correlation of a fact with an object, but rather the correlation of facts by means of the correlation of their objects. (5.542)

The logician or Samuel Beckett may point out that this formulation eliminates the aporia of infinite regression when an assertion is attributed to a subject (of the sort "I know that I know that I know" ad infinitum). But what interests us more is that the knowing self is in effect excluded from language and hence from being known. The knowing self is a transcendental eye that sees its world but cannot see itself seeing. Therefore, no metaphysical self is to be found in the world. Pursuing the analogy with the eye and its visual field, Wittgenstein states, "The subject does not belong to the world: rather, it is a limit of the world" (5.632). Wittgenstein's visual analogy comparing the subject to the eye that delimits the field of vision gives a kind of extreme formulation of the primacy of the visual; and it does so by giving ambivalent affirmation to the kind of solipsism that haunts the contemporary mind.

According to the Wittgenstein who was struggling with these issues in his *Notebooks,* solipsism is justified, for its ultimate implications would coincide with the demands of realism:

This is the way I have travelled: Idealism singles men out from the world as unique, solipsism singles me alone out, and at last I see that I too belong with the rest of the world, and so on the one side *nothing* is left over, and on the other side, as unique, *the world.* In this way idealism leads to realism if it is strictly thought out.[8]

But as the *Tractatus* shows, this "thinking out" is commanded by the visual metaphor that equates the eye with the self, so that "The I of solipsism shrinks to an extensionless point, and there remains the reality that is coordinated with it" (5.64).

The tension between the idea that the "world is my world" (5.641) and the idea that language is anchored in the world is not resolved in the *Tractatus.* Nor is it easy to see how men can use language to communicate if the equation of world, thought, and language entails that my language is my world. Or as Wittgenstein phrases it in one of his most seductive aphorisms: "The limits of my language are the limits of my world" (5.6). Pursuing this line of thought, one finds it difficult to see why one should not reverse the argument expressed in the *Notebooks* and declare that, on the one hand, there is only the self and its language, and that, on the other side of these idiolects, there is nothing. In any case, with this twist the *Tractatus* moves far away from positivism to open up on a metaphysical void of which Wittgenstein was quite conscious.

The final paradox about this book is that its author thought it to be a "metaphysical ladder" that the reader, once he had climbed it, should discard as nonsense. The book's concluding aphorism, perhaps the most famous in modern thought, should then be taken as a self-destructing statement that, acccording to one's disposition, leaves us with a world of meaningful empirical propositions or a realm of more authentic concerns:

What we cannot speak about we must consign to silence. [Wovon man nicht sprechen kann, darüber muss man schweigen.] (7)

Wittgenstein himself did put silence into practice for some time. But, with great honesty and courage, he came to realize that the *Tractatus* had to be done again. The result of that self-critique is to be found throughout his various later writings, especially in the *Philosophical Investigations.* To turn from the *Tractatus* to Wittgenstein's later work is, in effect, to turn from one of the most original and rigorous expositions of a representational view of language to a systematic critique of such a representational point of view. Perhaps "systematic" is a bit misleading, since the goal of Wittgenstein's second body of works is not to be systematic in themselves. Rather, Wittgenstein's intent is to destroy the very idea that there can be a systematic view of language, especially the kind of system proposed by the *Tractatus*. In brief, these later works offer a series of insights that attempt to dismantle—perhaps one might prefer "deconstruct"—those metaphysical views about language that give rise to those errors that are codified in (or as) traditional philosophy. Common to both the *Tractatus* and the *Philosophical Investigations* is the desire to put an end to metaphysics.

Wittgenstein's second philosophy, if such an expression is permissible, did not suddenly appear on the cultural scene in the way that the *Tractatus* did. His second body of thought was slowly elaborated after he returned to Cambridge and after, among other experiences, he had been a teacher in an elementary school in Austria. His experience with children and how they learned language became of fundamental importance to his thought. His later thought was initially disseminated by his teaching and conversations in Cambridge throughout the thirties and forties as he wrote and rewrote drafts of various projects. Such subsequently published manuscripts as *The Blue and the Brown Books, The Philosophical Grammar,* or *Zettel* show how laboriously he worked over his ideas as he sought to overcome the *Tractatus* and its metaphysics; whereas the smaller collections of aphoristic musings such as *Remarks on Colour* or the masterful *On Certainty* suggest the wide range of topics that his thought covered during these years. In their totality these works have quite arguably provoked more original thinking in such varied fields as the foundations of mathematics, philosophy of science, or language theory than any other body of philosophical work in the twentieth century. At least such is the case in the Anglo–Saxon world and, to a lesser extent, in the German world (where the Wittgenstein of the *Tractatus* often appears better known than the later Wittgenstein). It is hard to estimate Wittgenstein's influence in the Latin world, though recent work in France suggests that Wittgenstein is rapidly becoming known there as well.[9]

The first statement one must make when attempting to offer an exposition of Wittgenstein's later work is that any overly systematic presentation must be in a sense misleading. The purpose of the repetitive pages of minute analysis and questioning in that work is to examine one concrete case of language use after another in order to see what the initial errors of usage are that give rise to the subsequent errors that become the basis for philosophical systems. This strategy is grounded in the refusal to offer any systematizing that might be taken to characterize the "essence" of language. Yet, these investigations do offer a series of views about language, what we can call a series of heuristic axioms, that cumulatively constitute a theory of language. Taking as his first axiom that language has no essence, Wittgenstein insists from the start that no unifying trait or principle underlies all manifestations of language use. One can scarcely underestimate the importance of this axiom, since it justifies the techniques of analysis that constitute one of the most radically antimetaphysical visions in the history of Western thought. Indeed, I would argue that this emphatic denial of essence heralds as profound a change in twentieth-century thought as did the Cartesian revolution in the seventeenth century.

This rejection of essence is clearly set forth in the early *Blue Book*.[10] In this work Wittgenstein speaks of our "craving for generality" as the "tendency to look for something in common to all the entities which we commonly subsume under a general term" (p. 17). Problems of analysis arise because we approach language with "contempt for what seems to be less than the general case" (p. 19). If we look, however, at the real use of ordinary language, we find that "there is not one definite class of features which characterize all cases" of using a given word (p. 19). In the *Tractatus* Wittgenstein had attempted to draw the boundaries of language as narrowly as possible. He had wanted to find the essence of language, as it were, in the conditions of possibility of the pure proposition. Such a project had necessarily entailed his ignoring real language. By the time he wrote the *Blue Book* Wittgenstein had reversed himself totally, and when dealing with particular instances of real language usage, such as the meanings of the verb, "to wish," he was willing to pursue the endless variations of use that can constitute the meaning of a single word. Multiplicity of meanings is inherent in actual usage: "If . . . you wish to give a definition of wishing, i.e., to draw a sharp boundary, then you are free to draw it as you like; and this boundary will never entirely coincide with the actual usage, as this usage has no sharp boundary" (p. 19). Language has no essence, and thus no essential feature can be attributed to any given word. We are free to draw up definitions as the occasion and our purposes require. But we must not deceive ourselves by taking our definitions to be "complete," and hence as embodying a form of essence, the discriminating universal found in every application of the word.

If no word embodies an essence, if every word can be defined as sharply or as loosely as one needs, then how does one define that central word "language"? One might well ask at this point what kind of truth or generalizations can be offered about that series of phenomena we call language. If language is a series of sui generis manifestations that one can define arbitrarily, what kind of knowledge can we have of language? Or as Wittgenstein's adversary charges in one of the dialogues that Wittgenstein creates in the *Investigations:* "So you let yourself off the very part of the investigation that once gave you yourself most headache, the part about the *general form of propositions* and of language" (no. 65). In the later works Wittgenstein replies to this accusation by using the double-edged metaphor of games to describe and define language. First, to show what he means by games, Wittgenstein describes them as a series of variegated activities that share no single, essential feature but that can be grouped together in terms of their family resemblances or overlapping traits. The notion of family resemblances allows one in turn to apply the notion of games to language, for such a description of games suggests that they afford a singularly useful metaphor for describing all those various activities we mean by the word "language."

The notion of family resemblances bears a great deal of weight in making the notion of "language games" a plausible one. For the metaphor of family resemblances functions to describe how we can use generic words such as "language" or "games" to speak about the multiple specific things that have no essential commonality but that we speak of with a single word. To "see" these family resemblances that characterize all we call language, Wittgenstein asks us to look at what we call games:

> For if you look at them you will not see something that is common to *all*, but similarities, relationships, and a whole series of them at that. To repeat: don't think, but look!—Look for example at board-games, with their multifarious relationships. Now pass to card-games; here you find many correspondences with the first group, but many common features drop out, and others appear. When we pass next to ball-games, much that is common is retained, but much is lost.—Are they all 'amusing'? Compare chess with draughts and crosses. Or is there always winning and losing, or competition between players? Think of patience. In ball games there is winning and losing; but when a child throws his ball at the wall and catches it again, this feature has disappeared.

Which all leads to the following conclusion about family resemblance: "we see a complicated network of similarities overlapping and criss-crossing; sometimes overall similarities, sometimes similarities of detail" (no. 66). Wittgenstein wants to displace the notion of essence or universal trait with this concept of similarities that make up family resemblances. We identify commonality not on the basis of a single feature, but rather in the same way that we identify common identity in a family when, looking at a family gathered together or present in a family photo, we note a number of common features. No single member embodies all the traits, and yet we know that any given member of the family is part of the household. In the same way the series of similarities and nonexclusive features shared to various degrees by various games make up the family resemblances that characterize what we mean when we use the word "game."

Wittgenstein has, as several of his critics have noted, proposed a way of getting around the idealist-nominalist antinomy with regard to the status of universals. There is no "idea" of game in some Platonic heaven, nor is there some abstract concept of game that our minds have garnered from multiple examinations of sense data. What we call games—or language—can be defined with a great deal of latitude. Our definitions will change as our needs change, or as new games or languages evolve during the course of our history. This refusal of essence means that language can be defined by very flexible criteria, though, I hasten to add, it is not immediately apparent why the notion of family resemblances, as exemplified by all that one calls games, should lead to the conclusion that language is a series of games or *Sprachspiele*. Wittgenstein does use other metaphors to describe language; he compares it to tools and to the great variety of things we can mean by speaking of tools. But it is clear that games are the privileged metaphor for Wittgenstein, one that he uses throughout all his later writings.

The concept of play is a key concept for much contemporary thought; but it does not appear that Wittgenstein was interested in ludic activity as a kind of general explanation of culture, as were such theoreticians as Johan Huizinga or Roger Callois.[11] Rather, one might say that the play metaphor functions as another heuristic axiom for Wittgenstein, and in this respect it overlaps the formulations of other philosophers, anthropologists, and, as we shall see, novelists. And in terms of "family resemblances" it is striking that all three thinkers to be considered here resorted to ludic or play metaphors, especially chess and draughts, to talk about language. In the *Investigations*, when asked what a word is, Wittgenstein's answer is to say that the question is analogous to asking what a chess piece is (no. 108). Saussure had already used the analogy with chess to explain the nature of the linguistic system. And Heidegger came to use an analogy with draughts to offer an example of the autonomy of language. The comparison with chess in particular and ludic activity in general is a way of describing the autonomy of language that illustrates that it is a rule-bound activity that lies beyond the competence of any single speaker to alter. The recourse to ludic metaphors represents, throughout our cultural space, an attempt to rethink language in some way that does not make of the individual subject the primary locus for linguistic activity. These ideas will become clear, I hope, in the pages that follow.

The game metaphor and the attendant investigations into the following of rules and the criteria for the correct following of rules permeate Wittgenstein's later thought. There is, of course, more to a game than merely following rules. A broader, anthropological importance of the game metaphor is implicit in Wittgenstein's answer to his interlocutor in the *Investigations* when his adversary wants to know how many kinds of sentences there are. To which Wittgenstein replies that there are countless kinds. There are no fixed types, set once and for all, since new language games come into existence as others become obsolete and are forgotten: "Here the term 'language-*game*' is meant to bring into prominence the fact that the *speaking* of language is part of an activity, or of a form of life [*Lebensform*]" (no. 23). Wittgenstein seems to be making an anthropological statement to the effect that language, much like play, is a natural activity, embedded in our human history of being in the world. Language is enmeshed in all our activities, since language is constitutive of the sense of the world we live in.

Of course the game metaphor also stresses the rule-bound side of language. It was probably this side of game activity that impressed the metaphor upon Wittgenstein, as is suggested in the early *Philosophical Grammar* where he states that he is "considering language from the standpoint of play according to strict rules [*nach festen Regeln.*]"[12] Like most games, language is bound (usually) by rules, but following rules is only one, and not necessarily the most interesting, aspect of a game. As Wittgenstein later noted, rules may determine how far you can hit the ball in a tennis match, but not how high. Some aspects of the game are determined by rules; others are not.

Perhaps the most important aspect of the game metaphor is that it places language in public sight. The individual or inner subject cannot be the locus of meaning in language, for all the rules of a game must be a matter of common knowledge and publicly verifiable. Any appeal about what language may or may not mean, any question about the grammar of a given language game, is a matter of public perusal. In a sense there are absolutes in Wittgenstein's later philosophy, for if grammar is a convention established as part of the history of a given society's life form, the grammar of language games is nonetheless the final and absolute arbiter of disputes about meaning. The rules of the game exist publicly for all, and no one can deny them without ceasing to play the game, that is to say, without speaking nonsense. The import of such an absolute for modernist aesthetics would seem to be that the expression of the ineffable is an impossibility. Indeed, it is difficult to say what one might mean by the ineffable, since to say it would make it conform to the public grammar of language. The ineffable is truly the ineffable.

James Ramsay may have dreamed in *To The Lighthouse* of turning his private images into a secret language, but the force of Wittgenstein's analysis of the public nature of meaning would condemn that language to remain forever secret. Images may or may not accompany language as we speak it; but these have no influence on the way language works in the world. Wittgenstein's arguments against the possibility of a private language are motivated by his desire to show that what might take place in our "inner" self can have no bearing on the way language exists as a public and, in a game sense, absolute articulation of the world we share. With or without inner referents, a private language is an impossibility, for there would be no criteria for what this language might mean, either for the subject speaking it or anyone else. A private language might be seen to be as impossible as a private game, in that, if the rules of the game are not known by all, then none—including its inventor—can play it. Like the child who makes up the rules as he goes along in order to assure his chances for winning, the inventor of a private language cannot be given much hearing by his comrades. Moreover, insofar as modernist aesthetics made claims for the invention of private languages, for the expression of the ineffable inner world, it can be said that Wittgenstein's later thought is antimodernist, and such anti-modernism is no small component of all that one designates by postmodern thought today. With the game metaphor Wittgenstein at once severs language from images and from its relation to the private self.

The ludic metaphor underscores the public nature of language. Consonant with the notion of family resemblances, it also allows Wittgenstein to stress the indefinite number of games—of types of language use—that go to make up what we call language. There is something intoxicating about the plurality of games that Wittgenstein sees in the world and the freedom that this plurality offers one in defining the way language works. All the problems of thought seem to lie there before us, ready to be solved, if we are only attentive to the way we speak about them. The world seems no longer to contain hidden depths that language once could not reach. All lies on the surface, open to our inspection.

Yet the surface seems to be made up of infinite extension, and complexity has entered the world as its horizontal dimension. The indefinite number of language games entails an indefinite number of areas of investigation. This view of complexity can create great difficulty for the reader who wants some kind of delimiting principle to operate, since Wittgenstein's work often appears to mimic the complexity of language itself. Every verb Wittgenstein examines in these untidy investigations can enter into an indefinite number of games, the rules for which he elaborates by examining how the games are played. By describing the grammar of words, especially such "mental" verbs as to understand, to intend, to mean, to know, to believe, or to feel, Wittgenstein intends to lay bare those errors that have given rise to philosophical doctrines. The principle of the expansiveness of language and the indefinite number of games it can include is another heuristic axiom. Directed against philosophical thought that would privilege a few key meanings, this principle allows Wittgenstein to account for the wide play of meaning in language but also for the arbitrary and yet publicly verifiable ways we can frame definitions; and it accounts for the inexhaustible and often overlapping taxonomies that language proposes.

Such a view of the expansiveness of language could, of course, induce a mood of despair in anyone who was looking for a way to survey the totality of language. With reference to such a mood Austin jocularly remarked that one should not give up so easily in listing the uses of language, since, even if there were ten thousand of them, this would be "no larger than the number of species of beetles that entomologists have taken pains to list."[13] But this witticism misses the point, even if a list of ten thousand kinds of language use might seem adequate for most of our needs. (Actually a small dictionary, it seems to me, suggests many more thousand of usages than that.) In Wittgenstein's view the open-ended nature of language must be taken as an axiom that accounts for the changes that language constantly undergoes. Language changes as rapidly as does the world; it is as complex as the world, for our human world only exists as it is informed by language.

This relationship of language and the world may sound as if it is not too far from the view proposed by the *Tractatus,* and in one sense it is not. Wittgenstein's later work has, however, reversed the ontology of the earlier work. In the later work it is no longer the world that is mirrored by language. Language no longer performs a visual function. According to the later work, language articulates the space of all that we know as world. In the *Investigations* language is not in any respect a representation of the world, or a representation of thought that represents the constituent elements of the world. In this sense language can no longer be considered to be a form of nomenclature, a claim Wittgenstein elaborates at length at the beginning of the *Investigations*. In a rare instance of naming his philosophical opponent, Wittgenstein discusses there the Augustinian view of language as essentially naming. The institution of nomenclature is only one language game among many and a primitive game at that, as Wittgenstein observes. Children often play the game of naming when they are learning language, which might be one reason for the privileged role naming has often been given in explaining the way language functions.

Wittgenstein's experience as a schoolteacher undoubtedly taught him that asking how one learns a particular language game can give insight into the criteria for a correct understanding of the game's grammar. In teaching the names of objects, for instance, the teacher will often use an ostensive definition ("This is a . . . ") and point to the object in question. Though Wittgenstein recognizes that ostensive definitions are often a way into language, he also labors to show that they cannot be considered to ground language in a world that is beyond language. An understanding of the ostensive definition already presupposes a significant mastery of a good bit of language, of several different language games, which allows the child to make sense of the definition and how it functions within language. If one points to an object and says that it is a pencil, the child must already know, for example, that one is playing a naming game, since the pointing might have multiple meanings, or no meaning. The child must be aware of many conventions so as to understand that the teacher is not pointing at the shape, the color, the weight, the texture, the position—as well as understand what pointing means. Conversely, the question "What is X?" presupposes that the speaker disposes of a linguistic space—a space in his world—in which to order the newly acquired word or language function.

The thrust of many of Wittgenstein's demonstrations, as in the case with his commentaries on ostensive definitions, is to show that language games presuppose an organized linguistic space in which words and expressions function in order to be meaningful. In his first writings on language games, and later in *On Certainty,* he uses the word "system" to suggest how these games organize the space of meaning. But at the time he was working on the *Philosophical Investigations* the notion of system may well have appeared to suggest a too narrowly defined space, one whose limits should be traced with greater precision than he thought possible or desirable. In the *Philosophical Grammar* we see him working toward a definition of meaning that shows that the autonomous space of language can be encountered only from within language itself. Meaning is organized within the space of language itself. In that work Wittgenstein expresses this idea by stating that "the place of a word in its grammar is its meaning [der Ort eines Worts in der Grammatik ist seine Bedeutung].[14] This place can be shown by an explanation of a word's meaning, which in turn situates the use of the word

("Die Erklärung der Bedeutung erklärt den Gebrauch des Wortes" [p. 59]). Wittgenstein makes these formulations even more flexible in the *Investigations:* "For a *large* class of cases—though not for all—in which we employ the word 'meaning' it can be defined thus: the meaning of a word is its use in the language" (no. 43). Whatever influence William James may have had on Wittgenstein, it would be a mistake to see in this definition of meaning a pragmatist viewpoint. Rather, he is attacking any theory that would find for language some locus for meaning other than language itself, whether the theory is based on behavioral readings of language, idealist metaphysics, or logical atomistic distinctions of propositions and their logical form.

Wittgenstein's nearly obsessive attacks on the myths involving mental activity all aim to show that language and what we do with it are in a public space that needs no inner self or private subject to underwrite it. Let me give an example of my own to offer a sample of the kind of analysis Wittgenstein undertakes in this respect. Every reader will recall the famous scene in the Western novel *The Virginian,* in which, in answer to an unspeakable epithet that a villain has said to him, the laconic hero says, "When you call me that, smile." Such a response is a common language game, and the novel's narrator comments on it by calling on the metaphysics of traditional language theory: "So I perceived a new example of the letter that means nothing unless the spirit gives it life."[15] This comment is a good example of how metaphysics permeates everyday language, for the comment is, in fact, either false or superfluous. The Virginian has perfectly well understood the vile words; and his asking for a smile is in effect a request for a visible gesture that will change the context in which the words were uttered. The change of public context will change the words' meaning, which shows that meaning takes place in the world, not in any inner or spiritual domain. A smile would of course change the language game from that of insulting to one of teasing or mockery, language games for which one is usually not shot. The narrator, as a good metaphysician, would see the villain's inner self to be the true locus of meaning, and his insult to be a mere exterior expression of that inner realm. But smiles that act as semantic gestures are in the public space of which language is, in one sense, constitutive, for this is the only space in which meaning takes place. In short, as Wittgenstein puts it in a pithy phrase, "it would be stupid to call meaning a 'mental activity', because that would encourage a false picture of the function of the word" (*Zettel,* no. 20).

In the part of his investigations dealing with meaning, Wittgenstein's heuristic axiom is that, within a given context, the rules of grammar can account for all meaning. Every language game has a set of rules that, when framed much like a hypothesis by the observer, can account for that linguistic activity. The metaphysical self can simply be discarded as an explanatory principle. For example, to explain what we mean by meaning in the case of ambiguity it is useless to invoke the intention of a mind that somehow adds the "right" meaning to the ambiguous word:

If I say "Mr. Scot is not a Scot," I mean the first "Scot" as a proper name, the second one as a common name. Then do different things have to go on in my mind at the first and second "Scot"? (Assuming I am not uttering the sentence "parrot-wise.")—Try to mean the first "Scot" as a common name and the second one as a proper name.—How is it done? When *I* do it, I blink with the effort as I try to parade the right meanings before my mind in saying the words.—But do I parade the meanings of the words before my mind when I make the ordinary use of them?

By trying to discover wherein lies the "occult character" of mental processes, Wittgenstein comes to the conclusion here that it lies in misinterpretations:

When I say the sentence with this exchange of meanings I feel that its sense disintegrates.—Well, *I* feel it, but the person I am saying it to does not. So what harm is done?—"But the point is, when one utters the sentence in the usual way something *else*, quite definite, takes place."—What takes place is *not* this 'parade of the meanings before one's mind' ['Vorführen der Bedeutung' vor sich]. (*Philosophical Investigations*, Part II, p. 176e)

All sorts of things *may* of course go on in our minds when we speak. I may have various images; the word "green" may suggest my grandmother's garden; or the final syllable of "Guermante" may evoke the idea of the French aristocracy for me. But none of this is necessary for language to have meaning. My private world is indeed my private world, in Wittgenstein's view; and language is a totally public space, embedded in our social ways of being.[16]

If language lies so totally in the open to us, it might appear then that there could be little ground for the confusions known as philosophy. But, just as the *Tractatus* proposed a principle of error in language's ambiguity, the *Investigations* also offer a principle of confusion: "We remain unconscious of the prodigious diversity of all the everyday language-games because the clothing of our language makes everything alike" (Part II, p. 224e). Confusion arises because individual elements—let us say "words" for convenience—can be utilized in different games and, in so being used, change their function while they keep the same material form.

For this reason Wittgenstein frequently proposes analysis of how we confuse the proper ways of combining words in different language games:

I can know what someone else is thinking, not what I am thinking.
It is correct to say "I know what you are thinking," and wrong to say "I know what I am thinking."
(A whole cloud of philosophy condensed into a drop of grammar.)
(*Philosophical Investigations*, Part II, p. 224e)

"I know" in each instance appears to be the same words (a linguistic unit that one can call a fixed syntagm), but in Wittgenstein's perspective each instance of use would occur within a different language game. In the first instance the words occur within a normal language game for which the rules can be described. In this case one can also know when the rules are being broken. But in the second instance of use there is a confusion, since one is attempting to use "I know" as if one were talking about someone else. One is attempting to use "I know" as if one were still playing the first language game, or saying that "I know" what someone else is thinking. What "I" am thinking, however, is not an object of "my" knowledge.

This misleading analogy—and much of Wittgenstein's analysis turns on misleading analogies that occur when we confuse language games—causes one to use "I know" in a context where it makes no sense. Our linguistic space is so organized that there are no rules of criteria for playing the game "I know what I am thinking" in any normal context. What "I" thinks is not a matter of knowing at all. Moreover, once this misleading analogy has been allowed, it suffices to make merely one more deductive step for the "I" to proclaim that it is privy to private knowledge, to an inner metaphysical realm that no one in the exterior world can know. My private world may be private, but my relation to it is in no sense that of the knower to the known.

Grammatical confusion, or not looking at what the clothes cover, gives rise in this way to a belief in the metaphysical self and creates a host of epistemological problems that, in Wittgenstein's view, will simply disappear once one sees how language really functions. It is difficult to describe the world we will inhabit once Wittgenstein's analysis has had its way. It might be argued that if we will no longer be locked within the Cartesian self, whatever there is about us that might be beyond language will be more private than any solipsist's dream ever was.[17] Moreover, it seems clear that this view that language articulates what we call the world (and language here includes those scientific languages that order new regions of discourse) has given rise to the epistemological relativism that characterizes much contemporary theorizing about science as well as the nature of literature. Neither science nor literature can claim to come ever-closer to representing or knowing what once was called the structure of reality.[18] Reality only exists in function of the discourse that articulates it. Unlike the vision proposed by the *Tractatus,* with its world composed of atomistic facts mirrored by language, the *Investigations* and the other later works show no evidence of belief in any kind of final absolute structure. According to the *Tractatus,* language must reach the structure of the world, and logic sets the limits of discourse. But in Wittgenstein's later works logic and mathematics are merely systems among others, arbitrary absolutes, as arbitrary as the presence of life itself.[19]

Reality is in this view an unending process of articulation. Such is the force of the striking metaphor Wittgenstein uses when, asking what it would mean for language to be complete, he compares language to a city:

ask yourself whether our language is complete;—whether it was so before the symbolism of chemistry and the notation of infinitesimal calculus were incorporated into it; for these are, so to speak, the suburbs of our language. (And how many houses or streets does it take before a town begins to be a town?) Our language can be seen as an ancient city: a maze of little streets and squares, of old and new houses, of houses with additions from various periods; and this surrounded by a multitude of new boroughs with straight regular streets and uniform houses. (*Philosophical Investigations*, no. 18)

No city stops developing, though one could suppose that it might atrophy or die. Nor are there fixed boundaries to all that it might encompass. If, as we shall see, language for Heidegger is the house of being, for Wittgenstein it is the city of reality, with all the possibilities for growth and destruction that the comparison implies.

We live nonetheless in a world that seems to have, if not an absolute structure, at least a bedrock of certainties that allows us to live with a modicum of security. Our world seems to have enough stability to admit of norms for, say, sanity. At the end of his life Wittgenstein was attempting to describe that world and to show that much of our language acts as a series of ultimately unfounded but necessary assumptions that allow us to negotiate life without question. A central group of these thoughts, representing something of a philosophical anthropology, have been published in *On Certainty*. The starting point for this work is the epistemological dilemma brought up by the perennial question of certain knowledge. In a world in which the principle of causality is, at best, "a class name," and induction a convenient myth, wherein lies the certainty that might overcome the anguish we would all feel if we had to deal perpetually with a world without secure knowledge?

A philosopher in search of certainty, G. E. Moore, thought he had found a commonsense refutation of skepticism when he held his hand up in front of him and, echoing Dr. Johnson's comparable claim, proclaimed that he "knew" with certainty that that was a hand. But the Wittgenstein of *On Certainty*, building on the analyses of the *Philosophical Investigations*, states that one cannot take Mooore's claim to certainty seriously. Moore may be certain that that is a hand in front of him, but he cannot in any normal sense "know" it. Moore has confused language games, and it is simply not the case that knowledge is involved in his claim. Knowledge admits of doubt and of the possibility of being wrong. Knowledge sets forth criteria for error. What, asks Wittgenstein, would an error look like in Moore's case? Could he state that he once thought he knew that that was a hand, but was mistaken? To make claims for knowledge obliges us to ask what the criteria are for error or doubt. What could these criteria be when one holds up one's hand and says, "This is a hand," or when one says, "This is red," or "My name is Tom Jones," or "I am a human being"? For statements like these and countless others there are simply no criteria for doubt or for error. The rules of the language game involved do not admit such criteria. Hence, there is no way in a usual context to say that one "knows" such propositions, which in turn means that there is really no meaningful way to doubt them. Meaningful doubt presupposes the existence of public rules set forth within the space of a language game. Wittgenstein would hold, then, that at best Moore's curious asseverations, if they are not a sign of mental illness, belong to that bizarre language game known as philosophy.

We live in a world constituted by language games that can only be played as certainties, though future experience could conceivably give them the lie. I may state, as I learned unquestioningly from my teachers, that "This is a chair"; and the object may suddenly disappear. Something will then be amiss, but until that time, I shall continue to use my language as I learned it. A child learns that "This is a chair" and that "2 plus 2 equals 4." He does not learn that he "knows" such propositions. Each have the same degree of certainty in use. Indeed, we have no capacity to know exactly what it would mean if the propositions in these language games did not function as certainties:

> "I know that I am a human being." In order to see how unclear the sense
> of this proposition is, consider the negation. At most it might be taken
> to mean "I know I have the organs of a human." (E.g. a brain which, after
> all, no one has ever yet seen.) But what about such a proposition as "I
> know I have a brain"? Can I doubt it? Grounds for doubt are lacking!
> Everything speaks in its favour, nothing against it. Nevertheless it is
> imaginable that my skull should turn out empty when it was operated on.[20]

Such statements as "I am a human being" are not therefore matters of knowledge in any ordinary sense. These propositions are like a priori givens that allow us to inhabit a world. They constitute the countless operating definitions by which I first have a world, before I can have knowledge. To doubt these language games is to lose contact with the shared world of our language. If one truly doubted them, one would be, in the strong sense of the term, alienated from the world of one's linguistic culture.

To learn a language is to acquire what Wittgenstein calls a *Weltbild*, though the "image" in this notion is only one metaphor Wittgenstein proposes for our "world-picture" and is not to be taken with any special visual sense. Language is primary; it offers the system, the structure, or the background—to use Wittgenstein's other equivalent terms—that makes up the world, the context in which language games are mastered, the space in which they are organized and co-ordinated. Within the context of a given culture's *Weltbild* many language games function with a kind of logical necessity so that the world retains its coherence. Our certainties are an integral part of learning a language and acquiring a world. For, to return to the example of the child, the child learns many language games that he simply accepts as having the same degree of certainty that the philosopher would normally attribute to mathematics:

> We teach a child "that is your hand," not "that is perhaps [or "probably"]
> your hand." That is how a child learns the innumerable language-games
> that are concerned with his hand. An investigation or question, 'whether
> this is really a hand' never occurs to him. Nor, on the other hand, does
> he learn that he *knows* that this is a hand. (No. 374)

Certainty is concomitant with learning a language and entering the world that it articulates. There may be worlds that have other things to say about the hand held up in the air, but until one learns their language, one cannot do other than inhabit a world in which that, indeed, is a hand.

In epistemological terms Wittgenstein maintains that many so-called empirical statements are not garnered from experience at all; or, if one might point to where these statements once originated in experience, they no longer function as empirical statements. Consider the status of the proposition that water boils at 100 degrees centigrade. If I place a clear liquid on a fire and it does not boil at 100 degrees, I shall question my judgment as to whether the substance is water, not the supposedly empirical statement about the boiling point of water. We cannot, then, "compare" a good many empirical statements with the world, for they are in effect definitions of what makes up the world. There is no hard-and-fast distinction here, for Wittgenstein shows that such statements can vary in their function, not only in ordinary discourse but also in scientific discourse. Much scientific discourse is, in fact, the locus where language games become definitions of the world:

> It is clear that our empirical propositions do not all have the same status, since one can lay down such a proposition and turn it from an empirical proposition into a norm of description. Think of chemical investigations. Lavoisier makes experiments with substances in his laboratory and now he concludes that this and that takes place when there is burning. He does not say that it might happen otherwise another time. He has got hold of a definite world-picture—not of course one that he invented: he learned it as a child. I say world-picture and not hypothesis, because it the matter-of-course [*Grundlage*] for his research and as such also goes unmentioned. (*On Certainty*, no. 167)

Thus the "truth" of many of our statements belongs, as Wittgenstein puts it, to our linguistic system of reference, our *Bezugssystem*. And to ask if a statement "agrees" with the world is often simply a way of demonstrating what we mean by "agreement" (cf. *On Certainty*, no. 203).

Language and the system of reference it presupposes are the preconditions for all our knowing and doing. Many language games constitute a precognitive structure in the sense that many propositions of our language are presupposed by the very activity of "knowing" something:

> But I did not get my picture of the world [*Weltbild*] by satisfying myself of its correctness; nor do I have it because I am satisfied of its correctness. No: it is the inherited background [*Hintergrund*] against which I distinguish between true and false. (*On Certainty*, no. 94)

It seems important to stress that Wittgenstein is reversing our traditional attitude, inherited from classical metaphysics, that makes language subordinate to cognition. In this respect, Wittgenstein recalls Heidegger's attempt, in *Being and*

Time, to show that man's being in the world is not primarily, as Descartes, Locke, and Husserl had thought, a matter of cognition, or the relation of a knowing mind to a known world. Much like Heidegger, Wittgenstein wishes to show that a system of reference in preconstitutive of the world and its meaning and that the empirical model of language's fundamental cognitive role is in fact secondary to the world of preexisting relations that we learn when we learn language.

In *On Certainty* Wittgenstein again resorted to the notion of system to describe the network of language games that make up our world. It might be useful in this respect to anticipate a near homology with contemporary structuralist thought deriving from Saussure. Wittgenstein's reflections, like Saussure's linguistic theory of language, suggest that language, in informing our system of beliefs, creates a structure that lies beyond the individual subject's power to modify it or, at times, even to know it:

> Might I not believe that once, without knowing it, perhaps in a state of unconsciousness, I was taken far away from the earth—that other people even know this, but do not mention it to me? But this would not fit into the rest of my convictions at all. Not that I could describe the system of these convictions. Yet my convictions do form a system, a structure. (*On Certainty*, no. 102)

Within this system or structure we find our realm of certainties about the world so long as those certainties articulate a world that satisfies our human needs. Those certainties are not the same, needless to say, for modern Western man and medieval European man, nor for aborigines in Australia. And the differences in the system of certainties mean that men live in different worlds. After this discussion it should be clear that the difference in worlds men inhabit is *not* due to some visual trick in which each language acts as a pair of glasses that varies perceptual possibilities. World *as* language is a structure of interrelating certainties and possibilities for knowledge articulating what we can say to be the world.

To illustrate this difference in cultural worlds Wittgenstein asks us to imagine that a British scientist is suddenly placed in a culture whose system of reference includes the statement that the earth began to exist one hundred years ago. If this proposition were the background for many of the culture's language games, then one might well imagine that the scientist would be hard put to show that his system of reference is preferable. For to convince these people that his world view is somehow superior or more adequate, the scientist would in effect have to change their language and their system of reference. He would have no simple means of proving that his "knowledge" that the world is older than one hundred years is true, since this knowledge is knowledge only within the system of reference that makes up his language. Rather, he would have to try to convince this culture, or convert it to his belief. Such a conversion would entail adopting a series of many new language games. In an analogous sense, we see comparable conversions take place in our everyday intellectual dealings when people accept the language games proposed by various modes of explication, such as historical explanation, the discourse of Freudian analysis, or new scientific paradigms.

Of equal interest in this later anthropology is the way Wittgenstein plays with the possibility that the system might break down and that the definitions might no longer cohere. The history of Western thought and science demonstrates that such crises have occurred with increasing regularity in our own culture. But Wittgenstein is little interested in history, either of science or philosophy, and rarely alludes to it. Rather, the possibility that for any individual there might suddenly appear a disjuncture between language and experience interests him far more profoundly. If, for instance, in the face of all explanation Moore had maintained that he was not certain if there was a hand there or not, we should have called him mad. For madness is the condition in which we doubt language and the rules of language games; in which we are no longer certain how to follow the rules or if the rules exist at all. Wittgenstein himself was no stranger to the dangers of insanity, and the later writings return constantly to madness, in attempts to define those peripheries of understanding where the world of normal language encounters boundaries which it cannot cross. The same anguish Wittgenstein felt about trusting language, about what language can do or cannot do, underlies both *On Certainty* and the *Tractatus*. Both works speak of a need for language to offer a certainty that nothing else in the world will bespeak.

To lose certainty is to lose a world—the *Grundlage* for all asserting and inquiring (cf. *On Certainty*, no. 162). What if, Wittgenstein asks, someone were to doubt seriously that he had a body? As Wittgenstein observes, there would be no way that we could speak to him, for the common rules of a fundamental language game would be suspended. There would be no way we could attempt to convince him that he had a body, since such a conviction is one of the rules of language, a part of the system of reference, that is accepted without question. And if the doubter changed his mind, there could be no way of knowing why he did. (If he suddenly pinched his body and said, "Yes, it is a body," what would that tell us?) This doubt appears to be a central aspect of the schizophrenic condition; and Wittgenstein's preoccupation with the possible disjuncture between world and language parallels the development of a preeminently postmodern form of writing: the schizo-text that tries to place itself outside the pale of public language games.

With this reference to the schizo-text it seems appropriate to note that Wittgenstein, in his examples of doubting and their consequences, often recalls his near contemporary and fellow citizen of the Hapsburg Empire, Franz Kafka. Wittgenstein's prodigious variety of thought experiments are often like the kind of testing to which Kafka submitted the framework of rationality and certainty that characterizes our supposedly sane world. When Kafka's Gregor Samsa wakes to find himself transformed into a vermin, he tries to keep playing all the usual language games, for how can one doubt that one is a human being? In this disjuncture langauge maintains its power even if the world is berserk; for the giant insect soon loses his capacity to speak. The family is then able to assert that the insect is not Gregor, a proposition that is existentially false, but true from the point of view of the linguistic framework that allows us to make sense of the world. When one is no longer a man, logic must indeed take care of itself. In the same vein Wittgenstein asks:

> What if something *really unheard-of* happened?—If I, say, saw houses gradually turning into steam without any obvious cause, if the cattle in the fields stood on their heads and laughed and spoke comprehensible words; if trees gradually changed into men and men into trees. Now, was I right when I said before all these things happened "I know that that's a house" etc., or simply "that's a house" etc.? (*On Certainty*, no. 162)

What can one say about knowledge when vision refuses to obey language?

Presumably the Samsa family "knows" what it sees, though for the reader it is clear that Kafka is presenting a disjuncture between language and knowledge on the one hand, and vision on the other. And as the above quotation rather vividly suggests, Wittgenstein was also quite aware that there could be times when the world would break down; when vision would pay no heed to language; when the perceived world might indeed assert its primacy over the world guaranteed its certainty by and through language. Beginning with Sartre's *Nausea*, we shall see that the contemporary schizo-text arises at that point where, as in Wittgenstein's example, words and things go their separate ways.

In conclusion, however, I would stress that the force of Wittgenstein's work, as much in the *Investigations* as in *On Certainty*, is to demythologize the primacy of the visual. In the sections of the *Investigations* where he deals with misleading ways of talking about seeing, he seeks to lead us to the point where we no longer want or need to talk about mysterious hidden processes that take place when we see something. What we see we can describe, playing the multiple language games that make up description; and behind them lies no hidden self or a private cinema of ineffable vision. Pursuing these investigations in *On Certainty*, Wittgenstein proposes, in a style not unlike Heidegger's, that misleading analogies derived from an improper understanding of grammar have caused us to give the leading role to sight when we wish to talk about knowledge:

> "I know" has a primitive meaning similar to and related to "I see" ("wissen," "videre"). And "I knew he was in the room, but he wasn't in the room" is like "I saw him in the room, but he wasn't there." "I know" is supposed to express a relation, not between me and the sense of a proposition (like "I believe") but between me and a fact. So that the *fact* is taken into my consciousness. (Here is the reason why one wants to say that nothing that goes on in the outer world is really known, but only what happens in the domain of what are called sense-data.) This would give us a picture

of knowing as the perception of an outer event through visual rays which project it as it is into the eye and the consciousness. (No. 90)

This kind of demythologizing, which attempts to show how the privileging of the visual in knowledge and empiricist metaphysics go hand in hand, is perhaps the most important aspect of the legacy that Wittgenstein has left. Examination of the multiple functions of language has become a kind of final court of appeal for the investigation of myriad cultural activities, not the least of which, from our point of view, is literature.

Wittgenstein's example in philosophy is also characteristic of the kind of self-demystification that has become a primary activity of many thinkers and writers. I have stressed in this exposition certain of Wittgenstein's primary targets—the metaphysical self, the notion of essence, the belief in the representational function of language—because of the importance they have for both the theory and the practice of writing. But one might also note that there is a certain ambivalence in Wittgenstein's thought about the possibility of totally purging myth from our language and our habits of thought. For instance, certainty, and the concomitant kinds of knowing it vouchsafes, is a necessary myth that inhabits our language so that language, and hence our world, might exist at all. Moreover, Wittgenstein's hostile critics would charge that he contributed to the spreading of the most exemplary postmodern myth: the primacy of language. Ordinary language has often come to be viewed, as Austin put it, as embodying "all the distinctions men have found worth drawing, and the connexions they have found worth marking, in the lifetimes of many generations."[21] Wittgenstein would not have subscribed to this myth of the historical adequacy of language as our taxonomy of the world, for, in his view, history itself is a kind of myth, more or less adequate for explanations of various sorts, though rarely the best one. Yet, Wittgenstein was obliged to make of our received language, as the sum of our natural history, the final arbiter in matters of philosophic thought, which may well strike many—when compared with other thinkers' willingness to strip language of its received meaning—as an acquiescence to myth making. Wittgenstein was well aware of this danger, of the fact that language perforce offers us myths that are as necessary as the need for understanding itself. As he put it wryly in his remarks on Frazer's *The Golden Bough*, "Indeed, the elimination of magic has here the character of magic itself."[22]

2. Martin Heidegger

Much that is associated with Wittgenstein's name—logical atomism, positivism, or detailed linguistic analysis—contrasts vividly with the associations that Heidegger's name may evoke: existentialism, irrationalism, Teutonic abstruseness. Such antitheses have, undoubtedly, their share of truth, and they can account for the fact that Wittgenstein and Heidegger are sometimes opposed as the major representatives of the dominant tendencies in twentieth-century philosophy. But when one considers the central role that each of them assigned to language, especially in the later development of their thought, it is also evident that these thinkers had many affinities. Both desired, in their own way, to overcome metaphysics, and this desire led each of them to revise his earliest philosophical thought in a rather radical way. Heidegger, like Wittgenstein, first posited that meaning was derived from the world; but the metaphysical postulates such a view presupposes led him, again like Wittgenstein, to reverse his thought on language. In their later thought both men made language the central issue: for Wittgenstein language is constitutive of our world, whereas for Heidegger language provides our access to Being.

This distinction would suggest, however, that, if Heidegger began his career as a philosopher, he increasingly evolved toward a kind of thought that can best be described as religious, in the broadest sense of the term. Thus, after considering Wittgenstein as an exemplary modern philosophical mind, and before turning to Saussure for his development of scientific thought about language, I would propose that we approach Heidegger as a model for postmodern religious thought about language. Heidegger is not a theological thinker in any traditional sense; in fact, he is an antitheological thinker in so far as Western thought about the *theos* of theology is an adjunct to metaphysics. Heidegger's thought is religious in that it aims at finding those conditions of possibility that, Heidegger claims, once allowed the sacred to appear. Such conditions will appear once more when Western man learns again, as the ancient Greeks once did, to think about Being—and not merely about individual beings which, even when taken in their aggregate, can only be the object of metaphysical thought—thought that, as Heidegger puts it, separates entities from Being. In an era when the God once guaranteed by the principle of sufficient reason is dead and when technology is the latest outgrowth of the Western metaphysics that increasingly dominates the globe, Heidegger saw himself as trying to think back to earlier modes of thought.

In a sense Heidegger saw himself, as he said of the poet Hölderlin, as living in an era when the gods have flown and new ones have not yet appeared.

Heidegger likened his thought to paths that move ever closer to Being, and this comparison might well suggest certain analogies with Eastern religious thought, with Buddhism or, more especially, with Taoism. Heidegger did not draw directly on traditional religious sources for his thought. His work in its later development attempts to forge an original cosmology that, whatever its Greek sources, would supplant metaphysical concepts. In this way, one can again compare Heidegger with Wittgenstein, for his attempt to create a cosmology is motivated by a desire to replace old myths with new more satisfactory ones.

Heidegger refused to allow himself be called an ethical thinker; but he found in the domain of values the most urgent need for overcoming the kind of mythical hold that metaphysics has upon the Western mind. Since Plato and Aristotle, the sway of metaphysics has been uninterrupted in the West. Modern science and technology, conceived of as thought that deals only with entities, is the form metaphysics has taken in the twentieth century. And for Heidegger, it is the philosophical bankruptcy of that thought that is the source of what he describes, in the wake of Nietzsche, as modern nihilism: "What if even the language of metaphysics and metaphysics itself, whether it be that of the living or of the dead God, *as* metaphysics, formed the barrier which forbids a crossing over of a line, that is, the overcoming of nihilism?"[1] Heidegger's answer to this question he addressed to Ernst Jünger is that Western man should transform his relationship to language. He needs this transformation if he is to "cross over the line" and overcome metaphysics/nihilism. As any reader of Heidegger's later works knows, he undertook precisely to change our relationship to language, to change the way we experience language and hence our world.

Of the several perspectives that might allow an entry into Heidegger's thought about being and language, the one afforded by his attitude toward history is perhaps most central to our concern with literature. There underlies all of Heidegger's various declarations about Being, logos, poetry, and language a basic attitude toward temporality and history. This attitude is, to a large extent, a reaction to the modernist view of time as fall and of history as the process of absurd destruction. Few have linked this aspect of Heidegger's thought with the world view of aesthetic modernism, although his relation to proto-modernists and modernists such as Hölderlin and Rilke, Hegel and Nietzsche, make this affinity rather clear. Heidegger's reduction of history to a two-thousand-year period of decadence during which metaphysics has determined our relation to Being is, in fact, his version of the fall into time that Hölderlin expressed in somewhat similar terms in *Hyperion*. And much of Heidegger's development can be seen as a working out of modernist dilemmas, as a search for a way of overcoming the modernist view of the absurdity of temporality, as an attempt to recover the origins from which thought has been separated. Heidegger's relation to modernism is at times ambiguous, but the desire to abolish history—in effect to give the lie to Hegel—runs throughout his work.

To make this relation clear, one should recall that modernism developed as a quasi-theological response, usually transposed in secular terms, to a crisis in the interpretation of temporality that began roughly at the end of the eighteenth century. From Hölderlin to Joyce, with many variations along the way, the "modernist" has, as this curious term paradoxically reveals, lived his contemporaneity as a form of exile. The present moment is lived by the modernist as a form of fall into time whose process, whether in terms of the individual or transposed collectively in terms of history, leads inexorably away from privileged origins. The modernist dilemma has led frequently to a search for artistic strategies that might overcome one's exile in the present. This development in turn has engaged the writer in a search for privileged modes of revelation that would offer access to an ontologically superior realm, often in the past, transcending time and history. In this vein one can consider Mallarmé's dream of *Le Livre,* Proust's essences recovered from time past, Joyce's epiphanies, or Eliot's desire to make tradition a living presence as variant ways of seeking an ontological plentitude that exists as an atemporal presence. These projects are variations on the quest for an ecstatic openness in which, to paraphrase Rilke's Orphic bard, song would reveal true existence. Central to this modernist quest is the need for a language that can exist as a self-sufficient artefact, as the essential image beyond time. Existing as an autonomous image, this language would then be purged of time and could, like the works of Yeat's Byzantine goldsmiths, sing for all eternity. The modernist search for revelation inevitably becomes a search for a language that is more than language.

Within this general modernist context one can grasp the import of Heidegger's desire to overcome metaphysics by returning to the thought of those pre-Socratics who were not caught up in *Seinsvergessenheit*—the forgetting of the problem of Being as such. His solution to the modernist view of the fall into time is in a sense to abolish history, or at least the history of thought, by recovering the original ground for Western thought. In his first major work, *Being and Time* (1927), Heidegger clearly confronts the modernist vision of the fall into temporality. One sees this confrontation in his critique of Hegel's view of time and history, especially of the Hegelian notion that spirit *(Geist)* falls into time. In this work Heidegger reverses that protomodernist doctrine as he attempts to show that history exists only because man *(Dasein)* is temporal in his very being. Rejecting the metaphysical privileging of the "now" as the foundation of time, Heidegger analyses man's historicity to show that "authentic" temporality relies upon man's projection into the future, and that a true historicity also means a repetition of past possibilities. Heidegger's analysis of authentic historicity, rejecting the "now," also scornfully rejects what he summarily calls *das Moderne.*[2]

My claim that Heidegger desires to abolish history may be imputed to my holding too Hegelian a view of the nature of history. Yet, in the broadest sense, some such desire must be seen in Heidegger's preoccupation with history throughout his work, for why else would he want to rethink or undo what two thousand years of history have supposedly obscured? In another light, Heidegger's solution to the modernist view of the fall has a quite modernist ring, for his insistence in *Being and Time* on *Wiederholung* or repetition is also a manifestation of his desire to return to an earlier plenitude existing before Being's fall—a fall into history construed as a process of repression or forgetting. To counter this fall, Heidegger constantly claims that the privileged past can be made to perdure as a living present:

> But the tradition [*Uberlieferung*] of earlier thinking and what it thought is not merely a confused medley of laid-down philosophical views. Tradition is the present [*Gegenwart*], provided that we seek the thought that tradition has given us there where it most distantly comes to us in order to join us expressly to tradition.[3]

To this vision of tradition taken from *Der Satz vom Grund,* in which the past's pastness is overcome, one can add the Heideggerian insistence that we must think of Being as presence—*Anwesenheit.* The past would have being as tradition when it is thought as a past in the present; as *presence,* it would be. Offering a nearly modernist solution to the modernist crisis in temporality, Heidegger makes one think of, say, Proust and his desire to recover the fullness of time past as a present plenitude. Yet, in Heidegger's case, it requires only a slight shift in perspective for one to think that perhaps the past does not exist, only a radical presence or *Anwesenheit.* This is the view of temporality that Jean-Paul Sartre seems to have taken from *Being and Time.*

It would seem fair to say, then, that the central thrust of Heidegger's numerous commentaries on the history of thought is the exhortation to recover the past, the originating past of Heraclitus and Parmenides, that lies behind the metaphysical tradition. The recovery of this past demands an *Abbau*—a deconstruction—that will allow the presencing of the past to speak what history has repressed: some new determination of Being as Being.

Heidegger's thought must also be seen as a kind of dialogue with Kant, Hegel, and Nietzsche, often deconstructing them by using argumentative strategies borrowed from their works. Descartes and Husserl provide additional metaphysical models that Heidegger would undo. It is with these thinkers in mind that one can turn to Heidegger's first major and, for many, most important work, *Being and Time*. This work constitutes a seminal attack on the metaphysical underpinnings of modernism, for it attempts to articulate our experience of the world in terms that are not derived from traditional metaphysics, especially the epistemological tradition coming from Descartes through Kant and into Husserl. In short, *Being and Time* seeks to show that our experience of the world is not based on any subject-object dichotomy. By offering a new way of describing our being in the world, Heidegger joins with the later Wittgenstein, among others, in rejecting the Cartesian world view. But Heidegger is perhaps unique in the scope of his attempt to provide a full description of the structures of everyday experience. In one sense he has tried to be a modern Aristotle. Just as Aristotle derived much of his conceptual schema from the world of the Greek artisan, so Heidegger has entered the everyday world of the German peasant in an attempt to articulate the nature of everydayness.

Being and Time is also, again in the broadest sense, a postmodern religious work. It gives to be sure, an a-theistic description of contemporary man's dereliction, but one that could have been written by a contemporary Luther. A sense of original sin hovers over Heidegger's ontological descriptions of anguish and guilt, authenticity and inauthenticity, "thrownness" and "fallenness." For not only has Western man fallen away from the sense of Being during the two thousand years during which metaphysical thinking has separated him from the pre-Socratics; but man's everyday existence is a constant falling away from his own authentic possibilities. And as individual temporality is the ground for historicity, so, too, is the individual capacity for falling seemingly the source of the great historical fall that Heidegger wishes to overcome. *Being and Time* presents a secular transposition of many traditional religious motifs in its supposedly neutral description of the ontology of everydayness; but none is more persistent than the great Protestant theme of man's lost potential. Milton would have read *Being and Time* with no difficulty.

Being and Time, as now published, was to be the first part of a larger work addressing itself to the question of the sense of Being. The second part was never published, though in many respects all of Heidegger's subsequent work is a development and often a critique of the ideas presented in this unfinished work. *Being and Time* begins, in fact, by setting aside the question of the sense of Being. This question first requires an analysis of man, or *Dasein,* that being who is open to Being. Or so Heidegger reasoned at this point in his career as he set about to redefine man by laying bare the basic structures of what he calls *Dasein. Dasein* is the first of many striking formulations Heidegger coins in order to describe concretely man's being in the world. *Dasein*—being-there— stresses by its form that man is always already present in the world and not separated from it as mind from matter or subject from object. In contradistinction to Cartesian categories that separate a knowing self from an "objective" world that exists passively to be observed, Heidegger's *Dasein* is defined as *Erschlossenheit,* a term that stresses that man's being is a space of openness to the world as well as disclosure of the world. This definition of man as openness and disclosure is of central importance for a theory of language, for, as we shall see, it allows Heidegger to dismiss the notion that language operates as a form of representation, re-presenting objects to a distant subject, or re-presenting hidden thoughts of the inner self. Because man is the space of disclosure, Heidegger can interpret logos—taken as language or truth—as a "letting something be seen," to paraphrase one of his various formulations. In *Being and Time* logos and man's relation to logos have not yet become the center of Heidegger's thought, although his view of Dasein's disclosing openness orients all his subsequent thought on language.

Dasein is a space of disclosure that is first found *in* a world; it is not to be conceived on the model of an observer looking at a world apart from it. Heidegger's description of Dasein precludes any definition of self that would separate it from the world. However, something of a neo-Kantian framework seems to determine Heidegger's analysis of Dasein insofar he finds it to be constituted by various *Existential* or fundamental categories. The three principal categories or structures of being in the world are called *Befindlichkeit, Verstehen,* and *Rede.* None of these is easily translated. *Befindlichkeit* is mood, state of mind, the affective coloring of existence, or simply the state in which one finds oneself. *Verstehen* is roughly the understanding. And *Rede,* which Heidegger distinguishes from articulated speech, or *Sprache,* can be taken as the faculty for discourse. Important for our context is that Heidegger has placed the capacity for language on the same level as the emotive and cognitive faculties that traditional philosophy often ascribes, in a dualistic manner, to man. However, Heidegger is not interested in merely elevating the status of language. He wishes to redistribute, as it were, all these roles in a new intellectual economy in which metaphysical dualism is abolished. Discourse is constitutive of the disclosedness of being in the world, but so is mood or state of mind. As a generation of existentialists were to dramatize in various ways, anguish has a stellar role in *Being and Time;* for it can reveal nothingness, and this disclosure can, Heidegger claims, offer access to Being in its totality.

Heidegger's goal in *Being and Time* could be construed as a linguistic investigation, since he states at the outset that he wants to investigate the meaning *(Sinn)* of a word—Being. One might then suppose that language could offer an especially appropriate path to the knowledge Heidegger seeks, all the more so in that discourse is a fundamental structure in Dasein's openness to the world. However, in *Being and Time* Heidegger does not use the term *Rede* to refer to the ordinary language we speak to each other. Words are encountered within the world and thus, in ontological terms, can exist separately from discourse: "Language is a totality of words—a totality in which discourse has a 'worldly' Being of its own; and as an entity within-the-world, this totality thus becomes something which we may come across as ready-to-hand. Language can be broken up into word-things which are present-at-hand" (p. 204). Words can be encountered as tools of reference, like any other tools that "refer" to other purposes, or they can be encountered as objects of cognitive inquiry, like any other objects in the world. But discourse precedes this ready-at-hand and present-at-hand status that may fall upon "word things" or other tools. Again in a rather Kantian sense, discourse is the ontologically prior openness that would be the condition of possibility for actual articulated languages that can be found within the world.

At this state in Heidegger's thought real language is secondary to discourse. The capacity of discourse allows the articulation of those meanings that, through Dasein's openness, are given to the understanding. In *Being and Time* meaning is not, therefore, primarily encountered in language but in relations in the world that are disclosed through Dasein's openness. There is something tautological about this view of meaning as articulated understanding, for in one sense meaning is grounded in meaning. There is no appeal about meaning beyond disclosure. The web of meanings that Dasein encounters is part of a network of relations that are found in the world, primarily the network of relations among entities that Dasein discovers along with itself. Meaning is "that wherein the intelligibility of something maintains itself. That which can be articulated in a disclosure by something we understand, we call "meaning" (pp. 192-93). There is a semantic dimension to Dasein's world even before it is expressed linguistically. Words are derivative from this dimension: "The intelligibility of Being-in-the-world— an intelligibility which goes with a state-of-mind—*expresses itself as discourse*. To significations, words accrue. But word-things do not get supplied with definitions. [Den Bedeutungen wachsen Worte zu. Nicht aber werden Wörtedinge mit Bedeutungen versehen]" (p. 204). As Heidegger puts it with a curious organic metaphor, words grow to fit meanings that have been disclosed to Dasein's openness to the world.

Some would see in Heidegger's early attitude a residue of Husserl's phenomenology.[4] Meaning and real language are also separated in Husserl's early thought, for, to paraphrase Merleau-Ponty's critique of Husserl, the goal of phenomenology was to determine for all languages the universal forms of meaning that were necessary for any language to exist. In this perspective one can consider every empirical language as a partial realization of an ideal language existing before all languages.[5] Heidegger has considerably changed the context in which this separation of meaning and language occurs; and at no point does he envisage the possibility of the kind of universal grammar that Husserl, like many rationalists before him, hoped to discover and describe. In *Being and Time* meanings are articulated in the web of Dasein's concerned dealings with the world, and empirical language is a secondary level of articulation. The first level takes place in Dasein's concerned dealings with the world before any linguistic conceptualization can interpose itself between man's openness and beings that are revealed therein.

Early Heidegger shares with early Wittgenstein a distaste for empirical language and its ambiguity. Moreover, insofar as language is the locus of conceptualization, it would appear that language reduces Dasein's relation to the world to that of dealing with things present-at-hand, or beings considered as objectively viewed by a subject—the metaphysical relationship that underwrites modern science. To describe Dasein's concrete, everyday viewing of the world, Heidegger, again like an early Greek thinker working with ordinary perception, refuses language or the linguistic proposition its primary role in the determination of truth. Ontologically prior to the proposition's determination of truth, Heidegger claims, is truth as revealed in the world. And this revealing or unconcealment is the grounds of possibility allowing a statement to have truth when it corresponds to a state of affairs in the world:

> To say that an assertion "*is true*" signifies that it uncovers the entity as it is in itself. Such as assertion asserts, points out, 'lets' the entity 'be seen' . . . in its uncoveredness. The *Being-true (truth)* of the assertion must be understood as *Being-uncovered*. Thus truth has by no means the structure of an agreement between knowing and the object in the sense of a likening of one entity (the subject) to another (the Object). (P. 261)

To help us understand what he means by truth as uncoveredness, Heidegger asks that we consider what normally occurs when one says "The picture is on the wall" without looking at the object. The truth of this statement does not occur in someone's mind, even less in the statement: it occurs there on the wall, where the picture is, disclosed as being on the wall. Only secondarily, in the light of this disclosure, can one then maintain that truth is in the correspondence between the statement and the state of affairs, or between the statement and whatever the speaker might have in mind—which is the picture on the wall in the world.

This notion of truth as disclosure anticipates Heidegger's later formulations of truth as *alethia* or unconcealment. Whatever be the accuracy of his reading of the Greek—and it appears to be more than plausible—this reading again brings up Heidegger's ambiguous stance toward modernism. In *Being and Time,* while displacing the kind of subject-object relation that underlies the modernist primacy of the visual, he restores another kind of primacy by making disclosure the essence of truth and, as we shall see, of poetry and language. Later, one of his metaphors for Being is light-giver that allows things to come to be.[6]

In *Being and Time,* however, discourse is presented as concomitant with understanding. Discourse is openness to the concrete world, whereas language is a form of articulation that belongs to the world of cognition. This dichotomy means that language is considered as a mere conceptual system. And a goal of Heidegger's work here is to show that cognition is not a fundamental way of being in the world. The cognitive relation of a subject to an object is derivative from the everyday understanding and its immediate interpretation of what Dasein encounters in the world. This interpretation is a form of immediate seeing. For Dasein directly sees what is "environmentally ready-to-hand" as "a table, a door, a carriage, or a bridge" (p. 189). Understanding is a seeing that carries within itself an interpretative grasp. Derivative from this interpretation are multiple kinds of linguistic propositions, ranging from a pure pointing out *(Aufzeigung)* to statements of a purely cognitive sort. Heidegger understands the multiple types of language-use one might categorize, but he also wishes to bring them all back ultimately to some kind of disclosure that must be understood in visual terms. Heidegger's critique of the biblical view of language notwithstanding, one cannot help feeling that the biblical notion of logos as light has had a constant influence on the way Heidegger formulates his phenomenology of everyday being in the world. However that may be, Heidegger's attempt to describe how language functions without recourse to such metaphysical notions as universals or ideal concepts sets forth the scope of his project. It obliges us to ask if scientific or (what is the same for Heidegger) metaphysical descriptions of language fail to account for the way language is rooted in an immediate appropriation of the world.

Heidegger's separation of meaning and language serves to account for another central feature of being-in-the-world, for he must also explain why men's sense of Being is obscured. He must offer a view of language that accounts for why, in his perspective, men do not authentically communicate with each other. After all, one might very well ask, if Dasein is openness and disclosure, and if Dasein encounters Being in its openness, why do men have any difficulty talking about the sense of Being? Or, to introduce Heidegger's term for the social structure of our existence, if being-with-others, or *Mitsein,* is a fundamental category of Dasein's existence, why does Dasein's capacity for articulating what Heidegger calls *Mitsehen,* or seeing with others, go astray when it comes to communicating authentically with others? In short, what curse weighs upon the empirical language that we encounter every day in the world?

In *Being and Time,* by separating logos, discourse, and meaning from ordinary language, Heidegger is rather more metaphysical than he desires. One could charge that he creates a suprasensible realm of discourse, a metaphysical realm, where logos floats as in some Platonic heaven. This is not Heidegger's intent, and one could rejoin that such an interpretation reflects an inaccurate reading of what Heidegger means by truth as unconcealment. But the possibility of a metaphysical reading of *Being and Time* probably influenced Heidegger in his decision not to finish the work. Whether he is guilty of metaphysics or not, it is certain that in separating meaning from language, Heidegger sets up two realms, a higher realm of authentic meaning, and a lower one of empirical language. This strategy enables him to point to where authentic meaning might be found, if one were able to overcome the fall of language. For real language inevitably falls from the space of openness in which authentic meaning is articulated. The language we use to buy potatoes or teach philosophy falls into the realm of average everydayness—and therefore no longer has contact with Being. In this secularized transposition of the myth of the fall, language repeats the lapsarian drama of Western man.

In order to describe this fall—what one might call the original sin of logos—Heidegger uses the notion of *das Man* or the anonymous "they" that characterizes Dasein's mode of being in its average everydayness. Heidegger insists that this is simply an ontological category, though it is difficult to believe that this category does not have strong links with a certain right-wing modernist way of characterizing the masses. The notion's sociological overtones should not obscure its theological roots. *Das Man* participates in a network of concepts that describe Dasein's fallenness. In this state of fallenness, Dasein does not speak his own, authentic language; rather through each individual the "they" speaks a fallen language, *das Gerede*. This term has been translated as "idle talk," but that does not catch the full scope of what Heidegger implies: *das Gerede* seems to designate nearly every form of empirical language. Its power is limitless; for example, fallen language determines how the masses in their everyday existence think, see, and even feel:

> The dominance of the public way in which things have been interpreted has already been decisive even for the possibilities of having mood—that is, for the basic way in which Dasein lets the world "matter" to it. The "they" prescribes one's state-of-mind and determines what and how one 'sees.'
> (P. 213)

Das Gerede, the inauthentic language of everydayness, has the power to transform men into the kinds of automatons that Heidegger's contemporary Fritz Lang portrayed in *Metropolis*. Fallen language, moreover, sets the limits of the world of *das Man*, encapsulating him in an anonymous world characterized by curiosity and ambiguity.

Certain coincidences with Wittgenstein's early thought are striking in *Being and Time*. Neither Heidegger nor Wittgenstein provide an example in their early work of what would be an authentic articulation of meaning or an elementary *Sachverhalt*. Both distrust empirical language for its essential ambiguity, and both consign higher concerns to a realm of silence. In *Being and Time* authenticity is to be found in the authentic man's silent resolve to be true to himself and to the possibilities of his own historicity. Much as in the case of the *Tractatus*, *Being and Time* leaves one wondering how one could ever speak about one's deepest values and needs. Apparently these concerns can be shown or pointed out, but not expressed in the empirical language that *das Man* has appropriated. Yet, what Heidegger calls authentic existence, an existence maintaining a relation with Being, is essentially a problem of language in *Being and Time*.

Access to authenticity, and hence to a relation with Being, demands, according to Heidegger, an expressive discourse that, as a form of communication, would aim at bringing the hearer to "participate in disclosed Being" (pp. 211-12). Having separated discourse, meaning, and real language, Heidegger seems to have rendered impossible his own demands for a language that grants access to revelation. No example of authentic language is given in *Being and Time*— unless of course the work itself is to be taken as an example. And no real example of what might be an authentic life is offered, unless one takes at face value the example of the life of silent resolve that characterizes the higher consciousness to which disclosure is made. Perhaps the problem lies here in the way Heidegger, like many of a theological bent, is much more inclined to describe the fall than salvation. And the temptation to fall is great; being in the world is a form of

temptation in itself. In this context it is hardly surprising that everyday language
is a form of inauthenticity. Only silence can be meaningful.

There are several ways of interpreting Heidegger's failure to complete *Being
and Time* and the subsequent "turning" in his thought. The *Kehre* (reversal or
turning) that comes after *Being and Time* should not, however, be interpreted
as a radical rejection of his earlier thought. Heidegger's turning is not Wittgenstein's rejection. Rather, I think one can say that nearly all of Heidegger's later
work is an attempt to go beyond the impasse to which his vision of the fall had
brought him. In this regard his later work presents a constant reorientation of
his thought. Although often critical of *Being and Time*, Heidegger never repu-
diates it entirely. Perhaps the first essay to make this shift clear is "On the
Essence of Truth," first given as a lecture in 1930, though subsequently reworked.
In this work Heidegger's antihumanism comes to the fore. Man or Dasein is no
longer the privileged center of his thought or the space of disclosure through
which he might find Being. Though Heidegger does build on the analyses he
undertook in *Being and Time,* the main focal point of his thought is now Being.
And truth, in addition to meaning unconcealment, must be understood as a letting
be, as granting freedom to things to be what they are. If one were to try to offer
the most concise description of Heidegger's work after *Being and Time,* one
could perhaps formulate this work as a search for authentic forms of language
that will offer access to Being. In looking for such sources of authentic language,
Heidegger turned to those protomodernist and modernist poets who, from Hölderlin to Rilke and Trakl, offered the example of their quest for essential being
purged of temporality. Heidegger's meditations on poetry and language set forth
the central way into his attempt to recover a thought about Being.

With his 1935 essay "The Origin of the Work of Art," Heidegger began
tentatively the elaboration of a cosmology that, in this essay, takes the form of
a description of the ontology of a work at art. In attempting to formulate the
ontology of the artwork in nonmetaphysical terms, this essay also marks the
beginning of Heidegger's new way of thinking about language. Like the *An
Introduction to Metaphysics* of the same year, this essay makes language the
ultimate object of its inquiry.[7] In the former work Heidegger embarks on various
philological and historical investigations in order to recover the original meanings
of those Greek terms that still determine Western thought. In "The Origin of the
Work of Art" Heidegger goes beyond this project of recovery: here he advances
the claim that all language is originally poetry and, as such, founds what is.
This grandiose claim opens the way, moreover, for the development of Heidegger's own cosmology, a cosmology that presumably aims at ushering in a postmetaphysical era.

As is the case with much of Heidegger's work, this treatise on the origin of
the artwork (and finally on the artwork as origin) presupposes a familiarity with
the philosophical tradition and the way it sets limits as to the ways in which one
can think the subject in question. In the case of the work of art, Kant and Hegel

come to the fore. To free himself from the metaphysical determinations of the nature of the artwork, Heidegger must first reject the Kantian (and Goethean) notion of the *Geniebegriff,* or the concept of genius as the origin of the artwork. Heidegger attacks the notion that the metaphysical self can be the locus of origination for the work, for this notion implies a transcendent source as the ultimate place of the work's origin and meaning. Heidegger suggests a displacement of the locus of origination by asking if art itself is not the origin of the work. Heidegger's comments at the essay's outset anticipate much contemporary discussion of the source of art, not only by reducing the role of the artist but also by making the medium itself a key determinant in the significance of the work.

Hegel's metaphysical determination of the nature of art appears throughout these pages, and Heidegger has a much more difficult struggle with its implications, a struggle hardly surprising in one who was so often an anti-Hegelian Hegelian. Implicit throughout is a rejection of the Hegelian notion of art as the sensuous appearance of the Idea, a view of art that underlies much modernist thought about art as the revelation of essence. Heidegger has a more difficult time dealing with Hegel's contention that art, as a form of knowledge, now belongs to the past. In Hegel's historical schema, art no longer serves as an originating locus for truth. For Hegel art is a *Vergangenes,* a term for the past that indicates a past known merely as a past, having no relation to the present. Heidegger accepts the possible validity of Hegel's view of art, since he also accepts the view that most art exists as a mere present-at-hand, as so many "objects" of disinterested looking to be shown in museums or stored away for occasional inspection. Yet, he wants to argue that art can be a *Gewesenes,* a past that lives in the present and that can therefore determine the future. This way of reading art's historicity might well appear to have a Hegelian cast to it, and I think one might plausibly argue that Heidegger attempts to overcome Hegel with Hegel. Clearly Heidegger's treatise is a confrontation with the Hegelian view that with the coming to pass of the absolute Idea, with the advent of History, the need for art has been obviated.

In this confrontation with Hegel Heidegger must reject the notion that art was a product of the absolute mind at one stage in its development. For Hegel mind is the only subject of history, since history is the dialectical process by which mind comes to know itself. Parallel to this implied rejection of mind as the origin of the artwork, runs a shift in Heidegger's thought with regard to Dasein. Dasein, whose historicity provides the conditions of possibility for history, no longer occupies the center of this work. Dasein's eclipse means that Heidegger wishes to displace man and implicitly mind as the subject of his thought. Rather than placing Dasein's openness at the center of truth and meaning, Heidegger now emphasizes man as a receptor of language, truth, and logos. Increasingly logos, in a pre-Socratic sense, comes to the center of Heidegger's thought. In fact, to overcome the Kantian and Hegelian elaborations of the Cartesian subject, Heidegger grants logos a primacy that allows him to return to a world view in which the subject does not exist. Heidegger's interpretation of logos is not eccentric in this respect. With regard to language, the classicist Philip Wheelwright maintains in his commentary on Heraclitus that the pre-Socratic thought on speech and logos was radically different from our own:

> To a degree that our secular and colloquial habits of thought can scarcely comprehend, the ancient speaker was apt to regard his speaking not as a personal activity but as a voicing of a something greater—of a Logos whose character cannot be given, except haltingly and fragmentarily, in human utterance.[8]

And logos is "fragmentarily and haltingly" used by Heidegger for truth, *physis*, language, and Being, here and in the remainder of his work. Heidegger desires to renovate a vision of logos and the cosmos that he can oppose to the metaphysical determinations of man and being. In this sense he comes to say that language, not mind, the subject, or man, speaks. And not unlike the later Wittgenstein, Heidegger finds language to be the taxonomic source of all that is.

The displacement of Dasein as the focal point for access to Being obliges Heidegger to find some other privileged point of entry, namely, the artwork. But before Heidegger can show how art gives access to truth, logos, and Being, he must, much as he did for Dasein in *Being and Time*, lay bare the ontological structure of the artwork. Such a project requires that one know what is a work of art, for without such prior knowledge, how could one know what to examine in order to determine what is a work of art? Heidegger accepts the necessary circularity of such a project, for, as he exposed it in *Being and Time*, Dasein has a precomprehension of Being that allows one to interpret Being by entering the hermeneutic circle. Circularity—the fruitful tautology—is a necessary part of all thought.

Heidegger aims to rethink the ontology of the artwork in nonmetaphysical terms. By first noting that works of arts are "things," he can direct his deconstructive investigation against the various metaphysical determinations of "thingness" that he sees dominating Western thought. Not unlike Wittgenstein, Heidegger wishes to demonstrate the inadequacy of traditional notions of essence. To determine that the essence of a thing is to be a bearer of traits or to be a substance with accidents is to commit an assault *(Uberfall)* on the thing. Moreover, as Heidegger notes in making some rather acute linguistic analysis, the substance-accident model of essence is a displacement of grammatical categories whereby the subject-predicate relationship in a sentence is unconsciously transposed to account for the essence of nonlinguistic objects. A second metaphysical model defines a thing as the unity of a manifold of what is given in the senses ("die Einheit einer Mannigfaltigkeit des in den Sinnen Gegebenen").[9] But this determination dissolves the thing into sense impressions that have nothing to do with the specific object—the car in the street or the wind in the field—that we encounter. This rejection of sensory unity harks back to Heidegger's refusal of the subject-object dichotomy in *Being and Time,* for Dasein's encounter with things is always a direct, concerned viewing of specific things within the world.

There is finally a third determination of essence that has had a great deal of appeal for aesthetics. Nothing has seemed more plausible than to consider the artwork as a thing that is conceived as form and content ("geformte Stoff"). But this metaphysical pair derives from a view of those things that have been formed by man—essentially tools—and does not account for the essence of a simple natural thing, a piece of rock for example. Heidegger also questions how this pair can account for the difference between a work of art, a presumably self-sufficient being, and a tool that exists as a form of "servability" in a world of other-directed purposes. Tools, the primary things present in Dasein's world, exist as the ready-to-hand that makes up the world of meaningful reference and purposes; and a work of art is not encountered in the world in the same way as a tool. Nor is the work of art normally experienced as an object of disinterested contemplation, as the present-at-hand that is the object of the scientific mode of observation. This is the case except when it is transformed into the object of a science, of museum curatorship or commerce, and then the work of art no longer is fully a work of art. In its authentic mode of being, the work of art presents an enigma that metaphysics cannot account for.

If we are willing to accept the circularity in Heidegger's thought, that by definition art cannot be experienced as a disinterested object of contemplation without ceasing to be a work of art, then Heidegger has made problematic our traditional metaphysical underpinnings for discussing art—and perhaps for experiencing art. The next part of Heidegger's demonstration may call for a willing suspension of disbelief rather than a mere acceptance of procedure. Heidegger makes a creative leap when he calls upon his reader to follow him in an exploration of what might be the nature of tools. Tools or equipment apparently occupy a kind of half-way place between works of art and natural things. Thus an investigation of the nature of "toolness" might shed light on the nature of the artwork. To accomplish this, Heidegger, in a dazzling bit of legerdemain, chooses as his example of a tool a pair of shoes that happen to be found in a painting by Van Gogh. This choice brings him to a poetic leap—with Kierkegaardian overtones—that anticipates his vision of a new cosmology. The shoes in the painting reveal the pairing of earth and world:

> In the shoes vibrates the silent call of the earth, its quiet gift of the ripening grain and its unexplained self-refusal in the fallow desolation of the wintry field. This equipment is pervaded by uncomplaining anxiety as to the certainty of bread, the wordless joy of having once more withstood want, the trembling before the impending childbirth and shivering at the menace of death. This equipment belongs to the *earth,* and it is protected in the *world* of the peasant woman. From out of this protected belonging the equipment itself rises to its resting-within-itself.[10]

This movement first appears capricious on Heidegger's part, but when one views it as a leap within the perspective of his refusal of metaphysical determinations, one sees that Heidegger has used the painting as a creative bridge to go beyond metaphysics and the rationality vouchsafed thereby.

At this point it matters little if Heidegger sees the painting as revealing the essence of "toolness" to be reliability. For Heidegger is most interested, quite plainly, in describing the pairing of earth and world, a non-metaphysical coupling that marks his beginning attempt to think out, in the same terms, the ontology of the artwork and the ontology of a postmetaphysical cosmology. By using this pair of earth and world to describe the ontology of the artwork and by ascribing these notions to our "world," Heidegger has in effect proposed a nonrepresentational way of viewing how our world and the artwork share common ontological features. This move then allows Heidegger to bring together themes that existed separately in earlier works: art allows truth, a "letting be of what is," to occur as unconcealment.

In the work of art, there exists an opening between earth and world that allows truth to take place. Van Gogh's painting offers *aletheia*, the unconcealment that is prior to any determination of truth as a correspondence between a proposition and a state of affairs. The openness of *aletheia* is the grounds of possibility for seeing if any such correspondence has taken place. To the dubious who ask how one can test or prove Heidegger's assertion that the painting has offered the truth of the shoe-tool, no answer can be given in Heideggerian terms, and not merely because Heidegger demands a kind of Kierkegaardian leap. By equating logos with manifestation, and truth with unconcealment or disclosure, Heidegger has in effect precluded the possibility of a meta-discourse that could establish the criteria for such an assertion's validity. Such a meta-discourse would be, as the name says, a metaphysical construction that could not account for the specificity of *aletheia*. This position is not unlike Wittgenstein's in the *Tractatus*. In fact, in a curious way Heidegger has pursued a nominalist or empiricist position to its extreme consequences. Though his description of Dasein rejects any empiricist subject-object dichotomy, Heidegger's notion of truth as unconcealment, in disallowing a "realist" metaphysical belief in essence, makes immediate vision the criterion of truth. There is a significant difference with empiricism, of course, in that logos itself is the locus of vision where beings come to pass.

Since unconcealment takes place in the artwork, the question of the origin of the artwork can be framed as a question of the origin of truth; and Heidegger asks how truth is placed in the artwork. To pursue this line of thought, he turns to a work of art that is clearly nonrepresentational in nature, a Greek temple. This choice is hardly a neutral one for his purposes, since it easily allows him to append his cosmological construction to the Greek world view. For Heidegger, the Greek temple, like any work of art torn from its essential space and reduced to a mere present-at-hand, is a fallen form and can only be encountered as a *Gewesenes,* a form of pastness. Once again Heidegger's formulation aims to counter any Hegelian view that would see in the work some totally fallen form of historicity, a mere *Vergangenes*. But Heidegger, as he recognizes himself in the essay's epilogue, cannot really propose a satisfactory solution for the work's fall into time: Hegel might be right. Heidegger clearly wants to reverse Hegel and find a plenitude at the beginning of our history, not at its end. In this respect Heidegger's attitude toward history parallels that of many a modernist who could not accept the Hegelian vision of history as a solution to the "spirit's fall into time." Heidegger shares the modernist nostalgia for the past lived as a present plenitude that denies the present moment's fall from sacred origins. Heidegger's longing is, like Hölderlin's, a religious yearning. Thus he turns to the Greek temple and asserts that, when the temple was integrated into its space, it allowed the god himself to exist; it *was*, moreover, the god itself. The temple "ist ein Werk, das den Gott selbst anwesen lässt und so der Gott selbst *ist*" (*Ursprung*, p. 43). The sacred is—or was—abiding presence.

The example of the Greek temple affords Heidegger the occasion for a rather compelling application of his pairing of earth and world to describe the ontology of the work of art. This metaphorical pair can force us to consider our experience of art in concrete ways that are closed off to the rather weary pairing of form and matter. Form and content simply cannot be applied to much modern art and *a fortiori* to architecture. The earth is the work's closedness, its "thingness," its material presence against which it opens a world:

> Earth is that which comes forth and shelters. Earth, self-dependent, is effortless and untiring. Upon the earth and in it, historical man grounds his dwelling in the world. In setting up a world, the work sets forth the earth. This setting forth must be thought here in the strict sense of the word. The work moves the earth itself into the Open of a world and keeps it there. The work lets the earth be an earth. (*Poetry, Language, Thought*, p. 46)

The earth is the essential materiality of the work—sounds, stone, paint, words, or the earth—that in its "strife" with a world gives rise to that openness in which truth occurs.

Or, rather, the world of the work *is* that openness in which truth takes place: "The work as work sets up a world. The work holds open the Open of the world" (*Poetry, Language, Thought*, p. 45). The strife of the open and the closed, the world and earth, such are the elements Heidegger sets in play in describe the artwork. These elements also recall the ancient Greek cosmologists; and Heidegger echoes Heraclitus when he turns to the question of how truth establishes itself in the artwork. He first states that truth abides in the tearing strife between light and concealment. This answer is another way of phrasing Heidegger's view of truth and of his equating of unconcealment, disclosure, and logos. New at this point, however, is his contention that all art is *Dichtung* or poetry. *Dichtung* is not to be taken in the narrowest meaning of poems written on paper—Jacques Derrida has pointed out how greatly Heidegger distrusts writing[11]—but rather it should be understood in the broadest sense, as language.

All language is originally poetry. Such a claim is hardly original in itself, though it is perhaps unique as a contemporary idea (however, one recalls what Joyce did with Vico's ideas about language). What Heidegger is claiming, I believe, is that language conceived of as poetry, is coextensive with Being or logos and, as such, lets be what comes to be. Language, as poetry, is equivalent to the logos that allows the unconcealment that discloses truth and beings. Perhaps one might speak of a kind of metaphorical web of tautologies in this respect: logos, language, poetry, truth, unconcealment, and other terms are so many defining metaphors by which Heidegger hopes to bring one closer to Being. What is clear is that there is a shift in Heidegger's thought: Dasein's openness is no longer the primary openness for thought to interrogate. The work of art, or poetry in the broadest sense, is the openness in which logos can come to light. Language is no longer secondary to some realm of meanings articulated in Dasein's world; on the contrary it appears that Heidegger views language as articulating the world.

One might ask, however, what the relationship is between the originating logos and the empirical languages one finds in the world. Heidegger seems to anticipate this question by granting poetry in the narrow sense—written texts—precedence over other art forms. These examples of real language, properly understood, would bridge the gap between the realm of origination and the empirical world:

the linguistic work, the poem in the narrower sense, has a privileged position in the domain of the arts. To see this only the right concept of language is needed. In the current view, language is held to be a kind of communication. It serves for verbal exchange and agreement, and in general for communicating. But language is not only and not primarily an audible and written expression of what is to be communicated.

Rejecting the primacy of communication or of behavioral models for understanding language, Heidegger can assert that language as poetry bestows our contact with Being and hence beings:

Language alone brings what is, as something that is, into the Open for the first time. . . . Language, by naming beings for the first time, first brings being to word and to appearance. (*Poetry, Language, Thought*, p. 73)

The biblical overtones of Heidegger's description of the role of language are not surprising, but one wonders if such a description can tell us how logos sets itself in the text that we buy at the corner bookstore.

Heidegger's view of the primacy of logos has several consequences. If Heidegger means that language must be the mediator for all that comes into being, one might say, at the risk of being too psychological, that language is the mediator for all that man perceives. This view could be partially compared to Wittgenstein's attempt to define how language informs the world. With regard to works of art, the primacy of logos would impose the conclusion that non-linguistic art works "take place" in what Heidegger calls the "opening of saying and naming" (*Poetry, Language, Thought,* p. 85). In other words, for works of art other than poetry to have meaning, they must be mediated by language—which is a tautology if one construes "meaning" to signify linguistic meaning. Or, in a sense with which contemporary semioticians would agree, meaningful perception can occur only when mediated by linguistic structures. Heidegger would undoubtedly reject such psychological or semiotic terminology as a recuperation by metaphysics. But he does believe in some sense that language can mediate perception (which is not true of Wittgenstein). In *Being and Time* fallen language—*das Gerede*—has the power to institute mass thought, feelings, and vision. His claims for language (though one must ask which language) are just as great in his later essays; for example, in his "What Are Poets For?" of 1946 he states that language, presumably everyday language, mediates all human activity:

> It is because language is the house of Being, that we reach what is by constantly going through this house. When we go to the well, when we go through the woods, we are always already going through the word "well," through the word "woods," even if we do not speak the words and do not think of anything relating to language. (*Poetry, Language, Thought,* p. 132)

Language has replaced the subject as the central space of philosophical inquiry, since it is "always already" the grounds for any inquiry.

Heidegger's metaphor for language as the house of Being underscores that his claims for language are far larger than the idea that language mediates our vision of the world. This metaphor also points to the recurrent problem faced in his later work when he attempts to explain (to choose a neutral verb) how logos, Being, and language are joined. This problem underlies the increasingly complicated cosmology and attendant way of describing language that Heidegger developed throughout his later essays on Hölderlin and other poets as well as in his writings on language and the metaphysical tradition. I would maintain, however, that beneath these later works and the cosmology they propose lies the same drama of fallen langauge that Heidegger enacted in *Being and Time*. Only authentic language, or logos and its occasional manifestations in selected poets, can qualify as the house of Being. *Das Gerede* stands in implicit opposition to this language throughout the later essays. Ordinary language remains under the curse of the fall. It is true that in his last works, in which he uses the notion of play to explore the nature of language, Heidegger draws somewhat back from his fascination with the Augustinian and Lutheran tradition. By and large, however, the dichotomy of a superior realm and a fallen realm of discourse is never effaced from his thought. Poetic language offers access to the superior realm of origination, but it is not clear whether the empirical language of poetry is this language of origination in itself.[12]

"The Origin of the Work of Art" is a key text in Heidegger's articulation of his response to his failure to complete *Being and Time*. Having found in language as poetry the realm of authenticity that would allow at least a metaphorical approach to Being, Heidegger immediately began the series of essays on poetry and language that make up the core of his later thought. Especially in the work of Hölderlin—Hegel's university friend—did Heidegger encounter the purest example of a language attuned to the essential fall of history:

> For Hölderlin's historical experience, the appearance and the sacrificial death of Christ mark the beginning of the end of the day of the gods. Night is falling. Ever since the "united three"—Herakles, Dionysos, and Christ—have left the world, the evening of the world's age has been declining toward its night. The night is spreading its darkness. The era is defined by the god's failure to arrive, by the "default of God"[13]

Essential history—*Geschichte* as distinguished from the merely date-filled *Historische*—must be understood in terms of religious epochs. Poetry inaugurates this true history through the annunciation of truth, which is to say, with the advent of authentic language.

Presumably only two such inaugural moments have occurred in Western history: the time of the pre-Socratics and the time marked by Hölderlin. In this perspective one can say that Heidegger has attempted to displace the closure of history announced by Hegel in his *Phenomenology*. Mind is no longer the locus of the realization of history, since history only authentically occurs through language. The coming of language also means the advent of the sacred: "The sacred [*das Heilige*] sends the word and comes itself in this word. The word is the event [*das Ereignis*] of the sacred."[14] Hölderlin's poetry is one example of the originating calling of the holy that gives rise to an authentically historical event. Within this history-denying framework of history, Heidegger's later themes on language fit together to offer a cosmological vision that might displace the reign of metaphysics and the dominance of humanist views that see in man the measure of all things—man, the rational animal who has attempted to use his *ratio* for the conquest of the cosmos.

One of Heidegger's primary themes for an understanding of language is that the metaphysical view of essence must be subordinated to a more primordial understanding. The "essence" of language is not to represent a conceptual abstraction. One must admit there is something a little perverse about Heidegger's repeated use of the term "essence" or *Wesen,* when, quite clearly, he wishes to render problematic all those metaphysical oppositions, especially essence and accident, that ground metaphysical discourse. With regard to essence, he claims that the universal is an indifferent construct insofar as it can be applied to every particular. Such indifferent application means that the universal is in some sense inessential.[15] The essential in *Wesen,* or essence, is, as Heidegger claims to rediscover in its origins, the fact that it is part of the verb *anwesen,* to be present, and of *Anwesenheit,* presence, the essential trait of Being as defined by the early

Greeks. What is essential about something, what constitutes the *Wesen* that Heidegger uses idiosyncratically as a verb as well as a noun, is to be abidingly present. Meta-physical thought leaves *physis*, or Being, behind, as it attempts to reach an atemporal realm of universals. Heidegger believes his stress on presence introduces temporality into thought, for things must be considered within the framework of historicity.

Heidegger's language games call attention to features of the ontology of language that models of communication or expression do not identify. Language does perdure, it is abiding, we even understand "dead languages" from other eras, and this perdurance is perhaps as arresting a fact about language as the fact that it is a tool one uses (or uses up) or that it undergoes change in time. Heidegger's playful subversion of the notion of essence finds its final formulation in the following chiasmus: "Wesen der Sprache: Sprache des Wesens"—essence of language: language of essence.[16] This figure suggests that looking for an essence of language leads to a language of abiding presence, a language in which *physis, logos,* and Being are coterminous.

Heidegger's rejection of essence in any traditional sense remains ambiguous with regard to a possible interpretation of what literary language might be. One thrust is certainly a rejection of any symbolist or modernist views of language as a transcendent artefact outside of history. Language does not function poetically as the expression of an inner self mediated by an essential symbol, nor does it offer an essential image with some metaphysical provenance. When Heidegger turns to comment on specific poems, his rejection of the transcendental status of poetic images obliges him to explore these poems in terms of immanent oppositions or differences, an approach that often seems close to structuralist procedures. His refusal of traditional commentary is consistent with his views that the exegesis can only facilitate entry into the language of the poem itself. Yet, this procedure is not inconsistent with the modernist credo that a poem should not mean but "be." Ultimately the disclosure of presence through language is really not so far from the modernist search for revelation, even if Heidegger insists that the locus of disclosure is language itself. The same ambiguity with regard to modernist aesthetics haunts Heidegger's thought that we saw hovering about his attitude toward Hegel and the temporalizing of logos that characterizes the Hegelian system. The ambivalence undoubtedly springs from the same source: Heidegger's need to overcome the metaphysics of essence at the same time that he desires to utilize the notion of the fall into time and to keep the possibility of poetic language as a way of overcoming the fall. He wishes to reject Hegel while keeping an essential part of the Hegelian phenomenology of history; and he wishes to deconstruct essence while retaining a doctrine of essential poetic revelation.

In developing in his last writings his subsequent cosmology or what he calls the *Geviert*—the fourfold of men and gods, earth and sky—Heidegger elaborates a view of language as difference, which is to say language as the founder or solicitor of the differences that make up the world. Language is thus coextensive with Being. In this view language cannot be interpreted as a substance with an inner and an outer dimension, nor as a mirror that would reflect some transcendental locus of meaning. With the rejection of abstract essence, language can only be experienced from within; metaphorically speaking, from within the house of Being. This thought "on the way to language" necessarily rejects many of our commonsense notions about language, for such notions are usually unexamined metaphysical assumptions which have come to define what we take to be everyday language. Heidegger wants to recast entirely the way we think the relation of language to all other activities:

> If attention is fastened exclusively on human speech, if human speech is simply to be the voicing of the inner man, if speech so conceived is regarded as language itself, then the nature [*Wesen*] of language can never appear as anything but an expression and activity of man. But human speech, as the speech of mortals, is not self-subsistent. The speech of mortals rests in its relation to the speaking of language. (*Poetry, Language, Thought*, p. 208)

Real language is subservient to some more primordial language, the logos that determines what thought can be, and what can be thought.

This reversal of the Aristotelian tradition—or this return to Heraclitus if one prefers—means that language is not fundamentally a form of re-presentation of metaphysical entities (universals, ideas, or concepts) found in some other locus than language itself (say, in the Aristotelian soul, the Platonic heaven, or Husserl's transcendental consciousness). Language is autonomous. "Die Sprache spricht," as Heidegger laconically says in his later work; language, not the subject, speaks.[17] Which language? Although the later Heidegger does not frequently insist on the difference between authentic and inauthentic language, he assumes that when he qualifies poetic language as *Eigenlicht,* the opposition to inauthentic language is understood. Authentic language speaks, and we must be attentive to this language if we are to understand Being's call from within the fourfold.

Authentic hearing is also a part of language. Man must be able to hear if he is to make his own language correspond to logos that confers Being. The necessary precondition for hearing is stillness, the silence against which language differentiates itself. Saying stands out against silence. Heidegger's work also contributes heavily to that fascination with silence for which Wittgenstein's *Tractatus* has been more than a little responsible. Might one speak of a myth of silence in this respect? In any case Heidegger's later essays attribute as much importance to stillness as they do to the autonomy of language.

The breaking of silence is the condition for the advent of the holy. In the 1939 essay "Wie wenn am Feiertage . . . ," Heidegger makes this claim for the speaking *(Sagen)* in Hölderlin's poetry:

When the sacred beam strikes the poet, he is not torn away in the beam's flash, but rather is fully turned toward the sacred [*dem Heiligen*]. To be sure, the soul of the poet shudders and allows to be awakened in itself the stilled movement; but it quivers from remembrance and wishes to speak [*Sagen*] from expectation of that which happened before: that is the sacred's revealing of itself. The shuddering breaks the quiet of silence. The word becomes. The word-work that arises in such a way makes appear the mutual belonging together of God and man.[18]

The breaking of the stillness of silence and the self-opening or revelation of the poetic word occur against the backdrop of Heidegger's cosmological fourfold in which logos comes to bind together, in their difference, men and the gods, the earth and the sky. In *On the Way to Language* the notion of difference is also linked with the primacy of silence. Language is "the peal of silence" that allows the occurrence of difference, bringing about the *Unter-schied* (dif-ference, or the tearing asunder, as the Latin roots indicate) of world and things.

Language introduces the differentiation that allows world and things to exist separately, though they are united in the fourfold. By analogy, differentiation may throw some light on what Heidegger means earlier by calling Nothingness the veil of Being.[19] "What is" can stand out only against what is not, much as language needs silence in order to exist. Beings are "unconcealed" only against the undifferentiated totality that Heidegger alternately calls Being or Nothingness. In an analogous manner language can call things into being only against the undifferentiated stillness of silence. And this structural analogy would justify the metaphorical identity of language and Being, *physis* and logos. I stress the underlying unity of Heidegger's thought because it appears to me that the myth of the fall also underlies all these formulations. Heidegger's cosmology would find the origins of "what is" in pure undifferentiated being, in a primordial silence that can be likened to some form of paradise—especially when compared to the incessant noise that characterizes modern life. Our fall must be measured in terms of the distance that lies between our present corrupt state in which all language is appropriated by "publicity" *(Offenlichkeit)* and a pure state of holy silence.

The advent of the holy is, of course, not brought about by ordinary language's breaking silence, but by the poetic word or saying, conceived of as the autonomous speaking of language itself. The autonomy of language commands another major theme in Heidegger's work: language speaks essentially about itself. This theme is never elaborated in the later essays, since to do so would necessarily involve recourse to meta-linguistic considerations. Meta-linguistically, one can maintain, however, that language for Heidegger is essentially an act of self-representation or of auto-reference. Language is a self-contained series of differentiations that, insofar as it brings beings to light, brings itself to light. This view of language is reflected directly in the poems Heidegger chooses for commentary. They are poems about poetry (or that Heidegger interprets as being about poetry), self-referential texts about the advent of the word and hence about the advent of the holy or the sacred. They are poems about their own creation or the conditions of possibility for the advent of the poetic word.

The need to speak of self-referentiality without using the notion seems to lie behind Heidegger's use of the word *Ereignis*—event—or the moment in which language and Being are somehow joined. I have noted that in his early usage *Ereignis* is the mirror-image joining together of what is said and the saying in the advent of the holy. ("Das Heilige verschenkt das Wort und kommt selbst in dieses Wort. Das Wort ist das Ereignis des Heiligen.")[20] But Heidegger's later essays give a different sense to *Ereignis,* which most English and French translators would render as "the event of appropriation." In *On the Way to Language* the *Ereignis* is another tautological formulation for logos, grounding language in itself as the collector of what is said.[21] Language is self-motivated, for it is both what it names as well as that which calls the named into being. Heidegger has thus moved from a metaphor that might suggest a mirror image to one that would present language as self-mirroring, circularly present to itself as self-representation—if the idea of representation can still be used to describe this kind of tautological thinking that seeks to avoid every taint of metaphysics.

These reflections on mirrors remind us that vision remains a privileged theme throughout Heidegger's work, although the final essays reverse the direction of sight. Even in *Being and Time,* one might argue, language mirrors meanings that exist outside language. In the later essays the mirroring goes, as it were, in the opposite direction, for beings are called to be by language: they mirror the collecting of logos, they reflect the differences articulated by language. In *On the Way to Language* Heidegger continues to conceive of language as a form of manifestation, for "saying" is an opening to vision. "Die Sage ist Zeigen," as Heidegger says in his essay "The Way to Language":

> Saying is showing. In everything that speaks to us, in everything that touches us by being spoken and spoken about, in everything that gives itself to us in speaking, or waits for us unspoken, but also in the speaking that we do *ourselves,* there prevails Showing [*das Zeigen*] which causes to appear what is present, and to fade from appearance what is absent. Saying is in no way the linguistic expression added to the phenomena after they have appeared—rather, all radiant appearance and all fading away is grounded in the showing Saying.[22]

The tightly knit circularity of Heidegger's vision of logos and Being is powerful. All that is can be differentiated only against what is not, which presupposes the articulations of language. Nothing can be named without these articulations; and so, to be is to be in language, and to be in language is to be shown to be.

Whether one finds Heidegger's cosmology compelling or not, one can see that Heidegger is seeking to formulate a difficult aspect of the ontology of language. For if language provides access to what is, how can one speak of the relation of world and language? Can one separate them? In this view language cannot be considered another entity within an abstract domain of entities, which is, according to Heidegger, the way science views language. For if we encounter beings within the world only through language, then language itself must have a different order of being from beings themselves. This difference lies behind Heidegger's repeated insistence that one must distinguish between beings and Being, as well as his claim that language is not a being itself: rather, saying is Being. In a different perspective one might say that language has the same ontological features as the world and is the condition of possibility for there being world at all. Therefore, all the features we attribute to the world can be attributed to language and vice versa, for these features can only exist as discriminations made in language. This attributing of the same ontological features to world and to language is a strategy that Heidegger first used in "The Origin of the Work of Art." And, metaphorically, poetry, language, logos are all the same, according to the self-grounding tautology that underlies all of Heidegger's later work.

One should not be too quick to dismiss Heidegger's *Geviert,* the fourfold of men and gods, earth and heaven. The fourfold is another attempt on Heidegger's part to rethink our being in the world in non-Cartesian terms. If, as I have suggested, in *Being and Time* Heidegger sought to be our modern Aristotle, in the later essays he has attempted to be a postmodern Heraclitus, offering us a cosmology owing nothing to the metaphysical ordering that separates world and subject. I do not think that this world vision should be taken as mystical in any conventional sense, although Heidegger clearly desires to overcome metaphysics so that the sacred might appear once again to men. Heidegger's fascination with Heraclitus springs in part from the simple fact that the gods still spoke when Heraclitus lived, or so we can conceive. Moreover, Heraclitus is the thinker of difference, and his thought proposes a view of language as the source of all differentiations that make up the cosmos. As Maurice Blanchot has suggested, difference stands at the center of Heraclitus's thought as that unnamable that is always different from whatever might express it: all is articulated through difference, yet nothing can reduce it to the sayable.[23] The analogies with Heidegger's thought on Being are multiple, especially in the way Heidegger's conception of the fourfold attempts to recapture a sense of world that incarnates the play of difference that Heraclitus placed at the center of the cosmos.

Within the confines of the fourfold, language acts as the *Unter-Schied,* as the process of differentiation that holds apart the regions of the world while it joins them in the coherence that makes up a world. I would suggest that finally being and difference are another metaphorical pair that allows what is to exist. Difference is a tearing open, the strife that opens up the world when truth enters the artwork. Strife is a fundamental condition of world, or as a fragment of Heraclitus says: "Homer was wrong in saying 'Would that strife might perish from amongst gods and men.' For if that were to occur, then all things would cease to exist."[24] Heidegger's cosmology aims through this metaphorical language at bringing us back to a more primordial experience of the world. The metaphor of strife contributes to a portrayal of how the world is always an openness that is our openness, our receptiveness; and the metaphysical notion of a relation between subject and object—lifeless metaphors themselves—cannot describe this living in the cosmos. Men and gods, earth and sky, this is Heidegger's primordial experience in which differences coincide with language.

The notion of play is another key theme for our purposes that appears with increasing frequency in Heidegger's later writings. The play of difference joins together the four world-regions. Play is the antithesis of strife in that it unites what strife might appear to tear apart. In the relatively late essay "The Nature of Language," Heidegger proposes a way of viewing space and time as being joined in the play of the cosmos. They play out their reciprocity in the play space of primordial stillness:

> Time's removing and bringing to us, and space's throwing open, admitting and releasing—they all belong together in the Same, the play of stillness. . . . The Same, which holds space and time gathered up in their nature, might be called the time-play-space *(Zeit-Spiel-Raum)*, that is the time-space that gives free scope to all things. Timing and spacing, the Same of the time-play-space moves the encounter of the four world regions: earth and sky, god and man—the world play [*das Weltspiel*].[25]

Concomitant with the play of difference is the play of the same, holding together in the world that which is separated by strife. Formulated in this way, play is another metaphor for language and Being.

If Heidegger says in *Identity and Difference* that play is the essence of Being, it is not therefore, as George Steiner would have it in his elegant *Martin Heidegger,* because Heidegger finds the attempt to separate Being from beings to be merely a futile game.[26] Heidegger consistently made play at least a subordinate part of his thought. To philosophize is, as he often repeated, to think within the play-space of tradition *(Spielraum der Uberlieferung)*, though translations have usually lost the association with play *(Spiel)* contained in such German expressions. As a self-justifying activity, as a set of autonomous rules sufficient unto themselves, play is a complementary thought-metaphor for the kind of tautological thinking that Heidegger increasingly placed in the fore of his philosophy. Heidegger was not quick, however, to give play a leading role in his work. One can suppose that his Lutheran heritage would not let him easily embrace the idea that poetry could be play—mere play as Heidegger first phrased it. Yet, if logos can have no other ground than its own self-given rules, few other metaphors can offer access to thought about Being.

There are a number of references to play in "The Origin of the Work of Art." Most importantly, truth establishes itself in the *Spielraum* (free space, or room for "play") that strife opens within the art work, which parallels the Heideggerian assumption that art exists as an autonomous thing. Its autonomy is analogous to the autonomy that characterizes play or the play space. In the early essays on Hölderlin in the thirties, Heidegger draws back from the thrust of his own thought; he is fascinated by the idea that poetry corresponds to a ludic activity but cannot bring himself to use play as the kind of all-embracing metaphor that one finds in Wittgenstein. By the time he gave his lectures in 1951-52, gathered under the title *What Is Called Thinking?* Heidegger had accepted the idea that language is a play form. In keeping with his thought about the autonomy of language, he advanced the view there that language plays with man and his speech—man now understood as one of the regions making up the fourfold and hence one region in the play of difference that makes up the world.

Heidegger is a diffident ludic theorist, for the notion of play first appears in his work with the kind of pejorative connotation that one would expect only from a thinker who affirms the metaphysical division of the world into the real and the illusory. But any thinker who wishes to overcome metaphysics must overcome Plato, and play is one of the key questions with which the modern thinker can challenge the binary oppositions written into metaphysical thinking, as Plato himself knew when he anathematized mere play and illusion. To lead us into a thought that *is* play, in these lectures Heidegger first asks if it is merely playing with words when we attempt to give heed to the games of language and to hear what language says when it speaks.[27] This question throws light on what it means to say that man must "correspond" to language if he is to hear it authentically, which is to say, if he is to hear the call of Being. In what I take to be a nontrivial sense, man must play by the rules of the game, for the game of language has its rules; and these would be, in Heidegger's view, the laws of Being. I say a nontrivial sense, for giving heed to the games of language means more than obeying publicly-given grammar rules in order to form comprehensible sentences: creating significant utterances means using the restraints and licenses imposed by language to create the "full language" of a Hölderlin or a Rilke.

The game of language underlies what Heidegger calls the *Mehrdeutigkeit* of words, or what one translator calls the "meaning-fullness" of words. Another translation might propose "polysemy," for it seems clear that Heidegger, like the later Wittgenstein, came to accept the play of ambiguity as a necessary feature of language. Late Heidegger celebrates the polysemantic play of language that reaches its greatest elaboration in the "saying" *(die Sage)* of commemorative thinking. Every learner must master this commemorative thought by testing it:

> Here we recognize why every form of expression [*jedes Sagen*] of this sort struggles on in awkwardness. It always goes through the essential meaning-fullness [*Mehrdeutigkeit*] of words and phraseology. The meaning-fullness of language [*Sage*] by no means consists in a mere accumulation of meanings cropping up haphazardly. It is based on a play [*Spiel*] which, the more richly it unfolds, the more strictly it is bound by a hidden rule. Through this, meaning-fullness plays a part in what has been selected

and weighed in the scale whose oscillations we seldom experience. That is why what is said is bound by the highest law. That is the freedom which gives freedom to the all-playing structure of never-resting transformation.[28]

Increasingly, as Heidegger's thought thinks about limits, it proposes play as a model of how creation takes place within the restraints of law. The polysemantic nature of language is subject to rules. In this rule-bound freedom language offers the free play of unending transformations. Within the *Spielraum* of tradition, such play elaborates the meanings we take to be thought and culture.

Heidegger's thought aims here at reconciling freedom and necessity, and in making language the place of that reconciliation, Heidegger again seems very close to Wittgenstein and is the source for some of the later thought about play that characterizes the work of Jacques Derrida. He is even closer to Wittgenstein when, at the conclusion of his *Der Satz vom Grund,* published in 1957, he offers the image of the game of draughts (checkers) as the concluding metaphor for how one might describe an ontology of logos and Being that owes nothing to foundations provided by the principle of sufficient reason. Turning again to Heraclitus for a premetaphysical model of thought to validate his own thinking, Heidegger examines the following fragment on time as a thought that can give a résumé of the world's play; it reads in an English translation:

Time *(?Aion)* is a child at play, playing draughts; the kingship is the child's.

This is the translation that a cautious English classics scholar would propose, with the commentary that *Aion* "is mostly likely to refer to human lifetime, perhaps with the special connotation of the destiny which is worked out by the individual during his lifetime."[29] Heidegger sees in Heraclitus's playing child the founding and governing of all reason-giving *(Gründe),* the *archē,* the Being of beings, and thus he translates:

Fated sending of Being [*Seinsgeschick*], a child it is, playing, playing draughts [*Brettspiel*], a child's is the kingdom.[30]

Being and time—perhaps here is the solution to the work Heidegger left unfinished some thirty years earlier. Time as sending of Being, Being as play, all three are united in the ludic metaphor describing the play as the world and the world as play.

Heidegger offers the image of the child playing as his response to the principle of sufficient reason, the metaphysical postulate that states that everything has a reason or a cause. If one applies this principle to the child, then one asks why the child plays. Why is there Being rather than nothingness, why is there logos? In play, however, the "why" disappears: the child plays because he plays. And, as Heidegger says, the "because" then sinks away, losing its role as a link in the chain of sufficient reasons with which metaphysics would encircle the world. Being comes to pass as play, and the "why" resolves itself in the indentity Heidegger sees between Being and *Grund,* variously interpreted as *ratio,* ground, cause, reason. The child at his board plays, and it is within this *Spielraum* that he finds the kingdom of what is.

This metaphorical play ultimately represents a therapeutic end, for it wishes to cure us of the need to look for false questions and the pseudo-answers that inevitably follow. Heidegger's incessant questioning about Being appears, when taken in this light, to be far less obscurantist that many would claim, for his questioning eliminates metaphysical questions and distinctions: it reduces the realm of the problematic to the simple viewing of what is. Logos is play, and play is self-justifying. There are no reasons that transcend play or logos, or Being itself. By attributing once more the same ontological features to realms that we normally hold apart—to play, logos, Being, and time—Heidegger eliminates the need for finding differentiating essences. Play holds all together as the same— which strife holds apart in the play of difference. As the play of the same, time is the fated sending of Being, which in turn can be characterized as the process of play, as moves on a board, a child's activity for which there is neither a why nor a because. One plays because one plays.

Heidegger reduces the world to a meaningful tautology. With play as the privileged metaphor, he circumvents the great metaphysical principle of sufficient reason that has been the primary tool in the quest for origins. In saying that all has a reason or cause, traditional Christianity has, for example, traced the great chain of causes back to the self-caused cause, the God of Western metaphysics. The image of play makes meaningless any quest for an origin, since it offers a nontranscendental ground for Being and logos. Being comes to pass like the moves on a chessboard, according to the immanent rules that govern the game, or better yet—since the notion of immanence suggests a metaphysical pairing with transcendence—according to the free play of self-accepted laws that exist because they exist. There is a paradox in this point of view, since it might well appear that, in returning to Heraclitus for his image of play, Heidegger returned to the origins in order to find a thought that would abolish the metaphysics of origins. Such a paradox parallels Heidegger's ambivalent stance toward Hegelian history and the aesthetics of modernism; or the ambivalence of his rejection of the classical metaphysics that makes of vision knowlege, even as he interprets logos as showing. But with regard to play, Heidegger is an exemplary post-modern. Finding no ground for logos that would underwrite the arbitrary absolute that language seems to represent, he turned to play for the metaphor that allows him to escape from his own groundlessness. Like Wittgenstein, Heidegger leaves us with the world exactly as we find it—given in language, once we rid language of the metaphysics that has falsified our understanding of it. But unlike Witt-genstein, and more like the Didi or Gogo of *Waiting for Godot,* this postmodern thinker about the sacred also leaves us waiting for something else.

3. Ferdinand de Saussure and Jacques Derrida

In this chapter I wish to explore an exemplary scientific paradigm for the understanding of language. For this purpose there can be no more compelling example than that of Ferdinand de Saussure. Let us therefore make a historical turn and go back to that moment before the publication of the *Tractatus* when the then obscure Swiss philologist was elaborating the methodology that would be the basis for European structuralist linguistics. This science has also provided the conceptual tools for structural anthropology as elaborated by Claude Lévi-Strauss and for the science of signs that has come to be known as semiotics.[1] This historical reversal will be followed by another, for it will be useful to conclude this excursus into language theory by arriving in the Paris of the heady sixties. At that moment Jacques Derrida, pursuing the Heideggerian project of overcoming metaphysics, made a "reading" of Saussure that demonstrated the degree to which Saussure's thought belongs to the core of most thinking about language today. Derrida undertook to lay bare the metaphysical assumptions underlying Saussure's thought. But this reading could only be undertaken by using the axioms of Saussure's thought itself—as read through a Heideggerian prism. These meanderings through history will, I hope, show to what degree a remarkable consensus about many aspects of language theory has prevailed throughout the twentieth century.

In returning to that period at the end of the nineteenth century when Saussure was an academic philologist, working within the paradigms of the "New Grammarians," we should recall that he was also the contemporary of the philologist Friedrich Nietzsche, who understood well how systems of thought must work as a necessary consensus. There are historical limits that condition the possibility for thought in terms of the reigning systems of concepts, and Nietzsche saw this correlation of concepts to function as a historical law:

> That the separate philosophical ideas are not anything optional or autonomously evolving, but grow up in connection and relationship with each other; that, however suddenly and arbitrarily they seem to appear in the history of thought, they nevertheless belong just as much to a system as the collective members of the fauna of a Continent—is betrayed in the end by the circumstance: how unfailingly the most diverse philosophers

always fill in again a definite fundamental scheme of *possible* philosophies.[2]

The Nietzsche of *Beyond Good and Evil* saw the necessity of the systemic interrelation of thought at any time (of what Foucault would later call the possibilities of the *epistemē)*; and if we accept Nietzsche's reading of the systemic nature of thought, it was perhaps no accident that his contemporary Saussure made the notion of *system* the cornerstone of his thought about language. Moreover, Saussure was the kind of demystifier who would have quickly understood the kind of philology Nietzsche was undertaking.

For, among other things, Nietzsche was putting an end to the Lockean belief that ideas—the basis for language—arise passively from the reception of sense data. Ideas are bound up in language as systems existing in history.

To place Saussure in this context, with Nietzsche, is to suggest similarities that account for Saussure's belated appeal to our minds, well after the "Copernican revolution" he effected in linguistics seems to have been displaced by another "Copernican turn" by Chomsky and his generative theory.[3] Saussure belongs to the era of demystifiers that begins with Nietzsche and includes Wittgenstein, the logical positivists, and the early Heidegger. This era finds its final thinkers, it might appear, in the varieties of structuralist thought that have proliferated in France and Italy—and of which Jacques Derrida would be the latest product. Saussure, the philologist and inventor of modern linguistics, inaugurates a way of thinking that finds its full resonance when read as a response to nineteenth-century thought about language and, ultimately, to the way modernism attempted to revive the Western Platonic tradition.

Saussure's work in linguistic methodology was elaborated at the beginning of this century, during a teaching career that unfolded first in Paris, then in Geneva, where he taught until his death in 1913. Like Aristotle's work and much of Hegel's, Saussure's major work, the *Course of General Linguistics*, published in 1916, is based on collocations of notes taken by students. In its present form this work is based on three different courses on general linguistics that he gave at the end of his life. As such, the *Course* does not represent any final formulation. In its present state the book seems at times to be animated by two discordant impulses: to make language an isolated object of scientific inquiry and to show that language is a form of social practice. It has also been subject to criticism for supposedly utilizing elements taken from earlier thought on language. To be sure, Saussure was influenced by Enlightenment theories, but to point out this influence in no way diminishes the originality of his thought. His *Course* proposes an analytic methodology—in effect an all-encompassing scientific paradigm— that may well incorporate earlier views on language but that in its totality represents an entirely new means for explaining language. This methodology makes Saussure the father, or rather grandfather, of the modern study of linguistics; for the *Course* has opened a field of inquiry emblematic of the twentieth century's scrutiny of language as an object of scientific investigation.

Before Saussure, language had, of course, been the object of categorizing and of various types of grammatical inquiries (usually inherited from the Greeks, as far as Western thought is concerned). In the nineteenth century it had been the object of historical inquiries that, using models adapted from philosophy, history, and biology, had made great achievements in classifying various languages and in developing various taxonomies. But for modern purposes linguistics—taking language as a separate object of scientific investigation, using its own procedural model—begins with Saussure. Reacting against the models of organicity used by comparative grammar in the nineteenth century, Saussure stressed that the very nature of what philologists were investigating had not yet been defined by historical linguistics:

> This school, which had the incontestable merit of opening a new and fertile field, did not succeed in constituting a true linguistic science. It was never concerned with bringing to light the object of its study. Without this elementary operation, a science is incapable of becoming a method.[4]

Saussure criticizes those nineteenth-century comparatists who saw in language "an organism that develops by itself" and failed to recognize that language is the "product of the collective spirit of linguistic groups" (p. 19). This criticism might seem incompatible with the final words that the editors added to conclude the course, to the effect that linguistics has for its unique and true object language envisaged in itself and for itself. The editors have, to be sure, given us a *Course* that seems to reflect their preoccupation with isolating the study of language from its social matrix. But Saussure's thought also includes the procedural necessity of a methodological separation of linguistics from other sciences. Even in placing words in Saussure's mouth, the editors have not been unfaithful to the basic orientation of the course. Only after this separation is made can language be seen, in a Saussurean perspective, as a social product or a collection of social practices. Saussure's critique of nineteenth-century metaphors of organicity takes one step toward identifying the social locus of language, while his stress on the need for identifying precisely what language is shows that language is a unique phenomenon. Needless to say, this dual thrust to Saussure's thought has given rise to various interpretations as to how the *Course* should have been edited in order better to reflect whatever might have been Saussure's real thought.[5]

In the following discussion I propose to discuss the *Course* as it exists. Had Saussure lived longer, he undoubtedly would have given us a different book. What concerns us here is the *Course* as it has existed for a number of decades. The following exposition of its basic principles is perforce an interpretation, but one that many of Saussure's critical readers agree upon. Scientific paradigms must, after all, be transmissible. As my point of departure for characterizing Saussure's model for understanding what language is (and let us bear in mind the passage from Nietzsche), I take the premise that language is a system. Though some of Saussure's later critics have claimed that his conception of language as an autonomous system is either invalid or not consonant with his own premises about language being a sum of social practices, the description of language as a system is at the center of Saussure's thought. This characterization (or premise) makes language amenable to rational description. As such, the notion of system commands all the other perspectives in the *Course*. Certainly Saussure's formulations of system have, in various guises, found constant application in later linguistic thought, ranging from the models proposed by such European structuralists as Hjelmslev or Martinet to the transformational grammars of Chomsky and his followers. For example, Hjelmslev's *Prolegomena to a Theory of Language* sets forth a clear definition of system that has become the operational hypothesis for all linguistics after Saussure:

A priori it would seem to be a generally valid thesis that for every *process* there is a corresponding *system*, by which the process can be analyzed and described by means of a limited number of premises. It must be assumed that any process can be analyzed into a limited number of elements recurring in various combinations. Then, on the basis of this analysis, it should be possible to order these elements into classes according to their possibilities of combination.[6]

The description of the system will then, according to this structuralist credo, give rise to "a generalizing science, in the theory of which all events (possible combination of elements) are foreseen and the conditions for their realization established."

"Process" and "system" are new formulations for Saussure's distinction between *parole*, or individual speech acts, and *langue*, or language as a hypothesized system. This separation of the individual speech act and the system of which it is a realization is the first operative step in describing the system. One danger in such a structuralist approach to language is that the linguist invents a hypothesized model that he then projects onto the process of speech acts that supposedly embody the system. The hypothesized systemic model is taken to be the system studied. Such a shift hypostatizes the model and makes of the linguist's fiction a substantial reality. (Lévi-Strauss's application of Saussure's models has, for instance, been subject to such a criticism.) Saussure himself noted this problem when he remarked that it might appear that it is the observer's point of view that creates the object of his study.[7] This problem raises a basic problem of scientific epistemology. A model's giving rise to the object studied represents, it seems to me, a circularity that underlies much scientific method; one must look to other criteria to decide if an operational hypothesis is satisfactory or not. As Wittgenstein remarked about Newtonian mechanics, nothing is said about the world when it allows itself to be described by such a model—except that the world does allow itself to be so described. The question is how well.

The system that underlies the language we speak is not apparent to ordinary speakers of that language. As Saussure describes it, this system is a "complex mechanism" that cannot be understood except by "reflexive activity": "those who use it every day are profoundly ignorant of it" (p. 107). In stressing the unconscious nature of the system as mechanism, Saussure has replaced the organic metaphor, with its biological and historical connotations, that the nineteenth century had used to describe language. To be sure, he has replaced it with another metaphor, for however much the idea of system may motivate the choice of "mechanism," this descriptive term is equally metaphorical. This metaphor stresses at once the self-contained nature of language and the structuralist view of the language-machine as a system in which all parts are hooked to all other parts. As we shall see, this is a favored postmodern metaphor, offering the writer possibilities for affirming both his creativeness and his alienation.

This mechanism lies beyond our conscious mind. It can only be laid bare by the model that might illuminate it. As might be expected from a thinker who did not live to put his thoughts in final form, Saussure is not always consistent in his thought with this metaphor that presents language as a mechanism lying beyond consciousness. He also states that the system of language, though invisible to the speaker who makes use of it, is completely psychological in its ultimate reality: "At bottom everything in language is psychological in nature, including its material and mechanical manifestations, such as the changes of sounds" (p. 21). I take Saussure to mean by this statement that the material embodiment of language—graphic signs or oral performance—is a matter of indifference with regard to the system itself. However, such a formulation tends to suggest that the individual subject is the locus for the study of language. But this psychological particularization would make the notion of system ultimately untenable or inapplicable. The primary orientation of Saussure's thought argues clearly against a view of language as a series of psychological determinations. As the mechanism metaphor implies, his views also give support to the idea, comparable to Heidegger's later thought, that the subject is spoken by language. Or, as Jacques Derrida later formulated it in a thought that joins together Saussure and Heidegger, the subject only exists thanks to language.[8]

Saussure's view of system is not harmed by the psychologizing vocabulary, the "mentalism," that today seems to inhabit the *Course* as a reminder that Saussure lived most of his life in the nineteenth century. The twentieth-century linguist, as prepared by Saussure, need take note of individual speech acts only as manifestations of the underlying system. This system's locus is disclosed by the self-reflexive act that brings it to light. It exists in the public space of what we can call the space of description. In the *Course of General Linguistics* the system is described by a series of binary oppositions or pairings that are as powerful in their scope as they are exhaustive in their intent. Though Saussure did not explicitly set forth a binary creed as the ordering operation for linguistic description, binary ordering does constitute the heart of his methodology and has remained the major model for structuralist thought. In this discussion of Saussure, I propose to examine these binary oppositions and some of the problems they present for a description of the system that makes up every language. With this description of language as a system of oppositions, it would appear that Saussure believed he had laid bare for the first time what language is when considered in itself.

The first binary pairing in the system in operational terms is found in Saussure's principle that linguistics must be divided into diachronic and synchronic domains. In describing language one must distinguish between the study of the change of the system through time—the diachronic—and the description of the hypothesized static state of the linguistic system at any given moment in time—the synchronic. At every moment language is, as Saussure says, a current institution (*institution actuelle*) and a product of evolution through time. As a product of the past, language can be described diachronically. This was the principal preoccupation of nineteenth-century philology. For Saussure, however, linguistics as a science must give priority to the synchronic description of language as a fixed system. The primacy given to synchrony effects a break with those nineteenth-century studies of language that used biologically oriented models of evolution and taxonomy. It also marks a break with the historicism of the linguistic work that had developed from the time of Grimm, Rask, Schlegel, and Bopp and which, during Saussure's lifetime, had culminated in the studies of the Neogrammarians at the end of the nineteenth century.

To speak of this break is not to say that Saussure intended to disparage the historical study of language. Historical work interested him personally more than any other aspect of the study of language. The distinction between diachronic and synchronic linguistics, however, imposed itself upon him as a methodological necessity, as a way of introducing some rationality into the study of language. For, as Saussure saw, no reason, no cause, can be given for the diachronic nature of language. No satisfactory answer can be given as to why every aspect of language changes in time. Confronted with this fundamentally irrational side of language, Saussure felt, perhaps, that he must find a way of ordering the description of language that would be as rational as possible: hence, language as a fixed mechanism. The primacy of the sychronous language machine portended one of the most significant shifts in our contemporary intellectual economy. To generalize the primacy of this ordering entails the exclusion of history from our intellectual concerns. Such an exclusion is not the least of the dilemmas facing postmodern thinkers.

Working with the first premise, that language is a system, and having excluded the diachronic dimension from the space of his description, the linguist uses another set of oppositions to order the object of his inquiry: each instance of *parole* is an individual manifestation of the *langue* or the system of the natural language in question. Difficulties of translation arise from the existence in French of a third term, *language,* that, like *langue,* can be translated as "language."

Langage, as distinguished from *langue*, is the faculty of speech as opposed to a given natural "tongue" or *langue*. *Langage* can also mean a repository of signs or techniques for communication (in the sense of, say, *langage cinématographique*). *Langue* is, for Saussure, the system of the individual language such as French or English, whereas *parole* is the individualized utterance of that *langue* or language system. The same kind of distinction lies behind Chomsky's separation of competence and performance, in that transformational grammar also hypothesizes an internalized linguistic system in the individual that allows him to "generate" individual speech utterances in conformity with the rules of the system.[9] Semioticians have also used Saussure's distinction to specify that the *langue* is a code (an expression used only once in the *Course*), whereas the *parole* is the individual message expressed. In all these formulations language is considered an autonomous entity, a virtual code or system, that transcends any individual use of the system, and yet can be said to exist only as the totality of the individual language-users' possession of the code. Such a totality exists as a definition of what constitutes a language community.

If we say that the language system transcends any individual speaker's comprehension of it, we might well give the impression that Saussure's *langue* exists in some metaphysical heaven of ideal French or English. That the *langue* exists seemingly as an abstraction has certainly given rise to suspicions that it is a metaphysical construct, perhaps a Durkheimian creation, existing in some ideal realm apart from social reality. Such a suspicion strikes me as having little validity, for Saussure's description of *la langue* allows a reading that emphasizes its concrete social nature:

> If we were able to embrace the sum of verbal images stored in all individuals, we would touch the social bond [*lien*] that constitutes language. It is a store [*trésor*] placed, through the practice of speech [*parole*], in all subjects belonging to the same community, a grammatical system existing in virtual terms in every brain. (P. 30)

The abstraction *langue* exists as the foundation of a culture, as a collective realization, but one that can only be revealed in the space of inquiry.

There are other ways of describing the nature of *langue*. In Roland Barthes' semiotic perspective, it is not only a code but also a social contract. The contractual metaphor is sanctioned by Saussure's use of it in the *Course* (p. 31). Saussure may well have remembered this metaphor's success during the Enlightenment, especially in the work of a fellow citizen of Geneva, Jean-Jacques Rousseau. The metaphor likening the language system to a contract is felicitous in that it stresses the reciprocal bond linking language and culture and the type of access to communal membership that is essentially defined by language. This metaphor points, moreover, to affinities with Wittgenstein's view of language as the ethnological bond that creates a people's world view. Tullio de Mauro, for example, interprets the thought of the "later" Saussure—the Saussure of the third course—to be quite compatible with Wittgenstein's notion that language derives from a series of social practices that can be identified in a public space of social recognition.[10] Mauro is correct, though one scarcely need examine the manuscript sources to see Saussure's emphasis on social usage as the locus of the language system.

The distinction between a virtual system and individual instances of real speech brings up the question of the individual subject's capacity to deal, in some autonomous manner, with the system that lies beyond his consciousness. In purely methodological terms this was not a problem for Saussure, since the only object of linguistic inquiry is *la langue*, the sum of all individual cases of *parole*. And for Saussure it is only the operational hypothesis about *langue* that matters. Yet, Saussure did briefly address himself to the question of the relation between the subject and his language. These comments seem to anticipate Chomsky's view of the rule-bound freedom of the individual speaker: bound by a finite series of transformational rules, the speaker has the capacity for the genesis of an indefinite number of utterances. Saussure also sees in language a space in which freedom and necessity are conjoined:

> Language is not a function of the speaking subject; it is a product that the
> individual registers passively. Speech is on the other hand an individual
> act of will and intelligence, in which one should distinguish (1) the
> combinations through which the speaking subject uses the language code
> in order to express his personal thoughts and (2) the psycho-physical
> mechanism that allows him to exteriorize these combinations. (Pp. 30-31)

These remarks also seem to have a dual thrust. On the one hand Saussure does appear to vouchsafe the autonomy of the subject and the possibility of individual creativity—within the limits of the "psycho-physical" mechanism that underlies language. On the other hand, with a shift in perspective, these limits might appear to circumscribe severely the individual's autonomy. Moreover, the mechanism metaphor might appear to undermine the very act of will that Saussure here ascribes to the subject's use of language. As a passive receptor who acquires a language system in the same way he acquires the destiny prepared for him by biology and culture, the individual subject can be construed to be a mere topographical point in a space formed by forces that determine his entire being. Such an interpretation resembles, say, that of Lévi-Strausss, for whom Saussure, along with Freud and Marx, taught that "true reality" is never what is most manifest to consciousness.[1]

Meaning within the linguistic system is first to be defined in terms of the linguistic sign. Saussure uses another set of binary oppositions to define the sign: it is composed of a concept and an "acoustical image" or, as he prefers to say, a signified and a signifier. In common with the Wittgenstein of the *Philosophical Investigations* Saussure begins his definition of the sign by denying that linguistic signs constitute a nomenclature. Rejecting the common sense Occidental view that the sign is a noun referring to an idea or, more naively, to an object, Saussure rejected the Augustinian and the Lockean views of language in quick succession:

There is first of all the superficial concept that most people hold: they see in language only a nomenclature, an idea which does away with any research into the true nature of language. Then there is the psychologist's point of view who studies the mechanism of the sign in the individual. This is the easiest approach, but it does not lead beyond the individual performances [*exécution*] and does not reach the sign, which is social by nature. (P. 34)

Saussure shares with Wittgenstein and Heidegger the repudiation of the Aristotelian view of language as a representation of ideas in the soul or mind; and, as suggested before, he agrees with Wittgenstein that the social space of shared culture is the locus of the sign's functioning. The sign is transsubjective by its very nature. There are no private languages for Saussure any more than for Wittgenstein.

This rejection of the naive or traditional metaphysics of representation is the first step in defining the sign as the union of the signified and the signifier. If the sign cannot be defined in terms of representation—or if it cannot simply be identified with a word—then the linguist must locate it in terms of its place in the linguistic system. Representation and reference are therefore excluded as criteria for identifying a sign, a procedure that recalls Wittgenstein's demonstration of the difficulty of using ostensive definitions for knowing what a word means: one must already have an understanding of the linguistic space a word occupies before one can know how to use it. For Saussure, the autonomy of the linguistic system demands that signs be identified, both phonologically and semantically, in terms of their opposition to other signs. Signs derive their identity and meaning from their position in the space of the linguistic system: this position can be defined only by their opposition to and difference from other signs.

The notion that language is a differential sign system represents Saussure's greatest break with traditional views of language. As Tullio de Mauro has pointed out, from Plato to early Wittgenstein Western philosophy has agreed to the common premise that the signified—the concept or that to which the sign refers—could be defined in itself. This autonomy of the signified meant that the external form of the sign—material language—is only a negligible support for what is signified. Nineteenth-century historical linguistics had propagated this view in that it took as its object of study the transformations of the mere exterior or material forms of language. Saussure chastised this approach at the outset of the *Course* by declaring that the essential aspect of language has nothing to do with the phonic nature of the sign. The functioning of the sign cannot be grasped through its material forms, but only through its opposition to other signs, whatever be the morphological embodiment of the sign.

In defining the sign in itself as the union of a signifier and a signified, Saussure uses a vocabulary that, as Jakobson has noted, seems to go back to the Stoics. In anticipation of Jacques Derrida's charge that at this point metaphysics makes an entry into Saussure's thought,[12] one must point out that Saussure's use of such classical terminology takes place in an entirely new context. A more problematic issue is that, in defining the sign, Saussure's language suggests that he reverts to a kind of Lockean mentalism that is not consonant with his own view of language as a social practice: "The linguistic sign unites, not a thing and a word, but a concept and an acoustical image. The latter is not the material sound, a purely physical thing, but the psychic imprint of the sound; it is the representation for which our senses offer evidence" (p. 98). Clearly the concept is not the same as a Platonic idea, since it exists only in opposition to other concepts within the semantic space of a given language. Yet more problematic is the recourse to the "psyche" to define the signifier. This recourse does not square with Saussure's claim that the signifier is neither a material sound nor a purely physical thing. Derrida is right to point this out, especially with regard to writing, for if the signifier is in principle not tied to any material form—be it phonic, graphic, or whatever—then no form can be privileged over another. Yet, one should not be too quick to make Saussure a footnote to Plato. As Giulio Lepschy has noted, "psychic elements" in Saussure's language means essentially immaterial elements, and one can translate this notion into the modern sense of "abstract models."[13] Seen in this light, signified and signifier are both relational entities, to be defined in terms of their relative position to other signifieds and signifiers within the space of the linguistic system. They need no psyche for their existence, nor a Platonic heaven.

The definition of the linguistic sign is based in turn upon two axioms: the arbitrary nature of the linguistic sign and the linear nature of the language chain of signifiers. Saussure so highly valued the first axiom that in one lesson he called it the "first law" of linguistics. The principle of the arbitrary, as opposed to some motivated, nature of the linguistic sign is hardly new in itself. Before Plato this principle is to be found in Democritus and later in such thinkers as Locke—who found a lively opponent on the subject in Leibniz.[14] Within the context of Saussure's system, the principle of the arbitrary nature of the relationship between the signifier and the signified, between what, in one example, Saussure calls the acoustical image *boy* and the concept "boy," can account for a number of different features of language. Perhaps the most important is the way that the arbitrary relation between signifier and signified allows the diachronic change of language to occur unimpeded, without the linguistic system necessarily undergoing fundamental change. The irrationality of historical change corresponds to the arbitrary character of the sign.

In this respect Saussure makes a sharp distinction between the sign and the symbol. The symbol is not arbitrary, since it always has a degree of motivation to justify its symbolizing relationship. In this sense language is never symbolic. By radicalizing the principle of the arbitrary nature of the linguistic sign, Saussure demolished the underpinnings of aesthetic modernism. The *Course* can be read as something of an antimodernist manifesto, for it leaves no justification for a belief in the imagistic power of poetic revelation in language. To put this in a different light, Saussure brings a linguistic corrective to what Frank Lentricchia in a recent book calls the "naturalistic error" of those modernists who sought a motivated language:

The mainstream of aesthetic modernism (even the structuralist Todorov draws from it when he tells us that linguistic structure is a mirror of the structure of the universe) has primarily characterized itself not by its misleading propaganda against science and philistinism that the aesthetic world is a thing wholly apart, but by its claim that the aesthetic world plumbs the nature of things; and the pivot of this claim is the prior ontological claim for a natural bond between signifier and signified, and between sign and thing.[15]

Virtually every aspect of the *Course* is directed against this belief in a natural bond: the rejection of nomenclature, the dismissal of the naive metaphysics of representation, the reduction of the signified and the signified to relational entities. But it is the clear distinction between symbol and sign that is perhaps most telling as a critique of modernist views or, should I say, hopes about language.

Saussure's second axiom for defining the linguistic sign has equally antimodernist implications in the way it would undermine belief in the possibility of iconic or simultaneous representation. The second axiom is that the signifier has a linear and thus measurable character:

The signifier, being auditory in nature, unfolds in time alone and has those characteristics that it borrows from time: (a) it represents an extension [*étendue*], and (b) this extension is measurable in only one dimension: for it is a line. (P. 103)

Noting that this principle seems so obvious that it is often overlooked, Saussure goes on to state:

The entire mechanism of language depends upon it. By opposition to visual signifiers (maritime signals, etc.), which can offer simultaneous, intricate developments in several dimensions, acoustical signifiers have at their disposition only the line of time. Their elements present themselves one after another. They form a chain. This characteristic appears immediately as soon as they are represented by writing, and the spatial line of graphic signs is substituted for their succession in time. (P. 103)

In this view time seems to be an integral part of the ontology of language, or at least of spoken language. For the linearity Saussure speaks of can only be understood as a geometrical model drawn from our usual conception of the flow of time. To place time at the heart of the ontology of language creates significant problems. For the writer, the temporalizing of language means, in a rather perverse way, that all he says is condemned to the evanescence of the moving line. Modernism had reacted against this self-destruction inherent in language with its search for the icon. And postmodern writers find in this description of their language the conditions for their alienation from their own voice.

The model of language as a linear continuum, derived from the model of a linear temporal flow, obliges one to ask how discrete units of meaning are identified. This is a question of import primarily for linguists, since our daily meta-linguistic needs are met by using such approximate terms as "word."[16] But the linguist himself occupies no privileged position when it comes to language. In order to identify the sign, he must already know its signified—its meaning— which means that he must make an intuitive appeal to knowledge of a language's semantic segmentation of the linear flow. As Wittgenstein said, the way into language is through language, which finds an echo in Heidegger's belief that the way into language is the circular path of already being there. We begin and end in language. All three views here seem to be variants of a single demonstration of the autonomy of language and the primacy of the word.

When looking at the linguistic system strictly in terms of *la langue*, however, the *Course* does propose a conceptual way to consider the sign, and that is by separating the signifier and the signified in terms of their position on two axes. Signifiers can be isolated from other signifiers in terms of their opposition along a horizontal axis that corresponds to the linear chain of language flow. In turn, the signifier and the signified maintain a relationship along a vertical axis. Signification is characterized as a vertical relationship between the two faces of the sign, whereas the horizontal relationship of opposition is what Saussure calls value. Value is not one of the clearest notions in the *Course*, and at times it is difficult to see how it differs from meaning, signification, or what we would today call connotation. Whatever be the economic metaphor that stands behind the term, value is the horizontally differential organization of signs. Value presumably applies to both signifiers and signifieds. For practical purposes, however, it would seem that only by isolating the value of the signified can one then identify the signifier—so that a knowledge of meaning is still the way into language.

Value, difference, and opposition are three central notions in Saussure's view of how the linguistic system of functions both phonologically and semantically. These concepts are central, in particular, to his view that language is not a substance. Rather than as a substance, the linguistic system can be defined only as a set of formal relations: "Let one consider the signified or the signifier: language includes neither ideas or sounds that preexist the linguistic system, but only conceptual and phonemic differences which result from the system" (p. 166). All entities within the system function in terms of their differences from other comparable entities within the system. Signifieds or meanings can be identified through their difference from other signifieds; and signifiers, or the material forms of signs, through their difference from other signifiers (or, as a phonologist would say today of phonemes, through their correlative opposition of pertinent features).

A number of conceptual problems inhere in this view that signs can be identified only through their difference from other signs. Such a view presupposes that the linguistic system imposes conceptual differences and phonemic differences on the same kind of undifferentiated, linear continuum. The symmetry has an aesthetic appeal, but one can wonder how the signifier and the signified can impose the same kind of differential ordering, one on a sound spectrum, the other on a conceptual field. The notion of difference is without question a fundamental axiom in Saussure's thought and can, as an operational procedure, do without the notion of linearity. Difference functions as a negative notion that allows one to identify the signified or signifier in purely relational terms. Once differences have been established, it would appear that one can speak of the sign in some positive sense, much as we do of "words." The *opposition* between signs, as Saussure puts it in one passage, is like a positive relation between discrete entities (p. 167).

From Plato on, the metaphysical view of signs has been that each recurrence of the same sign can be identified as a recurrence because a universal is embodied in the sign. The next logical step says that this universal that confers identity must be somewhere other than in the sign. How could a sign be used to identify itself? The universal then becomes an essence, at once in the sign and elsewhere, allowing the identification of all different instances of the sign as the same sign. With this doctrine in mind, one can understand that the differential relation of signifieds is of the greatest significance. For this relation allows one to see, without recourse to a metaphysical doctrine of universals, how signs can have identity. Saussure offers an ingenious comparison to make clear his thought as to how signs have only a relational identity. He asks in what sense can we speak of the identity of such objects as express trains or streets, for which it would be most uneconomical to posit an essence. How does one define identity?

> The linguistic mechanism runs entirely on identities and differences, the latter being the counterpart of the former. The problem of identity is found everywhere; but, on the other hand, it overlaps in part the problem of entities and units, of which, moreover, it is a fecund ramification. The nature of this problem can be made clear when compared with a few matters taken from extra-linguistic domains. (P. 151)

And how can we speak of the identity of an entity such as an express train or a sign, entities that are always different instances of the same?

> Thus we speak of identity concerning the 8:45 P.M. Paris-Geneva express which leaves at intervals of 24 hours. In our eyes it is the same express train, and yet, locomotive, cars, personnel, everything about it is probably different. Or take the case of a street that is demolished and rebuilt. We

say it is the same street even though in material terms nothing subsists of the former street. Why can one completely rebuild a street without its ceasing to be the same? Because the entity that it constitutes is not purely material. It is founded on certain conditions for which chance materials are a matter of indifference: for example, on its position relative to other streets. In the same way what makes up the express train is the hour of its departure, its itinerary, and in general all the circumstances that differentiate it from other express trains. Every time the same conditions are obtained, the same entities are obtained. (P. 151)

And, as if in anticipation of Derrida's charge that metaphysics hides within the system, Saussure goes on to say: "And yet, these entities are not abstract, since a street or an express train cannot be conceived outside of a material representation" (pp. 151-152). With this formulation of difference, Saussure has struck a blow, as Jonathan Culler would have it, against "the metaphysics of presence" by defining identity in terms of common absences.[17]

Or has he? Certainly Saussure intends to do away with our recourse to a universal essence, defined as a positive idea, that allows us to identify each occurrence of a sign. In this respect Saussure's fundamental project can be compared with that of Wittgenstein and Heidegger in rendering essence problematic as the foundation of metaphysical thought. The difficulty that arises at this point in Saussure's thought is, as the above passage makes clear, the indifference of the material form of the signifier to the presence of the signified. The signified can be united to a phonic, graphic, or other type of signifier. One immediately wants to ask, What is the common X that can be united to all these material signifiers that gives them the same meaning? At this point the analogy with the train may well be inadequate since a train can only be identified as a train and not in a multiplicity of material forms. I shall return to the point in a moment; suffice it to say here that Saussure wants to propose a non-metaphysical way of identifying signs through their recurrence in a system of differences.

The play of these differential relations along the horizontal axis gives rise to value. Within the context of the autonomous linguistic system whose signs accrue meaning differentially, value would appear to be the way each sign system organizes these differences in various semantic fields. To make the difference between meaning and value clear, Saussure offers a comparative example drawing on French and English. *Mouton* has the same meaning as *sheep*, but it does not have the same value, since *sheep* has a differential value when contrasted with *mutton* in English. A problem of consistency again arises here, for strictly speaking, in Saussure's own terms, *mouton* cannot have exactly the same signified as *sheep*. No signified is defined except in terms of differences within the system of differences to which it belongs, in this case, the French language. Saussure frequently uses translation examples to which, strictly speaking, he is not entitled.

In illustrating value with such French synonyms as *redouter, avoir peur,* and *craindre* (all of which can be translated "to fear"), Saussure shows that part of value is connotation. Yet, how value differs from meaning is not made clear. With regard to these synonyms Saussure notes that, if one of them were to disappear, its contents would be divided among the remaining terms. It is difficult to see what "contents" might be, if it is not meaning. Value undoubtedly attempts to define what we would today call polysemy and connotation. For our purposes, the essential here is that, in defining value, Saussure is searching for a way to define the multiple relationships that signs maintain with other signs; that signs have meaning only in function of their relation to other signs; and that signifieds have conceptual value only in terms of their differential relationship to other signifieds. As part of the autonomous system of differences that make up the semantic dimension of language, the notion of value suggests that there is no intrinsic bond between reality and language. There is no necessary relationship between the so-called continuum of experience and those conceptual fields that organize what we take to be reality.

These comments do not intend to place Saussure in the same camp with those thinkers, such as Whorf and Sapir, who claim that language conditions the way we perceive reality. Rather, it seems to me that the social emphasis in Saussure's thought would better lead one to conclude that value represents the multiple ways a given culture, through its language, organizes its experience of the world. In this sense language articulates a societally shared world and, in terms not unlike Wittgenstein's, a culturally determined sense of reality. This interpretation finds support in Saussure's declaration that "the community is necessary if values that owe their existence solely to usage and general acceptance are to be established" (p. 157). The view that society articulates its world through language means that values are far more than a passive taxonomy reflecting whatever is exterior to language. In an active sense values are a priori articulations, or as Saussure put it in a letter: "As one progressively gets deeper into the material that is offered to linguistic study, one is increasingly convinced that the links that are established among things pre-exist, in this area, things themselves and that they serve to determine them" (p. 361). Parallels one can establish with both Wittgenstein and Heidegger reveal in this regard a larger consensus about language, a consensus that defines how we think about language today. To speak of the play of differences articulating a world points to analogies with Heidegger; whereas to comment on the a priori articulation by a language of a culture's reality is to offer a summary of Wittgenstein's thought.

In his discussion of system, difference, and value Saussure also uses the metaphor of play that Wittgenstein and Heidegger, in their comparable ways, used to explain the nature of language. When a future historian undertakes the project of explaining our contemporary fascination with chess, he will have to add Saussure to that list of thinkers and writers who have placed the square board in the limelight of our intellectual and creative concerns. Play, and especially chess, has become an almost obsessive leitmotif of the postmodern mind. For his part Saussure sees chess as the most elucidating metaphor he can offer to explain the linguistic system. With regard to the basic notion of system, for example, he insists that one must distinguish between that order of facts that is intrinsic (*interne*) to the linguistic system and that order of facts that is extrinsic (*externe*) to it. This distinction can be explained by comparison with the intrinsic system that makes up the game of chess:

> The fact that it [chess] came from Persia to Europe is an extrinsic matter; everything that concerns its system and rules is, on the other hand, intrinsic. If I replace wooden chessmen with ivory chessmen, the change is a matter of indifference for the system; but if I reduce or increase the number of pieces, this change profoundly affects the "grammar" of the game. (P. 43)

In proposing the comparison of language with a finite game-set, the chess metaphor also stresses that an analogy is to be drawn between grammar and a rule-bound type of behavior such as play. The metaphor elucidates, moreover, the structural view of language according to which all entities or minimal pertinent units are to be identified strictly on the basis of their position within the system. And it again shows that the various material realizations of language are secondary to its structure as a *langue*.

Saussure uses the chess metaphor to throw light on practically every other aspect of language; he is quite as enthusiastic about the game as Wittgenstein. Consider the distinction between the diachronic and synchronic realms. In likening historical change and fixed states to the moves in a chess match, Saussure claims that any given move in the game brings about a new fixed state that corresponds to the synchronic system at any given moment. After each diachronic change, after each move, the respective value of each piece in the game, or linguistic system, depends on the position of the piece on the board, much as in language each entity has value through its differential relation opposing it to all other terms in the system. And as in language, each fixed moment is only temporary; subsequent moves are inevitable.

Saussure recognizes that chess moves are intentional and that diachrony is unintentional; for diachronic change is irrational. Perhaps he should have also recognized another limitation. For Saussure, in using the chess metaphor to explain the nature of value, asserts that value in the system depends on an unchanging convention, that is, the rules of the game. These rules are unchanged by any given move and are the same before and after the game. It is misleading, however, to say that value can depend on immutable rules, since values, surely, can change as semantic shifts occur diachronically. To use the admittedly weak sheep-*mouton* example, there is no reason why we should not someday eat "sheep chops" as signs come to divide up semantic fields in a different manner. The history of any language is in part a history of the way words or signs have given up or acquired new values.

The chess analogy works well to elaborate the problem of identifying the entities that make up the system. In another comparison, which also throws light on the nature of value, Saussure asks us to consider the example of a chess knight. Can its material aspect—say, a plastic representation of a medieval knight—be considered an element in the game's system:

> Assuredly not, since in its pure materiality, taken outside its square and the other conditions of the game, the piece represents nothing for the player and can only become a real and concrete element once it has taken on its value and embodied it. Let us suppose that in the course of a game this piece happened to be lost or destroyed; can one replace it with another, equivalent one? Certainly, not only with another knight, but even a figure having no resemblance with it at all can be declared identical, provided it is given the same value. One can thus see that in semiological systems, such as language, in which the elements are held reciprocally in equilibrium according to determined rules, the notion of identity overlaps that of value and vice versa. (Pp. 153-54)

This comparison could support the contention that, in a Wittgensteinian perspective, the identity of a sign is given by its use. Value would then be the sign's grammar—or the rules of the language game. I should not wish to push this analogy too far, since Saussure's comparison with a chess knight is designed to clarify the nature of the linguistic system, the *langue*, and not the *parole*. The analogy points, nonetheless, to important convergences between these two thinkers, which in turn point to how thought about play organizes much of what we think we can do with language today. Perhaps most important with regard to play is that, for both Saussure and Wittgenstein, meaning or value is determined by a relation within the game space of language itself, not by some relation to an exterior realm.

Saussure buttresses his analysis with other analogies between chess and the linguistic system. Just as chess moves involve only single chessmen, so language changes involve only isolated elements, not the entire system. Each move, or diachronic shift, can have a different effect on the entire system, ranging from no effect to an enormous influence. Each moving of a piece, like each change in the linguistic system, creates a new state that is entirely distinct from any preceding static equilibrium that existed or that will subsequently exist. These comparisons underscore the fact that for Saussure, as for Wittgenstein and Heidegger, the game analogy is far more than a mere rhetorical comparison. To paraphrase Johan Huizinga, viewing language *sub specie ludi* is the beginning of a way of integrating language into a different, perhaps more complete way of viewing the relation between language and culture.[18] At the same time, this metaphor assures the autonomy of language by making it—like a chessboard—a self-enclosed space within which an indefinite number of rule-bound permutations can take place.

The chess metaphor is also motivated in Saussure by a recurrent desire to translate the notion of system into a geometric or algebraic set of operations. We have already seen this desire at work in the geometric spatialization underlying the distinction of meaning and value. The same attempt to offer a geometric model is found in the final pair of binary oppositions that describe the linguistic system. This pair is of particular relevance for throwing light on later attitudes toward voice in fiction, and I shall therefore give a fairly detailed discussion of their function. Saussure calls this binary pair the associative and the syntagmatic relations of language, though today the term "paradigmatic" has replaced "associative." These relations are again to be conceived of in terms of the relations of a vertical and a horizontal axis (on the model of a Cartesian coordinate system). The syntagmatic axis is the horizontal axis, or the linear flow of elements that combine as speech takes place:

> In discourse . . . words acquire relations, in virtue of their being chained together, based on the linear nature of language, which excludes the possibility of two elements being said at the same time. These elements are arranged one after the other along the chain of speech. These combinations which use linear extension for their support are called syntagms. The syntagm is always composed of two or more consecutive units (for example: re-read; against everyone; human life; God is good; if the weather is nice, we'll go out; etc.). (P. 171)

The syntagmatic axis defines the unfolding linear flow of differences in which every term, at every level of analysis, acquires value through its opposition "to whatever precedes or what follows, or both" (p. 171). Phonemes, morphemes (the smallest units of signification), and what Saussure calls larger "organized masses" (such as the phrases above) are defined by their opposition to comparable units along the horizontal axis (p. 177).

The system's geometry includes a vertical axis, or a vertical order of relations constituted outside of speech or actualized discourse. Consisting in all the possible elements that could appear on the horizontal axis, this vertical relation, existing *in absentia* as Saussure says, makes up the paradigmatic axis. This axis stands in a vertical relationship to each point of the horizontal chain. At each point of the syntagmatic axis an opposition occurs between what is actually said and all the elements that could have been said at the point. The vertical axis forms a virtual opposition between what is actualized and what could have been actualized. According to Saussure the meaning of any element derives from this virtual opposition. For example, when I say the syntagm "I see," the pronoun "I" derives its meaning from its opposition to all the units—nouns and pronouns, in traditional terms—that might replace the first person singular "I," such as "we," "you," "it," "Howard," etc. Syntagmatic relations actualize themselves in speech; they are nonetheless composed mainly of codified elements that make up the *langue* or linguistic system. The locus of paradigmatic relations would also appear to be the *langue*, for they are found in "the inner storehouse that makes up the language of each speaker" (p. 171).

There are a good many problems involved in this kind of axial geometry, especially with the notion that paradigmatic oppositions exist, like syntagmatic combinations, at all levels of linguistic analysis. Phonology is a closed system, which allows one to identify and describe the codification of permissible combinations and the virtual oppositions that exist when a combination is actualized The "p" of "pet" stands in virtual opposition of the "m" of "met" as a possible actualization in English. "Mwz" stands in opposition to nothing, since this actualization is not part of the system of possible phonemic combinations in English. In morphemic analysis the "re" of "redo" stands in opposition to the "un" of "undo," while it bears an associative relation to the "re" of "remake." Its meaning depends on both an oppositional and an associative relation. But in the case of the "I" of "I write," it is difficult to see how the indefinite number of possible oppositions, with no associative relations, enters into the genesis of meaning. The problem redoubles when one considers entire syntagms such as those given by Saussure in the quotation above. Such problems notwithstanding, this kind of analysis has brought about an extraordinary self-consciousness with regard to the limits of expressing original meaning in language.

Saussure's examples oblige one to ask how one knows what a syntagm is and where language as a system prepackages our meanings and perhaps thought for us. Saussure has no ready answer to such questions. In order to grant the individual speaker's freedom, he must grant him a great deal of latitude in combining signifying units along the syntagmatic axis. Yet, as demonstrated by Saussure's example, quoted above, of an entire sentence made up of two clauses, Saussure also believes that many combinations are codified in fixed syntagms. When the *Course* states that phonic and conceptual differences result from associative and syntagmatic comparisons, it offers little interpretative help by simply stating that both, to a large extent, are established by the *langue* (p. 177). This passage could easily be invoked to demonstrate that to a large extent all language consists in previously codified combinations that the speaker has little power to modify. With a little ingenuity one could establish parallels between Saussure's description of syntagmatic codification and Heidegger's view that most language is essentially the anonymous chatter that *Gerede* speaks through us as the voice of *das Man*. Such parallels are not fanciful, for structuralists have been more than a little inclined to read Saussure through this kind of Heideggerian grid.

The most insightful criticism of structuralism has come from the contemporary French philosopher Jacques Derrida. Often called poststructuralist, Derrida's work can be viewed to a large extent as an attempt to think Saussure's work through to some of its logical conclusions. I would maintain that a central impulse of Derrida's thinking is the desire to complete the rejection of the metaphysics of modernism and its theological underpinnings. Saussure's work suggests the forms this critique must assume, which necessitates an attack on much of what structuralism has borrowed from Saussure as well as a critique of the axioms that underlie part of Saussure's own thought. Derrida is also an inheritor of the thought of Nietzsche and Heidegger, and his reading of Saussure takes the form of a deconstruction or a demystification of the metaphysics that he sees functioning unself-consciously in Saussure's *Course* and in the thought of his structuralist inheritors. Derrida's project, like Heidegger's, aims at laying bare what he considers the "unthought" in structuralist thought. This laying bare shows that overcoming metaphysics demands a more fundamental questioning than structuralists have undertaken—even if this questioning, in pointing to the closure of metaphysics, also shows that we cannot hope to bring an end to metaphysics.

Accepting Heidegger's vision of Western history as the unbroken reign of metaphysics, Derrida's basic project demands the attempt to think through metaphysics to a position that cannot be easily defined within the limits of language, since language itself is a product of metaphysics. Such a dilemma obliges Derrida to elaborate deconstructive strategies that can think, as it were, beyond or, at least, to the limits of language:

> To deconstruct philosophy would be to think out in the most faithful and the most interior way the structured genealogy of its concepts; but at the same time doing so from a certain outside position that one could not name or describe. Deconstruction would determine what this history had forbidden or repressed, as it became history by this repression that is motivated somewhere.[19]

Although Saussure's thought, from Derrida's standpoint, is inscribed within this history, it is one of the first bodies of thought that offers a way to think beyond metaphysics. Derrida's deconstructive reading of Saussure means, in effect, the use of Saussure's own conceptual revolution to forge new tools for laying bare what appears, in Saussure's thought and in structuralism, to remain bound up with metaphysical determinations.

Derrida's work brings us, moreover, to a point at which we can begin to recognize the issues at stake in considering the homologies between thought about language and contemporary literature. In the first part of this book I have undertaken a kind of critical conspectus of several of the most important theories of language elaborated in the twentieth century. Derrida's work, however, is not exactly another theoretical activity. His essays are closer to a literary form of contestation and questioning; like many of the fictions I shall consider next, they act like distorting mirrors that reflect back toward theory a deformed image that demonstrates what was latent in that thought—whether it is the thought of Rousseau, of Lévi-Strauss, or of Freud. It is no exaggeration to state that increasingly Derrida has been as much a poet—a maker of words—as a philosopher. The two roles are combined in Derrida's essays, and in them philosophy reflects directly on literature as a kind of test case for philosophy's own dream of mastering language and its inherent conceptuality. In Derrida's essays philosophy becomes, one might say, a literary act, in which literature reflects on philosophy as a form of bad consciousness for philosophy's imperious dreams of power and manipulation of language. In this perspective Derrida is the Borges of philosophy who introduces the labyrinth into theoretical thought. Saussure's notion of difference becomes, in Derrida's work, a generator of semantic mazes in which words refer only to words, in an infinite play of difference for which there can be no center. Derrida's universe, like Borges's, is the infinite library; it is the house of Asterion in which the Minotaur imagines games for himself and his double as they go through the infinite, mazy doubling of courtyards and reflecting pools. For in Derrida's universe of infinite intertextual play and repetition, every place is any other place; every book is every other book; all is a paradigm series in which each element is at once aleatory and necessary.[20]

Derrida's deconstructive reading of Saussure relies upon demonstration that the *Course* is a repetition determined by the infinite text of metaphysics that writes what we take to be Western culture. Especially in Saussure's attitude toward writing—as opposed to speech—does Derrida find another instance of that recurring text. Metaphysics has always denigrated writing as a mere representation of the spoken word. This denigration constitutes what Derrida calls the phonocentrism (or logocentrism) of Western culture. Linking Saussure with the Plato of the *Phaedrus,* who saw in writing an inferior representative form much like mere painting, Derrida wishes to show that Saussure's exclusion of graphic signs from the linguistic system is more than an unwarranted methodological maneuver. This exclusion is an instance of repetition that obeys a law of necessity underwriting Western thought. Metaphysics must maintain that writing is merely an exterior representation having no essential link with the center of language—speech conceived as logos present unto itself. If speech were to lose this privilege, then metaphysical thought would be hard pressed to claim that being is always presence. Derrida accepts the Heideggerian perspective according to which being has always been thought of as presence (*Anwesenheit)*) and goes on to show that the model for this presence is speech itself, conceived of as the identity of speech (*phonē*) and logos, voiced in its presence to the inner ear. Writing merely represents this presence and suffers therefore from the same ontological inferiority that Plato saw in painting and poetry as representations of representations.

The anathema Saussure cast upon writing is, as I suggested, quite inconsistent with his own premises, for there is no reason within the system to privilege any material form of signifier over any other. This point has been made by a number of later linguists. But only Derrida has made the case for reading Saussure's fulminations against writing as a sign that metaphysics is speaking through Saussure, demanding that a "center" be maintained in discourse. One can, as is Derrida's constant strategy, read Saussure against Saussure. The doctrine that language exists only as a set of differential relations suggests that there is no fixed center to discourse. Signs exist only in their difference from other signs. As Derrida would have it, the privileging of *phonē* throughout the history of Western thought has served the metaphysical need to guarantee, in spite of the differential nature of language, the existence of a center to discourse. The privileging of speech as logos recurs as a law of the history of Western thought:

> The center receives, successively and in an ordered manner, different names or forms. The history of metaphysics, like the history of the West, might be taken to be the history of these metaphors and metonymies. The matrix form would be . . . the determination of being as *presence* in all the senses of the word. One could show that all the names for the foundation, the ground [*principe*] or the center have always designated the invariant of a presence (*eidos, archē, telos, energeia, ousia* [essence, existence, substance, subject] *aletheia*, transcendentality, consciousness, God, man, etc.).[21]

Opposing this center is any antimetaphysical vision that would decenter discourse, transforming language into the play of differential meaning. Such is Derrida's claim for Saussure as an antimetaphysician: Saussure's thought about the differential nature of language frees the signifier from any ground that would root it in some form of logos conceived as presence.

The metaphysical side of Saussure recurs in later structuralist thought, as Derrida attempts to show by quoting Roman Jakobson's claim that the Saussurean definition of the sign simply updates Stoic thought about language.[22] The structuralist definition of the sign is another unconscious metaphysical determination that allows a Platonic vision of logos to dominate our thought:

> The *signatum* always referred, as to its referent, to a *res*, to an entity created or at any rate first thought and spoken, thinkable and speakable, in the eternal present of the divine logos and specifically in its breath. If it came to relate to the speech of a finite being (created or not; in any case an intracosmic entity) through the intermediary of a *signans*, the *signatum* had an *immediate* relationship with the divine logos which thought it within presence and for which it was not a trace.[23]

Saussure's thought again allows a way of thinking around this metaphysical view of the sign as a form of direct revelation of essence. Saussure's model of the differential determination of signs breaks all contact with a transcendental sphere. Signifieds only exist differentially, and, as difference, each signified contains the trace within it of all the other signifieds that allow it to exist as a differential entity. Saussure's semantics depends, then, not on the immediate presence of a meaning-giving logos, but on the absence-presence of traces of the entire differential system.

Saussure's comparison of the sign with a piece of paper also first appears as

an image of the traditional way in which voice and essence are unified; the
Course makes the following comparison:

> Language is also comparable to a sheet of paper: thought is the frontside
> and the sound is the backside; one cannot cut into the front without at
> the same time cutting into the back; in the same way, in language one
> cannot isolate either the sound from thought, or thought from sound;
> one succeeds in this only by an abstraction. (P. 157)

But, read antimetaphysically, this passage offers a comparison that refuses the
separation of meaning from its material signifier within a system of differential
relations. Every concept is manifested only in the play of those relations, in
conjunction with a signifier, and in no other sphere.

It seems to me that there is a far more consciously antimetaphysical strain to
Saussure's thought than Derrida allows, especially insofar as Saussure rejects
any conceptual realm that might preexist the actualized linguistic system. One
might suppose that Saussure's banishment of writing from the system was an
inconsistent step by which the linguist avoided facing the problem of defining
the status of the signified that can be conjoined to both a phonic and a graphic
(or any other form of) signifier. And, since I do not find it especially economical
to read all the history of Western thought as a footnote to Plato, I think Derrida
does not give Saussure his due when he reads Saussure's privileging of speech
in linguistics as one more traditional recourse to the union of logos and *phonē*.
Yet, Derrida is surely right to oblige us to ask what is the status of the "x" that
can be the signified of various signifiers. The problem of universals is hardly
moribund, even if Saussure's thought forces us to approach this topos in terms
immanent to the linguistic system.

Derrida pursues the implications of Saussure's thought by designating with a
special name the signified that every signifier can manifest. He christens this
signified with the name of "arche-writing" (from *archē* or origin). Or, more
globally, arche-writing designates the play of differences that make up all signifying systems. The study of arche-writing would be grammatology. This Borgesian science need not actually exist in order to perform its critical task of deconstructing the unthought center of those sciences that believe themselves un-
tainted by essentialist underpinnings. In his reading of Saussure in *Of
Grammatology* (1966) Derrida's attack on the logocentrism of structuralism is
based as much on later developments in linguistics as it is on Nietzsche and
Heidegger. Grammatology unfolds in fact as a kind of textual game in which
one confronts texts and brings out the conflicts that lie within. For the notion of
arche-writing, the Danish linguist Hjelmslev is of special importance. This structural linguist made refinements of the notion of signifier and signified that can
be "read" against Saussure to show that one need not privilege any form of
material embodiment of the signified. Along with Hjelmslev one can call upon
one of the founders of the notion of semiotics, the American philosopher Charles

Peirce, to show that the notion of meaning Saussure develops can only result in a semantics of decentered meaning. In his thoughts out of season Peirce found the locus of meaning in the infinite play of reference among signs. According to Peirce each sign has an interpretant that can itself become a sign in the indefinite deferring to other signs that constitutes the process of meaning—in short, semiosis.

Grammatology is, then, the practice of reading texts against themselves, semiotics against semiotics, structuralism against structuralism, in a Nietzschean celebration of the destruction of the presumed center of thought. Reading Saussure to go beyond Saussure, Derrida formulates the concept—or nonconcept—of arche-writing as the locus for the play of meaning. One must say nonconcept rather than anticoncept, since the notion of "anti" would suggest that Derrida's terms are somehow negative mirror opposites of the metaphysical concepts that they seek to displace. In the case of arche-writing one may well feel that such a term has reintroduced a metaphysical determination into our thought. It does have a Kantian cast to it. For all its stress on play and difference, arche-writing is a transcendental concept that serves as the ground of possibility for the linguistic taxonomies that constitute the world. Derrida himself might agree with this critique, since it confirms that we cannot think beyond metaphysics. All we can do is, in a Heideggerian move, place these concepts *sous rature*, erasing them by putting an "X" on them. This gesture recognizes that metaphysics returns to inhabit even thought that would attempt to think beyond the limits of metaphysics and hence language. By allowing us to continue to read what has been obliterated, the erasure shows our distance from the concept that we continue to use even while recognizing that we are still within the economy of metaphysics.

Arche-writing is one among many nonconcepts that Derrida has elaborated, but for our purposes it is perhaps the most important. Arche-writing should break the hold of the metaphysics of presence while at the same time it functions in the space once filled by notions of logos. Like Heidegger, moreover, Derrida posits with this term an origin-less origin to language, the "always already" present arche-writing that unites all signifieds in the differential movement of meaning. A philosopher of the contemporary analytical persuasion, with a Wittgensteinian sense of the way metaphysics results from misuses of language, might wish to point out at this point that Derrida has elaborated a rather complicated way to judge that the problem of origins is a pseudo-problem. Derrida might also well agree with such a judgment. But he would reply that the analytically inclined philosopher fails to see the full complexity of the relationship of speech and writing. Traditional thought would without exception make writing derivative from speech, with all the ontological implications that Derrida has called to our attention. Paradoxically, however, once we see there are no grounds for privileging any signifier over any other, we also see that the system of differences that underlies any semiotic system is more like writing than like speech. Like writing in the ordinary sense, the system of differences perdures. Its material form is arbitrary and a matter of indifference with regard to its functioning as difference. The system functions in the absence of any apparent origin, such as the speaker or subject that speech seems to presuppose. Arche-writing is truly autonomous.

This latter point brings up a critique that both Heidegger and Derrida would address against analytical and structuralist understandings of language. Both of the latter tend to privilege a communication model of language, which implicitly reintroduces the notion of origin into language, to wit, a sender, a subject, or a speaker.[24] But writing—in both the sense of archē and the ordinary sense—can function without any immediate sender or receiver of an intended message. Writing can, moreover, function without immediate context. And unlike speech, writing or the system of differences is a permanent inscription; it does not, as Derrida remarks, disappear in the very act of its appearance. Thus, as Heidegger had insisted about language as advent, when understood as a permanent trace language does not need a communication model to underwrite its functioning. When language is understood as arche-writing, information theory loses its dominant role as the explicator of language. There is no privileged model, for there are multiple types of signification that can emerge from the play of difference. Derrida's work actively undermines the essence of language that information theory proposes in complete indifference to its metaphysical foundations. One can imagine that Wittgenstein would not have objected to this aspect of Derrida's work. Nor would he have disagreed with Derrida's claim that language understood as the play of difference grants language the autonomy of play. Wittgenstein would, however, have surely objected to Derrida's claim that this play always entails an excess of meaning that can never be delimited by any attempt to assign a center or a final meaning to discourse. For the poet-philosopher Derrida the system of differences generates forms of play whose meaning always surpasses any attempt to limit their possibility.

I have used the word "system," but this concept should now be placed under the appropriate *rature*. Derrida's views of difference and the play of meanings it generates will not really be accommodated by the notion of system. No system can contain the play of *différance*—note the graphic change that neither French nor English will differentiate orally. *Différance* is the neologism that Derrida coins in order to name how signs function differentially in opposition to other signs at the same time that they depend on deferring and referring to other signs for their meaning. In Saussurean terms, signs mean insofar as they function diacritically, through their differences; but meaning is also engaged in movement toward other signs, and hence signs perpetually defer. The sign is not a full presence in itself, but always sends us toward something other than itself, those other signs whose traces it bears. Insofar as one can speak of foundations in Derrida's a-metaphysical world, *différance* is the foundation of conceptuality: "Every concept is . . . inscribed in a chain or within a system within which it refers to the other, to other concepts by a systematic play of differences. Such a play, that of difference, is no longer simply a concept, but is the possibility of conceptuality, of conceptual process and systems in general."[25] The Kantian ring to the idea that *différance* constitutes the conditions of possibility for conceptuality calls forth another erasure. *Différance* is another non-metaphysical concept that, like Heidegger's *Unter-schied*, calls into question the metaphysics of presence. Heidegger and Derrida differ substantially, however, in their ways of questioning. Heidegger attempts to think *through* presence, past metaphysics and its history as it were, to some primordial notion, whereas Derrida attempts to think beyond traditional concepts by undermining them from within. Derrida has little interest in the pre-Socratics, since the origins of metaphysics are "always already" operative in our thought. One must plot strategies for thought within their limits. Finally, Saussure's differential theory of meaning gives rise to a thought about *différance* that can in turn undo the metaphysics of presence in which this thought was presumably embedded.

Différance pointedly illustrates Derrida's deconstructive strategy: it undoes structuralist thought by using the structuralist principle of differentiality. A comparable strategy commands Derrida's use of the notion of "trace." The play of difference, the movement of arche-writing, comes to pass through the institution of the trace—*la trace instituée*. With this term Derrida is trying to think the nature of the sign in a way that recognizes at once its status as cultural artefact and its status as the founder of the differences that institute culture itself. "Trace" suggests that meaning is immanent in the movement by which signs defer to signs, a movement in which traces of other signs exist in every sign. Every meaning, in its institution as differeence from other meanings, holds in itself the trace of those meanings from which it differs. Trace is a complementary concept to *différance*, for it designates the effect of the play of *différance*. Every element in language is at once a movement toward another element—through reference—and a discrete entity made of traces of those other elements.

Derrida is attempting, with the notion of trace and *différance*, to propose an alternative to thinking in terms of simple presence. And with the notion of trace he believes he has found a way to show, as he puts it, that nothing in language, neither individual elements nor the system, is ever fully present—or fully absent. Language exists only as the text, the tissue of movement of deferring traces. This play of movement of the present-absent traces, in the play of *différance*, can be called spacing (*espacement*). Recalling the way words are typographically disposed, as well as the temporality of language's spatial unfolding, spacing is another term that suggests that the language system's play of *différance* can best be called a form of writing, not of speech. The dynamic notion of spacing also suggests that we must replace static notions of structure or system with descriptive terms that emphasize movement, force, production, and play. For language's differing and deferring will always carry the play of meaning beyond any statically geometrical structure that would arrest the production of meaning. For the writer, Derrida's description of texts seems to grant writing a status in the production of culture that has limitless possibilities.

Derrida's conceptual inventiveness is exhilarating. In a world in which the divine guarantees of logos have disappeared and essentialist thought has lost its power to convince, Derrida proposes conceptual play as a substitute for theologically underwritten meaning. This exaltation of play marks, too, the antimodernist side of this artist-thinker, for Derrida's decentering games are opposed to any "poetics of presence" or modernist theology of the Book.[26] Decentering play is the antithesis of the modernist attempt to render iconically the presence of essence. Derrida's attack on essentialist thought proposes a demystification of the notion that logos is immediately present in the immediate presence of speech to itself, as a kind of transparency in which voice and inner ear are united. This attack also includes a sharp critique of the belief that language can function iconically as an image of some presence. Western metaphysics is rooted in the primacy of the visual, in what Derrida calls in an early essay a "heliocentric" metaphysics that has used the metaphor of light and dark as its founding metaphor.[27] But visibility is not, in any sense, an essential part of language.[28] Saussure's rejection of the motivated symbol finds a more radical development, then, in Derrida's attack on an aural or a visual center to language.

To disallow a center to discourse amounts to explicit rejection of the theological structure that we have seen at the heart of aesthetic modernism. The search for the essential image that modernism proposed was based on a displaced theological quest for revelation; the making manifest of the invisible through the visible signifier, the word incarnate. Derrida moves beyond Heidegger's meditation on the theological nature of Western metaphysics. His deconstruction of the metaphysics that Western man has used to interpret language proposes a broad interpretation of the history of our culture and its theology:

> The subordination of the trace to the full presence summed up in logos, the humbling of writing beneath a speech dreaming of its plentitude, such are the gestures required by an onto-theology that determines the archeological and eschatological meaning of being as presence, as parousia, as life without *différance*: which is another name for death, an historical metonymy where God's name holds death in check. That is why, if this movement begins its era in the form of Platonism, it ends in infinitist metaphysics. Only infinite being can reduce difference to presence. In that sense, the name of God, at least as it is pronounced within classical rationalism, is the name of indifference itself.[29]

In the last chapter of this study I shall return to Derrida's view of history in order to criticize it. Here I wish to stress the antitheological side of his analysis of writing. This analysis, after Heidegger's, is emblematic of what I would take to be the antitheological climate of postmodernism (or antimodernism), though one might suspect that such antitheology is the theology of our times. In any case, no other thinker has so clearly laid bare the metaphysical and theological premises of aesthetic moderism. One may wish to take issue with Derrida's total view of history, but one must nonetheless read him as the postmodern thinker par excellence.

With regard to literary practices Derrida's notions of trace and *différance* find homologies in various contemporary forms of intertextuality that writers have sought to develop. "Intertextuality" will recur in this study as a key notion for understanding one aspect of postmodern literature. Derrida's writings are exemplary of the postmodern awareness that, if the word no longer represents a theological form of presence, a manifestation of some transcendent logos, it can be taken as the trace of all other words. Texts are a tissue of all other texts. Perhaps the key postmodern understanding of writing is that every text, consciously or not, is penetrated with and composed of traces of other texts. Such an understanding of writing further entails the belief that the ultimate locus of meaning is never one text, centered upon itself, but all the other texts that inhabit writing in a free play of *différance*. Intertextual relationships are the basis for the indefinite possibilities of the genesis of meaning in writing. This view of writing has profound anthropological implications, for the ultimate space of meaning becomes the entire space of culture itself as encoded in language. Derrida's view of intertextuality is, in some senses, comparable to Wittgenstein's proposal that our world of meaning, our *Weltbild,* is the totality of our language. No longer does logos, or God, or his romantic substitute, the author, determine meaning; the determinants of meaning are simply meanings themselves, in the self-enclosed play space of language.

The recurrence of the play metaphor in Derrida's writings suggests other affinities with Wittgenstein and Heidegger. But, in conclusion, let us rather render homage to that other chess player, the Saussure who, unbeknown to himself, gave us *différance* with an "a." And to the Derrida who, in playing with Saussure, seeks to overcome the condemnation that Plato placed on art, painting, representation, and writing as mere play. Play will also take us into postmodern spheres of exploration, into fields of "infinite substitutions within the closure of a finite set."[30] Such is, according to Derrida, the play of language. And if language is a chess match, who would blame writers for turning their works into games within games? Before beginning to negotiate this labyrinth, perhaps we should return to Plato and representation. Let us ask what the poets today think themselves to be doing when they play those games known variously as representation in language or, more recently, as the weaving of tissue-texts, the playing of chess-fictions, or simply as writing.

4. Representation

Traditional language theory and traditional literary theory have jointly held that language and literature represent. They are acts and arts of representation. In the case of language, representation brings forth ideas that preexist language; in the case of literature, representation produces, through language, the appearance of various forms of essence, the Idea, or in later theory, the essence of a particular self. The attack on the metaphysics of representation that has run like a leitmotif throughout the preceding pages may suggest the tenacity with which metaphysical notions of representation determine our thought. Perhaps the reader will wish to imitate Heidegger or Derrida and place an erasing X over the word ''representation'' in the following considerations. For this very contesting of the role of representation shows that representation constantly returns to inhabit those works—philosophical and literary—that would call it into question. By representation, I do not mean reference, though these are interrelated notions and function in often analogous ways. I understand by representation the way language and, by extension, literature function through their linguistic structure, a structure that is always displacing the word or the work toward something else. Reference—or the relationship of that structure to the order of the real—will occupy us in subsequent considerations.

Many works of literary and intellectual history, moreover, hold that literary works are or contain representations of philosophical ideas. In this view literary works are, as Plato claimed, representations to the second degree. In works of intellectual history this point of view allows for an easy ordering of relations and influences in terms of abstract entities, of ideas as leitmotifs that are subject to taxonomies or hierarchies. This is not the point of view of the analysis I now wish to propose, though the fact that I have chosen to consider literature after my exposition of the thought of several philosophers might suggest that philosophical thought has some kind of priority here, be it temporal, analytical, or ontological. I do not intend any such proposition, and I hope already to have shown in a few cases how parallel concerns of artists and thinkers, *Dichter und Denker,* seem to spring from a larger field of analogous concerns. In the following pages I prefer to speak of several different kinds of relationships between philosophical thought and writing that go to make up a large part of the common space that we call contemporary culture. A central aspect of these relationships is found in various types of homologies one can discern between literary concerns and philosophical thought. Representation provides a central space for homologies between reactions against metaphysics by both writers and theoreticians. This reaction leads both groups to a self-interrogating stance in which language seems to question its own possibilities. Moreover, literature often functions as a negative representation of philosophy, as a distorting mirror that sends a parodistic image back to philosophy and to philosophy's claims to order the world. This kind of representation, for which I consciously select iconic metaphors, offers a play of representation against the dominant claims of philosophy as moral tutor. This contestation also points to common concerns that are central to the way we identify ourselves and our culture in the late twentieth century; or, to use the verb we shall not cease to query throughout this chapter, how we represent ourselves to ourselves.

In philosophical thought the status of representation has been made problematic by considerations of the nature of meaning. In various ways the writings of Wittgenstein, Heidegger, and Saussure have brought about a shift in our views about where to locate the realm where meaning occurs and which language presumably "represents." This shift has scarcely brought about a uniformity of views, and our contemporary ideas about representation can be characterized by a fairly clear opposition between two outlooks. In terms of a theory of language this opposition turns on whether one considers the locus of meaning to be the world or to be language itself; or, in other terms, whether the world articulates language, or language articulates world. This opposition is illustrated, for example, in the shift that occurs between Wittgenstein's *Tractatus* and his view of language as iconic representation and the views propounded in the *Philosophical Investigations*. Parallel to Wittgenstein's shift is Heidegger's "turning" and his change of viewpoint after *Being and Time*. And analogous to Heidegger's later granting of primacy to language over world is Saussure's thought about language as an autonomous system. Saussure's point of view is somewhat more ambiguous, and his thought could probably be interpreted in nearly opposing ways. But the later interpretation by thinkers such as Roland Barthes and especially Jacques Derrida have made of Saussure's *Course* a seminal work proposing semiotic autonomy. Derrida's view of meaning as *différance,* as the infinite play of differing and deferring, constitutes perhaps the most radical attack on a classical view of representation: there is no locus for meaning, only movement, dynamics, play.

The tension generated by these different views about meaning and representation, often held at different times by the same thinker, has undoubtedly been largely responsible for pushing language to the forefront of our contemporary intellectual and artistic concerns. The empirical impossibility of deciding if language limits my world or articulates it, if language is a form of revelation of being or a simple recording instrument, if language *is* world, all these questions have also played a role in making language the burning issue for many writers, those who live by language. Writers' responses to views about language are essential to their craft, however, whether they come upon these views in the writings of a Heidegger or a Wittgenstein or elaborate them themselves within the general climate, or epistemē, of our language-obsessed time. I reiterate that my purpose here is not to study influences. One chooses one's precursors in a multitude of ways. Rather, I want to trace out some of the limit-ideas that operate in culture, and the reactions to those limits.

The view that language in its autonomy articulates (the) world can elicit varied reactions. On the one hand, many writers feel a kind of despair that, because fiction is merely language, it is cut off from a, or the, world. Language is, as the German novelist Dieter Wellershoff puts it, split between an ''experienceless general speech'' and a ''dark, fragmentary murmuring of dream.''[1] Language can thus be experienced as a form of splitting, isolating us from some authentic realm of essential concerns. But this view is hardly the only one. The belief in language's autonomy can also give rise to an often joyous affirmation of fiction's power, as language, to define the world and hence reality. For the French novelist Alain Robbe-Grillet, fiction, in its status of autonomous language, has the power to create the world anew, innocent and purged of all repressive ideologies.[2] And in other writers one finds embodied the paradox of partial belief and partial disbelief with regard to the competing claims of language theory. Not the least interesting aspect of contemporary culture is that many believe simultaneously that language articulates the world and that language cannot reach the world.

A model for this kind of paradox is to be found in Jean-Paul Sartre's *Nausea* (1938). In its strident antimodernism, it offers an exemplary demonstration of how a crisis about the nature of language comes to inform a fictional work. Sartre is of course a philosopher, though one should not take his philosophical work as the determining source from which *Nausea* borrows its ideas for purposes of representation. In writing *Nausea* during the thirties, Sartre was as much drawn to Kafka's vision of metamorphosis as he was to the theorizing of Husserl and Heidegger. Sartre's revulsion at metamorphosis, or the world's instability, when contrasted with the autonomy of language, is more important for a reading of *Nausea* than his views on the transcendental ego. This novel is paradigmatic, then, in that it has as its focal point an exploration of the relation between language and the world. Profiting from this exploration of language and the unstable world, *Nausea* also launches a fierce and parodistic attack against modernist aesthetics; Sartre intends to show that language can never endow a hypostatized nature with some form of religious presence. What language can represent is another matter, and in many respects I would propose that Sartre's ambiguities about representation mark the beginning of our postmodern paradoxes.

Nausea is a fictional diary kept by a modern historian named Roquentin. Roquentin not only records his own life in language, but he also entertains hopes of resurrecting an enigmatic eighteenth-century character named Rollebon. A would-be Proustian, Roquentin learns that restoring time past is an epistemological impossibility, when he discovers that he can invent any number of narratives, which is to say any number of linguistic constructs, that would account for the limited set of data he has gathered about Rollebon and his intrigues. Representation of the past is, Roquentin concludes, always an arbitrary invention. It differs little from the writing of a fiction. This discovery initiates a process that leads Roquentin to discover that language has no more hold on the world in the present than it has on a world that hypothetically might have existed in the past. There is a fundamental ontological gap that separates language and the world. *Nausea* brings forth a dramatized series of revelations—and relevation works here as the negative counterpart to modernist epiphany—that compel Roquentin to see quite literally that the world is an absurd and often disgusting overfullness of amorphous existence that nothing, least of all language, can account for. In contrast to the world's jelly-like, amorphous being-there, language is a realm of pure and ideal concepts that floats over being, hovering in its detached autonomy with all the self-contained indifference of a mathematical theorem.

The form of Sartre's novel, a diary written by a historian who is now presumably dead, aims at giving the equivalent of an immediate seizure of the revelations that Roquentin is obliged to undergo. At first daily objects provoke a bizarre sensation in Roquentin, for in their obtuse specificity things refuse to enter into the linguistic web of meanings that should firmly fix them in their place in preordained taxonomies. The order of conceptual taxonomy that language offers has no real power to stabilize things, to separate them out into clear categories, or to force them to obey definitions. Critics have found a Cartesian dualism in this vision, but surely it is one Descartes would have had trouble recognizing. Words and things have taken on a preponderant role. In a moment of Cartesian introspection Roquentin encounters no privileged inner dimension, no stage of an inner drama. All he finds is a flow of words. In this moment of hyperbolic doubt Roquentin discovers a perverse *cogito:* I do not think, therefore I am. Even if I think that I don't think, the flow of words keeps me existing. In Sartre's parodistic stream of consciousness, Roquentin discovers himself existing as language representing itself to itself as language.

This *cogito* leads to the conclusion that the self exists only insofar as language grants it existence to it. But language is detached from being, and anything that exists as language, such as stories or tales of experience or narrations of adventures, perforce has nothing to do with existence. One's identity is of course involved with such narratives, for identity depends upon narrative continuities linking past to present. Roquentin's identity would, in part, be that of an adventurer (before he ended up doing research in the "Mud-city" library). Adventures, as Roquentin comes to see, are made of language and, like histories, only exist insofar as they are told. They have nothing to do with the flow of contingent events that make up existence in the world, no more than historical narratives have any contact with those past events that quite simply no longer exist. Adventures, stories, and narratives—made of language and its self-sufficient concepts—are essences that exist in a place that has no point of contact with being, with the messy realm of amorphous protuberances that impinge upon Roquentin's consciousness. Stories are generated by the internal connections existing within language. Like all essences they precede existence and are logically self-sufficient. They represent nothing in the world of existence, as Sartre seems to want to show when he juxtaposes Roquentin's reading of a Balzac novel with the trivial events that make up this disgruntled observer's experience in a café. There is something paradoxical in this juxtaposition of "real" fictional language (quotations from *Eugénie Grandet*) with fictional language that purports to offer the immediacy of the real, or the shapeless contingency of experience. *Nausea*'s fictional language wants, without irony I think, to give access to a contingent world that would presumably be *the* world—and it is this world that is contrasted paradoxically with the world of noncontingent being that Balzac once created for us. This is not the last time that we shall encounter such a paradox about real fictional and fictional fictional language—a paradox that later writers will abolish by reducing all language to the same status of intertextual fiction.

Roquentin's spirited disquisitions on the ontological separation between language and the world serve Sartre's larger attack on romantic and modernist aesthetics. As Roquentin's nausea increases, he rages against poets and priests who see in the world as a great metaphor for God. At certain moments Roquentin appears to be a nascent linguistic philosopher, for he demonstrates with gusto that errors in the use of language (the belief, for example, that analogy can apply to things) lead to bad metaphysics. In an encounter with a streetcar seat, for example, he uses an entire range of metaphors in an attempt to reduce the seat's thingness to something he can handle. But calling it a dead donkey on which he is astraddle does nothing to assuage his anguish or his nausea. When freed from the signified that Roquentin tries to impose upon it, the thing is an amorphous "X" that undergoes free metamorphosis.

Roquentin's subsequent encounter with a tree root is the final negative epiphany that turns the modernist notion of visual revelation on its head. Roquentin experiences the root as a revelation of the absurdity of being but also as a disclosure of the essentially ineffable nature of the world. Language fails in the presence of the tree root. Sartre then has Roquentin write, for the first time, in the past tense, for language can not mediate directly such a revelation. Roquentin finds a choice number of grotesque similes to describe his vision of the ineffable. His characterizing the absurd over-fullness of the tree root as a dead serpent or as an ignoble marmalade is less paradoxical than it might appear. A strong element of parody sounds throughout this epiphany. Sartre apparently had Virginia Woolf in mind when he thought about the proper way to look at trees; and the novel itself makes quite clear that the description of the root is a parodistic inversion of modernist values, as well as a sarcastic rebuttal of the Nietzschean idea that the world is animated by a will to power. Perhaps more surprising is the way Sartre seems to have mocked the Heideggerian notion that the world as world can reveal itself in moments of *angst*. But the Sartre writing *Nausea* was in the mood to spare no one.

The parody of modernist revelation notwithstanding, there can be no doubt that it is an "unhappy consciousness" that finds the world on one side of a chasm and articulated relations of pure linguistic constructs on the other side. This disassociation of language from the world brings about the dissolution of those norms of certainty that go to make up what Wittgenstein calls our *Weltbild*, or world picture. Once the order of language no longer holds, the constant menace of metamorphosis poses a threat to sanity; for how can one live in a world in which, as Roquentin imagines—as did Wittgenstein—the most incredible transformations are plausible? What is to stop a side of meat from beginning to crawl bloodily about or people's clothes from taking root in them?

By separating language from the world in such a radical fashion, Sartre arrives, not too surprisingly, at a vision of total ontological instability. This same ontology of language also leads Roquentin to believe that he might find a partial solution to his misery if he were able to write a novel. In writing he might find some kind of vicarious participation in a realm of motivated or noncontingent being, the realm of autonomous and ideal concepts that makes up language and consequently novels. Language, books, the library, all constitute an order having some kind of inner necessity. They are an arbitrary absolute, to be sure, yet nothing in existence can touch them. As Roquentin observes, Saint Denis could walk through the Bouville library, holding his decapitated head in his hands, but that would not have the slightest effect on the A to Z order that rules over the alphabet and the absolute ordering of books on the shelves. The rationalist belief in necessary truths of reason that not even God can change finds new life in this faith in the order of the library. But Roquentin is perhaps the first thinker to have seen in language the locus of these absolute rational orderings.[3]

One may doubt that the Leibnizian Roquentin finds salvation in a book. Proust took his narrator into old age, which meant that the narrator still had the possibility of using a limited future to write the work that would overcome time. *Nausea*, however, is the diary of a dead man. There is something morbidly ironic in the novel's form, since it presents the last pages of a man who wrote no other book. The novel's form functions a bit like the spike in the officer's head at the end of "The Penal Colony": we see no promised redemption.

Nausea is one of the most significant literary landmarks of the decade that saw the demise of modernism, and it initiates us into the problematics of a work that interrogates its own status as language. In its parody, sarcasm, and anger Sartre's novel vehemently rejects the possibility of revelation, of a transcendence beyond language, while it acerbically demonstrates how it conceives the limits of language, in a demonstration that points to the madness that lies just beyond what little security language can offer. The novel is a kind of testing ground for at least two theories of language. On the one hand, Roquentin seemingly wants language to function as a delimiting nomenclature, as a series of labels that would nail things in their place; on the other, his view of language's divorce from the world forces one to conclude that language, in its autonomy, can only represent itself. Roquentin would like to encounter a world that is as well-ordered by transparent relations as the one depicted by the language theory of the *Tractatus*. But his nausea obliges him to reconcile himself with the helpless a priori nature of language that exists as a series of autonomous concepts related only to each other. This clash of theories sets out parameters within which much of the exploring and interrogation of language in fiction has taken place in the several decades that have passed since Sartre published what was to be a work unlike any other he wrote.

Sartre's later change in attitude about language in *What Is Literature?* shows that he could not tolerate his own nihilistic paradoxes. This essay certainly marks a retreat from the radical separation that characterizes *Nausea*'s view of language. Sartre's ambivalences are also characteristic. Many postmodern writers would like, in a Wittgensteinian sense, for language to "reach" the world. But these writers often find that the evidence forces them to accept Roquentin's unhappy impasse: language represents and even refers only to itself. The conclusion then seems to follow that literature, as a pure linguistic construct, can represent only itself and its own functioning. Or it can represent only its attempt to go beyond itself toward that domain that Wittgenstein called the mystical and that Heidegger relegated to silence, some realm fuller than language or one accessible only to an authentic, but never found, language. The postmodern lives with a kind of nostalgia for the modernist belief that language is rooted in the essence of things.

Theories of the autonomy of language have made of language, at least for some writers, the enemy that writing must get around. These writers feel they must elaborate strategies of self-representation that can confront and perhaps overcome the a priori autonomy of language, whether language be conceived of as system, world view, or the advent of being. The very autonomy of language challenges the writer, in an impossible move, to write around his language. A master strategist in this game is Vladimir Nabokov. His work provides a useful counterpoint to many of the kinds of self-representing narrations and meta-fictions—self-designating works—that have proliferated since World War II, especially in the United States, France, and Latin America. Nabokov accepts the self-contained play of language and uses it as a celebratory game. Moreover, Nabokov perceives something supremely comic in the immanence of meaning to language alone, in the way words can mirror only words, and representations can demonstrate only themselves. And it is especially comic that characters, these deluded creations, never seem to know this. As master game-strategist Nabokov uses a variety of tricks to give the impression that he rises above language and gives the world its due. In his best work—*Pale Fire, Lolita, Bend Sinister, Transparent Things*, to name a few titles—Nabokov elaborates a subtle, comic play between his characters and a world of which the reader catches glimpses. He presents a comic conflict between those who are caught up, often solipsistically, in language that purports to be *the* world and a larger world that can impinge upon these linguistic-born illusions with often catastrophic consequences. Not unlike his contemporary, Borges, Nabokov accepts the rule-game that narrations replicate by producing illustrations of their own limits. He often dramatizes this rule of the game by ironically placing doubles for everything in the novel within the novel itself. Few works abound in so many comic forms of self-representation.

This practice of inner doubling is true even of Nabokov's early fiction, for example, in a novel like *Despair,* written about the same time Sartre was setting out to write *Nausea*. *Despair* (published in Russian in 1934) is the paradigm for the novel that ironically plays with its self-contained nature. In it the reader confronts a work in which events, objects, and even the first-person narrator— or so the narrator believes—are doubles for other events, objects, and characters in the novel. In his review of the novel Sartre saw how this doubling was a kind of self-intoxication:

> One day, in Prague, Hermann Karlovich finds himself face to face with a vagabond "who resembles him like a brother." From this moment on he is haunted by the memory of this extraordinary resemblance and by the growing temptation to *use* it; it appears that he feels it is his duty not to leave this prodigy to his state of a natural monstrosity and that he feels the duty of appropriating it for himself in some way. He undergoes, in a certain sense, the vertigo of the masterwork.[4]

Hermann, a narrator who would pass himself off as an actor, is taken in by the vertigo of the perfect double, the dream of absolute representation. He has encountered, in his dementia, not a mere simulacrum, but a perfect synonym of himself.

The dream of literary representation has always been a kind of full synonymy, despite the iconic metaphors that have always surrounded the claims of representation. Nabokov exploits with ironic deftness the necessity for literature to be a nonvisual mirror of the double; nonvisual, because the reader can quite literally never see the double. Hermann's claims to have encountered his double can never be evaluated. And this impossibility for verification then works to undermine any belief in claims for doubling, mirroring, representing. All that fiction trades in is verbal synonymy, something demonstrated all the more acutely by the severe problems Fassbinder and Stoppard faced when they attempted to transform *Despair* into a film. Hermann's double exists only in language, his demented language. Closed in upon itself, this language is a literal double for this first-person novel. Insanity is no counterproof to the proposition that the autonomy of language undermines the very notion of representation, though in Nabokov's hands the closure of insanity becomes a double for the closed nature of language. One immediately wants to ask if language theory is not guilty of some complicity in the appearance of madness as a general theme in contemporary letters.

Even poor Hermann must acknowledge that his writings lacks those iconic qualities that we are wont to take as the very criteria for what constitutes representation:

> How I long to convince you! And I will, I will convince you! I will force you all, you rogues, to believe . . . though I am afraid that words alone, owing to their special nature, are unable to convey visually a likeness of that kind: the two faces should be side by side, by means of real colors, not words, then and only then would the spectator see my point. An author's fondest dream is to turn the reader into a spectator; is this ever attained?[5]

Wanting the "plain crude obviousness of the painter's art," Hermann must work with mere language, mimicking thus the plight of the modernist who longed for the verbal icon in order to fix his own essence. Hermann's plight is also the mad dilemma of all who would escape from language, or at least such are the ironic implications of Nabokov's fictional strategy. His first-person narrator is quite contradictorily ensconced in language, whatever be his protests about the inadequacy of mere language. His first-person world is quite literally his language.

Which perhaps explains why Hermann, in spite of his iconic yearnings, has a distaste for mirrors, those reflectors of true doubles that Stendhal proposed as the model for mimesis in fiction. A hatred of mirrors, to paraphrase Borges, is a beginning of an understanding of postmodern fiction, for as producers of doubles mirrors augment the illusion of being and foster metaphysical illusions. One might suspect that Hermann shares some of Nabokov's aversions, for, as representations, mirror-images work best to trap the unsuspecting, like mirrors set for dull-witted birds. Hermann is not dull-witted, but he is duped by his own verbal contrivances, which is to say he is taken in by the belief that his language mirrors *the* world. This is plainly not the case, for the reader can observe, along with the ironic author, occurrences of which Hermann is ignorant. The reader is seemingly privy to a larger world, or so Nabokov would have him think. The reader notes that the yellow post present at the lake where a seducing relative entertains Hermann and his wife is doubled in the form of the yellow scaffold that is present on a stage set when the police come to arrest Hermann, the would-be actor, for the murder of his double. The patterns of these multiple inner doubles in Nabokov's works act as cues that the reader is to look beyond the characters' language for a world. They offer a self-consciously ironic portrayal of the way we expect sense to be generated by recurrence, doublings, and synonymies. In this way Nabokov offers a larger world, one transcending the characters' language, while undermining to a second degree our belief in having found a world beyond language.

Like many of Nabokov's protagonists, Hermann is attentive to his "inner world," and he frequently narrates dreams. Nabokov uses these dreams for purposes of analogy. This is not to say that dreams are offered for their symbolic value. On the contrary, Nabokov is quite antisymbolist in his approach to meaning in the literary text, as are most post- or anti-modernist writers. He uses dreams precisely to show that inner life is no repository of hidden symbolic substrates. A dream can of course be used as a metaphor. As metaphysician of the void, Nabokov conceives dreams as offering privileged analogies for the situation of a man trapped in the delusions that language promotes. But metaphor is not symbol, and every reader knows that Nabokov refuses the possibility of any symbolic reading of his works or, a fortiori, of the dreams contained within. Nabokov's rejection of symbolism—Freudian or any other variety—is more than a cranky dislike. This hostility is part of a more general refusal, one that I take to be characteristic of postmodern writers in general, of the idea that language can be subject to any court of appeal other than its own self-contained surface. Latent contents, hidden depths, signs grounded in something other than signs— these are ideas that have failed to survive as part of the modernist legacy. Structuralist attempts to redo Freud notwithstanding, most postmodern writers, like Nabokov and Wittgenstein, are very wary of the idea that language could have a hidden dimension such as some secret, occult motivation.

In very precise terms the antipathy or distance that many feel toward Freud takes root in a refusal of the kind of motivated discourse that such a symbolism demands. In short, this motivated discourse denies the arbitrary nature of the sign. In retrospect it is clear that Freud and his psychoanalytic theory of symbolism present homologies with the modernist quest for a locus of revelation. From this angle Freud appears to be a quintessential modernist insofar as the unconscious, with its storehouse of time past, can be compared to the modernist domain of revelation, waiting to be seized in the form of iconic symbols. By contrast Nabokov's self-conscious play with ironic doubles exults in the arbitrary relations that obtain between signs. There is, for Nabokov, no other discourse than this manifest play of autonomous language. There is nothing beneath this verbal surface. The novel's surface is all that the novel is: a self-enclosed structure of self-mirrorings, offered as so many language games, with only an occasional catastrophe to recall the void that waits on the other side.

Nabokov's work evinces the common interest, shared by fictions and theories of language, in challenging the Cartesian view of representation. The Cartesian view of representation makes of language an actor who is the expression of a private drama played before an inner self. Language expresses this drama and somehow crosses over from the inner world of thought into the world of shared extension. Nabokov parodies this kind of theater in various ways, frequently by the hyperbole of the utter solipsism in which he enfolds his characters, as in, say, *Pale Fire* or *Lolita*. In *Despair* this mockery takes the form of allowing

Hermann to act out the role of a Cartesian observer, looking at the inner drama of his private theater, which in Hermann's case is clearly a form of madness. Not only does he find his self as a double in the world, but he also is granted the Cartesian ecstasy of the split self. He has the capacity to disassociate himself from himself and to regale himself with the spectacle of his making love with his wife. As self-observing voyeur, Hermann's situation duplicates that of the Cartesian self, the privileged introspective spectator watching the drama of his own impressions.

Nabokov's parody, as well as Sartre's transformation of the *cogito*, Wittgenstein's endless explorations of psychological statements, and Heidegger's attack on the notions of subjectivity and objectivity—in short, all the attention that the twentieth century has given to Descartes—reveal how much the Cartesian model of self and language still have appeal, especially insofar as Descartes' thought offers a model of representation that breaks out of language. In securing the self as the stage of representation, Descartes refused to allow language to disrupt his thought. In the *Meditations,* at the moment of the hyperbolic doubt to which the *cogito* will bring a principle of certainty, language menaces the entire process with its endless chains of definitions. Descartes has no need for, indeed categorically refuses, the play of difference as he goes in search of certainty:

What then did I formerly believe myself to be? Undoubtedly I believed myself to be a man. But what is a man? Shall I say a reasonable animal? Certainly not, for then I should have to inquire what an animal is, and what is reasonable; and thus from a single question I should insensibly fall into an infinitude of others more difficult.[6]

It does not seem exaggerated to propose that three centuries of Western culture have been built on this refusal to allow language to inundate inquiry and representation with endless semiosis. From Wittgenstein's search for the indefinite number of criteria or rules for language games to Derrida's doctrine of *différance,* an infinitude of questions about language has been raised that locks the contemporary thinker into language, and apparently nothing but language. Descartes might think his fears were well founded.

Neither Sartre nor Nabokov makes the infinite chains of definitions and the bifurcating taxonomies that language offers into the structural principle of their work. For the Sartre of *Nausea,* it is the world, quite freed of language, that might enter into any kind of combinatorial possibility. And Nabokov's ironic narrating intelligence, wary of the delusions of words, serves to keep language in check, although *Pale Fire* and its demented play of gloss between poem and commentary shows how arbitrary taxonomies generated by language can take over the novel and become the stuff of its world. A number of writers could be listed as among the first to allow the combinatory possibilities of language to generate the world of their fictions—Raymond Roussel, Queneau, a certain

Joyce—but it seems to me that Samuel Beckett is perhaps the most public example of a writer who, especially in his early work, plays inventively with the autonomy of language.

Signs offer access only to other signs and to the taxonomies they generate. To offer a Beckett-like example of how this recognition can in turn generate a novel, let us pursue the earlier Cartesian question, "What is man?" This in turn leads to the question as to what is a reasonable animal. In all good logic it should also lead to the question as to what is what, and this query, allowing all possible homophones, gives a title to one's exploration, *Watt*. And if one pursues the question as to what is *Watt*, one finds oneself embarked in a questioning about questioning that makes meta-questioning the substance of fiction. The reader finds himself embarked on the hunt for the meaning of meaning that Descartes had banished from his search for a locus, the certain self, where the drama of certain representation could be enacted, to the greater applause of a self-confident self.

To ask what is what is an interrogative form that poses the question of the status of meta-language and meta-linguistic concepts. Fiction obliges us then to consider one of the most vexed issues in all theoretical discussions of language in the twentieth century. Early Wittgenstein denies the possibility of a meta-language, while Heidegger, in a comparable move, denies meta-linguistic considerations any value except that of mere metaphysics. Structuralist and positivist thought has by contrast made much of the notion of meta-linguistic discourse, finding in this concept the solution to a good many problems of classification of language. Beckett's work brings us to considerations of the way fiction takes upon itself, for better or worse, meta-linguistic explorations as it questions its own status as discourse, its status as a verbal construct to the second degree within the autonomous reign of language. In Beckett this questioning that questions itself is the heart of the black comedy in which the narration undertakes a futile quest to find its own meaning. In one sense Beckett comes to define postmodernism for us as a comic despair about language that, locked in its autonomous meanderings and arbitrary orders, can offer only mindless taxonomies that order the writer's pursuit as he meta-linguistically pursues a meaning in his pursuit. The movement of the work becomes, as it doubles back upon itself, a metaphor for the endless meta-linguistic questioning and questing, as for example in the case of Molloy's journey. Wishing to go and see his mother and somehow later ending up in the room that is the space of writing, he ends his trip in a ditch, although not without first learning a meta-linguistic lesson:

> Yes, even then, when already all was fading, waves and particules, there
> could be no things but nameless things, no names but thingless names. I say
> that now, but after all what do I know now about them, now when the
> icy words hail down upon me, the icy meanings, all the world dies too,
> foully named. All I know is what the words know, and the dead things, and

that makes a handsome little sum, with a beginning, a middle, and an end as in the well-built phrase and the long sonata of the dead.[7]

The consistent meta-linguistic position of the Beckett narrator requires him to use language to decry language, those foul words, separated from things, those dead things, that refuse to allow words commerce with them, except for a bit of useless naming.

The language system is a series of dead codifications, and yet the narrator gets around it to tell a tale of sorts. In his Beckettesque book on Beckett, Hugh Kenner would, for instance, tell us that *Watt* narrates perhaps the most universal of all tales: "Watt enters, there is no knowing why, the employ of Mr. Knott. His duties are rudimentary. He stays an indefinite length of time. He is then replaced, as appears to be the custom, and leaves. That is the entire plot, and whoever chooses to see in it a metaphor for human life is welcome to do so."[8] Watt comes to Knott, for what what does not always come meta-linguistically to naught? Set within this degree-zero world every interrogation can only come to naught when confronted by the infinite possibilities of the flow of language. In *Watt* Beckett has created a fictional space that is not unlike that of Kafka's *The Castle,* though with a difference of emphasis. The interrogation that Beckett's characters undertake dissolves itself in the multiplying meanings that language allows, whereas Kafka's land surveyor, in seeking to interpret the dictates of the Castle, seems to look for a locus of revelation that would ultimately be beyond language, if there were anything beyond language. The interrogation set loose in Beckett churns out a possibly infinite number of solutions for the questions one poses, since language is merely so many arbitrary and overlapping articulations, and finally a comic repeating machine. Beckett may not have read Wittgenstein until 1961, and thus some twenty years after he began to write *Watt.*[9] But in *Watt* the reader finds a book that proposes the same sense of the arbitrary nature of language games, of the indefinite possibilities for analysis of language games, and the same meticulous proliferation of language games, as Watt experiments with the various grammars that might fit the case.

This proliferation accompanies the narrative development or, if one prefers, the meta-linguistic interrogation that asks what is what. How can it be, wonders Watt, that a dog was always ready to eat the remains of the unbelievable mixture of all known liquids and solids that made up Knott's singular diet? Since Watt's words had not yet begun to fail him, and hence his world had not yet become totally unspeakable, Watt can speculate for a number of pages on diets, dogs, and arrangements for their intersection with all the exhaustiveness that possible linguistic combinations allow; or at least he can speculate on a sufficient number of dog-diet combinations to suggest that there is an indefinite number of them. And, if we may believe the narrator, a certain Sam, one possible combination of dogs and diets includes the existence of a family with a kennel of famished dogs that can be counted upon to relish the slop.

And such is the case, at least fictionally. Words may be split from things, but this has little effect on the capacity of linguistic taxonomies to generate (fictional) being. They bring into existence the Lynch family, a linguistic specification that allows a good many more pages of taxonomic orderings to describe the permutations of degeneracy that characterize this tribe's relations. But such mere semantic existence is not altogether satisfying, not for a language philosopher such as Watt who is in search of "semantic succour." Not only is Knott's existence, like that of a good many fictional characters, attested to only by those verbal speculations that surround him, but even ordinary objects seem to resist Watt's attempt to fit them out with words and thus to endow them with a bit of meaning. He wishes that words would aid him in "foisting a meaning there where no meaning appeared."[10] He desires that things conform to those neat concepts that language brings with it in its presumed ordering of the world; and so he *looks* at things to see if they consent to being named, which is to say, to embody an essence:

> Looking at a pot, for example, or thinking of a pot, at one of Mr. Knott's pots, of one of Mr. Knott's pots, it was in vain that Watt said, Pot, pot. Well, perhaps not quite in vain, but very nearly. For it was not a pot, the more he looked, the more he reflected, the more he felt sure of that, that it was not a pot at all. It resembled a pot, it was almost a pot, but it was not a pot of which one could say, Pot, pot, and be comforted. (P. 79)

And mere pragmatic considerations will bring no succour:

> It was in vain that it answered, with unexceptionable adequacy, all the purposes, and performed all the offices of a pot, it was not a pot. And it was just this hairbreadth departure from the nature of a true pot that so excruciated Watt. (P. 79)

As a meta-linguist Watt is also an anguished metaphysician. Essence refuses to leave language and come down to the world. Heidegger and Wittgenstein might both feel vindicated in their respective assaults on essence; or at least it is an interesting thought experiment so to imagine. No essence "pot" comes to assail the *Ding* pot, nor does Watt's craving for generality modify the world of pots. And he certainly has a Wittgensteinian crimp in his thought.

This comedy of essence is complementary to Sartre's radical vision of the separation of concept and world, and it is also parallel to Nabokov's attack on symbolism and the possibility of motivated doubles, analogies, and representations. This sort of attack on modernism and the belief in symbolic revelation finds its motto in the concluding line of *Watt,* the last line of a book the writer did not deign to finish: "No symbols where none intended." Beckett's separation of language and world obliges one to ask what it would mean to *create* a symbol, a motivated sign-relation between world and language, between *representata* and *representans.* One could presumably create a symbol by intending it, by a mental act that would transform the signifier even though, to all appearances, the signifier remains unchanged. If one accepts the Cartesian schema of representation, this transformation of the signifier would take place on the hidden stage of the Cartesian self where intentions represent themselves to us as unmediated events in the drama of language. But as Watt's pot shows, the separation of language and world makes this representation invisible. There is nothing in the world of pots that corresponds to that immaculate concept of pot that we behold in our inner representations when we are in the thrall of metaphysics. One may, as Wittgenstein did not quite put it, strain with intentionality: "pot" will never leap from the inner world to the outer.

There is a constant Wittgensteinian side to the comic critique Beckett makes as he sends Watt looking for public meanings that might also have meaning for him. Were Watt successful in finding a bridge going from private meanings to public ones, he might well intend a symbol. But Watt can never get beyond public appearances, as when, for instance, he interrogates the meaning of the presence of two piano tuners:

> Thus the scene in the music-room, with the two Galls, ceased very soon to signify for Watt a piano tuned, as obscure family and professional relation, an exchange of judgments more or less intelligible, and so on, if indeed it had ever signified such things, and became a mere example of light commenting bodies, and stillness motion, and silence sound, and comment comment.
> The fragility of the outer meaning had a bad effect on Watt, for it caused him to seek for another, for some meaning of what had passed, in the image of how it passed.(P. 73)

The image dissolves in memory, and, as Wittgenstein stresses, there is no criteria in one's mind for what a true memory might be, its relation to the world, or what it might mean. Nor is there a meaning hiding behind the surfaces, however much Watt might wish it. Watt has not, we are told, seen a symbol since he was fourteen or fifteen. His lack of symbolizing capacity is tied up with his incredibly defective memory, for how could he remember what meaning he intended in the first place? Watt's recall of past meaning, refracted through a decaying memory, narrated in scrambled syntax and disordered lettering, and told to a listener who has no aptitude for listening sets forth an enactment of symbolizing on the Cartesian stage of representation. Beckett wrote one of the best introductions to Proust available, and *Watt*, by utter negation, continues that exploration of Proust and the recall of time past, one of the "bad effects" we saw above.

To summarize my argument to this point, I am proposing that the antisymbolism that runs in various forms throughout contemporary fiction seems to demand that the writer take refuge in various forms of auto-representation or meta-linguistic strategies. For if the postmodern cannot accept the belief that either language or mere intention can ground his writing in a transcendent symbol, in some motivated mode of revelation, the belief in the autonomy of language allows him to turn to strategies of self-representation and to ground his fiction in language as language. Numerous labels for this strategy have been proposed—meta-narration, fabulation, surfiction, self-referentiality, *récit spéculaire*, the technique of *mise-en-abyme*. All these terms refer to the ways contemporary fictions attempt to represent meta-linguistically their own functioning—or dys-functioning. Beckett exemplifies the writer who comically engages in this self-representation is such a way that he disparages the idea of a meaningful meta-language. This writing against oneself is not the least interesting aspect of Beckett or of much of postmodernism in general.

One can of course find antecedents for this kind of self-representation in the history of the novel, beginning with the inaugural work, *Don Quijote*. Closer to the present, it has been argued, erroneously I believe, that *Remembrance of Things Past* narrates its own genesis. Kafka's texts overlap with much postmodern meta-fiction in that they indirectly represent their own dysfunctionality as quests for representation of the Word, the Law, or perhaps Logos. And *Finnegans Wake*, the work some would name as the inaugural work of contemporary fiction, includes many elements of auto-representation, such as the "letter" episodes. In my own readings of Joyce's last work, I have nearly always found that the interpretive principle of self-representation nearly always sheds some light on the *Wake*, the universal work that narrates everything, including perforce its own functioning. But by and large modernism made the creative act a form of thematic representation. In Proust and Mann the theme of the artist's salvation through writing reflects indirectly on the status of the narration that embodies this theme. In brief, the modernist work of Woolf or Rilke does not allegorize its own functioning.

Beckett's allegorization of the work's autonomous status springs in part from a comic play of the author and the narrator's self-dramatization, a play that runs through *Murphy, Watt, Mercier and Camier,* and into the trilogy of *Molloy, Malone Dies,* and *The Unnamable*. This play of travesty-narrators narrating their narration undermines the attribution of any locus of narration (as well as the modernist and new critical belief in the iconic autonomy of the isolated text). The only locus can be that vast semiotic space that is narration itself. *Molloy,* for example, opens with the vagabond narrator Molloy describing how he is writing in his mother's room, and, then, through narrative slight of hand, Beckett sets him to describing his travels as he goes in search of his mother. Molloy's unsuccessful journey, an epic reduction of all epics from the *Odyssey* to *Ulysses,* is a double for the narrative's attempt to come to an end, to find a meaning, to be something other than a dysfunctional representation of its own movement. But the tale cannot come to an easy end in a ditch, for in the novel's second part Moran is sent after Molloy, in a second search that mirrors the first. The novel's movement suggests an infinite play of mirroring regressions as one meta-linguistic act attempts to explain another, in the infinite regress of language's failure to designate anything except, fleetingly, itself.

This regressive mirroring destroys the hope that there might be a transcendental signified existing beyond the play of proliferating stories. Homologies with Derrida's thought are germane here. Not even the author, Derrida's final absent center, can be taken as a source of ultimate meaning, for he is, as *Watt* comically shows, just another narrator, a Sam included with a Watt, Malone, Murphy, and the others. Intertextual reference also enters into the comic regressions, though Beckett's antisymbolism uses it characteristically to undermine the genesis of meaning by representation of other texts. *Molloy* presents an intertextual panorama playing with this kind of reference. Within the confines of this novel Beckett makes allusion to most of the important works of Western literature from Homer to Dante and from Goethe to Joyce; to most of the systems of Western thought and science from the ancients to the present; and to most of the major religious and ethical views that have held sway over the Western mind. As a kind of meta-text to the major texts that make up Western culture, Molloy demonstrates the inadequacy of all these texts to account for Molloy's misadventures and his pointless narration. These symbols of Western culture are as dysfunctional as the narrative quest that in its helter-skelter way embodies them. Brother-images in their decomposition, Molloy and Moran, philosopher and theologian, dig a great cemetery for the symbolic constructs that once gave the Western mind the illusion that it had the capacity to order the world.

Beckett's ambiguities about surfiction or the possibility of a meta-linguistic act that might bring meaning into the meaningless autonomy of words encompass much of the range of attitudes and techniques that characterizes postmodern fiction on the question of self-representation. The breadth of responses is wide. John Barth and William Gass, Claude Simon and Alain Robbe-Grillet, Julio Cortázar and Juan Goytisolo, these are some of the names that come immediately to mind when one considers the diversity of meta-narrational strategies that form the gamut of contemporary fiction. Attitudes toward these narrative strategies strongly resemble attitudes toward meta-linguistic concepts that one finds in language theories. Theories that place an emphasis on communication accept meta-linguistic operations as a necessary procedure for self-reflexivity; whereas other theories, ones as diverse as those of the *Tractatus* and of Heidegger's writings on the *Geviert*, reject the notion of mega-linguistic concepts as mere metaphysics or as a contradictory aporia. Within their theoretical frameworks both points of view seem plausible. In spite of the logical difficulties attendant upon the use of self-referential language—consider the ever intriguing paradox of the Cretan liar—I find it difficult to see why the necessity of meta-linguistic operations should not be accepted. Heidegger's tortured example shows the difficulty of speaking about language, indeed, of viewing language as essentially a self-reflexive activity, without recourse to some kind of meta-linguistic procedure. (And Beckett, never afraid of contradiction, shows that these procedures must perforce issue in infinite regress.) Most postmodern writers accept the necessity of self-representation, though not all are willing to dramatize this representation as a meta-linguistic act. One can accordingly, after Beckett, note two primary tendencies among contemporary writers. Many engage in overt dramatization of their works' self-referentiality. Typically, as in Beckett's fictions, the narrating voice describes its struggle with language and comments on its own fictionality. This kind of meta-narration has become something of the rule, for example, among so-called experimental writers in the United States for the past decade or so.

Another tendency, however, does not make explicit the meta-linguistic procedure by which the work shows that it is representing itself. The ancestor to this kind of fiction is Kafka's work, with its inscription within itself of doubles that represent the text itself—such as the writing machine of "In the Penal Colony." To illustrate this kind of meta-linguistic operation in a postmodern novel, I shall turn now to Robbe-Grillet's *Jealousy* (1957). This work shows a refusal of explicit meta-linguistic comments, while engaging in a number of strategies to make the work speak about itself. In a Heideggerian sense, the language speaks itself, but with no recourse to a reflexivity that might be called metaphysical. It brings itself to light, as Heidegger would say, by bringing beings into a world.

In *Jealousy*—or *la jalousie,* a word meaning both an emotion and a set of blinds—Robbe-Grillet does not overtly dramatize the way the novel represents itself. There is no authorial intrusion in the flow of description, and the narrator never establishes a meta-linguistic level that calls attention to the act of narration. Within the writing itself Robbe-Grillet repeats motifs that act as so many indices of self-representation, though this function may not be immediately evident. The novel never explicitly names itself as the object of representation. Further to complicate the fiction, *Jealousy* appears, as a number of critics have noted, to be a first-person novel written about the pronoun "I". The novel can be construed as reporting what might be seen by a jealous husband who obsessively ruminates on the appearances created by his wife and her supposed lover. The husband would be, according to this interpretation of the novel's rhetoric, the "I" narrator who does not speak his own name—which would make of him the most non-reflexive first-person narrator in the history of fiction. The novel also narrates, in the form of descriptive fragments, various hypotheses about the couple's conduct. None of these hypothetical fragments or fantasies is differentiated in any way from what the reader might take to be an "objective" description narrated from the point of view of a first- or third-person narrator.

In *Jealousy* Robbe-Grillet systematically avoids any type of meta-linguistic statement. This lack of reflexivity appears to offer a world of sheer presence. I must immediately make exception for the novel's title, which names the novel's informing principle. In this novel Robbe-Grillet sets forth a world entirely informed by an emotion, as seen through the blinds of "jealousy," with no attempt to simulate the reflexivity that codes of verisimilitude normally demand. The novel is a world written as a hypothetical text generated by an emotion, or the representation of the world as the text of jealousy. Representation is given as functioning in terms of a selected model for writing, and in this way Robbe-Grillet affirms the primacy and autonomy of language over world. The novel could be viewed therefore as unfolding the tautology that jealousy is jealousy, a formulation that suggests the circularity of criteria of this kind of model of self-representation. In elaborating this tautology, Robbe-Grillet writes a novel in which emotion informs the world, which is to say that the emotion is a text that generates hypotheses as to what the world might be. And the obsessive generation of hypotheses is precisely what we call jealousy. In his essays Robbe-Grillet appeals to Heideggerian thought to justify his presentation of the world of his fictions as a mere given "there." But one might also suggest that Robbe-Grillet explores the ways that the language games making up "jealousy" can identify a world, a near-demented one lying on the edge of normal certainty and its language games.

The various hypotheses, repetitions, speculations, and seeming fantasies in *Jealousy* present a model of a world written as a limited language game. It is an obsessively self-contained form of discourse, based on what appears to be a limited number of combinatorial elements: a wife, a presumed lover, possible secret letters, assignations, excuses, arrangements of chairs, drinks, a recurring centipede, as well as the plantation setting that is meticulously described. Such self-containment would seemingly preclude the possibility of a meta-discourse— and what is less self-reflexive than jealousy? Yet, the novel is a constant meta-fiction insofar as it demonstrates its own functioning. In a way that recalls Heidegger's definition of poetic language as self-representation without meta-language, Robbe-Grillet allows every recurrent motif in the novel to be read as a double for the novel itself: the row of trees that, according to the observer's position, change their arrangement are like the labyrinth of writing; the wife's blue writing paper whose message, left traced on the writing pad, cannot quite be deciphered; the native who sings what one can only suppose to be an intelligible poem or song; or the novel about colony life that the wife and her presumed lover Frank read and comment upon as if it narrated, in a deficient way, the lives of real characters. This novel within the novel is an especially pointed form of self-replication.Though presented as part of the "natural" environment of the novel's world, it is an ironic *mise-en-abyme* or inner duplication of the work's presence in the reader's world and of the way *Jealousy* seeks to disrupt our conditioned responses in reading. This duplication underscores how the rhetoric of irony has taken on a major meta-linguistic role in much of postmodern fiction.

Jealousy and reading have analogous roles in the sense that both seek to interpret signs. We see here a clever series of overlapping analogies, for the husband-reader tries to interpret the signs of the novel just as the wife and Frank interpret the signs of the novel within the novel. Neither interpretation is apparently bound by the formal rules that logic imposes for weighing evidence, for both engage in contradiction:

> The main character of the book is a customs official. This character is not an official but a high-ranking employee of an old commercial company. This company's business is going badly, rapidly turning shady. This company's business is going extremely well. The chief character—one learns—is dishonest. He is honest, he is trying to re-establish a situation compromised by his precedessor, who dies in an automobile accident. But he had no predecessor, for the company was only recently formed; and it was not an accident. Besides, it happens to be a ship (big white ship) and not a car at all.[11]

This passage is a description of the novel within the novel. The fictive novel's oblique overlapping with *Jealousy* is clear in the detailed references, especially the reference to a car accident and the big white ship. A car accident is one of the novel's fantasy events, and the big white ship on a calendar cover functions as a kind of projective image in the jealous speculations about what the wife and Frank might have done while shopping in a port city. Neither interpretation—of text or text in a text—is directed by logic. And this absence points, I think, to an even more interesting issue, the status of logic in representation.

I have already noted how Beckett is willing to pursue the contradictions inherent in meta-linguistic procedures. Robbe-Grillet eschews explicit meta-representation, but works in ironic modes that also flaunt the irrational nature of their operations. Logic is plainly being given the short shrift here. This refusal of logic is not an isolated phenomenon in the history of thought in the twentieth century, and the nature of logic has been a recurrent topic in all thought about language. Beginning with Frege and Russell at the beginning of this century, and continuing with Wittgenstein's response to these thinkers as well as with the irrationalism of a Heidegger, logic has seen its status as an arbiter of language both glorified and rejected. Whatever later scientifically inclined empiricisms have made of logic, it seems safe to say that logic has by and large lost the governing role that earlier thinkers in the century attempted to attribute to it. Twentieth-century writers have also arrived at the judgment that, as in Wittgenstein's view, logic is one activity among others, a set of conventions among others, or, as Heidegger would have it, one more guise of metaphysical thought and its dominance.

This widespread refusal of logic as the arbiter of discourse is also part of the revolt against the conventions of realism that relied on logic as part of their scaffolding. There is of course no intrinsic reason why meta-linguistic operations in fiction should be viewed as incompatible with realism, even if self-referential language is fraught with seemingly illogical paradoxes. The realist's distrust of meta-discourse has historically been the case, as Flaubert's work shows. The combined forces of the felt necessity of self-representation and the diminished status of logic, moreover, have contributed to eliminate realism from much contemporary fiction. Robbe-Grillet's example in *Jealousy* is instructive. As autonomous language, Robbe-Grillet's fiction is a self-representing set of combinatory elements that evinces no need to respect what logic would decree to be permissible combinations. And these permissible combinations have traditionally set the limits for what we have come to accept as realism. Robbe-Grillet's work has increasingly sought to expand the range of narrative combinations that can be unified in the play of self-representation. In *Jealousy* the laws of psychology might seem to underwrite the contradictions therein; in later fictions Robbe-Grillet relies almost entirely on the tautology that fiction is fiction in order to justify creating a space for his combinatory play.

Meta-linguistic operations and logic have a problematic status in most language theory as they do in contemporary fictions. The writer's grasp of this question, intuitively or self-consciousnessly, is of fundamental import for the structure of representation in his work. To reiterate, the practice of self-representation is hardly unique to contemporary fiction.[12] But clearly the generalized practice of self-representation in much contemporary fiction is hardly the fortuitous appearance of a rhetorical technique. Its full significance for our culture can be measured in part by the parallel that one finds in the generalized rejection of representation in contemporary language theories and their views of language's autonomy. With Heidegger in mind, one might say that literature, as language, is constrained to be a form of *necessary* self-representation; for, insofar as language brings being to light, it brings itself to light as a form of self-reflexive advent. My continued use of the term ''representation''—I can find no other— should not obscure the fact that the practice of self-representation necessarily aims at abolishing the kinds of distinction between *representata* and *representans*, between the inner and outer dimensions of language, that the traditional metaphysics of language has promoted. But my continued use of the term ''representation'' also points out that the matter of representation is hardly a dead issue. For the recourse to self-representation can also be a despairing strategy by which the writer seeks to represent anything at all.

In a different light I would also invite us to consider the question of self-representation as an epistemological question that is common to both language theory and literature. Although most postmodern writers have given up on finding revelation, salvation, or transcendence in fiction, they have not necessarily given up claims for literature as a form of knowledge. And Wittgenstein's investigations into the way language is inherently a form of knowledge of the world should bring in view homologies with fiction. Many writers would argue that literature is a kind of model for the construction of reality in the same way that language games allow the articulation of the various taxonomies and models that literally articulate or construct what we take to be the real. Literature distinguishes itself from ordinary language by being a conscious and self-given game for the articulation of multiple areas of the real. Robbe-Grillet, Julio Cortázar, and William Gass write not as if the world existed for literature to mirror it, but rather as if literature, as a language game, could offer various grammars for ordering the world or worlds.

Literature comes to consider itself functioning like a scientific model or hypothesis, or like a secondary system within the general system of language. Like scientific language games, literary constructs are a constant addition to Wittgenstein's city of language, though postmodern suburbs are scarcely so tidy, one might think, as those added by organic chemistry or quantum mechanics. From an epistemological standpoint, self-representation or meta-linguistic procedures are part of the necessary operations by which literature translates its self-consciousness of itself as linguistic construct. The underlying axiom here is, especially for a structuralist understanding that knowledge derives from the self-conscious construction of a model, that no knowledge exists without knowledge of that knowledge (and Beckett's infinite regress returns to haunt that self-reflexivity). This axiom is part of the understanding of the active role played by models in articulating the world. Connections among things in the world do not exist apart from the language that states them. And the number of possible linguistic constructs that might supply those connections is indefinite. Therefore, as writer-philosopher William Gass argues, the model is not responsible to some order in things but only to itself. The scientist and the writer are merely obliged to be conscious of their procedures: "The model is not to be confused with the world of ordinary experience, and the connections it establishes, made possible entirely by rules of representation the scientist adopts, are not connections in any sense inherent in things."[13]

The epistemological status of literature as model or system can of course be granted to any piece of literature from any historical period. But this recognition is part of a postmodern understanding of literature that derives from the Borgesian conviction that, if fiction can propose an indefinite number of orders, it is because there is no order apart form the linguistic construct that articulates that order— fictions are all. Many a contemporary writer confronts the blank page with a kind of vertigo at the prospect of the taxonomic freedom that it presents. Yet, this freedom can also be a source of doubt or discomfort. In the case of a Beckett it leads to a constant epistemological satire, in which the text is reduced to a demonstration of its arbitrary foundations. For a Borges this freedom allows a more ironic detachment: all orders are equally valid because equally invalid. Gnostic theology imposes the same claims on our attention as does a gaucho epic or a medieval bestiary. In the works of both Beckett and Borges, the result is a powerfully ironic distancing from the very belief in the autonomy of language that vouchsafed language's power to create multiple orders. As Michel Foucault notes in a commentary on Borges, the celebration of incongruous classifications, of a kind of heterotopia, undermines our belief in the possibility of language.[14] Language is a form of utopia in that, because of its apparently natural taxonomies, it seems to guarantee the order of the world—a notion that is at one with Wittgenstein's thoughts on certainty. The proliferation of orders and classifications produces a malaise, a lack of certitude about any order. In the work of Robbe-Grillet this destruction of certainty may promise new freedoms, but in other writers—a Pynchon, a Heller, or a Roth—it often calls in question the capacity of language to guarantee certainty and sanity.

Finally, in a purely literary perspective, self-representation imposes itself as an almost necessary technique for the genesis of meaning in texts that want to be more than mere language. Meta-fictional strategies designate this language as language that wills to be fiction or literature, which is to say a special institutionalized form of language that exists with its own peculiar autonomy. The autonomy of language that is true of every form of language characterizes literature particularly, that form of language which exists only by virtue of its linguistic self-consciousness. Meta-narration can be an essentially conservative strategy that allows fiction to generate meaning by self-reference to the entire canon of literature. By making of itself one more accretion in the intertextual realm of literary texts, postmodern fiction assures itself an identity as it also valorizes the entire history of its genesis. Reference to this unlimited intertextual realm known as literature is a form of self-representation in that it allows multiple self-mirrorings within that self-proclaimed autonomous world of discourse that we call literature. Meaning is generated by the play of representation within this empire of self-reflecting orders, taxonomies, and hypotheses about being, in short, all the accomplishments that the Western (and Eastern) imagination has given us in two thousand years of fictions. When Beckett's Molloy cannot remember whether he crouched like Dante's Belacqua or Sordello; when Robbe-Grillet's works play with Kafka's Franz-Frank in a recurrent paronomasia; when Philip Roth's narrator in *The Great American Novel* echoes Melville by opening this rival to *Moby Dick* with "Call me Smitty"; or when John Barth, using language that can only be experienced as the language of literature, introduces his hero in *The Sot-Weed Factor* as a "rangy, gangling flitch"; then the work has designated itself as another verbal construct whose meaning can only be derived from its connection or its lack of connection with the great heterotopia of imaginary orders.

By contrast to these postmodern works, the realist work refuses the autonomy of language. It frees itself from the necessity of questioning and portraying the status of language in the work; this means that it need not reflect on its own limits as language. Realism basically accepts language as it is and, in so doing, accepts that language is in the service of the world. In *S/Z* Roland Barthes has attempted to show that realism depends actually on the nonreflexive play of codes of representation that combine to offer what a given culture at a given time determines to be the real.[15] Realism demands a language that ignores its own status as a determinant in the circulation of codes that constitute the real. As a response to realism, the postmodern writer uses self-representation so that his fictions dramatize their knowledge of themselves as language—a drama often as disturbing as it is clarifying.

Realistic representation has not had its final word; and if postmodern stragegies seem today to have reached something of an impasse, then we may well expect to see a revival of interest in realistic rhetoric. But any new form of realism will have to take into account the theory and practice that have undone our commonsense beliefs in language's function as representation. As a fictional mode, realism has had an uninterrupted development since the Renaissance, one paralleling those changes in science and philosophy that had, many believed, brought us into closer contact with the real. Realism equated the real with those types of essences that it located within the Newtonian confines of a public and linear space and time. Unquestioning of its own language, realism tacitly accepted the anthropology that its language encoded. The real demanded only a narration that respected the public rules of plausibility, those cultural codes that, embedded in language, prescribe the conditions of possibility of the real. To this circular operation realism added one more that assured the flawlessness of its claims: the narration carries inscribed within itself self-effacing codes of representation that declare that this narration is the real. Though grounded in its own rhetoric, the realist novel assured us that it opened on to something that was other than language.

The realist writer today must confront the difficulties involved in all these points. Language theory does not allow an easy acceptance of the belief that the real consists in types or essences, though Jacques Derrida takes great pains to show that this metaphysical thinking still determines much of what we call modern thought. Nor can the contemporary realist accept without question the transparency of a language that, he must suspect, articulates the real he wishes to transcribe. For many writers the idea that language itself is somehow the locus of the real is an intolerable notion. It is especially intolerable if the writer accepts in addition a view of language akin to that proposed by the *Tractatus* or by Heidegger's drama of fallen language. In the first instance the real can only be the truncated world of atomistic propositions; and in the second the world is reduced to the inauthentic determinations with which *das Man* circumscribes his world.

Some such views of language seem to me to be present in the most important postmodern attempts at realism. Borrowing from painting, I would call these attempts hyperrealism, for this kind of realistic representation limits itself in general to the surfaces of things, hyperbolically accentuating the sense of a world in which there are no depths, only the descriptive immediacy of flat surfaces. There are American and French practitioners of hyperrealism, but primarily German and Austrian writers come to mind as those who have pursued this postmodern form of realism to the limit: Dieter Kühn, Thomas Bernhard, Gerhard Roth, or Uwe Johnson to offer a few names of writers of quite dissimilar temperaments. The hyperrealist writes as if he feared his language could not, to call upon the *Tractatus,* quite reach the world; or if it does, it can only be the world that fallen language articulates as clichés, platitudes, and banalities. And threatening the entire attempt at a seizure of some real beyond language is the capricious autonomy with which language can construct its own world.

Perhaps no better example of this kind of anxiety about language can be found than in the work of Peter Handke, the Austrian writer who says that, having seen the flight of Marx, Freud, and structuralism, among other productions of "Universal-Pictures," he now desires to be impressed only by "the weight of the world."[16] Handke's work has constantly demonstrated the difficulty in feeling that weight. In *The Goalie's Anxiety at the Penalty Kick* (1970), for instance, Handke portrays an alienated, working-class protagonist, living in a contemporary urban environment, who commits a gratuitous murder for which neither narrator nor character offer a reason (though there are intertextual resonances with both Kafka and Musil's *Man Without Properties*). Motivation—the creation of something deeper than the surface event—does not interest Handke. What is of importance here is to dramatize the split between the narrating language and what might be the novel's center of reference—a world. The enactment of the split between the character's consciousness, as given through language, and a problematic center of discourse culminates in the goalie's losing language. He then attempts to represent the world to himself in pictographs. It is as if he had studied Saussure and had thereby grown satisfied with the indirect symbolic function of phonetic lettering. With his pictographs he wishes to find a direct iconic seizure of the world. For this lost soul language has lost its anchoring in the world.

Like many hyperrealists Handke uses deadpan narration as he relentlessly explores realistic narrative codes to demonstrate that language does not reach the world. Like Nabokov, Handke is exploring the limits of sanity, though with none of Nabokov's humor. When language does not reach the world, when it closes upon itself, then language in its own self-representation is a condition of madness. In Handke's novel the protagonist Bloch is nearly paralyzed when, in conversing with some girls, he is caught up in the infinite play of language referring to itself:

> Bloch . . . explained, whenever he mentioned a name, whom he was talking about. Even when he mentioned an object, he used a description to identify it.
> When the name Victor came up, Bloch added, "a friend of mine," and when he talked about an indirect free kick, he not only described what an indirect free kick was but explained, while the girls waited for the story to go on, the general rules about free kicks. When he mentioned a corner kick that had been awarded by a referee, he even felt he owed them the explanation that he was not talking about the corner of the room. The

longer he talked, the less natural what he said seemed to Bloch. Gradually it began to seem that every word needed an explanation. He had to watch himself so that he didn't get stuck in the middle of a sentence.[17]

Bloch finds his sanity in danger when he gets caught up in the play of *différance*, in the chain of definitions that Descartes banished when he wished to secure the self. Handke's wish to feel the weight of the world seems to be a desire to overcome his own vision of how language dissolves the real into its unending semiosis. In this sense Handke's novel expresses an oblique critique of those theories that would rob man of the world and leave him with the insane vertigo of language forever spinning away from some mythical center.

Wittgenstein insisted that explanations must end somewhere, but hyperrealists often refuse explanation altogether, as if this refusal would protect them from being swept away by language's autonomous play of *différance*. Deadpan positivists, they rely on the atomic proposition to exhaust the surface of the world. The *Tractatus* is not the best guide to writing novels, however; this reduction of language inevitably turns against itself in a kind of parodistic rage or despair. In its most parodistic extreme this about-face undermines realism as much as any other postmodern hyperbole does. Consider the following, an entire one-page episode from a 1973 novel by Gerhard Roth, a Viennese doctor, in which the reader is offered a typical day in the life of its protagonist, Kalb:

> On the plate lay a tomato. The bottle gave off a noise as the cork was pulled out. He took out his pocket handkerchief and cleaned the chair before he sat down. In the tomato was an elliptically shaped tomato seed. A sudden smile flitted playfully over Kalb's lips. His bladder was burning. Was there knocking on the door? Were the room's walls bending? He had smoked too much. The crack in the ceiling. The burn on the tablecloth. The leftover food on the tablecloth. He heard a vacuum cleaner humming through the wall. DESCRIPTION: He unbuttoned his shirt collar. He untied his shoes. END OF THE DESCRIPTION.[18]

Appropriately titled *Der Wille zur Krankheit: Roman ("The Will to Sickness: Novel")*, Roth's work presents an ironic transcription of "states of affairs" *(Sachverhalten)*. The two questions in this passage remind the reader that there are an infinite number of such states of affairs. The "episode" ends with a self-reflexive bit of derision, calling attention to the language as description or representation *(Schilderung)*. The net effect of this hyperrealism is to suggest that there ought be a meta-linguistic position from which one could speak about these propositions, but that such a position must be beyond language, and beyond a silence protected by irony.

With this realization some writers, in their despair over the very being of literature as language, find quite simply that literature is impossible. This realization does not stop them from writing. The continuing representation of the impossibility of representation is, in fact, beginning to constitute a venerable tradition, running from Kafka through Beckett and culminating in various post-modern variants, including hyperrealism. A parallel reaction to the despairing view of language's autonomy, however, is to move in search of a meta-linguistic place whence to speak of literature and its difficulties. This move often results in the creation of meta-texts about fictional texts that do not exist, in the wake of Borges's frequent demonstration that imaginary works of the imagination are quite as useful as real works of the imagination. In other words literature moves, in quest of a stance on language, toward an increasingly philosophical form of writing, taking refuge in a theoretical discourse about its own possibility. The mixing of theory and illustrative practice recurs throughout most postmodern texts: in Latin Americans such as Cortázar, Fuentes, or Sarduy; in French writers such as Sollers or Simon; and in Americans such as Sorrentino, Sukenick, or Federman. To illustrate this point I shall consider another German-language writer who offers a nearly pure example of the temptation to abandon the practice of fiction in favor of a literature that becomes a kind of second-order theory about its own existence.

Helmut Eisendle is another Austrian whose work shows the importance of that country for an understanding of our postmodern dilemmas. His *Jenseits der Vernunft oder Gespräche über den menschlichen Verstand* takes the reader "beyond reason" for "conversations about human understanding." This eighteenth-century-sounding title points to how this *roman* reverts to the philosophical dialogue as a way justifying its discourse about discourse. There is a "realist" cast to the work, though it entertains intertextual play with that prerealist world of Enlightenment texts where fiction and philosophy were wedded by the delightful excesses of the allegorical mind. "Beyond Reason" entertains the hypothesis that the real is theory, theories about language, and that the task of literature as representation is to represent theory, the play of theories, theories that exist only *in* language. The conversations about human understanding take place between two contemporary tourists who, spending their free time on the Spanish coast, imbibe great quantities of brandy and truly find themselves liberated from the constraints of reason. Beyond reason, they have leaped beyond logos to a reeling meta-linguistic place where they may confront Heidegger and Wittgenstein. But in being beyond reason, like many a postmodern, they also survey the limits of sanity.

The questioning of language, the meta-linguistic leap that such questioning demands, inevitably brings the postmodern writer to see that he is risking the certainty without which one falls prey, beyond reason, to dementia:

Doubt about reality is madness. Doubt is delusion. All turns about delusion and ends in it, every sentence, every word, every expression can be a beginning. Beginning insanity. The world came into the world with language; in language insanity shows itself. A name, a word, a concept is a guest of the real. My name is Schubert. I am a guest of reality.[19]

Precarious guests of that dubious host, Eisendle's conversationalists echo Hei-degger, Wittgenstein, and an imaginary scientist named Misley as they ruminate upon the possibility of finding a meta-linguistic locus that might be more than mere language. Language discourses only about language; and even scientific concepts, those most privileged guests of reality, are merely definitions of other definitions. Not unlike the Wittgenstein of *On Certainty*, they find language ultimately is a matter of belief, of accepting a *Weltbild*, or finally, from their radical viewpoint, it is theology:

> Measurability of man. Belief and quantification. The dogma of a world
> view *[Weltbild]*. Science is dogma. Psychology and theology. In all speaking
> and thinking is found theology. Spirit, consciousness, the self, concepts
> whose foundations rest upon the dubious ground of chance thoughts. (P. 69)

Wittgenstein's demonstration that language provides the criteria for certainty and knowledge means, for these chatty neopositivists, that all knowledge is reduced to theological acceptance, to blind faith. The examination and demystification of theories leads no more toward certainty or knowledge than would the blind acceptance of the reality of the world, or of a fictional world. Language imposes the necessity of belief or the alternative of madness. Reason and unreason are wedded in their joint appearance through language.

At the end of the novel the second conversationalist, Estes, sits down to write and to affirm the possibility of a kind of minimalist fiction. He begins to type the same manifesto with which a first-person narrator opens the novel:

> Ask for nothing from the reader except that he allow himself to be locked
> in the cage of a word-mesh. Forget all of literature. Participate in the
> fabrication of fictions, studies of a dying culture, in the illusion of reality,
> in contributions to a critique of language. Arrange a mass of unordered
> thoughts and feelings in an incoherent, meaningless succession. Remain
> distant from literature's necessity, its usefulness, its meaningfulness, or its
> tasks. Turn one's self, one's consciousness inside out and make oneself
> available, always with the protective rampart of possible invention.
> Every word can be a lie. What remains is a succession, a novel, an action,
> a nothing. (P. 153)

With this Beckett-like self-exhibition the novel turns itself inside out in a Möbius strip movement. The meta-commentary at the end is the same as at the beginning, and the novel begins to write itself again in an infinitely circular movement. Eisendle has found perhaps the only way to write a meta-fiction that does not run the risk of becoming an infinite regress of language about language; it is a meta-fiction that repeats in endless circularity its own conditions of possibility.

Within the Möbius strip of *Jenseits der Vernuft* Eisendle has taken the reader on a vacation from reason so that he might survey the linguistic fictions encoded in language that he normally believes in. Representation is representation of a kind of sparring match with language during which the antagonists throw more shadow blows than real ones, precisely because they never really quite get beyond language to encounter some opposition that would be more substantial than the unsubstantial flow of words that surrounds them. The conversationalists dream of an order beyond the orders of language, an order for which, by definition, there can be no word or concept, for the order would be then recuperated by language. Perhaps Heidegger's authentic silence is a pious contradiction. So in a quiet despair or resignation one accepts the necessity of writing—"I" or Estes—about the conditions of writing which lead to a discovery of the conditions of writing. . . . .

To conclude, one can observe in Eisendle, as in numerous other writers, that the separation of theory and imaginative practice has increasingly ceased to exist. Representation has become perforce representation of a theory of representation, or a contestation of what are taken to be the reigning theories of representation. This blurring of the distinction between theoretical and literary texts goes in both directions, and the theoretical writing we have been considering has also increasingly come to resemble literary texts. Wittgenstein's late dialogues, Derrida's essays playing with the signifier, or Roland Barthes's last works often cannot be distinguished in kind from the self-reflexive writing one finds in Eisendle or other contemporary Germans, in the self-representations of a French writer like Philippe Sollers, or in the fragmented theorizing that occurs in American writing by Federman, Sukenick, or in a different, pop, vein, Barthelme. Emblematic of this disappearance of conventional boundaries is one of Barthes's last works, his *Fragments of An Amorous Discourse*. What one might take to be a theoretical work explicitly eschews any form of meta-linguistic discourse in order to let a special form of language speak "directly." Appealing to the linguist's need for a direct intuition of language through the "linguistic feeling" one has for language, Barthes asks his reader to use the same feeling to guide him through this work offering a repertoire of amorous figures. Barthes entices the reader to enter immediately into a world of language as a fish into the sea, or as a lover into this world of feeling. Barthes proposes a work of language theory that does not speak *about* language, but in which language speaks. His proposal that one listen to language introduces the inquiry of the next chapter: who does speak in these works—is it language itself?

5. Voices

The ambivalent and opposing attitudes that characterize postmodern views of representation find comparable polarities in what many contemporary writers believe can be said in literature today. By using the verb *to say,* a verb that can encompass writing as well as speech, I wish to introduce here what is at once one of the simplest and most complex issues in literature. We all know what it means to say something, and in literature much is said, left unsaid, said by implication, or perhaps cannot be said. In literature as in life, moreover, we tend naturally to assume that saying something takes the form of voice, springs from a voice, and, whatever be the rhetorical distinctions we make between natural and fictive discourse, implies a space whence a voice speaks. The notion of saying implies, then, a two-way passage, from a space without to a space within and back, from the outer space of grammar to an inner space of semantics, or perhaps the passage from the public system of language to a unique realm that we might call soul or self. From Wittgenstein to Derrida, modern language theories have rendered problematic the relationship that exists between voice and discourse. If today, as some critics would have it, no literary text can ever completely assume a ''natural'' status for the voice therein, contemporary writers have nonetheless made the status of the voice that speaks within a text a theme, often the central theme, of much of their work.

The puzzlement and malaise about the status of voice that one often encounters today does not represent so direct a break with modernist concerns as does the postmodern rejection of essence or the pursuit of symbols. Rather, this aspect of contemporary fiction strikes me as a more direct outgrowth of modernist concerns. I would propose that contemporary questions about who speaks and from where correspond to a shift in the practice and theory of fiction that was largely initiated in the thirties. This shift leads from the modernist conception of fiction as vision, and language as iconic plenitude, to postmodern interrogations of literature as saying and voice. This change in viewpoint parallels the breakdown in belief in an iconic or representational function of language. As we have seen in the preceding chapter, this breakdown in the belief that repre-

A portion of this chapter originally appeared in ''Wittgenstein, Heidegger, the Unnamable, and Some Thoughts on the Status of Voice in Fiction,'' in *Samuel Beckett: Humanistic Perspectives,* edited by Morris Beja, S. E. Gontarski, and Pierre Astier. Copyright © 1983 by the Ohio State University Press. All rights reserved.

sentation can transcend itself has increasingly led to the felt necessity that literature must somehow speak about itself. This evolution—a rather rapid evolution to be sure—has been accompanied if not accelerated by the crisis-creating questions that language theories have forced writers to ask themselves. To give some sense of this evolution, before turning to specific considerations of language theories and contemporary fiction, I should like to deal with some of the contradictions about voice that are present in modernist writing. These considerations should help us better understand some of our later anxieties about what can be said in a literary text.

To this end I turn to two late modernist works, both published in 1936, Faulkner's *Absalom, Absalom!* and Celine's *Death on the Installment Plan (Mort à crédit)*. Both of these writers pushed modernist notions about writing to extreme conclusions, and in so doing they marked out ways of writing that continue to determine much fictional practice today. With regard to voice, Faulkner's work represents a highpoint in the modernist quest for essence at the same time that it often dissolves this quest into a fragmented play of voices. Céline carries out a form of subversion of modernism, for his work often inverts the quest from within, revealing and reveling in the nihilism attendant upon the belief that literature could anchor itself in its own fullness. Céline inaugurates much of the linguistic experimentation that characterizes contemporary attempts to define voice through the form of its language. In the context of world literature, these two writers set forth most of the limits within which subsequent postmodern voices attempt to express themselves.

Absalom, Absalom! is set in a realist framework, though the fragmentation at work in the novel makes it difficult to say if the public space within which it unfolds is Mississippi, the American South, or perhaps the entire space of Greco-Judaic culture. Spatial fragmentation parallels a suggested collapse in temporal coordinates. Faulkner drew back from entirely losing the clarity of a realist scaffolding, as witnessed by his appending a narrative calendar to the end of the book. Thus aided, the reader is assured that the novel is founded on a public chronology, one encompassing the immediate narrative. This narrative runs from 1807, a date that marks the birth of the character Thomas Sutpen, to 1910, the date of the destruction of the Sutpen mansion by fire. 1910 would be an arbitrary date for the conclusion of what is the chronological narrative of historical time. But, as we know from *The Sound and the Fury,* 1910 is also the date of narrator Quentin Compson's suicide. It is therefore the necessary date of the end of narrative time; it marks the limits of the voices that narrate the history of Sutpen's coming to Mississippi, his founding of a family, and his destruction under the curse of blood and race.

In Faulkner's novel, history—the history of Sutpen's attempt to found a dynasty—is a product of multiple voices. But these voices are subject to a larger history that seems to lie outside their capacity to say it. The unsayable is the bedrock underlying the layers of voices that tell the tale of Sutpen abandoning his son Charles Bon because of his son's Negro blood and of Bon then returning with the threat and the desire to marry his half-sister. In orchestrating the various tale-telling voices, Faulkner dissolves the codes of realism into a play of self-sufficient voices that hear only themselves, that think that they can establish the fullness of the real, but which actually celebrate only their own saying while never exhausting what might be said. As Derrida might have it, in the presence of the Faulknerian voice to itself there is created the illusion of a presence, of a plenitude that is the fullness of being itself.

First one hears Rosa Coldfield's voice, supposedly recalled by Quentin Compson. Rosa is Sutpen's sister-in-law. He would later have married her, had she been willing to see first if she could give birth to a son by him. Then one hears the voice of Quentin's father, recalling his own father's voice as it recalled Sutpen's voice, among other voices directly presented in the text. And finally there is Quentin's voice accompanied by the voice of his roommate Shreve at Harvard, recalling, recreating, pursuing the past through their voices and others' voices:

> They stared—glared—at one another. It was Shreve speaking, though save for the slight difference which the intervening degrees of latitude had inculcated in them (differences not in tone or pitch but of turns of phrase and usage of words), it might have been either of them and was in a sense both: both thinking as one, the voice which happened to be speaking the thought only the thinking become audible, vocal; the two of them creating between them, out of the rag-tag and bob-ends of old tales and talking, people who perhaps had never existed at all anywhere, who, shadows, were shadows not of flesh and blood which had lived and died but shadows in turn of what were (to one of them at least, to Shreve) shades too, quiet as the visible murmur of their vaporizing breath.[1]

The authorial comment underscores how the voices of Quentin and Shreve have reached back into the past and encountered shadows, emblems of the silence they would voice, of that lack on the other side of the full voice.

Faulkner's meta-commentary endows his novel with a dimension of self-knowledge: inscribed within the novel is the awareness that the voices turn about themselves in a moment in time, a privileged moment in history, for which they can never give a total or even an adequate account. Sutpen's moment is forever beyond a defining shape. The voices are seemingly full because of their autonomy; but the voice is also, as Quentin's grandfather says, "that meager and fragile thread . . . by which the little surface corners and edges of men's secret and solitary lives may be joined for an instant now and then before sinking back into the darkness where the spirit cried for the first time and was not heard and will cry for the last time and will not be heard then either" (p. 251). This disjuncture between the power of language and the impotence of its cry is central to what is said about Sutpen. In terms of the codes of realism Sutpen's life is

completely illuminated. At the same time as *Absalom, Absalom!* gives the reader
this exhaustive realist portrayal, the novel obliges the reader to look beyond the
narration toward some shadowy place to which the voices have no access. Sutpen
escapes the voices that would interpret him, and the place he inhabits might be
compared to a kind of silence that dwells in speech. Faulkner's novel invites a
Heideggerian reading.

A rhetorically oriented reader will probably feel that the reason one never fully
grasps Sutpen is largely a matter of perception. Since each narrating center of
consciousness has only "seen" part of Sutpen, no total view can emerge. This
narrative model may well apply to earlier modernists, but the recourse to perception to explain the limits of narration in Faulkner obscures the way he has
used narrators who have never seen Sutpen. Faulkner is at once more traditional
and more contemporary than a Henry James or a Proust. He has asked his reader
to listen to voices, to attend a series of representations of speech acts, that in a
paradoxical way proclaim their own fullness and authenticity even as they fail
to lay hold of Sutpen, of an essence, of a history. Rather than history, these
voices affirm the power of myth and literary language (and in this affirmation
of myth Faulkner is resolutely a modernist). Precisely those two narrators who
have never seen Sutpen, Quentin and Shreve, are the principal creators of the
language that mythically enshrines Sutpen. In "overpassing" from the known
to a self-sufficient mythic voice, it does not matter which of them speaks, as
Faulkner says, "since it was not the talking alone which did it, performed and
accomplished the overpassing, but some happy marriage of speaking and hearing
wherein each before the demand, the requirement, forgave condoned and forgot
the faulting of the other—faultings both in the creating of this shade whom they
discussed (rather, existed in) and in the hearing and sifting and discarding the
false and conserving what seemed true, or fit the preconceived—in order to
overpass to love, where there might be paradox and inconsistency but nothing
fault or false" (p. 316). The voice's self-sufficiency can be likened to a nuptials—
speaking and listening conjoined—in which what is said joins itself to itself,
and to which there is no referential dimension (like an advent of being through
language that suggests another Heideggerian dimension to Faulkner's modernism).

Faulkner's work presents a shift from the kind of search for totality characterizing the novels of earlier modernists. His novel's failure to lay hold of
Sutpen's essence is not of the same order as, say, the Proustian narrator's failure
to grasp the true Albertine. For Proust narration must confront an epistemological
dilemma born of the limited nature of the knowing subject, limited in space and
time as well as in terms of his continuity. For Faulkner this epistemological
question is quite secondary; his voices give primacy to their task of creating a
mythic fullness. There is a striking analogy to be drawn here, I think, with the
side of Heidegger that grants to the essential word the task of conferring being.
Faulkner's preference for myth over history is an ontological, not an episte-

mological, choice. It is a preference for the advent of the word in all its fullness over the absurd chronologies that make up the fallen realm of history.

Faulkner's disdain for reference and history, even when he attempts to conform to the canons of realism, is not the least of his paradoxes. A second paradox, characterizing both Faulkner and Céline, is a disdain for the written signifier, the graphic sign that must transpose the living voice. This disdain is complementary to Faulkner's attitude toward history. As opposed to the autonomous power of the full voice, history exists, much as in *Nausea*, as signs on scraps of paper. These written signs are dead letters, often existing as letters from the dead, such as one sees in the letter that Charles Bon wrote to Judith. Read some fifty years later by Quentin, this letter from the dead takes note of its incongruous nature with an ironic invocation that denies its status as voice and invites future philosophers to meditate on the ontological divide between the letter of history and the living sound of speech:

> You will notice how I insult neither of us by claiming this to be a voice from the defeated, even, let alone from the dead. In fact, if I were a philosopher I should deduce and derive a curious and apt commentary on the times and augur of the future from this letter which you now hold in your hands—a sheet of notepaper with, as you can see, the best of French watermarks dated seventy years ago, salvaged (stolen if you will) from the gutted mansion of a ruined aristocrat; and written upon in the best of stove polish manufactured now twelve months ago in a New England factory. (P. 129)

Here a "dead tongue" denies its status as voice. As a letter, all it can give testimony to is the absurd produced by history. The ironic derision of the letter—in the sense of graphic representation and of epistle—sets off the letter's incapacity to offer a vision of events that is more than a concatenation of the meaningless.

This derision signals the kinds of ambiguities that have come to beset contemporary attitudes toward the voice and the letter, though the postmodern no longer expects his language to seize some mythic fullness or essence that is beyond history. He is more likely to expect the letter, the fixed codes of writing, to be the place where the fallen word of *das Man* awaits him. Nor does the postmodern seek that plenitude in some pastness, for, like Faulkner, he realizes that the act of speech is always in the present. The voice that utters is always a present act, whatever be the past that it aims at recovering. But after Céline can the contemporary writer even trust the fullness of the present voice? Faulkner granted the voice at least the possibility of triumph through myth, but with Céline the voice comes to lose every privilege, even before it is betrayed by its transcription as a letter.

Contrasting Céline with Faulkner provides us with an overview of the positive and negative poles of modernist attitudes toward the voice and writing. Céline takes on the modernist task of recalling time past through the creation of a voice that, in recreating writing, seeks to abolish the ossified codes of writing. Céline, with less intellect but more rage than many of his contemporaries, viewed writing as a repository of what has already been said. He is prototypical of the self-abolishing writer who views writing as the death of what can be said. Writing is the codification of a dead past, and creation—that most theological of metaphors—demands that the life-breath of living speech be infused into these dead letters. For Céline this entailed the fabrication of a written spoken language, one based to be sure on the codes of popular spoken French, but one aimed primarily at destroying the written syntagms of the letter and at restoring the life-fullness of immediate speech. Through this destruction of the codes of writing, through this restoration of a *parole vive,* Céline's novels, not unlike Proust's work, aim at forcing the past to explode into the present, embodied in the rhythms of the immediate presence of oral language.

The desire to create a form of writing that would destroy writing inaugurates a certain contemporary desire to raze every repository of the past. In works such as *Journey to the End of Night* (1932) and especially *Death on the Installment Plan* Céline's project is to abolish the time past that his works apparently set out to recover. In the Célinian novel an older narrator tells the tale of his youth, of his adventures and misadventures, of his coming of age, in a language that mimicks a-temporal presence, absolute presence defined as the instant of speech. This oral language that should offer a redemption, an infusion of life into dead creation as well as an exorcism of the past and all its misery, is a deceptive language. Rather than purging the past of its malice and delirium, this language acts more like a Pandora's box from which spring all the past's evils. Céline's living language allows the past's dementia to erupt as a living presence into the present; and the voice that desires to be a form of ecstatic opening onto a living plenitude, purged of the dead past, finds itself to be a victim of the very language it has forged. The voice is engulfed by a demented logos beset with the madness and evil that are the essential traits of time unfolding. Dependent on the absolute present of the narrating voice, Céline's work cannot unfold as history but only as the perpetual repetition of the same, of the madness that invests all language.

That speech is madness, that writing is the codification of past delirium, that logos is essentially diseased, these are Célinian variations of modernism that have scarcely yet played out their role in determining postmodern attitudes. Perhaps no more apposite prefiguring can be offered in this respect than the beginning of *Death on the Installment Plan,* where the older narrator, sick and feverish, and profiting from his delirium to recall his past, lies in his bed in what is clearly a parody of Proust's recumbent, if transcendental, narrator. Céline's narrator is a feeble meta-narrator who, before turning to madness past, vaunts the source of his creativity:

Fever or not, I always have such a buzzing in both ears that it can't get much worse. I've had it since the war. Madness has been hot on my trail . . . no exaggeration . . . for twenty-two years. That's quite a package. She's tried a million different noises, a tremendous hullabaloo, but I raved faster than she could, I screwed her, I beat her to the tape.[2]

By being more delirious than madness itself, the narrator can create his "music," for music would be the form of pure emotivity, of emotion present to itself with no need for a semantic intermediary, that is the image of life that triumphs over writing, the past, and death.

In Céline's hyperbolic work, however, delirium inverts everything; and if he can proclaim that his is the organ of the universe, it is because he has, roaring in his head, an avalanche of trombones and three thousand five hundred and twenty-seven birds (pp. 39–40). Music is the rhythm of madness; and meta-commentary is delirium about delirium. When this parodistic self-reflexivity gives way to the recall of time past in Céline, the music of the voice's presence to itself is revealed to have been madness then, too, though a form of comic dementia that destroys writing and releases folly as the present voice.

As with Faulkner, the Célinian voice posits a realm of silence that might be more primordial than the voice itself. The Célinian voice strains hopelessly to exhaust all that might be said in order to reach that place of silence.[3] But the task is hopeless, and silence is merely a utopian abstraction, a negative counter-pole, to the dementia that invades the voice and reigns supreme in Céline's works. As with Faulkner, silence would be something other than the language that the work needs for its existence and which the work could reach only by abolishing itself. In *Absalom, Absalom!* silence might be the place where absolute truth takes refuge, a kind of mythic locus beyond myth. In any case silence is posed here, too, as a utopian locus, beyond the solipsistic myth-making voices of *Absalom, Absalom!*

Céline's and Faulkner's novels are not without homologies with the ideas of those language theorists that we have been considering; and these homologies present a determining configuration of many of the themes that constitute the center of contemporary literature. Céline and Faulkner share with Heidegger and Saussure the paradoxical devaluation of writing that Derrida claims to be a foundation of Western logocentrism. This devaluation of writing by theorists and writers commands a central position in twentieth-century attitudes toward language. After Céline, however, it seems to me that we also find a concomitant devaluation of voice. For contemporary writers, writing and speech are caught up in the same suspicion of language in general as autonomous system or fallen logos, as truncated propositions or mere *Gerede*.

Parallels between Céline and Faulkner and the Wittgenstein of the *Tractatus* may have also suggested themselves in the course of this discussion. One cannot overestimate the importance that the *Tractatus* has had and continues to have as the locus classicus of a view of language and representation that can assign both a positivistic and a mystical limit to speech. Faulkner and Céline each subscribe to what I am tempted to call the modern myth of limits, for it is not at all evident to me that one can meaningfully speak of limits to language. The very notion that there are limits to language can only have meaning when contrasted with something that might exist on the other side of language. The *Tractatus* makes this opposition of the linguistic and translinguistic all the more pointed by suggesting that the limits of my language are the limits of my world. Not only does the *Tractatus* cast doubt upon my language by implying that it is somehow less pure than perfect constructs such as logic and mathematics, but it also posits silence as the place where dwells the really important things I should like to speak about, would language but enable me to say them.

The view of voice proposed by the *Tractatus* is of course also considerably different from that we have found in Céline or Faulkner. The *Tractatus* depicts a voice that does, however, speak in a number of postmodern texts. The only voice that speaks meaningfully, according to the *Tractatus*, is one that is certain of a limited number of atomistic propositions. Translating the seeing eye, this voice of iconic duplication can say nothing about itself, for the speaking self is excluded from the world that discourse can represent: "The subject does not belong to the world: rather it is a limit of the world" (5.632). Incapable of speaking about what it is saying, the voice can only be a recording of states of affairs, a hyperreal catalogue that excludes itself from its listings.

Wittgenstein's shift in thought from the *Tractatus* to the *Philosophical Investigations* provides little comfort, moreover, for those traditional humanist views that assume an unmediated relationship between self and voice, voice and discourse. In the *Philosophical Investigations* voices arise as a form of participation in the various language games that take place in the indefinite number of public spaces constituting language and the world. If one asks where the self is that is the origin of the voice, the answer seems to be that the self is only a kind of abbreviation for talking about the multitude of ways in which voices enter into language games. If taken as a substantial entity, the self is a metaphysical error arising from a misunderstanding about the nature of language. The locus of speaking might appear to be language itself.

Faulkner and Céline share with Heidegger a certain myth about the superiority *silence* of silence; and, as I have suggested, Heidegger's work suggests parallels with Céline's in the way it places in doubt the capacity of the ordinary voice to master its speech. In Heidegger's early work there is really no such thing as an individual *God's death.* speaker, only *das Man*, the anonymous "they" that speaks in its inauthentic voice the fallen logos of everyday existence. The only authentic voice is the voice of silence that stands opposed to the "they" that speaks a language of publicly determined meanings, a language that has fallen from the plenitude of authentic being. Although Heidegger declares in his later writings that language is the house of being, this characterization does not necessarily mean that ordinary speech is no longer fallen logos. When he summons the poet to become a speaker of authentic language by listening to the call of Being and by letting logos speak through him, this call can have meaning only if it also means that the poet must give up ordinary language. And when speaking this authentic language, the poet does not give voice to his own language. Language speaks through the poet, a proposition that expresses another form of rejection of the Cartesian self that believes itself empowered to use language to mediate its thoughts. It is autonomous language that, in speaking, differentiates Being against the backdrop of silence. Saying—*die Sage*—manifests Being as Being itself. Heidegger's claims for language evacuate the self from language. They might well also leave an ordinary mortal, someone less than a Hölderlin, or perhaps a Faulkner, in doubt about the ordinary language that he finds in his mouth: for most contemporary writers Heidegger's description of fallen logos rings much truer to their experience than does his vision of the possibilities of poetry.

And finally I should recall that the status of voice is made problematic by the opposition between Saussure's granting the individual's capacity to speak a unique *parole* and his declaring the individual to be a mere repository of the autonomous linguistic system. Certainly later structuralists have emphasized the second half of the opposition, whether they have been animated by a Marxist desire to demystify consciousness or a Heideggarian impulse to lay bare the inauthenticities of received language. Saussure's view of language as a system functioning beyond man's consciousness stands behind Foucault's well known and rather apocalyptic statement that man is dead. It also underlies Derrida's contention that the subject is constituted through language. Much contemporary fiction attempts precisely to ask and sometimes even to answer the question as to what voice can be said to speak if the speaker is a storehouse of his culture's linguistic system, of its codes, syntagms, and potential paradigmatic options. In this context the writer's suspicion of the very act of writing takes on additional twists. Not only can writing be viewed as ontologically inferior to the fullness of the voice; it can also be viewed as the most rigid embodiment of those fixed codes that deny the writer his voice. Writing seems to threaten the voice—an intolerable state of affairs for the fiction writer whose voice can, after all, only exist as writing. Céline lived this paradox to the edge of madness, and beyond; and it is still a paradox that animates contemporary practices of writing and antiwriting.

Man may be dead, but this death does not prevent him from speaking, as witnesses Beckett's prolonged sonata of the dead. Again, it seems to me that this elusive Irishman's fictions present exemplary illustrations of the questions and paradoxes that modern language theory brings up about what a voice might or might not say. Central to all of Beckett's fiction, especially to the works written in French and even more particularly to *The Unnamable,* is a constant self-interrogation about the status of the unhappy voice that speaks, about the voice's reaction to the language it speaks, and about the locus whence it speaks.

Let me recall in this regard how the unnamable comes to be the final speaker in the trilogy of works published as *Molloy, Malone Dies,* and *The Unnamable.* As the first decaying narrator, Molloy speaks to us about his journey. Then follows Moran's voice narrating his attempt to join Molloy. Both of these voices seem to be present to the Malone of *Malone Dies* as he, another bedridden speaker, talks about his narration and offers up the tale of Macmann. This bloody tale comes to its end with Malone's declaring that he will never say "I" again, although he immediately breaks his vow as he concludes the tale of a homicidal outing from the insane asylum. The refusal to say "I" brings the reader to the voice named "the unnamable." He begins his speaking with a question: "Where now? Who now? Unquestioning. I, say I." The original "Dire je" conveys even more forcefully the imperative sense of the voice that must order itself to use the first-person pronoun and hence force itself reluctantly into complicity with the structure of language. His questions underscore at the same time the separation that exists between voice and language. For *The Unnamable* takes the reader into a narrative space that is inhabited by a voice that cannot speak except in nearly contradictory fashion to assert that it is not his language that speaks, thus it is not he who really speaks, even if the I-voice appears to have no choice about using this language in order to decry this intolerable situation. The unnamable finds himself narrating the impossible quest to get around language. This speaking must perforce fall back onto language, onto stories, pseudo-narrations, other voices and laments, if the quest is to exist at all.

Beckett's reduction of fiction to this kind of self-reflexive rumination obliges us to ask what it means to say that voice and language are separated. For the unnamable's plight is grounded in comic non sequiturs that can illuminate the way much of contemporary fiction functions and, moreover, show how theoretical concerns have become the very stuff of this fiction. Or perhaps one might more precisely ask how literature seeks strategies for overcoming its own unhappy belief in language theory.

The homologies between Beckett's literary performances and the philosophical ones I have outlines are many. Of greatest significance is that they grant plausibility to the seemingly paradoxical assertion that voice and language can be separated, that there is indeed a place where, as the unnamable puts it, "language dies that permits of such expressions."[4] The unnamable's paradox first sends us back to read Heidegger again and ask if we have found that region of intersection between the realm where authentic language is heard only in silence and the realm of average everydayness where the babble one hears belongs to the anonymous other. The unnamable, if he dreams of silence, seems to reside precisely in that region where the only language he finds is, by its very ontology, the language of everybody, and hence nobody. His narrative trajectory wants to move toward a paradoxical ending that the other's language prevents from taking place:

All this business of a labour to accomplish, before I can end, of words to say, a truth to recover, in order to say it, before I can end, of an imposed task, once known, long neglected, finally forgotten, to perform, before I can be done with speaking done with listening, I invented it all, in the hope it would console me, help me to go on, allow me to think of myself as somewhere on a road, moving, between a beginning and an end, gaining ground, losing ground, getting lost, but somehow in the long run making headway. All lies. I have nothing to do, that is to say nothing in particular. I have to speak, whatever that means. Having nothing to say, no words but the words of others, I have to speak. (P. 314)

As pure voice the unnamable can do nothing, for in Beckett's world to say is to do, and he cannot speak since he has no language, except the language of everyone and no one. The unnamable thus sits chattering, looking across a silent space at Heidegger's authentic man, that hero who remains locked in his quiet resolve. Yet, the unnamable's antics let us know that he exists, however paradoxically, and by contrast one might well suspect that quiet authenticity is a figment of a loquacious philosopher's imagination.

The unnamable is a clown version of the man who would live authentically by speaking his own language. He is a clown who stands in relation to his own discourse much like the philosopher who uttered the axioms of the *Tractatus*, a work of metaphysical nonsense whose goal, according to Wittgenstein, was to annul itself. Yet, the unnamable is inescapably trapped in a bizarre public space where voices reverberate everywhere, public voices that seem to be a pluralization of *das Man*:

It must not be forgotten, sometimes I forget, that all is a question of voices. I say what I am told to say, in the hope that some day they will weary of talking at me. The trouble is I say it wrong, having no ear, no head, no memory. Now I seem to hear them say it is Worm's voice beginning, I pass on the news, for what it is worth. Do they believe I believe it is I who am speaking? That's theirs too. To make me believe I have an ego all my own, can speak of it, as they of theirs. Another trap to snap me up among the living. (P. 345)

The schizoid unnamable here presumably demands an idiolect that would express his absolute specificity, for the self that is spoken by public language is mere convention, a trap designed to ensnare it as it transforms one into otherness.

Beckett's narrator is keenly aware that language is a publicly determined repository of usages, and he also has a profound sense that his (or their) language is a social contract. The social bond that language requires is but another form of pluralized otherness, and the unnamable refuses the social glue even as he affirms, in common with structural linguistics and the Wittgenstein of language games, the social basis of all language:

> It's of me now that I must speak, even if I have to do it with their language, it will be a start, a step towards silence and the end of madness, the madness of having to speak and not being able to, except of things that don't concern me . . . . Not to be able to open my mouth without proclaiming them, and our fellowship, that's what they imagine they'll have me reduced to. It's a poor trick that consists in ramming a set of words down your gullet on the principle that you can't bring them up without being branded as belonging to their breed. (P. 324)

Wittgenstein often said that to understand how a language game is played, it is often helpful to see how it is learned. The unnamable here shows his familiarity with the most general pedagogical principle the tribe possesses for insuring that the linguistic system will be, literally, internalized. The system must be internalized and contractually obligatory if one is to speak, to be named, and that contractual alienation is what the unnamable would refuse.

Thus the language of the "tribe," as Beckett puts it in French, cannot be the language of the voice that is engaged in a curious struggle for sanity. To speak a single word is, as the unnamable says nonetheless, to enter into complicity with the tribe's codified system—or perhaps into complicity with the tribe's way of theorizing about its linguistic system. To speak is to force the voice to enter into an alterity that can only be a form of alienation. Even to say "I"—that "putain de la première personne"—is to accept the linguistic token that designates all voices. To say "I" is to accept the hoax fostered by the tribe's system of pronouns: for can "I" be "I" if every voice is "I"? Structural linguistics may point out that such a pronoun functions as a shifter on the paradigmatic axis of discourse, but this will bring little semantic succor to the speaker who feels that precisely such a semantic feature makes a mystification of the whole notion of personal identity.

In this novel Worm doesn't speak, nor, declares the unnamed narrator, does he; and Mahood is aphonic. With this voiceless cast who can, then, speak in this text, except perhaps language itself? On the other side of language there might be—farcical hypothesis—a self possessing a voice unmediated by language, the pure self of Wittgenstein's *Tractatus* or Heidegger's unalienated man. Except, of course, that this view of the separation of language and self is a schizo-comedy that takes desperate delight in its own impossibility. In this respect Beckett's work ushers in the era of the schizo-text that is perhaps the postmodern text par excellence. Beckett's work gives full expression to the voice alienated from itself, the voice for which the first- and the third-person pronoun are a matter of indifference. The speaker lives the "I" as an "it," for the voice is present to itself only as otherness:

> My voice. The voice. I hardly hear it any more. I'm going silent. That is to say I'll hear it still, if I listen hard. I'll listen hard. Listening hard, that what I call going silent. I'll hear it still, without hearing what it says, that's what I call going silent. Then it will flare up, like a kindling fire,

a dying fire. Mahood explained that to me, and I'll emerge from silence.
Hearing too little to be able to speak, that's my silence. (P. 393)

And the notion that one might listen to one's voice as the voice of someone else
brings us to the paradox that one might speak silence.

Beckett's narrators speak clamorously about silence. Like Wittgenstein's
metaphysician in the *Tractatus*, Beckett's narrators spend enormous amounts of
logical energy saying the unsayable and speaking about the unspeakable. As in
the case of Heidegger's vision of authenticity, one has the feeling that silence
would be a kind of utopia where the voice, divested of the tribe's language,
would have direct access to itself. In silence, speaking and listening, I and it,
would no longer be separated. The voice would be a pure self in which, as
Derrida might describe it, consciousness would be fully present to itself as a
plenitude unmediated by the alienating otherness of the tribe's linguistic system.
Yet, Beckett's is a self-reflexive comic vision, and his noisy praise of silence
mirrors Wittgenstein's dream of purity and Heidegger's claims for authenticity,
as in a distorting mirror:

> with regard to me, nice time we're going to have now, with regard to me,
> that it has not yet been our good fortune to establish with any degree of
> accuracy what I am, where I am, whether I am words among words, or
> silence in the midst of silence, to recall only two of the hypotheses launched
> in this connexion, though silence to tell the truth does not appear to have
> been very conspicuous up to now, but appearances may sometimes be
> deceptive. . . . (Pp. 388-89)

Appearances may be deceptive; yet despite one's worst intentions, it does
appear that merely saying "I" fosters the illusion that a self has been created,
that a character is present, that a voice speaks. The tribe's linguistic system has
many powers, and Beckett's narrators are constantly playing with variations on
the idea that naming suffices to grant existence or to offer being. Heidegger's
poet may have the task of authentic naming and hope to confer being against
the backdrop of silence; but Beckett's unnamable narrator clearly wants to resist
the power of language to hustle him into existence. To say "I"—how can this
confer being, when it offers existence to every "I" and thus to the pluralized
no one?

In Beckett's work and in many other contemporary texts we find a comic
equivocation about the nature of language. On the one hand these texts declare
that merely to name cannot of course confer existence, and that to accept the
deceitful appearances of mere pronouns is to give consent to a fraud fostered by
language. But, on the other hand, it is precisely the nature of literary language,
or a feature of the ontology of fiction, that to name *is* to confer existence.
Heidegger can, in his later writings, play with one side of this equivocation,
and Beckett, as if in response to Heidegger's extraordinary claims for poetry,

can play with the other side. Both are right, of course, for to name in literature is to confer being, merely fictive being, yet being nonetheless.

Beckett's equivocation with regard to fictive and nonfictive language also functions as critical irony. By allowing his narrators to act as if they were dealing with nonfictive language, Beckett allows them to undertake an ironic critique of errors that can only exist as illusions in the realm of nonfictive language. The schizo-text comically blurs the line of demarcation between fictive and nonfictive text in order to live out the madness that our various philosophical systems would ascribe to our daily lives. The schizoid suspension of logic allows the unnamable to live his narrative project as an experiential critique of language theory, much in the way Wittgenstein flirted with madness when he created such antimetaphysical fictions as the following: "One may say of the bearer of a name that he does not exist; and of course that is not an activity, although one may compare it with one and say: he must be there all the same, if he does not exist. (And this has certainly already been written some time by a philosopher.)"[5] Seen in this light the claim of Beckett's characters not to exist is at least as comprehensible as the claim to say "I" might confer existence.

Measuring the distance from Céline and Faulkner to Beckett may allow future historians to measure one of the major displacements of the sense of self that has occurred in Western history. Or, if the displacement is probably not so great as it seems to those of us living through these times, it is likely that Beckett's works will have the status of a major prelude to the great proliferation of postmodern texts of the past two or three decades that propose a kind of inverted therapy. Beckett's work offers, with constant irony, an inverted therapy for the unquestioning acceptance of fictive language and its pretensions to found self, world, or being; and, by implication, all hyperbolic claims for language's founding powers. Beckett's work, with its sardonic contradictions, is a prelude to those postmodern works whose voices know not whence they speak or speak from that equivocal space called the text. Many of these later works would go further than Wittgenstein or the unnamable in denying that language can reach any private sphere, that there could be such a thing as a private language, or in questioning if there could be a self that might exist beyond the voice that is created by language. Others follow another implication of Beckett's work and unfold according to the assumption that since the self must be translated by what is other than the self, the self is permanently alienated from itself, alienated in the tribe's fallen discourse. This point of view can exacerbate the suspicion that character and self may be only functions of language, mere aspects of rules of grammar that we have hypostatized into metaphysical entities.

If few of these later works seem to have Beckett's richness, perhaps it is because they fail to allow for the negative hypothesis that there might be a not-I, a self to be translated by what is other than the self of language, alienated in the tribe's fallen discourse. Beckett's unnamable stands as a contradictory protest against, as well as an ironic affirmation of, the idea that character and self may be only functions of language. He obliges the reader to ask himself if he can really be happy with the belief that his voice grants him a self merely because the rules of grammar have been misinterpreted as substantial categories? These various notions about voice, intertwined in Beckett's work, open up a postmodern space of narration in which most writers tend to hear either of two voices: voice as an automatic product of language, generated by pronouns, and often a comic automaton spoken by language; or as something separate from language, though forced to borrow from language to speak, often from the fallen language of everydayness or from the public delirium that I shall designate here and elsewhere as "pop." These views of voice and language tell us much about what has happened in contemporary fiction to what once was called character. Characters around 1900, as Queneau shows in his *The Flight of Icarus* (*Le Vol d'Icare*, 1968), had such ontological substance that they could be stolen or could even decide to abandon the novel in which they were to appear. No such fears of losing a character, I should think, need haunt the writer for whom a character is simply a repository of the tribe's syntagms or is a pronominal function.

One might suspect that more is at stake, however, than simple grammar lessons when a writer attempts to show that voice in fiction, as in life, is a pronominal function. For many writers this reduction of voice to a position within a linguistic system is another way of launching an attack on the tenets of bourgeois ideology or classical humanism. Writers find in this theoretical position a launching pad for works that wish to effect revolutionary transformations of literature, of views about the nature of the subject, and, in more general terms, of ideology. Although one can think of a good many German and American writers to whom this description would apply, it is more often writers working in French and Spanish who have been attracted to theories that voices, mere products of a cultural system, are masks for such metaphysical constructs as the bourgeois "individual": Alain Robbe-Grillet, Claude Simon, Philippe Sollers, Julio Cortázar, Carlos Fuentes, José Donoso, and Juan Goytisolo are some names, with all the necessary modifications for individual cases, that immediately come to mind. A quick survey of writing in the United States, Germany, or Austria would suggest that recent writers in these countries concentrate more on the struggle to get around fallen logos, often in the form of the commercial everydayness of pop culture. These writers seek ironic voices that can speak around language, from a locus of values which, if they are not revolutionary, would at least offer resistance to the destruction wrought by contemporary culture in its multifarious ways, including the destruction of language. These generalizations are useful within their limits but should not cause one to overlook how profoundly a reaction to fallen logos or pop permeates writing in the Romance languages, nor how a profound desire to transform ideology often emanates from these ironic silences lying behind the textual facades of much writing in German and English.

I propose to spend the rest of this chapter examining some of the ramifications that these views about the status of voice have had in contemporary fiction. I shall begin with the view that voice is a product of language. To prepare for this examination, let me offer a somewhat more detailed exposition of the structural linguistic theory that seems to have directly and indirectly created the climate in which writers can treat characters as nominal or pronominal functions. The work of Emile Benveniste, drawing on Wittgenstein and Austin, represents a direct development of Saussure's thought, and it can be of great use for understanding much contemporary thought about literature. Benveniste advances the claim that what we take to be subjectivity arises from the functioning of pronouns in the linguistic system, "ego" being originally the first-person marked form of the verb "to be." Subjectivity is linked to the way "I" exists in discourse. This pronoun is a unique word in that its only referent is the present instance of discourse: "I" can only exist in and by the speech act that profers it. As such, "I" has no referent other than the utterance in which it occurs. Since "I" only has reference to the speech act in which it takes place, this means that it is always a self-referential speech form.

Consciousness of being a subject arises only through the contrast of the "I" in face of the "you" that constitutes, according to Benveniste, the other pole of the axis of discourse. "I" presupposes the other, for the axis of communication demands the polarity of I/you. I shall leave aside at this point a possible Heideggerian critique of Benveniste's privileging a communication model. Of immediate interest to us is his claim that the self arises from the individual act of discourse and the concomitant implication that the self can only exist as a present instance of discourse, whatever be the tense of the verb used in the utterance. For, according to Benveniste, all our notions of temporality find their roots in the self-referential present moment of the "I." Our notion of time is derivative from this anchoring moment in discourse; and all other notions of temporality exist only through their articulation in the tense structure of language.

The present moment is therefore the primordial temporal position from which all our subjective reckoning of time flows; and that present can only be defined in terms of the moment in language where the "I" is articulated. (As might be expected, Derrida has done a deconstruction of this version of the metaphysics of presence.) There is no other criterion and no other expression by which one can indicate "the time at which one *is*" except to define it as the moment or the time "at which one is speaking."[6] The eternal present is the eternal repetition of the present instance of discourse, which means that linguistic time is self-referential. Whence the conclusion: "Ultimately, human temporality with all its linguistic apparatus reveals the subjectivity inherent in the very using of language" (p. 227).

Benveniste presents a powerful version of the autonomy of language that reduces Kantian questions of self and time to linguistic matters. The circularity of Benveniste's thought undoubtedly accounts for much of its power: the speaking voice grounds the absolute present which in turn localizes the speaking voice. Subjectivity is a condition of language which in turn is the condition of possibility for subjectivity. Benveniste's granting language the founding role in the creation of the ego proposes a powerful model for liberating the notion of the self from all ideological encumbrances. The self exists as a moment of the voice reflexively present to itself through language, a moment of the pure presence of voice to itself, as Derrida would say. Moreover, in ideological terms the voice confers a self that is free from past and future. The ego is, then, a radically defined moment of public subjectivity, as public as language itself.

Several consequences result from the point of view that language is the condition of possibility of self, the ego, or person. First by experimenting with pronouns and nouns the writer might discover new domains of self and identity. Or, at the very least, one might get rid of a good many mystifications about "man" and "identity." Discovering the power of language to confer identity can come as a liberating surprise to those who have accepted the received ideology of self, such as, for instance, Cortázar's Oliveira in *Hopscotch* (*Rayeula*, 1963):

> he had found out (first off) to his surprise and (later) with irony, that an awful lot of people would set themselves up comfortably in a supposed unity of person which was nothing but a linguistic unity and a premature sclerosis of character. These people would set up a system of principles which had never been legalized basically, and which were nothing more than a concession to the word itself, to a verbal idea of strength; rejection and attraction were subjected, displaced, gotten out of the way, then replaced by their verbal equivalent.[7]

Oliveira, an existentialist of the Saint-Germain des Près era, makes a discovery that could well turn him into a determined structuralist, an intellectual metamorphosis common since the fifties. There has been a certain complicity between the existentialist and the structuralist; structuralist notions of subject have given the existentialist a kind of imprimatur for his notions of the self as a blank space of total freedom, at least when it comes to the writer's freedom to redefine the coordinates of self in fiction.

This redefinition of the coordinates of self finds expression in the postmodern attempt to write a new kind of fictional autobiography. The great modernists in the first part of the century, writers as diverse as Colette, Rilke, Musil, Proust, and Joyce, made great use of the form of fictive autobiography as well as their own autobiography in their fictions, and in so doing their practice contributed significantly to the spread of the idea that the primary function of literature is to explore and defend the self—a notion that would have been incomprehensible to most writers in earlier times. Céline's example could serve to convince a good many writers that the self is best explored at some distance. Today it is certain that postmodern writers find the very idea of a substantial self entirely problematic. Contemporary explorations of the self as a kind of autobiographical fiction are accompanied by a linguistic consciousness that places in question an easy acceptance of the pronoun "I" and the fictions it fosters.

A writer such as Michel Butor, for example, is extremely aware of his literary historical situation with regard to both the achievement of the modernist tradition and the necessary consciousness about language that contemporary literature has imposed upon the writer. In his *A Change of Heart* (*La Modification,* 1957), one of the earliest examples of the French "new novel," this awareness is evident in his decision to abandon the pronoun "I" as the center for a fictional auto-biographical narration of a change of consciousness. Nearly throughout the work he uses the second-person pronoun *vous,* the formal form of address. Butor reverses the direction of discourse in terms of its normal axis. In narrating from the pole that is rarely if ever used as the principal pole in fiction, he gives the impression of an unbroken direct address in which "you" are a Parisian busi-nessman, about to go to Rome to join the woman for whom you are going to abandon your wife:

> Before you knew Cécile, even though you had seen most of the sights of Rome and enjoyed its atmosphere, you hadn't had this love for the place; it was only with her that you began to explore it in some detail, and your passion for her colors all the streets of Rome so thoroughly that when, in Henriette's presence, you dream of Cécile you're also dreaming of Rome in Paris.[8]

According to Benveniste's schema the "I" presupposes the "you"; but in Butor's novel the formal "you" does not refer to an "I" except perhaps by implication. The novel seems to speak in a dialogue with one side missing. The repeated direct address produces near total reflexivity; and in effect the novel does narrate its own genesis. Making explicit the underlying tautology of most narrations, the novel tells the events that precede the decision to narrate the narration that tells the events.

Without the intervention of the self-consciousness given by an "I," the ul-timate effect of the "you," however, is to depersonalize the discourse. It is as if a personless "they" were speaking. The voice defines itself as something of a negation of personality, like the voice of *das Man,* as it ranges over the past and the future, telling of the affair and imagining its outcome. This effect becomes clearer when, in sleep and dream, a second or a mythic voice using *tu,* or the intimate form of address, narrates the change of heart the protagonist undergoes. Butor has recourse to a Faulknerian use of voice by allowing a second voice capable of narrating beyond the real to intrude in his text. The "thou" of myth sets off the "you" as the voice of everydayness, capable only of the kind of sentimental discourse of which a certain kind of sentimental Italian movie gives the best example. Finally this play of pronouns redefines fictive autobiography by diluting the narrating self into a formal play of discourse.

To return to the work's self-reflexivity, at the conclusion of *A Change of Heart* the "you" assumes an imperative force, commanding the reader to see that he has been witnessing the narration of the genesis of a potential autobiography.

The trip to Rome now completed—the modification of intent now undergone—
"you" decide to transform "your" decision into a book:

> The best thing, surely, would be to preserve the actual geographical
> relationship between these two cities
>   and try to bring to life, in the form of literature, this crucial episode in
> your experience, the movement that went on in your mind while your body
> was being transferred from one station to another through all the
> intermediate landscapes, toward this book this future necessary book of
> which you're holding in your hand the outward form. (P. 249)

The narration has told the tale of a modification, as part of the ongoing spinning-
out of a self, narrated by the "you" that generates the text. Your self has been
defined as a play between the modalities of anonymous and mythic discourse.
And the final disclosure of self-representation shows that you are the product of
your narration, of the language that will be organized in the book you have just
finished reading/writing.

This kind of text that plays with pronouns and the axis of discourse often
implicates reading and the reader, calling reflexive attention to the way readers
are inscribed in the narrative. Juan Goytisolo's *Juan the Landless* uses the *tu* or
"thou" form with verbs in the future tense, to project a future first-person
autobiography that would exist beyond the codified forms of today's narratives.
In an act of reader-oriented aggression the Spanish writer projects a future
language that will destroy from within all the repression that Spain's traditional
values have encoded in both literary forms and language. This is, in effect, an
imagined destruction of the present-moment Spanish reader who can enter into
Goytisolo's imprecations only through their shared tongue. The apocalyptic voice
projected from Goytisolo's fantasy autobiography contrasts markedly with the
listless autobiographical voice of, say, the hyperrealistic cataloguing of a Peter
Handke: the narrating "I" in his *Short Letter, Long Farewell* (*Der kurze Brief
zum langen Abschied*, 1972) appears to be merely appended to a list of descriptions and events, the limit of a *Tractatus*-like world that could not exist without
the "I" but which in no way seems to impinge upon it. The reader is called
upon to read an "I" for which no "you" is ever evoked in the world of facts.
Beckett, Robbe-Grillet, Tony Duvert, Ludovic Janvier, and other, younger
French writers, in giving a ludic development to the schizo-text, often make no
distinction between the "I" and "he." The indifference to the choice of pronouns
makes of the voice therein both the subject of discourse as well as the object.
The axis of discourse to which the reader is accustomed is subverted, when it
is not a subject of mockery. The text no longer relies on the dichotomy of the
"I/you" to define the realm of the person, which can then no longer be juxtaposed
against "it" or the third-person realm of the nonperson in order to define the
objective world. At once a form of ideological therapy and an expression of
schizoid separation of voice and language, these texts, perhaps not unlike the

products of boisterous mad scientists, experiment with pronouns to see what new forms they might generate.

Perhaps the fundamental question behind these dislocations of the axis of discourse bears upon the criteria for identity of the voice that speaks in fiction and the certitude with which the voice can speak. These are overlapping issues, for criteria of identity often provide the criteria for the degree of certitude that the reader can attribute to the narrating voice. Much contemporary fiction attempts to undermine these certitudes or invent new criteria for something other than the traditional certainty that the reader can attribute to, say, the objective voice that speaks in the realist text. The first-person narrator of the traditional fictive autobiography has always had a more dubious status than the seemingly anonymous voice of the realist text that speaks about the third person—the third person being the object of the discourse that unfolds along the "I/you" axis. For the self-reflexivity of this "I" motivates the suspicion that the narration may be inaccruate, mendacious, or an overt lie. But the voice that speaks only of the third-person other in the realist text has often taken on the status of an oracle: Flaubert could not be wrong about the color of Mme Bovary's eyes. A structuralist understanding of the functioning of the parts of discourse, of the way they naturalize these conventional certainties while masking the identity of the voice, is undoubtedly responsible in part for the kinds of texts that flaunt the way grammar is at work in every narration. Moreover, Wittgenstein's search for the many kinds of criteria for certainty and identity that are masked by the seemingly identical exterior forms of language is similar to the writer's attempt to invent or discover new forms in language for redefinitions of self and its way of being in the world, which is to say, in language.

Let us concretely illustrate these comments by turning to one of the most remarkable novels to explore the functioning of pronouns and the voices generated by them. I have in mind one of the earliest of what has come to be called the "new novel" in Latin America, *The Death of Artemio Cruz* (*La Muerte de Artemio Cruz,* 1962) by Carlos Fuentes. A mixture of fictive autobiography and biography, the very title prepares the reader to open a book that reverses conventional biography: *The Life of* ***, the received form of which Boswell bequeathed to the English-speaking world. Fuentes has done more than grace his novel with an ironic title. He has also narrated a work in the first-, second-, and third-person singular, creating thereby a prototype for the self-conscious exploration of the axis of discourse in contemporary fiction. In the juxtapositions of the three voices that emerge from the novel the reader is obliged to look for confirmation and contradiction, incoherence and myth, in a work that poses questions about possible criteria for the identity of the voice narrating a life, which is to say a death.

It is revealing that most criticism of *Artemio Cruz* that I have read explains the use of *yo, tu* and *él* in terms of some kind of psychological representation or in terms of a modernist point of view, that is, vision analysis. These readings achieve a kind of approximate if misleading truth; for at this time Fuentes was working with Faulkner's model of multiple voices as a way to create narrative dissemination. I use Derrida's term "dissemination," because it suggests most aptly the way the novel refuses to grant a privileged narrating center to any one voice but rather spreads meaning among several centers, each of which may contest or modify the other. An "I" narrates the present of an aging Mexican capitalist millionaire who is dying. A "thou" is addressed, often in the future tense, by a voice that comes from an unnamed source, perhaps from the subconscious, from the domain of myth, or perhaps from an alter ego. We have no ready criteria for identifying this voice. And the third-person narration, narrated by the omniscient narrator who is the "objective" voice of literature or of history, tells the tale of Cruz's past, the story of the young Mexican revolutionary who later becomes the very bourgeois who has betrayed the revolution. This past-tense narration sets forth a masterful portrayal of the play of revolutionary forces, so masterful that many readers probably forget to ask how the three directions of discourse fit together. Fuentes demonstrates, as did Picasso on occasion, that postmodern writers can rival with the old masters in story narration, much as the modern artist can "draw" when he wants to.

Fuentes's early work is not self-reflexive in the way of works by Butor, Robbe-Grillet, Goytisolo, or even as in his own later *Terra Nostra,* but *Artemio Cruz* is perhaps all the more effective in that it can purport to give us a realistic portrayal of a self in history while exploring how the structure of language informs that portrayal. The voice of the "I" marks the moment of the absolute present, or the present of enunciation, which is ironically the moment of the body's dissolution. The present instance of discourse is concretely rooted in the body; as in Céline, fever is as important a component of the voice as is the narration itself. Fuentes presents, in harmony with this kind of structuralist understanding of pronouns, the "I" as irremediably cut off from the past. This is the sense of the scene when, in the presence of his wife, Cruz tries to remember his son, killed in the Spanish Civil War and left to rot as carrion:

> And she does not know that there is something worse than an abandoned dead body, that the ice and sun buried him, that his eyes, picked out by birds will be eternally open: Calina stops rubbing my forehead with the cotton and moves away and I don't know if she is crying: I try to raise my hand and reach her, the effort stabs me with pain from my arm to my chest and from my chest to my belly: in spite of the abandoned body, in spite of the snow and sun that buried him, in spite of his eyes open forever because eaten by birds, there is something worse: this uncontrollable vomiting, this overwhelming desire to defecate without being able to. . . . [9]

Certitude for the "I," existing as the center of the present instance of narration, is the present state of the body. This bitter realization is accompanied by the further manifestion that only the present moment offers criteria for certitude and identity, since the "I" is radically cut off from any contact with the past. The passage continues denying any contact with the past:

there is something worse: not to be able to remember him, to remember him only by pictures, the things he left in his bedroom, the notes he made in his books: but how did his sweat smell? and nothing repeats the color of his skin: and worse that I cannot think of him now that I can no longer see him and touch him. . . . (Pp. 234-35)

The autobiographical project is circumscribed by the limits of the pronoun that grammatically as well as existentially—and one adverb implies the other in Fuentes—cannot transcend a present discourse rooted in the "nowness" of the body. Time past cannot enter into this project, and the "I" voice can only speak self-reflexively of its own limitations.

The voice using "thou," apparently addressing itself to Cruz as well as to the reader, often speaks in a kind of mythic future tense that appears to want to deny the radical presentness of the autobiographical moment. In this case, the mythic figure could be interpreted as a kind of modernist promise of transcendence, a Faulknerian paean celebrating myth over history. I suspect, however, that Fuentes has, in this narration in the future tense, called upon one of Borges's philosophical fictions, especially the one developed in "A New Refutation of Time." According to this critical fantasy the consequence of the autonomy of the present moment and the self-sufficiency of psychic states is that the self is a superfluous notion and that time is an unfounded assertion. Borges's ironic development of the implications of these philosophical principles allows the writer the freedom to indulge in mythic or fantasy play underwritten by axioms about the self locked in the present moment. The voice of direct address can, for example, promise "you" survival:

You will survive; you will rub the sheets again and know that you have survived, in spite of time and the movement that second by second shortens your fortune: the line of life lies between a paralysis and frenzy. (P. 198)

Time is an invention of men needing to frame discourse, and there is no time other than the time men invent:

you will invent a time that does not exist, and measure it, you will know, discern, judge, calculate, imagine, predict, and you will end by thinking that there is no other reality than that created by your mind; you will learn to subdue your violence in order to subdue that of your enemies: and you will learn to rub two sticks together until they burn, because you will need to throw a torch into the mouth of the cave and frighten the beasts that see you as no different from themselves. (P. 199)

And all this will continue until "you" split the atom.

The future-tense narration addressed to the *tu* enacts perforce a universal allegory that can be ascribed to anyone or to any receiver of the grammatical shifter. As with Butor, one is initially disarmed by the second-person address, because conventional expectation wants to find the ''I'' of the axis of discourse implied by this form of address. With no ''I'' given, the speaking voice seems to emanate from no particular place, a creation of discourse to which the reader responds with conditioned reflexes. ''You'' are ''you,'' no matter what the voice says. The ''you'' has the uncanny power to confer identity on the self that is absent from the discourse, to generate a semantic presence for which there is no rational justification other than the structure of discourse. The repetition of the second person, in *Artemio Cruz* as in *A Change of Heart,* gives the impression that the writer has created a reversed form of autobiography, although in Fuentes's novel the reversal cuts his fiction lose from the existential moorings of the solitary ''I.''

The third-person narration—the voice of literature or history—is the voice to which one is obliged conventionally to attribute certitude. Third-person narration is, as Benveniste says, the voice of the nonperson defined as discourse directed at the other as that which is objectified. In *Artemio Cruz* this discourse about the nonperson or the objectifiable competes with the two voices emanating from the two poles of the personal axis of discourse. The third-person narration is in the past tense, the traditional tense of realism, when not of the real itself. For Western realism has come to encode the real as that which can be objectified as the having been, not as the currently ''is,'' and the present tense is rarely used as a realistic tense in our literary tradition. The voice speaking in the third person, when contrasted with the other two voices, is a voice of negation, announcing the past tense as the death of what is narrated. The objective history of Artemio Cruz is, then, the death of this man, as any objective voice must be if it defines itself as objective only because it has been, has become a solidified bit of past to be arranged in an ossified chronological unfolding.

The voice using the second-person address can promise survival because the past is nothing except a death; the future is nothing, however, except a myth; and nothing can really be said to exist except the present-moment utterance—a self-reflexive death rattle. One can cavil at this existential bleakness. What is significant here is that Fuentes's use of the three persons of discourse poses the kinds of questions postmodern writers ask when they attempt to find a voice for biography, be it fictive or nonfictive, that does not derive its criteria for meaning from the automatic play of pronouns. Conversely, of course, some writers want precisely to show that it is the automatic play of pronouns that is responsible for all the metaphysical illusions we hold about voices. An especially deep suspicion surrounds the third person, for it seems to be a form of alienation with regard to the primary axis of discourse, the ''I-thou'' axis that must be exploited to enter into any kind of subjectivity. Moreover, the third-person pronoun, manipulated by the masked voice of omniscience, also masks the very fact of the conventionality that underlies its guaranteed certainty. The realist voice is viewed, by many writers, as the voice of bad faith (and the existentialist roots of this view go back at least to Sartre). We must take note of a paradox here, since the third-person narration in *Artemio Cruz* does appear to offer, in terms of the codes of realism, a retrieval of time past squarely grounded in Mexican history. The mechanics of realism work efficiently to satisfy the reader that there is a history here, a tale of commitment, ambition, and struggle that in some "objective" manner can be said to apply to Mexico past and present. When facing such a "readable text," to use Roland Barthes's term, the poststructuralist reader can borrow an explanation from Derrida and say that the power of the codes of realism are such, that even when deconstructed by the general textual matrix in which they occur in *Artemio Cruz*, they still force assent: they constitute a certain definition of the real, and who can deny the real? In fact, the autonomy of language can scarcely better be demonstrated than in this play of writing that shows how it forces assent to what it says while laying bare its conventionality. In later work, such as *Terra Nostra*, Fuentes attempts to contest from within these received codes of writing and reading the voice of history. But *Artemio Cruz* is likely to remain a more important touchstone for postmodern fiction. It carries to an exploratory limit a writing of biography-autobiography that does not allow one any longer to overlook the codes that establish the difference between the voice that utters the "I" of identity and the voice that utters the "he" of the identified.

Artemio Cruz remains perhaps more on the existentialist side of the passage that had led many writers to a structuralist understanding of writing and to a view that language is essentially autonomous. When in a more literal sense, the writer accepts that it is language that speaks in his writing, then he may well feel that only by working against language can he find a voice, by inventing new language games or by subverting old ones. The self, the voice that might say "I" or indifferently "he," the voices of the tribe's others, the presence of the text itself, all are spoken by language; and hence for some writers, the criteria for who says what become either impossibly problematic or the matter of new game rules, or both. After Beckett, one may think of the French new novelists with regard to what amounts to a breakdown concerning certainty about who speaks and from where: Nathalie Sarraute's undifferentiated "sub-conversations," often the embodiment of anonymous *Gerede,* Robbe-Grillet's shifting narrators who are doubles of each other, or Robert Pinget's narrator-less tales that tell tales render reading a kind of hermeneutic activity for which the rules demand that the reader not be able to assign a textual voice. Such is the case, for example, in Robert Pinget's *Passacaglia (Passacaille,* 1969). In this novel voices proliferate in such a way that no central narrative locus can be found, only thematic modulations that, as in a musical score, offer a series of variations on the theme of a narrated death or deaths. It is not certain who has died where or when in this novel—this uncertainty will of course eventually be part of everyone and anyone's tale. In a world in which voices are constituted by language's autonomous displacement of pronouns, uncertain certainty is a fundamental language game.

Pinget's moving novel, beginning in the third person, commences its narration by setting forth the scene of writing in a French village:

> In the glacial room was leafing through the book, December evening, the clock was showing the maid's time, the rain was beating down on the cobbles in the courtyard.
> An April shower, the garden swamped, the plan for the greenhouse on the lower level, two notes from a blackbird resuscitated his childhood, everything would start again in the spring.
> That murmur interrupted by silences and hiccups.[10]

Omitting a pronoun or noun in the first sentence, Pinget plays on the paradigmatic possibilities of an indefinite number of choices at that point in the linguistic chain. Any masculine third-person singular pronoun or noun would seemingly fit into the telling of the telling, of language speaking its eternal taxonomy of births, seasons, and deaths.

In spite of the verb tenses, time is left undetermined in Pinget's work. Inflections marking tenses are merely signs within language, and any event can come before or after any other. Verbs in any tense suffice to generate narration. These narrations, then, go to make up those unfolding discourses that, in Pinget, bear much resemblance to the voice of *das Man*, the anonymous *Gerede* that speaks through everyone or as it speaks in the novel,

> Then the other man left and towards the end of the day someone apparently saw him over by the marsh, they heard about it at the café where conversations intersect and intermingle, anyone who isn't really listening doesn't follow what's being said and with the help of booze everything merges into a sort of monotonous drone which is always the same, come winter, come summer, so that you could. . . . (P. 23; author's suspension points)

As in this passage, Pinget's language of idle chatter can reflect upon itself and, as a kind of comic meta-language, tell about its speaking. The voices that proliferate are the voices of everybody, hence nobody, the booze-inflected telling and talking of the anonymous "they" reflected upon by a language that represents its own speaking. This telling and talking has no locus except the present instance of discourse, there is no time past, no memory except as it exists in verbal construct. Like a decentered version of Faulkner's orchestration of voices, Pinget's voices add details to details, compounding probabilities and uncertainties, so that a narrator ironically notes at one point that it would take him "till tomorrow or even longer to restore verisimilitude to his tale" (p. 55).

As one might well suspect, third-person narration and its conventional certainties are not the only item on Pinget's agenda. An "I" intervenes late in the novel; but it no more gives a center to the narrative voices than do the multiple third-person possibilities. The "I"—much as in Beckett—is a mobile token, quite literally a shifter, that might be said by anyone, servant or master, or perhaps even by the idiot who appears in the last third of the novel. Pinget's schizo-text takes on at times a Shakespearian grandeur. The separation of voice and language, and the uncertainty about which voice is spoken by the language that does not belong to it, is a form of sound and fury giving voice to an existential forlornness:

> Sitting at that table a few hours earlier, found dead on the dunghill, a
> sentry was on guard, he had seen no one but the deceased one cold, grey
> day, must have gone over to the slit in the shutter and apparently distinctly
> saw him put the clock out of action and then sit there prostrate in his
> chair, elbows on the table, head in his hands. (P. 94)

This final passage in *Passacaglia* dramatizes a postmodern tragic moment in the tragedy of telling tales: the reader looks in upon the place of death, where an unnamable writer, in dying, produces a dead text. Language, like a tragic destiny, speaks its characters and their fate, in supreme indifference to the illusion of individuation. Pinget's work reveals that all telling is repetition of the same tale, comic in its foreseen linguistic taxonomies, but capable of a Nietzschean sense of the tragic in its dissolution of all into language's "murmur interrupted by silences and hiccups."

Pinget's example may cause many readers to ask if this means the writer has given up his own voice. One answer that some writers would offer to this question is that it has been a delusion for writers ever to have thought that they had their "own" voice, and that today no writer can hope to have a voice when all he can speak is a language that is somehow ontologically deficient. This distrust of language has broader implications than the exploration of the automatic generating powers of language, since belief in fallen logos affects a wider spectrum of writers, often including those who have not articulated narrative structures that consciously play with pronouns or linguistic functions. Many a contemporary writer feels little self-consciousness about using pronouns; it is the rest of the language he finds at his disposition that strikes him as being beyond his power, beyond his voice, in short, the product of a language system over which he has no control. He feels he must contrive a voice or voices by overcoming some fallen form of logos or some linguistic system that manipulates him as much as he speaks it.

Given the totalitarian nature of fallen language, it is not surprising that contemporary writers in search of a voice constantly employ parody. In parody lies the hope of destroying this language from within, or at least making it speak against itself. Parody has become a staple of contemporary American fiction—far more so than in the other literatures I am considering—and the number of examples one can find is considerable. The Fiction Collective offers choice material in this respect, and Ronald Sukenick's *98.6* is among the most interesting. This novel plays with the typical American worry about American identity, though with a new twist. The novel presents an America known as Frankenstein as its fictional space; here, in the book's central section, the children of Frankenstein seek to create a new America, a countercultural community of utopian drop-outs. In its self-reflexivity the work is typically postmodern: a novelist named Ron lives at the commune and works (or doesn't) on a novel at the commune. And it displays its postmodern concern with language in speaking of a dream of a language beyond the corrupted and fallen language of Frankenstein. But the novel must reckon with the language it has, the language of liberation in the sixties that undergoes a fall and becomes the cant of mindlessness, as the reader sees in the following considerations about one of the commune's female characters:

> Dawn is riding up the old logging road on her stallion Lawrence. She's worried about Lance. She's worried about Cloud. She's also worried about herself. She's worried about Lance because Lance has stopped paying attention to her. She's worried about Cloud because Cloud has started paying attention to her. It's true that Dawn is a superliberated woman on the other hand it's also true that she depends on Lance in a way to hold her together. At one time Dawn was a go-go-dancer under the name of Dolly Dawn. Dolly Dawn was topless and bottomless. Dolly Dawn liked being Dolly Dawn. Dolly Dawn was so liberated she could exploit her own exploitation. She liked being a sex object. It really turned her on. It turned her on because it turned off something she really wanted to turn off.[11]

The parodistic allusion to D. H. Lawrence—appropriately a stallion—and his sexual politics, the childish syntax of the language, the repetition of ideological notions that have become media and journalism clichés, the general inversion of what is usually taken as a liberation ideology, all these parodistic dislocations produce an ironic series of collisions in which language stands out as language, as a kind of public *Gerede* that defines consciousness. At the same time, as the final sentence suggests, this passage asks for another language, one freed from that fall that menaces every word in Frankenstein. One may doubt that such a language will ever be found there, for the only alternative language offered in *98.6* is called "BJORSQ," a kind of "language people don't understand," dreamed-up by a paranoid writer.

If BJORSQ is the only language one can find beyond parody, then parody plainly has its limits for escaping the fall, all the more so in that parody turns quickly into hysteria and enters into paranoid fixations about the world to which fallen language delivers us. In the interests of an approximate typology one could say that the paranoid discourse is the American contribution to the more general category of schizo-text that I have been discussing. This variant—that of a Roth, a Pynchon, and a Sukenick—derives from the belief that beyond the fallen or demented surfaces of language there must be a conspiratorial domain where something is really said. This domain cannot be directly voiced by the writer. He can only give voice to the language of the world while trying to find messages coming from some other place. The paranoid text suggests the structural equivalent of a *Tractatus* that has lost its certainty—or a less heroic version of *Being and Time*'s division of the world into that given by *Gerede* and that one yet to be found in silence. This paranoia is also a comic commentary on the philosopher's privileging of silence. For what if, in silence, there is to be found, not spiritual or mystic concerns, or authenticity, but the orchestrators and origins of the Célinian madness that the writer finds erupting in his language?

The *Tractatus* is, I would submit, a proto-schizoid text in its dividing of self and world, in its separation of the source of voice and the object of voice. Its narrating voice belongs to a self that is not in the world but is the limit of that trivial world that can be exhausted by atomistic propositions. In much American fiction the analogues of these propositions are those of the cant, cliché, and fixed syntagms that make up a special American idiom of fallen language, often with pop inflections.

In contrast with American exploitation of pop culture, and perhaps drawing directly on the *Tractatus*, many of the works of what I am calling German-language hyperrealism present this kind of fallen idiom in forms more clearly influenced by a positivistic reduction of the world to intolerably trivial limits. As an example of this kind of hyperreal fallen discourse I offer Dieter Kühn's *Ausflüge im Fesselballon* (roughly "excursions in a captive balloon," first published in 1971), although works I have referred to by Handke and Roth in the preceding chapter might also be evoked. In Kühn's novel one finds exemplified a day in the life of a German schoolteacher, whose narration is an ultimate example of the world reduced to the simple proposition. What voice can be said to speak when no more is said than:

> Stack of notebooks left, the corrected notebooks right, a new stack of notebooks left, the corrected notebooks right, a new stack of notebooks left, the corrected notebooks right, a new stack of notebooks left, notebook on notebook, after notebook on notebook: two three stacks per week makes around thirty centimeters of notebooks each week, stacked on the left, carried over to the right, notebook on notebook after notebook on notebook on notebook, one meter twenty centimeters per month. . . .[12]

The voice is the autistic voice of the proposition that measures and hence finds exact analogy between its language and its world. Such a positivistic quantification results in a demented reduction of the world, but it can claim, in its own terms, to exhaust it. Such desire to control with absolute precision, to speak without fault, is a form of hysteria; and from one point of view, it corresponds to the tight-jawed determination that the criteria for certainty will be simple and clear. Many would maintain that such a voice of certainty is in fact the voice of hysteria that speaks from most places of power and decision making. And perhaps one could speak of a new form of realism in which the shape or structure of the voice in fiction coincides with the shapes or structures of voices of power in the world.

Dieter Kühn would probably endorse such a view, for his novel is a clever satirical orchestration of a number of such voices, though the dominance of these voices echoing truncated language seems to preclude the explicit presence of any other kind of voice. Kühn integrates into his work, as the voice with which characters speak to themselves, voices from the media that seemingly only need to be quoted in order to parody themselves. This frequent reduction of the world to pseudo-positivist descriptions or to the language of insane triviality that characterizes media slogans brings up a sociological question about the production of such language. This type of reduction is often predicated on the assumption that contemporary society, in a totalitarian way, manufactures languages that displace all others. The only thing that the writer can say is formed, as it were, by the molds that fabricate the discourses of consumer society or pop culture. If the writer, taking clues from Saussure, views language as a sclerotic collection of fixed syntagms, or if he finds it reduced to a quantifiable series of truncated atomistic propositions, or if, in agreement with Heidegger, he sees language as a fallen or sullied public logos—or accepts some combination of these three points of view—then it requires little imagination for the writer with a certain sociological sensitivity to see that the major source of such language is the marketplace as determined by advanced capitalist society. To such a writer language comes as a manufactured product to be sold in the form of so many imaginary and often insane discourses that purport to be adequate to the needs of contemporary man. Fabricated discourses, invented to meet the needs of capitalist market drives, proffer so many voices to be mimicked, like garments turned out for the season's fashion dictates. These discourses include not only the language of advertising, magazines, TV, and the general commercialized ideology promoting a fantasy world of needs and drives, but also the languages of comics, movies, trivial literature, and pop music. To live in this society means to many a contemporary writer, if he opens his mouth, that he immediately finds the commercial tribe has already stuffed words down his gullet. And if he should invent something new, he must entertain the suspicion that he will hear it on television next month, used to sell cigarettes to future victims of lung cancer.

Pop language exercises an ambivalent fascination, however, and writers' responses to the kinds of myth elaborated by pop cultures are varied. One need think only of the equivocal responses found in the pop art of the sixties to consider how "pop," as a cultural category, can both seduce and repel. Or, in cinema, one should consider the ambiguous responses of Fellini and Godard to the pop myths and culture that are at the basis of their own postmodern reflections on the nature of film. Brecht claimed capitalism was bringing about its own demise by elaborating pop myths that as de-psychologized modes of narration would cause bourgeois ideology to explode from within. Most, though not all, contemporary writers have given up a belief in such Marxist dialectics, but many—a Sukenick or a Robbe-Grillet—do respond to the general category of pop as to a kind of mythic discourse that can be spoken against itself or against those social conditions that produce it. Yet pop culture attracts for other, perhaps more dubious reasons, for one cannot overestimate the universality of pop as an idiom that has infiltrated contemporary culture in every European language. To the extent that American capitalism has dominated the creation of the language of advertising, movies, comics, and magazines, the mythology of pop presents an American idiom spoken throughout the world. Every child in Buenos Aires, Paris, Havana, or Budapest feels that King Kong is part of his language (and Goytisolo can use him as a character in a Spanish novel with no fear of mis-translation). The bibliography to Oswald Wiener's novel *Die Verbesserung von Mittel Europa* has as many references to Donald Duck as to Heidegger. Pop culture attracts because it proposes the only universal idiom today, a twentieth-century church Latin as it were. The semiotician could claim that pop is a universal *langue* of which much contemporary fiction is a *parole* realized in local dialects.

The voice of pop has been perhaps exploited by none better than Donald Barthelme, one of the writers most sensitive to the loss of a full voice that modernism once offered (modernism, or "the dead father" who continues to accompany us as one can discover in the novel of that name).[13] Barthelme's stories are marvelously absurd repetitions of our pop syntagms. These repetitions testify at once to the way the idiom of pop has seemingly displaced those claims literature once made to having its own voice and to the black humor that such a displacement brings about as a response to this loss. The title of Barthelme's *Come Back, Dr. Caligari* (1959) underscores with ironic equivocation the way in which literature calls upon pop for its idiom. Perhaps there could be no more appropriate emblem of ambivalence for pop's attraction than Caligari, at once a mad scientist and, in the final framed narrative of the film imposed by the producers, the beneficent doctor who takes care of the mad. Barthelme is some-thing of a Caligari himself, as he mixes motifs taken from movies, cartoons, and Madison Avenue with the clichés of a certain highbrow *Gerede*. It would be too simple to say that this mixture produces a satire of American life, though there are many elements of satire in Barthelme's work. Satire would be the response of the sane, but Barthelme's hyperbolic mixtures result in the creation of a mad recording machine for the voices of hysteria, repeating themselves in such a way that language loses all reference except to denote its dysfunctional nature.

Caligari, we know, was mad, but he did manage to be placed in charge of the asylum. The guardians of the language of high culture may judge pop to be mad, but, as we see in Barthelme's work, it is the idiom of pop that integrates all languages into itself, including the language of high culture, reducing them to sign systems that designate themselves as mythic constructs. In the story "At the Tolstoy Museum" of *City Life* (1968) one can visit a temple of high culture where the display of thousands of pictures of Tolstoy makes us ask what is the meaning of the manufacture of images connoting "high culture" in a world where the fact of pop proliferation shows they no longer denote anything. They circulate as mythic images of "culture" in a space where they have as much significance as the images of *Teenage Werewolf* or *Beast with a Thousand Eyes*— to mention two of the films that have invaded the world in "Hiding Man," another story from Barthelme's *Caligari*. In that collection's story "The Piano Player" we find a *Look* magazine image of the ideal family in which pop and high culture coexist: one daughter eats Silly Putty while another reads *The Rise and Fall* and dreams of being an S.S. trooper. Any text, including the one you are reading, can be reduced to pop *Gerede:* in "The Joker's Greatest Triumph," literary criticism can be transformed into another robot discourse. Marc Schorer's description of Sinclair Lewis can just as well be applied to the Joker as an explanation of his cartoon-strip behavior. Barthelme creates, if creates is the word, quintessential pop in this tale, for he narrates quite literally a tale of Batman and Robin, with contemporary adjustments, since Robin studies French at Andover and Batman keeps a bottle of B and B in the Batmobile's bar.

A "serious" writer's narrating a tale of Batman is perhaps the reverse image of capitalism's using Rembrandt to sell beer and shampoo. In the first instance we are quick to ascribe an ironic voice to the text, though I am not sure that the ironic voice really deflates the power of pop. In the second, in the appropriation of Rembrandt, we clearly see the conversion of a language of culture into a myth that is used to connote a system of values and value-charged associations that can seemingly appropriate anything. In Heideggerian terms this fallen discourse simply determines everything. In self-defense Barthelme's irony functions like the placing of a frame around a Campbell's soup can or the hanging on a museum wall of an exact reproduction of Steve Canyon and his forty-five. With these gestures the utter conventionality of pop discourse stands forth. Perhaps we are critically disengaged from it by a voice that calls upon us to be aware, but, I think, pop remains the dominant idiom, like the voice of the master, Caligari, running the asylum. In its mythical completeness, in the way it subjugates all discourses, pop is a totalitarian discourse, if merely because in its completeness as myth it needs no other discourses. There is no possibility for meta-linguistic criticism in the seamless world articulated by pop. The self-reflexive language of doubt does not occur in the language that promises the paradise of a roll-on deodorant or the apocalyptic retributions of a Clint Eastwood movie.[14]

For other writers, moreover, pop releases a deep-felt nostalgia for a world of mythic purity or a world articulated in terms of clear absolutes. Though the language of pop might appear to be a form of fallen logos, in its almost religious simplicity it can appear to be a language of transcendence—of a kind of camp transcendence that can make Bogart appear to be the embodiment of a good number of values that one would like, in nostalgia, to resurrect. In Peter Handke's *Short Letter, Long Farewell* the writer protagonist lives in a world made up entirely of artificial and manufactured sign systems that enclose the urban spaces and freeways where he travels. During his trip across America, as he goes west while pursued by an estranged wife who wants to kill him, he finds that his journey's natural conclusion is an interview with John Ford, the Hollywood director whose Western movies have given a shape, through their mythic plots, to the writer's trip west to California. But Handke, the pioneer who travels in a rent-a-car, reading the romantic novel *Der grüne Heinrich*, traverses a landscape that bears little resemblance to those created by Ford's famous panoramic shots. And "Green Henry's" nature has given way to a landscape composed entirely of signs—in the two or three senses of the word—that are drawn from the language of pop. Handke's deadpan realism surveys a *landschaft* that is a page of pop script as he travels to the Mecca of pop culture in search of an encounter with a great creater of movies. The novel lays bare the world as a place of fallen nature, or nature transformed *into* pop signs and language. Against this background it also betrays its nostalgia for pop myths that might transcend the very pop that has created a civilization composed of freeway lanes, telephone poles, and advertising signs.

Pop often enters into contemporary fiction, by way of film, for movies have become a part of the tribe's language that both attracts and repels writers, though most postmodern writers strike me as inveterate movie-goers. Movies offer writers the example of a pop language of ready-made myth. A postmodern classic using this language is Manuel Puig's *Betrayed by Rita Hayworth* (*La Traición de Rita Hayworth*, 1968), a novel in which all the voices seem to derive from the movies. Or one could say it is a novel through which the movies speak a kind of autonomous language. In this work the reader finds a series of voices, excerpts from diaries, letters, inner monologues, that in speaking the *porteño* Spanish of Buenos Aires speaks the idiom of Hollywood. Thus, when a family is about to witness a baby die, its loss can be expressed only through responses they have already seen in the movies:

> at the beginning Toto didn't like the baby's face, he says to me "the baby isn't so handsome" and I tell him it's because he's not too well, and there's some danger, and Toto says "If he dies it's like *The Great Man's Lady*, when Barbara Stanwyck's newborn baby dies on her" and I calmed him down saying he wasn't going to die and "If he dies it would be like in a movie, don't you see?" he says to me, and "If you could choose a movie to see again which would you choose?" Toto asked, and I read his mind and said "Hmmm . . . *The Great Ziegfeld*, did I guess right?", and he said "No," but then he said "Yes, *The Great Ziegfeld*, me too." I think I'd die of sadness in the movies if I had to see *The Great Man's Lady* again.[15]

The Heideggerian would undoubtedly point out how the idiom of the movies dissipates any authentic concern with death in these people's lives and that this Hollywood-produced *Gerede* has alienated them from any encounter with their authentic possibilities. In less dramatic terms one can see that *Betrayed by Rita Hayworth* offers a troubling example of how the anonymous other speaks in a singular voice. Speaking the manufactured movie language of macho fantasies and feminine dreams of love that never ends, these characters give voice to a pop discourse that seems to be the natural stuff of life. Puig's work disconcerts precisely because this seemingly fallen language appears to be naturalized as our normal language.

Perhaps it is a primary function of fiction today to make certain that no form of discourse becomes naturalized, even if one can propose no effective counter-discourse to pop. To their credit American absurdist writers have continued a kind of guerrilla warfare with those pop discourses that permeate every aspect of our life. I use the word "absurdist" in a general way to characterize much of the most important American fiction of the past two or three decades. Absurdist strikes me as a useful term to designate those postmodern novels that work in modes of radical discontinuity and that, using large doses of black humor and frequent irrational transformations, explore a space that from the outset is given as incommensurable with the language to be used to explore it—which is to say, the absurd. In these works—those for example of Heller, Roth, Barthelme, Coover, Kesey, Brautigan, Vonnegut, Pynchon—the narration is set in scenes of war, insane asylums, or Southern California, places that are metonymic spaces representing the book's own production. These places serve to designate the book's impossible task of finding a voice capable of speaking the absurd languages spoken therein, or a language adequate to the absurd. There is a Célinian side to this task of uttering the unsayable in a language invested with the insanity of the place that produces the language. Explicitly or implicitly the absurdist novel must contest its own language and, by so doing, refuse a natural status to any contemporary discourse.

The most grandiose demonstration of this contestation, pushed to a logical self-destruction, is found in Pynchon's *Gravity's Rainbow* (1973). The reader who does not read to the end this violent and confusing work of comic genius will not discover that finally he and the narrator are inscribed in the novel together, in a final melded voice of pop delirium, projected within the cinema that is now the target of the descending rocket that Blicero and the Schwartz-commandos have launched:

> The film is broken, or a projector bulb has burned out. It was difficult even for us, old fans who've always been at the movies (haven't we?) to tell which before the darkness swept in. The last image was too immediate for any eye to register. It may have been a human figure, dreaming of an early evening in each great capital luminous to tell him he will never die, coming outside to wish on the first star. But it was *not a star,* it was falling,

a bright angel of death. And in the darkening and awful expanse of screen
something has kept on, a film we have not learned to see . . . it is now
a closeup of a face, a face we all know—[16]

And the rocket closes in, on the film we have been watching, as some final
messenger from the place where the mad conspiracy that the paranoid dreams
of truly reigns.

The narrating voice in *Gravity's Rainbow* marks its self-consciousness about
its status by inscribing itself at the end within the pop schizo-text. The above
voice comes at the novel's conclusion from a viewer, split from himself, as he
observes his own narration played on the movie screen. The narrator/reader/
viewer is inscribed in a text that culminates in the narration of its own obliteration:
as the rocket descends, the novel is shown to be a self-annihilating Möbius strip.
What has been played out in the novel has been a movie scenario of pop voices,
a delirious series that is designated finally as separate from the instance of
narration itself. This split between the voice as spectator and the voice's language
is analogous to the schizo split that Beckett posits at the heart of *The Unnamable*
and finally at the heart of all speaking. Pynchon's omniscient narrator, in tracing
the disintegration of the main character, Tyrone Slothrop, is omniscient in that
he gives voice to all the mad fantasies that this cinema of the absurd can speak,
which allows him to narrate, in a series of radical discontinuities, everything
from the tales of a kamikaze squad to dithyrambs about the V-2. But at the end
this voice acknowledges that it has been speaking the voices emanating from a
screening of our delirious recent history, a movie of fragmented voices, of pop
images, and paranoid imaginings. The narrator is, in this sense, as much spoken
as speaking, spoken by a language whose goal is to narrate its own destruction.
Hence we have the rocket that falls, a messenger from that space on the other
side of language.

Pynchon's finale precedes a noisy return to silence, though it is hardly that
silence endowed with a quasi-mystical aura that the Wittgenstein of the *Tractatus*
and the early Heidegger located beyond the language of the empirical world.
Pynchon's novel, like many of the works I have discussed here, suggests that
contemporary fiction, in its comic or hysterical validation of the insights of
language theories, also functions as a savage critique of what the theorists propose
as a description of what our voice can say. In conclusion—before the rocket
arrives that will bring silence—let us note that this critique takes the form of a
debilitating ratification or a parodistic pursuit of the logic of theory. Saussurian
linguistics, for example, tells us that in uttering a *parole* we enter into a contract
with the shared world of a linguistic community whose basis is the common
system of *langue*. Postmodern fiction, in the wake of Céline, and beginning
explicitly with Beckett, shows that the voice is nothing but the demented belch
of some collective monster, an alienated utterance of the tribe, that speaks through
us with its deceitful, shifting pronouns. Other writers have developed this schizo-

critique in ways that undermine our notions about certainty of the self and world; for the language that encodes the tribe's certainties is nothing but a machine for producing discourse, a producer of ideology and myths, relying on its autonomous functions to mask the codes that underlie it.

Postmodern writers have created voices that resemble the description of voices given by the Wittgenstein of the *Tractatus* or the Heidegger of *Being and Time*. In light of Wittgenstein's view of the poverty of empirical language or Heidegger's strictures about the fallenness of everyday discourse, the schizoid split with ordinary language appears to have the force of a logical necessity or an ethical imperative. Perhaps postmodernism begins and ends in this necessity of disassociating the voice from the language that speaks it. Silence might be preferable to giving voice to the alienating speech of others, especially in those forms of loss and madness that one finds not only in pop and the absurd, but also in the ordinary fallen language of everyday existence. But to be a writer who refuses language is a contradictory position.

This impasse undoubtedly has its roots in earlier periods that one can trace historically according to the defining model one uses. Contemporary contradictions can be viewed as the closure of the reign of metaphysics or of the Renaissance, as the last gasp of romanticism, or as an outgrowth of modernism. But these periodizations do little to assuage the condition of the postmodern writer (and reader) who lives this impasse as a unique moment in which he is condemned to end before he can begin. The changing status of logic I spoke of in the preceding chapter finds another role in this contemporary impasse about the writer's voice. The devaluation of logic allows him to speak forth, to write on in contradiction with his insistence that he has no language. To paraphrase Beckett, he speaks his alienated voice as a situation in which he has nothing to say, but, even worse, nothing to say it with. Or, to quote another writer whose schizoid withdrawal sings forth in low-key, contradictory laments, the voices of confinement that the Austrian Thomas Bernhard orchestrates assure us that "Very early we know . . . that we do not think with our brain and cannot speak with our language; and yet all our life we think with our brain and speak with our language."[17]

The jubilant energy of postmodern fiction arises, in a nearly dialectical fashion, when the postmodern accepts this contradiction as a challenge, and pursuing his alienation, hyperbolically assumes the otherness of language, its schizoid structures, and its pop dementia. By assuming these voices in their most grotesque and delirious forms, he can attempt to explode language from within—and with language the limits of selfhood that humanism has assigned as the limits of reason since at least the Renaissance. In this way arises the postmodern alternation of voices, of silence and madness, loss and jubilation, deadpan realism and irrational exaltation. Within this oscillation one finds nearly all the voices that make up the range of contemporary fiction. Within this fluctuation arises what I would call an attempt at redefining sanity, at founding a literature of freely

sanity

given play that wants to understand the ontology of language as a means to guarantee the possibility of literature. The play metaphor in modern language theories now takes on its full importance for the way it suggests that language is best used when literature acknowledges and explores its nature as language, which is to say play.   *playing w/ language*

6. Play

The voice that assumes madness and its language in a text is playing at madness, for true madness would leave in its wake only silence.[1] But one can play with the voices of dementia, invent games for fallen language, and seek play strategies that convert this language of otherness into literary language. The schizoid voice knows that it must play with and against language, since the alternative to "shapelessness and speechlessness, incurious wondering, darkness, long stumbling with outstretched arms, hiding" is to enter into the game, to play, as Beckett's Malone puts it at the outset of his prolonged death: "This time I know where I am going, it is no longer the ancient night. Now it is a game, I am going to play. I never knew how to play, till now. I longed to, but I knew it was impossible."[2] In *Malone Dies,* as in many of Beckett's other works, the schizoid voice recognizes that play's the thing, for nothing except play could offer even a semblance of justification for its otherwise absurd existence. Facing "shapelessness and speechlessness," the storyteller plays, because play is the only self-justifying undertaking he can find. By making of his tale a self-conscious game he can perhaps transform his narration into something other than a litany of fallen language, stuffed into his mouth by the tribe's linguistic system. Play's autonomy promises, if faintly, the possibility of creating a necessary order in the midst of absurd fallenness.

Modern language theories agree in telling the storyteller that, whenever he tells a tale, he has already started to play. They are basically at one in telling the writer that to use the tribe's tongue is to undertake a ludic activity whose rule-bound forms are grounded only in themselves. Literature—inventing fictions, narrating tales, writing texts—would therefore be so many language games, play in language to the second degree, or perhaps moves on the chessboard of being. In this light the writer can view his struggle with language less as a condemnation to defeat than as an agonistic encounter for which he can invent some of the rules. He finds himself in the position of needing to invent rules and make them explicit so that his fiction does not appear to receive passively its game plan from sources other than itself. Self-representation is imposed as a kind of necessity, for the writer must lay bare the rules of his game—within the game itself. This laying bare of the rules within the game-construct itself is perhaps imposed by the nature of play, for one can maintain that there is no play that is not accompanied by an awareness of play. To play without being conscious that one is playing seems contrary to our notions of what it means to play. Self-representation is often representation that assumes its consciousness as play.

To assume a ludic consciousness, a consciousness other than one's world-oriented consciousness that characterizes normal *da-sein,* is also to divide oneself into a player and, implicitly, one who knows he is playing. Play carries with it a divided consciousness that obliges one to enter into full acceptance of the game while one watches oneself accept this state.[3] At the same time play promises a way to overcome a schizoid stance toward language by granting the writer ludic autonomy, it reinforces the divided sense of the self that is turned toward itself in reflection upon itself as player. As Beckett's work playfully shows, there is no contradiction in finding in the same text the schizoid voice and the proclamation of play that reflects upon the text's self-consciousness as game.

For the writer the play metaphor offers the possibility of wresting rules of the game from the welter of competing discourses, truncated languages, and totalitarian codes that make up his world. It allows him to dream of his writing as its own principle of sufficient reason, originating itself in itself as play: it plays because it plays, like the Heideggerian child of Heraclitus. The child plays on the chessboard-cosmos of language, the closed space in which the infinite permutations of being unfold according to the immanent rules of their unfolding. Perhaps the fall can be overcome; or perhaps the fall never occurred. There is only the constant repetition of the cosmic roll of the dice as what is comes to be.

Another impulse lies at the heart of play: to kick open the closed space and experience the exhilaration of the body's vertigo. Agon, mimicry, and perhaps cleansing destruction—these urges also motivate play.[4] Behind parody, behind the play against language lie these urges to create other games, physical games that engage language in its material as well as its conceptual being. As Wittgenstein insisted, there are multiple games to be played and an indefinite or open number of play spaces to be explored with language. Moreover, the power of the play metaphor is such that all can be converted into a game. Metaphorical transfer is a language game itself, and, in the play of metaphor, language and play entertain those mutual relations that make up the indefinite play of meaning (and meaning as play). If every feature that can be ascribed to games can, with metaphorical adjustment, be used to describe language and writing, then metaphorical exchange imposes play at every juncture in writing. There is no escaping the play of play.

Games—some games—have rules. Language is characterized by rules. And, at least when viewed in post-facto terms, fictions are created by rules of selectivity that generate their combinations. Ludic models that posit rule constraints and utilize probability also define the ground rules for other areas of knowledge, not least of which are biology and physics.[5] The multiple spaces of provisional order that we encounter—games, language, narrations, laws, probability models in sciences—all entertain metaphorical exchanges in terms of the way they organize chance and necessity. In this sense there is no simple opposition of illusion and reality, since all contemporary constructs of reality are ludic models offering multiple and perhaps complementary ways of ordering rules, criteria, and models for the play of what is. (Recall *ludere:* ludic, to enter into illusion, play, game; here is perhaps the basis for Nietzsche's critique of science as the will to illusion.)

All seems to move in a great *Spielraum*, and one might argue that Heidegger's cosmology is but another metaphorical extension of what the play of language itself allows. Language speaks: it defines the multiple rules of the game it contains. To play, one must submit to the rules, one must accept the necessities brought about by the role of the dice. The rules are arbitrary, products of chance, but act as a necessity if the game is to continue as a game. Language and games are the play of arbitrary absolutes that could have been quite different from what they are. But once they exist, the realm of chance is transformed into necessity. Saussure's chess system has its arbitrary history, its chance origin, and its unexplainable diachronic changes. As a synchronic system, however, it imposes the game's rules with the fiat of a god. It is true that the notion of system can be defined without recourse to ludic metaphors, but it is also true that the very notion of system derives much of its plausibility from the way it is characterized as a game construct with ludic autonomy and rule-bound enclosure.

The play metaphor is in some respects a two-edged sword: with regard to the writer's revolt against or acceptance of what is, it cuts both ways. In some writers I think that it works both ways at once, for they attempt to revolt against fallen discourse at the same time they feel compelled to accept the play rules that prescribe what kinds of games can be played in the chaos.[6] The writer who, like Wittgenstein, Saussure, and Heidegger, is seduced by the chess metaphor may find in it a model of how at least a provisional order can be introduced by fiction into an otherwise absurd reign of disorder. Within the closed space of the chess game the writer can hope to find the model for how to create, with a finite number of elements combining according to the finite number of rules, the paradigm of what a limited combinatory order is.

Within the limited field of order, a provisional acceptance of the world seems plausible. In the hands of a Derrida, however, this model of limited order loses whatever solace it might have offered the writer in search of order. In Derrida's version of the book as chessboard, it becomes "a field of infinite substitutions in the closure of a finite ensemble" for which is no center that might arrest the "freeplay" of substitutions.[7] *Différance* ascribes an infinite play to meaning in language; it is a process of infinite deferring and differing that refuses any arrest to the play of meaning. Derrida's description of language aims at the destruction of what Heidegger calls onto-theology and the metaphysics of presence; but it also affirms that the chaos that the modernists sought to overcome must now be recognized as a fundamental state, traversed by a play of meanings that is constantly in movement. According to Derrida's game rules, there is no center to discourse, no possibility of even metaphorically finding a spatial state of arrest in language, of an iconic seizure of a static moment of transcendence. Derrida's work brings certain contemporary writers' jubilatory acceptance of the labyrinth to the philosophical playing field.

Perhaps the most striking similarity offered by the view of language as play, characterizing both language theory and writers of fiction, is found in their therapeutic aims. I stress this therapeutic urge, because it seems to me that this is one of the curious and most important attributes of contemporary fiction. Not only does this fiction inscribe within itself the rules for how to play the game, it also wishes to disabuse us of the wrong ways to play the game. Of course, much of this therapy is directed against the same metaphysical determinants of thought that Wittgenstein, Heidegger, and Saussure sought, in their respective ways, to cure us of. In fiction these determinants are especially prevalent in the form of the metaphysical notions about what writing is: its function as mimesis and representation, the belief in ideal meaning or essentialist signifieds, the subordination of writing to the metaphysics of history, or the text as the representation of the substantial self. The play metaphor is often conceived to be a medicine, a pill to cure the reader of ill effects produced by the pills of some earlier doctor. This play therapy is designed to restore a state of health in which the reader accepts fiction for what it is: language, nothing but language, and nothing beyond language. Perhaps one could liken this to psychiatric therapy that aims at ridding us of delusions of grandeur. Literature can have nothing to do with anything that lies outside the game space of language, simply because there are no rules for how to play these games beyond language, at least not available to literature, which is a play of language within language. Yet language is world, the play of the world, which leaves no small room for a playground.

Before turning to some specific writers, I might anticipate an objection to privileging the twentieth-century use of play metaphor and admit that it is quite true that contemporary writers are hardly the first to have invoked a theory of play. In a different historical perspective one could point out that artists have on more than one occasion defended their right to play in the face of imperious philosophical judgments that condemned art as mere play. With the demise of neoclassicism's claim that literature could be knowledge, for example, Addison exalted the play of the imagination as a way of endowing literature with a function; this was in reaction to Lockean epistemology's denial that literature could have a cognitive capacity. Or one might recall that Schiller defended art as play, seeing in it the highest use of the human faculties; this was a defense of art against the onslaught of Kantian metaphysics and ethics. Philistine distrust of art is certainly part of the Western tradition, beginning, as Derrida would point out, with the inaugural distrust that characterizes the Platonic condemnation of art and representation as, again, mere play. Platonic metaphysics affirms the ludic side of mimesis in order to denigrate it, and this suspicion that play has an ontological deficiency has undoubtedly not yet said its last word.

What appears quite distinctive for the contemporary writer is that modern thought about language offers play as the very model for describing the ontology of language and discourse. With the advent of linguistics, with philosophy's attempt to abolish its traditional foundations, and, I add for illustrative purposes, with the contemporary elaboration of many new game models for scientific projects, the writer can affirm with far less diffidence that his task is to create play forms. The postmodern lives in a world in which play has become a generalized and shared therapeutic metaphor to describe the ontology of both language and fiction. The recognition of the commonality of the play metaphor to both philosophy and literature turns the traditional tables. For insofar as literature celebrates itself as a self-conscious ludic construct, it offers models to philosophy as to how theory might conceive its own discourse.

For an example of a writer who demonstrates that the play metaphor characterizes all systems of thought and representation, I turn again to Luis Borges, who started publishing stories in the thirties, that decade of fruitful transitions. The stories in *Ficciones* (1945), his best-known collection, are extraordinary game systems in which philosophies, cosmologies, our various *Weltbilder,* are unmasked as rule-bound constructs of the fantastic, which is to say, playing mind. And fantasies are shown to function as systematic constructs springing from the play impulse toward order. The creation of systems that order a world is a gratuitous form of play, and, as such, all are equally worthy of interest. Or, conversely, as the narrator of "Pierre Menard, Author of the *Quijote,*" somewhat cynically notes, there is no exercise of the intellect which is not, in the final analysis, useless. Pierre Menard's own extraordinarily useless game is a case in point: he undertakes to rewrite the *Quijote* as a word-for-word reproduction of itself.

Borges's story of this second *Quijote*—an imaginary *Quijote*—is a teasing kind of therapeutic thought-experiment that invites us to contemplate the way meaning is the product of diachronically given rules for the genesis of meaning. The exact reduplication of Cervantes's novel by a Frenchman at the end of the nineteenth century would result literally in the same novel. The word-for-word rewriting would mark the successful completion of this absurd game. But the second *Quijote* would have, one can imagine (and even verify), quite different meanings for whoever might play the game of explaining these meanings. This second version would be the same, but different, deriving its meanings from the totality of nineteenth-century language games that surround it, as well as from a kind of intertextual play with the "original" novel. The original, the "real" fiction, would determine in part the meaning of the derivative meanings, and, one might well imagine too, the second *Quijote* would change the meanings we could attribute to the first. I have twice used the verb "imagine" in this discussion, since the second *Quijote* of course does not exist. Or rather it exists only in the game "Let's imagine that . . . " or "What if . . .," which are literary

games par excellence. Borges's genius is to make these games into games explicitly about literature, beliefs, philosophies, and systems of representation. In
this way Borges shows that meta-linguistic texts are language games, too. The
second *Quijote* exists only as imagined in a game, and if that game is also called
"reading," then it exists an infinite number of times, in an infinite number of
places, which is every time a reader reads the book and rewrites it in his imagination. A labyrinth is always lurking in the recesses of Borges's work, for it is
a metaphor with as much convertibility as the play metaphor of which it is a
specification.

Unlike many younger writers, Borges does not propose a theory of play, for
such a theory would be only one more fictional system to which the playing
skeptic could give only metaphorical assent. As "Pierre Menard" demonstrates,
Borges's *practice* of play dissolves all beliefs, myths, philosophies, and metaphysics (a branch of fantastic literature according to Borges) into a labyrinthine
play of ludic hypotheses. One can only demand of these hypotheses that they
respect the rules that generate them. For any play model to have power, the
aesthetic power that will make it effective, it must be worked out with a kind
of demonic consistency to its own intrinsic rules. Borges's fictions are the model
for stories that work as games of the liberated imagination. This imagination
can entertain any fantasy so long as that fantasy obeys the inner logic of its own
rules. This logic is given by language, by premises couched in language that,
merely because they are in language, command assent. A constant therapeutic
point of these fictions is the demonstration that *all* systems are games that seduce
by virtue of their consistency as language games. It seems to me that Wittgenstein
makes this point, in an analogous way, in *On Certainty*. Linguistic constructs,
obeying arbitrary rules, come through overlapping consistencies and mutually
supportive definitions to constitute what we take to be reality at any given moment
in history.

The power of such consistent play in "Tlön, Uqbar, Orbis Tertius," worked
out with the "rigor of chess masters," suggests that the taxonomic autonomy
of language automatically compels assent to its orders when these orders are
perceived as rigorously consistent (the criteria for rigor constitute another game
played *within* the language system). An imaginary encyclopedia—a compendium
of linguistic taxonomies—can transform "reality" by providing a world view
that is simply superior to the one found in other books. Borges's works anticipate
in comically outrageous ways some of the conclusions that one might draw from
the post-Bachlardian epistemology of a Thomas Kuhn and a Michel Foucault:
the models that knowledge proposes as the real come in a series of ruptures,
one model displacing another, and each bringing about a new world. What we
take to be reality at any given moment is merely a game construct, a successful
model, drawn up in accord with arbitrary rules, that succeeding and more seductive models can easily replace in the minds of men if these models can impose

their rules as the criteria for a successful game. When the superior language of the Encyclopedia of Tlön invades the earth, who can be surprised if the natural taxonomies of English, French, and Spanish disappear:

> Almost immediately, reality yielded on more than one account. The truth is that it longed to yield. Ten years ago any symmetry with a semblance of order—dialectical materialism, anti-Semitism, Nazism—was sufficient to entrance the minds of men. How could one do other than submit to Tlön, to the minute and vast evidence of an orderly planet? It is useless to answer that reality is also orderly. Perhaps it is, but in accordance with divine laws—I translate: inhuman laws—that we never quite grasp.[8]

All order is perforce human order, given through, and understood in, human language. Borges's anthropomorphism works subversively to underscore the provisional nature of any fiction (literary, philosophical, or scientific) that we construct for ourselves. And it places us on guard against the temptation to believe in those orders that attempt to present themselves as the natural order of things, those sources of fanaticism that are the very antithesis of the free play of the skeptical mind.

The passion for symmetry, another variant of the play impulse, leads to the creation of orders that might be likened to so many anti-entropic moments of organization in a universe that is given over to increasing chaos. As every reader of Borges knows, Borges's favored image of that symmetry is the labyrinth. This metaphor for writing and reading conveys a sense of both the enclosed nature of the ludic space and the play that can unfold therein, such as the minotaur's games in "The House of Asterion" (this story appears in the collection *El Aleph* [1949]). Fictions are labyrinthine constructs generated by the play principle of repetition; they are "gardens of forking paths" in which symmetries are created by the infinite possibilities of choice that allow the indefinite proliferation of possible orders. (And I leave it to the more mathematically minded to pursue analogies here between Borges and the decision trees that are central to Von Neuman and Morgenstern's theory of games.) The play impulse that would reduce chaos through the repetition of symmetries, a repetition that creates the labyrinth, finds a counterpart, in Borges's fictions, in the entropic play of chance that increases disorder. The desire to dominate chance carries with it the need to flaunt the aleatory side of the game by making visible the role of the dice that imposes a rule decision at each fork in the labyrinth. *Alea*—a dice game—is another privileged metaphor for the arbitrary rules that are the absolutes of the game, conceived of as rules for language use and the rules of selectivity that generate a fiction.

Borges's work sets out the parameters for the postmodern collaboration with chance. The creation of a necessary system must follow the chaotic unfolding of the chance diacronic antecedents that, in Saussurian terms, lead to the present game. Or, metaphorically, every gallery taken in the journey through the labyrinth, each order proposed in the elaboration of a fiction, is determined at each juncture of decision by a role of the dice: this is the aleatory. Our constructs of reality are therefore so many repetitions in an "infinite game of chance." In "The Lottery in Babylon" the reader finds this view of chance portrayed in an elaborate fictional conceit in which every element presents a metaphorical side of the game of chance. The tale is first of all an allegory about itself, since in it we discover that it is our need to augment chance and to vary our accounts of ourselves that lies behind our inventing fictions in the first place. Fictions are lotteries, and behind the lottery lies chance—or the Company—but what can explain the Company's refusal to disclose whatever might be the basis for its aleatory results? This desire to know generates more fictions:

> That silent functioning, comparable to God's, gives rise to all sorts of conjecture. One abominably insinuates that the Company has not existed for centuries and that the sacred disorder of our lives is purely hereditary, traditional. Another judges it eternal and teaches that it will last until the last night, when the last god annihilates the world. Another declares that the Company is omnipotent, but that it only has influence in tiny changes: in a bird's call, in the shadings of rust and of dust, in the half dreams of dawn. Another, in words of the masked heresiarchs, *that it has never existed and will not exist.* Another, no less vile, reasons that it is indifferent to affirm or deny the reality of the shadowy corporation, because Babylon is nothing else than an infinite game of chance. (P. 35)

Babylon, when called the Hebrew Babel, is also the place that legend offers as the source of languages in a fallen world, and perhaps we might see in this "infinite game of chance" an allusion to language itself as the ultimate game in the mirror play of self-allegorization. A game in language, the Borgesian text uses self-representation to create a play of mirror symmetry by which the work represents its own game structure. And this game structure is generated by the same aleatory processes that the story presents as its ostensible subject. A lottery in Babylon can only represent a lottery in Babylon, or the play of chance that is a text and its subject.

All orders come from Babel insofar as language informs our human taxonomies. In this sense it is evident that we inhabit by definition the "Library of Babel" (as another of his stories is called), the universe of all orders, potential and actual, that language might contain. But in this infinite library it is a matter of pure chance as to which taxonomical texts we shall encounter in our quest for order. Our version of the real, that we receive from those texts in Babel, is quite aleatory. Of course it is the perennial dream of literature and philosophy to discover the single order that will obliterate all others, or, to invoke Mallarmé again, to make the one role of the dice that would abolish chance. The history of literature, philosophy, and science would be the story of successive findings of the ultimate Book, as well as the story our successive losses of belief in that

Book. But the search continues through the infinite number of hexagons making up the library, for the very notion of the infinite number of possible books available seems to promise mathematically the finding of the ultimate order. This unbearable certitude leads to the creation of literature, philosophy, and science; to the proliferation of sects; to a quest throughout the (infinite) library:

> The certitude that some shelf in some hexagon held precious books and that these precious books were inaccessible, seemed almost intolerable. A blasphemous sect suggested that the searches should cease and that all men should juggle letters and symbols until they constructed, by an improbable gift of chance, these canonical books. The authorities were obliged to issue severe orders. The sect disappeared, but in my childhood I have seen old men who, for long periods of time, would hide in the latrines with some metal disks in a forbidden dice cup and feebly mimic the divine disorder. (P. 56)

Borges is a poet, so perhaps one can laughingly forgive him for this derisive image of poets: old men in a latrine who combine the aleatory with the mimetic as they attempt in their play to find the hidden order of the world. Is one to see here, in addition, a critique of modernist ambitions?

Borges work brings us to the postmodern recognition that the aleatory cannot be abolished (though Mallarmé anticipated as much, in anguish, with his *Coup de dès*). Rather one must accept the play of chance by using various forms of mimicry while maintaining one's lucidity about the limits of representation. One has no choice but to play; and yet one can never suppose that the arbitrary combinations of letters—the building blocks of the library—will ever imitate infinite chance in its totality. Borges is fascinated by the hubris of representation and mimesis as forms of play that wish to rival the divine play. For example, the gnostics held that mimesis was at the basis of creation and that the universe was a mirror image of the heavens. But such mimicry gives rise to paradoxes that human play cannot resolve: in such a view must not Judas be a reflection of God? The play of mimesis is founded in the metaphysics of the visual. The mirror recurs in Borges's work, since it is the image for the confusion that mimetic play brings into the world. It promises to abolish chance, since it produces a *certain* representation of the mirrored. In practice, however, mirrors compound images of being, multiply imaginary orders, and allow the fantastic proliferation of symmetries that quickly become labyrinths.

Facing the mirror and its representations, the reader resembles the archetypical detective Erik Lönnrot, who must decipher the clues he finds in "Death and the Compass." By misreading the clues he ends up in the labyrinthine villa where his enemy waits to shoot him. Hermeneutics is a game, though for the detective it is a deadly one: mirrorlike parallels and repetitions lead the quester into a space where losers lose their life, philosophers as well as "mere" detectives and readers. Such are the wiles of mimesis. In the self-mirroring allegories that

Borges proposes, where the fiction is a game, the reader-detective is thereby a player. This metaphorical implication multiplies other metaphorical parallels of players facing texts as mirrors, mirrors facing other text-mirrors, in a play of self-contained reflections in which the negotiator of the labyrinth may well lose himself. Losing at this game is another form of therapy that works by dissolving textual absolutes into a play of intertextual reference, often through imaginary reference to the reflections of imaginary texts. To say that this play of mirrors deconstructs the primacy of the visual is to say that Borges undoes the meta-physics of representation by exploiting all the paradoxes to which representation can give rise. His narrative voices obey the rules of the narrative construct whose logical implications they pursue with ironic unflappability as they demonstrate the paradoxical conclusions to which forking paths can lead.

Borges has become something of a patron saint for many contemporary writers, especially in Latin America but also in Europe. To a lesser degree this role has been played in the United States by a writer whose views of play give less emphasis to the aleatory and more to the self-conscious side of play. I refer again to the Russian-American Nabokov. In ways at times more subtle than those of Borges's work, Nabokov also pursues therapeutic aims in novels whose nar-rative space is cordoned off as a closed playing field. Like Wittgenstein Nabokov aims at curing his readers of such maladies as *profunditis,* a neologism I offer to designate the need for organic symbols that might transcend language and express unconscious or invisible depths that lie outside the public space of the world as it is. Borges's fictions present various parallels with modern attempts to cure us of metaphysics, and in a comparable fashion Nabokov's novels dem-onstrate in their self-conscious play that the world is what it is—a variety of games played in language as so many taxonomical variations. The world consists in verbal surfaces: it is nothing other than the playing fields that his novels offer as so many game constructs. But only through these constructs can one enter into the game—and hence a world.

Within the play space that Nabokov cordons off, usually with self-conscious irony, the narrative game-master allows a limited number of elements to undergo permutations according to the rules of a game plan, in the manner of a Saussurean chess system. Nabokov's need to delimit a self-consciously enclosed narrative space explains many of his narrative strategies. In such works as *The Defense, Despair, Laughter in the Dark, Pale Fire, Lolita,* and *Transparent Things*—to offer samples from a career that approximately parallels that of Borges in span-ning a good part of the twentieth century—Nabokov uses weak, deluded, or insane characters for his central focus so that he can keep his narrative space from opening up too much. Though often for purposes of parody, Nabokov does stay on the realist side of fiction in his respect for the canons of verisimilitude (*Ada,* for example, being a grandiose representation of the representation of a world). He therefore usually restricts the game space to an area that might be plausibly located within his characters' reach, within their consciousness or grasp of understanding. The effect of this restriction is to create a novelistic world that, so delimited, can be likened to the chessboard on which these pawns repeat their trajectories as they move to an inevitable checkmate, usually to an exemplary if predictable death. The prototype for this narrative game strategy is *The Defense*, a novel originally written in Russian in 1930, which is about a chessmaster named Luzhin whose limitations lead to a nervous breakdown. Nabokov's forward to the translation of the novel, done years after the novel was first written, still echos with the ironic voice of the narrative game-master who relishes "taking advantage of this or that image and scene to introduce a fatal pattern into Luzhin's life and to endow the description of a garden, a journey, a sequence of humdrum events, with the semblance of a game of skill, and, especially in the final chapters, with that of a regular chess attack demolishing the innermost elements of the poor fellow's sanity."[9]

The Defense sets the pattern for the Nabokovian game. In an agonistic encounter a narrator reveals his ironic presence and mastery over narration as he checkmates his opponent, the protagonist. This ironic presence constantly affirms that ludic artifice is at work even as the novel unfolds according to more or less realistic conventions. These realistic conventions are, in Nabokov's works, the game rules that can be as self-consciously used as any set of rules for the delimiting of his play spaces. This game strategy can also accommodate a first-person narration, as in *Lolita* or *Pale Fire*. In these works the presence of the master player is often revealed through other indices, in the fabric of the narration itself or in plays on words, through devices of which the protagonist may not be conscious, but which endow the work with its ironic and at times parodistic play. By implication the reader, too, is involved in the play, for he must attempt to solve the various enigmas and word-plays the text poses if he is not to be defeated. In *Lolita,* for instance, Humbert Humbert tries to catch up with Claire Quilty in a pursuit across America that requires the slightly mad satyr to decipher clues that Quilty has, so Humbert believes, left in motel registers. Humbert plays a game that obliges the reader to play at least two, for he must decipher Humbert's words before going on to play at figuring out the puzzles that Quilty may or may not have left behind. The reader's relationship to Humbert is parallel to Humbert's to Quilty, for he must play at deciding which words are animated by a signifying intent beyond their surface meaning. (The impossible game of symbolism that Nabokov takes delight in parodying is present obliquely in many of his works.) Humbert's narration is sometimes reliable, but the reader must determine when. In the case of *Pale Fire,* with its play of mirroring between a fictional poet's poem and the fictional meta-fictional commentary, Nabokov carries this type of game to its limit. He forces the reader to work from the mad commentary to the poem and back in an attempt to construct a realistic exegesis of the relationship between the exegete and the poem. The utter implausibility of this task serves all the better to lay bare the ludic nature of those rules for realistic interpretation that guide the reader in his construction of a meaning for the text.

This ironic play proposes a therapy for our naive acceptance of rules as absolutes true to some hypostatized nature of things. However, there must be rules, however arbitrary, for the game to exist. Nabokov shares a certain consensus with Wittgenstein about the rules: the world's hidden depths disappear in their works as they reveal the game plan that allows, in all its rule-bound arbitrariness, the elaboration of novels, or forms of behavior, ways of understanding the world, in short, the world itself. Nabokov, no less than Wittgenstein, is an inveterate investigator of the taxonomies given by the play of language; and one can understand the attraction that entomology might have had for Nabokov as one exploration of the way the world and language mesh in a field that attempts to delimit rigorously its language game.

Nabokov's work consistently affirms the autonomy of play by affirming the artifice of his rules of creation. In his short work *Transparent Things* (1973) he gives one of his best late performances in a display of the surfaces of artifice. In this novel he characteristically kills a character named Hugh Person: Who?—*personne* or "nobody" when the French pronunciation of the novel's Swiss location is used. Through ironic doublings—transparent "tralatitions" as this novella would have it—Nabokov sets forth the ground rules of the metaphorical play. Through the circular play of the metaphor of play nearly every element in the fiction offers itself as a double of other elements in a closed set of combinatory pieces that the narrator uses in the sport of assassinating characters. For example his *personne* returns to Switzerland with his father at the novel's outset. While dawdling in a shop with his father, Hugh notes, among other things, a "rather fetching green figurine of a female skier made of a substance he could not identify through the show glass," though a parenthetical narrator tells us sotto voce, "(it was 'alabasterett,' imitation aragonite, carved and colored in the Grumbel jail by a homosexual convict, rugged Armand Rave, who had strangled his boyfriend's incestous sister)."[10] The narrator gamester shows with this parody of the omniscient author that he is clearly superior to the *personnage* whom he will checkmate, for Hugh has no taxonomical *connaissances* in mineralogy. But more important is the way Nabokov sets out in the parenthesis the combining elements of his game set, for each of these elements is combined and repeated, with ironic reversals, as the narrator proceeds in varying the positions of his pieces: Hugh will strangle his wife Armande in her sleep and, for killing this player-skier, he will be interned by those "Freudian witch doctors" who specialize in finding Oedipal symbols in dreams and novels.

Wittgenstein, Saussure, and Heidegger give us, joined with the examples of Borges and Nabokov, a number of homologous viewpoints for understanding the role of play in contemporary culture: as a model for scientific models, as a form of therapy to dissolve received errors, as a mode of thinking beyond metaphysical determinations, and as a model for constructing interpretations. With such overdetermination—and one could also adduce examples of ludic thought from other areas—it is not too surprising that much of contemporary culture is dominated by what I am tempted to call the ideology of play. I have developed at some length the role in play of Borges and Nabokov because it seems to me that these two modern—or postmodern—masters set forth between them a kind of rough topography of literary play that finds its full meaning when juxtaposed with ludic thought about language. Since the late fifties many writers have been attracted, on the one hand, to the chance side of games, to the Borgesian roll-of-the-dice aspect of aleatory structures and decision trees, to the arbitrary juxtapositions that can arise when one attempts to overcome fixed codifications, or to a kind of solicitation and exploitation of chance. Writers undertake the celebration of the aleatory in the hope of inventing new language games, and sometimes in the hope of overcoming the rules of the game. Such hopes can foster apocalyptic illusions about radically redefining the very nature of language and thought. Other celebrations of chance give rise to various sorts of assemblages, montages, or aleatory textual collisions that proclaim meaning to be the fortuitous organization of the random. One may see certain modernist roots to this writing, for Mallarmé, too, dreamed that the chance play of a finite set of phonemes might eventually give rise to an Orphic explanation of the earth.

For some writers, on the other hand, play entails the ostensible affirmation of the rules of the game. Accepting the necessity of rules of discourse, made aware perhaps by linguistics or semiotics of how determining these rules are, these writers work with the sense of their writing as the production of a system, of a closed field of self-conscious and self-reflexive transformations and permutations. Nabokovian celebrators of artifice, writers of this sort create works that designate themselves as chessboards, mathematical combinations, sports, mobiles, or types of machines that manifest themselves as self-contained systems. The opposition between these tendencies is clearly not a neat one, and one should retain a Wittgensteinian sense of the multiple forms of activity that manifest the traits of play. These tendencies derive from the multiple and often opposing impulses of play itself: the desire to find exhilaration and liberation in chance and in the overcoming of causality; and the converse desire to introduce regularity into disorder, to make experience obey self-given rules, to reduce chaos to an arbitrary but absolute play of recurrent forms. These impulses can very well inhabit the same novel, much as they can coexist in, say, a football game, a chess match, or in the invention of a mathematical theorem. In the rest of this chapter, I shall explore these two broad types of play in fiction. Though I shall make fewer explicit comparisons with language theorists, the categories their thought has established are presupposed throughout this discussion.

A postmodern *locus classicus* of a work that purports to offer an aleatory structure is Cortázar's *Hopscotch* (*Rayuela*, 1963), a work whose game title also emphasizes the rule-bound nature of this narration that can be played in more than one way. This Argentinean novel proposes a form of therapy for our need to read novels as linearly constructed causal chains. This therapeutic intent is clear in the way that the novel gives the reader two options (at least) for reading, options that in turn should cause him to question his belief in the metaphysics of linear causality that underwrites narrations. He should ask what need to hide the aleatory is hidden by the fiction of causal anchoring. For his first move, according the novel's Table of Instructions, the reader may read the novel in a traditionally straightforward "linear" fashion in the sense that he can read it sequentially from chapter 1 to chapter 56. In this way the reader follows the narration of the events dealing with the Argentinean protagonist Oliveira, a prototypical alienated intellectual looking for the kind of meaning of life that Saint-Germain des Près existentialism put into the literature textbooks in the fifties. The novel's events take Oliveira from Paris back to Buenos Aires and a possible suicide as he works in a Célinian mental asylum. The reader may, however, play according to another game plan and, following other instructions, skip from chapter to chapter according to a prescribed ordering that leads back and forth in the book. Following this plan the reader encounters chapters that were "expendable" if he stopped at chapter 56. By following what appears to be a nonlinear order, the reader finds new passages and different textual juxtapositions.

Cortázar's novel brings up interesting problems with regard to concretely realizing aleatory projects that in Borges's work are usually imagined possibilities of texts. The second order of reading is a prescribed order and is really laid out with all the rigor of the normal "linear" order offered by the unfolding of pages. The second order appears aleatory only through contrast with the received order of reading given by the book's format. Some readers may feel that the contrast succeeds in revealing that the normal linearity of the bound book is merely one order among many possible orders, one arbitrary rule of the game of reading-writing among many conceivable rules. And of course this revelation also suggests that the contrasting order of reading is also arbitrary. But this second order, as it jumps from chapter to chapter, flaunts its arbitrariness as an imposed convention, as a rule of reading that the reader must also accept with complete consciousness. One could of course go a step farther in this play of artifice and cut the book up, then glue it back together according to the second order of reading, and an unsuspecting reader would experience the aleatory as the normal—which is an attractive bit of textual gymnastics that would lay bare, at least to an exterior observer, the arbitrary decisions that go into transforming narrative order into a necessity. The point, however, to Cortázar's two orders is that the reader contrast the game plans and, hence, conceive of the multiple narrative arrangements possible for any fiction. Finally, this novel is not really an actualization of the aleatory; it is a contrastive representation of skipping on the textual board space, prescribed by Cortázar's own rules.

The representation of chance also suggests that one could read *Hopscotch* in any order one desired, letting a real roll of the dice—or throw of a stone—decide where one would begin and end and in which order. For the reader who accepts Cortázar's gambit will find that reading the chapters in any order whatsoever is quite as satisfying as reading them according to the table's second ordering. I harbor the suspicion that these multiple readings are most satisfactory when we, inevitably, read in the normal linear fashion the first time and have a fairly normal plot line against which to juxtapose all subsequent discoveries. But this game of juxtaposing can produce meanings that, in terms of these game rules, are quite as interesting as any other, perhaps more so. Cortázar makes the reader aware that the genesis of meaning in a text always depends on a series of rereadings that produce meanings as much in accord with the reader's game plan as the author's. Finally Cortázar's play-metaphors anticipate Derrida's description of the way the genesis of meaning, as play, abolishes the notion of a single meaning of a text, of any form of writing. There is no center to the board on which one skips, from position to position, in the movement of play.

The concrete actualization of the aleatory in fiction remains a limit notion for postmodernism, and I am not certain it has ever been better realized than by Raymond Federman's flippant instructions for *Take It or Leave It* (1976), according to which one can read its numberless pages "in any order one likes." One fiction that has attempted to integrate the aleatory by changing its format as a book is Marc Saporta's *Composition No. 1* (1962, translated in 1963). The reader may shuffle the pages of the novel exactly as if he were playing with a deck of cards and then read it according to the resulting order (or orders, since one can shuffle the pages as many times as one wants or at any point in the reading). Saporta's work appears to offer an indefinite if not infinite number of narrative connections, like a Borgesian series of forking paths that, in principle at least, could never be exhausted. In practice, however, Saporta's game of narrative poker confirms in an interesting way that narrative and linguistic structures operate as separate systems, much as structuralist analysis of narratives has proposed. They cannot be so easily assimilated as many postmodern writers have supposed as they sought to introduce play at every level of writing: at the level of micro-units such as phonemes or syntax as well as at the macro-level of narrative units of discourse. In his experiment in aleatory structure Saporta is obliged, for purposes of minimal narrative continuity, to make of each page a mini-narrative unit that is complete in itself. Each page contains a coherent scene. In other words, the forking paths do not function at the level of syntax or the sentence, but only at the level of larger narrative units. There is nothing really aleatory at all about the individual narrative scene contained on one page—say, each of the various repeated scenes that go to make up the seduction/rape of a German maid. At most one might say that shuffling the pages introduces aleatory variations at the level of the narrative scene. It is much as if one were to take a movie, cut the film with scissors at the end of each shooting scene, mix and then splice the pieces of film with no attention given to continuity (a bit as Alain Resnais seems to do at times). A reasonably sophisticated viewer would have no trouble in reading the film in terms of flashbacks and flash-forwards, or in allowing for a calculated indeterminacy.

Saporta's work sheds a great deal of light on the difficulty involved in creating aleatory structures, as opposed to the conceptual games that recognize, after the fact, the existence of aleatory structures at work everywhere in the universe. In the same vein I would compare Saporta's semi-aleatory work with William Burroughs's supposed textual montages based on cut-ups. It may well be the case that Burroughs uses chance cuttings, along the line of my film example, for the composition of his novels; but there is nothing within the structure of these fantasies that can be read as aleatory. The mechanics of textual production convert the arbitrarily selected material into the absolute presence of the unique textual order. Saussure's lesson can be taken to heart with regard to the distinction between the chance play of arbitrary forces that lead to a present system and the rigorously necessary character of the system when considered at any given moment in time. Whatever be the play of chance that led to the creation of a fiction—and nothing but a play of chance-decisions can ever lead to that theological metaphor we call creation—the present text imposes itself as the necessary set of selections generated by an arbitrarily given, but absolutely valid, set of game rules. Saporta's aleatory shuffling method for the distribution of scenes gives a margin of freedom in the play against necessity. But it is a small measure of freedom compared with the necessary rule-constraints that are at work at all other levels of narration: from the phonemic to the semantic. Other writers dream of introducing the aleatory at these levels where language binds us with its absolute rules of play. The play with pronouns reflects one aspect of this play with and against the necessities of syntax, one aspect of an ideology of play that dreams of instituting the writer as a player who can equal, not God, but the dictionary and its power to define.

Cortázar's hopscotch, much like Saporta's poker game, invites the reader to skip from narrative block to narrative block. Each of these blocks has its own integrity. However, the dubious reader may feel that any text that invites its own decentering is another variant of the schizo-text whose refusal of a narrative order or center brings with it the fragmentation of the world. Whether that fragmentation be produced by the reader or the writer, it will seem to the doubting reader to be another text that denies a single order of reading. With its implied denial of a center to the world, the ludic text is undoubtedly in many cases a sign of schizoid disintegration, which is perhaps why the *rayuela* in *Hopscotch* is drawn upon the pavement of an insane asylum. If one cannot sort out the competing narrative orders that would make sense of the world, if there is no longer a single world at all, then it seems right to affirm that one has reached a Beckett-like end-game in which play serves as the final gesture for warding off the onset of madness.

There is, however, a Nietzschean side to this exaltation of the plurality of narrative orders and the game that refuses to choose among them. In this Nietz-schean sense, play grants the exaltation of a superior freedom that affirms the ontology of the many against the reductive views that would always force one to choose the unique, the centered, the ontology of single presence that is at the heart of Western rationality. The danger of schizoid fragmentation and the Nietz-schean affirmation of play often inhabit the same text, such as we see in *Hop-scotch* and, in an analogous way, in Derrida's writing on *différance*. This Nietz-schean affirmation of the multiple can suggest another analogy between Cortazar and Derrida: the affirmation of intertextual play as the ludic nature of meaning. Meaning in Cortázar's novel is in part derived from the play of reference among its various chapters and their orders. Directing the reader to other chapters, the expendable chapters serve to show that reading is a kind of skipping through a play space made up, in utopian terms, of all the texts in the world. In reading these chapters one must be prepared to enter the imaginary encyclopedia of total culture, represented by the way Cortázar uses numerous quotations taken from a prodigious variety of sources: Lévi-Strauss, Meister Eckhart, Lezama Lima, George Bataille, Artaud, blues lyrics by Duke Ellington—these kinds of texts complement the copious paraphrases of Camus, Sartre, and Freud that make up the conversations of Cortázar's loquacious characters. These quotes and para-phrases are so many synecdoches for all the texts that could be quoted in the circulating play of reference that can draw upon any and all texts that make up the utopian space of culture. To read any text is to cross over into the play space of intertextual reference—analogous to the play space of *différance*—that implies the totality of all possible readings.

In these expendable chapters Cortázar invents an imaginary man of letters named Morelli who, though characterized as pedantic, stupid, and confused, is also quoted for his insights into metaphysics, language, and literature. Morelli is the imaginary theorist who completes, in a Borgesian way, the realm of "real" texts that Cortázar quotes. Morelli is representative of the Borgesian realm of all the imagined texts that might go to complete the play of reference among real texts, imagined texts, texts imagined in imagined texts, ad infinitum. What for Kafka in *The Trial* was the impossible situation of the hermeneutics of hermeneutics, of the infinite regress of the interpretations of interpretations, becomes in the postmodern novel play within the labyrinth of a potentially infinite intertextual deferring.

One image of this infinite play is given in Cortázar's homeless hero's search for a totality, conceived of as a mandala or the infinite circle of the cosmos. Like many a contemporary, Oliveira finds less succor in the vision of the mandala than he finds distress in the dictionary. I have spoken of the postmodern desire to rival, in the creation of game rules for grammar, syntax, and semantic use, the dictionary as the ultimate empire. In Oliveira, Cortázar has created a character who wishes to play word games that would detach language from a cosmos of preexisting signifieds and signifiers. Coming in the wake of the *Wake*, and bearing some affinities with writers as diverse as Michaux, Pinget, and Arno Schmidt, this existentialist hero wants to overcome the codification of fixed language rules by inventing a language that might suggest new ways of playing language games. Consider chapter 68:

> As soon as he began to amalate the noeme, the clemise becgan to smother her and they fell into hydromuries, into savage ambonies, into exasperating sustales. Each time that he tried to relamate the hairincops, he became entangled in a whining grimate and had to face up to envulsioning the novalisk, feeling how little by little the arnees would spejune, were becoming peltronated, redoblated, until they were stretched out like the ergomanine trimalciate which drops a few fileures of cariaconce.[12]

As Gregory Rabassa's marvelous translation shows, Oliveira is revolting against what he calls the cemetery: the dictionary and its supposedly dead rules for language use. *Hopscotch*'s freeing of the signifier in this very funny word play represents the dream of new language games that would liberate the hero, if not the reader, from codifications in which the same way that the book's aleatory structures might liberate the reader, if not the hero, from the received order of narrative discourse.

Cortázar's play with the shape of linguistic signifiers is another kind of post-modern limit game, and it shows again that the received rules of the linguistic chessboard are difficult to get around. To create this wonderfully suggestive piece of nonsense Cortázar has had to respect both the rules for phonemic combinations and the rules for the normal syntax of the Spanish language. Because he has respected these rules, his semantic inventions appear to take on the semblance of near sense that they have. Cortázar's semi-invented signifiers are, moreover, a representation of what an invented language might be, and not really an actualized invention. The game consists here in tantalizing the reader so that the reader attempts to extrapolate meanings from suggested ones, partly on the basis of their place in the syntactical structure, partly because the reader can recognize some morphemes. It is instructive to recall, too, that in *Finnegans Wake* Joyce also respects, by and large, the rules of syntax while attempting to condense the greatest number possible of signifieds into a single signifier. Cortázar, however, is not playing the same game as Joyce: in this passage he is playing with the resemblances of signifiers in order mechanically to produce the form of meaning, much in the same way that highly codified or dead discourse—the fallen speech of everydayness—is mechanically produced without question. Cortázar's play with the signifier has more parallels with Heidegger than with Joyce.

The examples of Cortázar, Burroughs, and Saporta make clear the difficulty involved in actualizing aleatory play in discourse even if fiction itself can be understood, in theoretical terms, as a production due to chance. One of the best examples of a work that explores precisely this dilemma is an American novel that uses the national sport as its game metaphor, Robert Coover's *The Universal Baseball Association, Inc., J. Henry Waugh, Prop.* In Coover's novel the baseball game in question is not, initially at least, the kind played in Fenway Park and Yankee Stadium. Coover's game is a table game, played by rolling three dice. The dice throws generate the moves in this board baseball game that occupies most of the time of the novel's protagonist, a game "creator" whose name J. Henry Waugh recalls that of the original creator-artist Yaweh. Yaweh-Waugh has created his own game cosmos; but the creator is also a frustrated accountant, an ineffective keeper of books, who really lives for orchestrating probabilities and keeping the records of his imaginary league. Waugh uses chance to set his games in motion, but in accordance with rules: he has invented an incredibly elaborate system of rules that govern how rolls and sequences of rolls are to be played out. Not only do the dice cast ordinary events such as hits and runs, but also extraordinary events such as the death of players and hence, finally, life histories of all the players and their consorts who make up the universal league.

The keeping of baseball records depends on the keeping of books and the writing of accompanying narratives. Each roll of the dice produces hits, runs, and errors that in turn produce an ongoing history that, like a Borgesian encyclopedia, comes to possess such a powerful presence that it generates a world, and finally the world, at least the world created in the game novel at hand. In the final chapter of *The Universal Baseball Association* Waugh, like Voltaire's watch-winding deity, has set the world's mechanism in motion and has seemingly retired or died. Or, alternatively, the eternal laws of chance have combined hits and errors whose unforeseen probabilities have resulted in this world, a baseball world that is perhaps no more fantastic than the one that the random encounter of a few amino acids has created (and in which you and I, my reader, apparently live). Years after the disappearance of the universal baseball league's creator, in the book's final chapter, the baseball players gather to celebrate a ritual game that reenacts the founding of their league in its present form. The league is a metaphor for the play of the world, the cosmos as *Weltspiel;* it is also the players' shared community that imposes rites, language, and a world view. Some players entertain doubts about the origins of the game, but finally they must accept it if they are to remain players in the game, members of a community, participants in a world. The rules of the game are the only grounds for certainty about their identity and their existence. Coover's ballplayers suggest a number of parallels with Wittgenstein's language user. Only a superior intelligence, say, that of a reader who knows the evolution of the game and the league's history, can doubt the formulas and rules that make up their game, their systems of beliefs and language. Coover's work affords of course this superior perspective, and the result is a near satire of our acceptance of language's *Weltbild* and its innumerable statements that have no explanation except that they exist as part of our language-baseball games.

In addition, the parallels with the sacred texts we once accepted as our history reinforce the parody of our world construed as divine text: Henry J. Waugh's one intervention into the history of his league is to suspend the play of chance, fix the dice, and kill a pitcher, one Jock Casey. Thus, a JC is the victim of the deity's only interference with the normal chance course of events. Although somewhat facile, this parody does bring up what I take to be a more interesting issue. The myth of the creator that the romantics borrowed from creation myths and transposed for the needs of romantic aesthetic ideology has continued to influence our thought about the genesis of literary texts. (And I admit that "genesis" is probably no more innocent of theological associations than the word "creation.") The creation myth gives the appearance of a perduring center to the "created" work, a locus outside the work in which the meaning of fiction can be grounded. As a "creation" the work becomes a kind of epiphanic revelation of the creator. With its mock theological baseball game, with its league and its creator, Coover's novel forces one to reevaluate the role of the creation myth: what does one make of a beer-drinking creator whose only active role in the history of his league has been to cheat by violating his own rules of neutrality? The real creation of the league and its history occurs when the play of dice is harnessed to the rules of the game. And as Coover relentlessly shows, the game metaphor supplants any other description as the best account of what unfolds in the work. This imperious metaphor ursurps all others, and Henry's rousing session in bed with a prostitute can be as adequately described in terms of hits, runs, and errors, as can the so-called creation of a fictional world or a real universe.

In its play the imperious metaphor of play obliterates distinctions between the real and the illusory, relegating them to a realm of metaphysical distinctions. In the first part of *The Universal Baseball Association* the reader may make an effort to distinguish between narration that depicts Henry and his life, and narration that presents events in the ball game. Within the confines of the novel, however, there is no ontological difference. There is no feature that differentiates what is posited as the novel's "real" world—the one that Henry inhabits—and the imaginary world of the dice-generated baseball league. There is nothing in language itself, at least in the play of fictive language, that allows such a differentiation. The dice Henry rolls in the "real" world set the game in motion, but the narration telling the adventures of the imaginary players differs in no way from narration about the dice-roller himself. Coover again plays with the equivocation that language is being, understood as "real" and fictive being, and refuses any meta-linguistic attempt to designate one language as simply illusory, mere fiction within fiction. The dice can generate the same narrative structures for realms offered as either fictive or real, and therefore the same world for imaginary lusty baseball players as for a miserable accountant whose addiction to play causes him to lose his job.

The roll of the dice presides over the elaboration of a series that, once entrusted to narration, becomes a history having its seasonal repetitions and generational cycles. Henry's random rolls of the dice produce for his players so many narrative choices that, when organized into larger linguistic units of meaning, seem to possess a necessity that is perhaps superior to ordinary life—especially Henry's ordinary life, spent in a dismal bachelor flat, and sustained on pastrami sandwiches and beer. One might wish to argue that it is this reconciliation of chance and necessity that gives narration an aura, a certainty, that allows it to obliterate the real, or in this case, Henry's life. Moreover, without attempting to make reading an aleatory process, Coover's novel has allegorized its own process of coming into existence through random choices that, when completed, stand as a kind of necessity for the reader.

By way of a brief excursus, I might add that in Coover's novel, as in those of a number of other American writers, one finds an understanding of fiction as a kind of engineering game. These game strategies aim at creating communication machines that attempt to overcome entropy. The probability that each roll of the dice should lead to the creation of a greater, rather than a lesser, amount of order or system is, in an entropic universe, the least probable occurrence. The organization of information in an isolated system—such as a novel—is a rather unlikely event in the flow of random happenings that make up the universe. Inscribed in Coover, Barth, and especially Pynchon's work is a consciousness of the improbable effort required to achieve negative entropy, or a superior level of organization, in a world in which the drift toward the random and disorder is the most probable event. This awareness of the very unlikely nature of obtaining a high level of organization, one that can yield a high level of "information," also explains the postmodern concern with chance and the aleatory. Chaos is the rule, and this belief results in a rather ironic view of the struggle that the writer undertakes with the random, the fortuitous, or the aleatory. In these usually, but not exclusively, American texts engineer-writers often use game theory as a way of playing against the second law of thermodynamics. The organization of play within the heart of chaos relies upon the elaboration of anti-entropic strategies that celebrate the momentary taming of the random while affirming that this game is only an exceptional moment in the otherwise straightforward process of general entropy, the measure of the passage from order to disorder.

This understanding of fiction also convinces writers that they must elaborate their game rules and demonstrate their organizing power. Artifice must be shown, for the formal play of the game is in one sense the very object of the demonstration. In France, this kind of demonstration has come to constitute something of a literary tradition. Were one to give a full exposition of ludic experiments in French fiction, one might begin with Raymond Roussel and the surrealists and survey a development that finds a certain logical climax in the work of Raymond Queneau and the group of mathematicians and writers he gathered together under the name of Oulipo, or the Ouvroir de littérature potentielle. These writers, including such novelists as Georges Perec and Italo Calvino, continue to meet and look for new game models with which to generate literary texts.

Wittgenstein's use of engineering models is relevant for an understanding of this play, and one is tempted to call the workers of Oulipo a group of playful engineers, engaging in civil engineering in Wittgenstein's city of language as they attempt to build new suburbs that will have more than a few affinities with the new faubourgs added by the sciences. This sense of textual engineering also characterizes the work of two other contemporary French writers who attempt to found fiction as a self-demonstrating play of self-given rules, Alain Robbe-Grillet (an agricultural engineer by training) and Philippe Sollers. I shall call on these two writers to round out the illustration of the spectrum of contemporary play options. For, as ideologues of play theory, they both plan for literature new game plans that will radically renovate the old city of language. They plan a kind of urban renewal that will rid the city of the bourgeois ideology that inhabits the older quarters.

Robbe-Grillet's claims for play theory and for the freedom of the writer to invent freely the rules of his writing as game have evolved as part of his assault on the belief that something lies beyond language that it would be the writer's obligation to translate into language. Robbe-Grillet's early essays on the future of fiction as well as the axioms of his earliest novels suggest remarkable analogies with Wittgenstein's rebuttal of the contradictory belief that there might be metaphysical hiding places outside of language that one could somehow speak about. Much as the later Wittgenstein sees the world as a public openness in which all we can know is articulated through publicly verifiable language games, so does Robbe-Grillet, in his essays and novelistic practice, claim that the world is a public space that exists only as the surface of what we all can see and articulate: there are no hidden depths, no forms of transcendence. This view entails a number of consequences for the practice of fiction. Most interestingly, according to Robbe-Grillet, the writer should avoid metaphors, since the romantic and modernist use of metaphor has, if I may borrow Wittgenstein's term, bewitched our imagination by creating the linguistic illusion that man lives in a universe with which he can have communion. Organic metaphors are anthropomorphizing figures that lead writers into metaphysical errors and delusions about the relations among man, language, and the universe. Figural descriptions suggest that one can use language to reach out beyond language to some form of transcendence and perhaps revelation. Though one might accuse the Robbe-Grillet who endorses the metaphors in play theory with a certain lack of consistency, his antimodernist views about organic metaphor are comparable to Saussure's rejection of the motivated sign. Both aim at undermining any view of language that would make of it a metaphysical form of representation.

Robbe-Grillet's refusal of metaphysics is part of the radical contemporary therapy that would cure the writer of bourgeois humanism with its belief in essence, nature, causality, and the primacy of the self and its representation in literature. For Robbe-Grillet, play theory has come to fill the void left by the death of humanism. In his earliest essays, however, he was hesitant to state that a purely ludic view of literature underwrote his own practice of fiction. In attacking the metaphysical description of literature that attributes to the text a form and a content, it is clear that Robbe-Grillet, much like Heidegger, was attempting to deny the imperative that makes form subservient to something that transcends it—a content—and that thus makes the work of art disappear as such. In *For a New Novel* Robbe-Grillet used the game metaphor to buttress his argument that literature, like a game, should liberate itself from this subservience by recognizing that a novel is a self-contained system. The system operates according to an internal necessity that must perforce appear as gratuitous from the point of view of any external system of reference.

   In his later writings and lectures, as well as in his novels and films, Robbe-Grillet has become the most seductive spokesman for the ideology of play, developing multiple arguments that call for the death of seriousness and the overthrow of those oppressive game rules encoded in realist fiction. One's reaction to these polemics, as well as to their realization in novels and films, will depend in large measure on the degree to which one identifies the artist's freedom to create new game rules with a politics of ludic liberation. Robbe-Grillet fully intends that the writer's demonstration of freedom be the first step in the creation of a new order of politics situated on the other side of the tyranny of representation. This tyranny can perhaps be best characterized by Derrida's description of classical representation as the ordering of a present space—stage or text— by an absent space, the absent God, author, or represented text of classical theater.[13] The present act of representation is always subordinated to an absent center, a guardian of meaning. There is also a surrealist side to Robbe-Grillet's games, for they seek, in parody and derision, to lay bare a common system of codes that underwrite the values of work, seriousness, beliefs in depth, and the logic of representation.

   My earlier discussion of Robbe-Grillet's work takes on its full significance when considered in the light of Robbe-Grillet's elaboration of his notions about literature as a play space. *La Jalousie* is a game set of self-referential permutating elements; whereas a later work such as *Project for a Revolution in New York* can be likened to a pop combinatory game in which proper names and pronouns circulate as so many interchangeable masks. The way in which Robbe-Grillet attempts to create an anti-representative novel is perhaps clearest, however, in a work such as *In the Labyrinth* (1959), whose title openly manifests its game status. This play space includes within itself its inner and its outer, mirrored in a labyrinthine play of inner mirrorings and duplications. *In the Labyrinth* is a rather extraordinary example of the kind of *Selbstdarstellung* that Hans Gadamer sees as characterizing play,[14] for the novel is generated by a picture hung in the inner space of a room in which the, or a, narrator takes refuge from the outer space of symmetrical streets and repeating house façades. The outer space is where a nameless, Kafkaesque soldier wanders in quest of an unknown person to whom he must deliver a box that perhaps contains a message. The two spaces exist in opposition within the book, like a representation and the absent space of the represented, or like two opponents looking over a *damier*, the checkerboard tablecloth that is found both within the narrator's room and within a scene set in the novel's outer space. In the movement of narration, inner and outer are only relative positions in the game, for the image within the room can become a scene within the outer space of the novel, and the movement of the quest situated in the outer space finally moves into the inner space of the room. The labyrinth is formed by the play of symmetrical representations generated between the two spaces in the book. In this way the novel proposes hermeneutics as a game for which the rules must be elicited from the novel's own practice of writing. Exterior rules cannot be imposed. Robbe-Grillet discards a number of familiar rules, such as the principle of noncontradiction and the rules for temporality and chronology that are dependent on this principle. It is as if we were invited to play chess in a non-Euclidean game space. Yet Robbe-Grillet's novels are systematic in a nearly Saussurean sense. They obey rules, given within the text, such as certain types of opposition and recurrence, with a quasi-mathematical rigor. If the reader is to play the game, he is obliged to accept a ludic pact that takes him into a text that seeks to invent new language games and, perhaps, new modes of articulating the world.

Rules for Robbe-Grillet's game fictions are immanent to the text and are to be derived from the actual textual performance. In the case of his contemporary Philippe Sollers, however, we find novels, if such is the proper term, which have become rather pure meta-fictions that act as rule books for potential fictions, for performances without an execution as it were. This is especially true for novels such as *Drame* (1965) and *Nombres* (1968), works for which at this writing there is no translation. The novels are comparable to the kind of philosophical activity that consists in setting forth the rules for philosophy's conditions of possibility, such as one finds to a greater or lesser extent in Wittgenstein, Heidegger, and Derrida. The game consists in defining the game or in reflecting on the rules of possible games. One may also see Borgesian antecedents for this kind of self-reflexive play that comes close to transforming itself into meta-theory, or perhaps theory that plays at being theory.

Sollers enlists a series of familiar metaphors in his description of the plans for his writing machines. Writing is a Mallarméan drama, a self-conscious scene of writing; it is a Saussurean chessboard as well as the Heideggerian play of the cosmos. *Drame*, more single-mindedly than *Nombres*, metaphorizes its space as a play area in a theatrical sense. In this "drama" Sollers reduces narration to its most relentless form of meta-narration. In narrating nothing, except the rules for the theatrical play of narration narrating itself, Sollers produces a poetic text that has some of the celebratory effects of a Saint-John Perse. Within the

meta-narration potential fragments arise, resembling memories or perhaps the
call of the world, reminiscences of love, the sea, a port, the sky. These fragments
are inscribed within a series of self-reflexive descriptions in which pronouns are
not used to produce a play of fictive reference or to create a play of voices.
Rather the pronouns, alternating "I," "thou," and "he," appear to be actor-
like tokens or chessmen used to produce modulations in the game in which
language acquires consciousness of itself.

Drame reads like a description for a writing to be, but also like an injunction
calling for the creation of writing as pageantry:

> Now, the curtain is rising, he recovers his sight, escapes, sees himself in a
> struggle with the spectacle that is not within—nor without. So he goes
> on stage as if for the first time. Theater, this: one begins again. A chaotic
> and irresistible parade, crowds, cries, acts, words, furtive landscapes,
> what silence. You have the choice and more than the choice. The answer
> will tell you if you invented it. No more delay. It's up to you.[15]

The passage's final line, "A toi"—"It's up to you," enjoins the addressee,
language itself as it were, to become public spectacle, to recognize itself as the
public theater of our social rites, and to overcome the alienation that makes of
language a private theater of the self's hidden stage. "A toi" might also be
translated "It's your cue" or "It's your move." The latter reading would then
stress the chess metaphor that lies behind the moves of the pronouns as counters
on the board. *Drame* is written in the form of sixty-four segments, which, as
Sollers's cover notes rather insistently state, allows one to read the entire book
as an elaboration of the favored postmodern chessboard metaphor. The shifting
play of different metaphorical descriptions in *Drame* serves as an illustration of
game rules that call for play to liberate the text as a field of polysemic exchanges.

Despite its extreme attempt at setting forth a fiction that illustrates only its
own game plan, *Drame* remains centered within most of the parameters we have
seen characterizing the conjunction of language theory and textual practice. The
novel declares, in a language that must be taken as language speaking, that the
major obstacle to its creation of spectacle is language itself, the fallen logos that
is codified in received writing. Hence writing must look for something beyond
language:

> The only problem is to find words. Or rather to seize upon the incessant
> gravitation that unbeknownst to me uses up words (and which to speak truly
> is something other than words even if I can name them in no other way).
> On the one hand there is this language, this already dead writing—that was
> one day definitively classified—already lived as if it had disappeared.

This Beckett-like aporia—one names the unnamable only with names, dead
names, used names—can only be expressed as a blank on the page:

> On the other hand there is   (A dot on whiteness, that's it.) (P. 111)

In a sense narration has dictated a game plan to be played against itself, and here declares its own checkmate. Yet, Sollers will have his language fall and then undergo resurrection, for the ambiguous pronoun *il* awakes one morning within the text to find that "he" has written it. Language has given birth to some form of being. The game text, in describing the failure of language, has, by this description, engendered its own being; it has given birth to itself in a kind of parthenogenetic reproduction that once more bespeaks the autonomy of language.

Parthenogenesis offers an apt metaphorical description of *Drame* and of those contemporary texts that seed themselves as self-generating systems within the general system of language. In *Nombres* Sollers picks an explicitly different biological metaphor, for, in writing a tandem text to Derrida's theorizing, he wishes to fashion writing that is a receptacle for all the seeds blown through the space of culture; he wants to engage in a process of dissemination needing multiple textual sources of germination. One need not restrict oneself to this biological metaphor, however, for *Nombres* is equally well understood as a piece of meta-engineering or another game plan for a self-contained machine. Like one of Tinguely's meta-machines that produces only its own process, *Nombres* is a machine-*jeu* in four sequences setting forth its own movement. *Jeu* should be taken here, as in *Drame,* in its multiple senses of drama and acting, or chance, gambling, and play in the cosmic sense of what is, the *Weltspiel.* For all this, the book is an even more unreadable work by traditional criteria, since it is a game plan for the process of meaning, and not an actual production of meaning, if such a distinction is plausible. This plan can be achieved only through a play of internal metaphor in which every element in the text would be a metaphor for the text's *jeu,* in a play of internal self-reference in which all the cogs of the machine are used to turn other cogs, directing energy, like meanings, throughout the closed system. This self-contained mobile of kinetic displacements can be another metaphor for the dissemination of meaning from one signifier to another, from one player to another, from one text to another in the imaginary and real library that inhabits this book. This machine is an intertextual mobile insofar as its parts are constituted by pieces taken from countless other machines that we call books, which is to say, is filled with direct, but unattributed quotations from many other works. The unconvinced reader may well see in *Nombres* one of Rube Goldberg's more elaborate inventions, and in a sense he would surely be right.

Three of the four sequences in *Nombres* are in the imperfect tense, and one is in the present tense. They do not follow each other sequentially; rather, the sequences are broken up and the fragments are intermixed throughout the book. Each fragment has a number that identifies it and the sequence of which it is a part. The numbers and subnumbers of this textual format recall the *Tractatus,* in a kind of intertextual allusion designed seemingly to bring logical and mathematical theorizing within the novel's ken. As in *Drame* the juxtapositions of tenses and pronouns attempts to show how these purely linguistic elements function as potentialities and potentiators of discourse. The shifter "I"—in its "perpetual slippage"—turns on the game machine, as the ink-river flows. The self-referential "I" describes perforce itself, but this description establishes the axis of I/we that can in turn speak of him/her. The nearly literal translation of language theory into a textual practice that wills itself to become fiction shows, I think, to what point not only language theory but our fantasies about language theory have become the stuff of our fictions. Dreams of Wittgenstein, Heidegger, and Saussure—as well as the direct influence of Derrida—recur as so many leifmotifs here. The broken sequences may aim at breaking up the metaphysics of linearity that Sollers, with Derrida, sees as part of the foundations of Western logocentrism, but these ruptures also produce a kind of alogical space in which theoretical phantasms recur obsessively.

Sollers wishes, of course, to undermine our attachment to traditional metaphysical views of language and the genesis of meaning in discourse. To this end he presents us with bits of mathematics and some Chinese ideograms, forms of writing for which traditional metaphysics offers inadequate accounts. Sollers was something of a Maoist when writing *Nombres,* but the presence of the ideograms seems motivated by the desire to introduce that "other" form of writing that Saussure had contrasted with the linearity of phonetic alphabets. Phonetic and ideogrammatic types of writing contrast in their basic ontology. The ideogram's presence would, in Sollers's view, contest the linear flow of his phonetic writing by their spatial unfolding. Mathematics, Sollers seems to believe, also in some sense imitates space. "Numbers" could also contest phonetic and logocentric linearity as a language with more spatial dimensions, as a spacing and perhaps as the play of *différance.* Derrida, in *Of Grammatology,* had already called mathematics a nonlinear language, and Sollers seems to have seized upon this idea as part of his therapeutic attack on logocentrism. I leave a discussion of the adequacy of this notion to mathematicians, though my own impression is that, in the wake of Wittgenstein, a view that the foundations of mathematics are a matter of arbitrary, human invention does overlap with a view that language games are multiple and have no metaphysical foundations. There is no simple ontological bond between mathematics and space. On the other hand, however, much modern thought on mathematics is overtly and aggressively Platonist.

The dominant metaphor for the play of writing in *Nombres,* as in *Drame,* is the scene or the stage, but enlarged in *Nombres* to include a cosmic image of the locus of creation that is engendered by the divine play of numbers. *Nombres* is also a cosmology, the description of the *Weltspiel,* in which the advent of being takes place within the self-contained closure of the world stage. Sollers equates the four walls of the traditional stage (one wall is removed, of course, for the spectators) with the fourfold that Heidegger made the root of all things, with *Geviert* or the labyrinth of four squares. Numbers come to play as the fourfold, which can be taken as the play of the cosmos, and also as the play of the four arms and legs that mirror the center of creation in its sexual sense. The fourfold of coupling is a series of combinations within the finite but continuous *ensemble* that goes to make up the play of being.

These few examples will, I hope, suffice to show the kinds of metaphorical play that go to make up this primer in discourse about discourse. Existing as a past that is only a modality of discourse, and as a present that speaks itself as the ongoing instance of present enunciation, this novel proposes itself as a germinating machine whose only goal is self-production. But that insemination demands reception of other seeds. "Seminaque innumero numero summaque profunda" is the incipit on *Nombres*'s title page, and this unattributed quote from Lucretius stresses both in its presence and in its meaning that the novel seeks to germinate itself through the play of intertextual references.

This practice of intertextual germination brings me back to the subject of intertextuality as play and to the final point I should like to make about literature as play. Intertextuality, as practiced by Sollers and many of his contemporaries, is clearly a form of play, one buttressed by theories of meaning as ludic activity or as the play of *différance*. *Nombres* is full of quotations from other texts, and part of the game consists in the very fact that Sollers does not make attributions. He uses these borrowings as part of the material of his discourse, and it is up to the reader to identify the various writers and theorists, often of Marxist-Leninist provenance, whose texts enter into the texture-tissue of the writing. In theoretical terms Sollers is practicing, in a literal sense, what theory holds that all writing does: germinating its meanings through the dissemination that all texts practice as they refer to each other in the great labyrinthine hothouse of culture. To read, to write, is to play a kind of hopscotch, to leap from writing to writing in the never-ending play of codes that refer to other codes.

Nombres undoubtedly reaches a limit point for the illustration of the rules of the game of intertextuality, or the game in which the text is constructed as a closed space in which other texts are recombined to create an ongoing game set for the production of meaning. Intertextual play is, moreover, a key example of how the contemporary mind mixes theory and practice, for writers—starting with Roland Barthes—often fail to maintain a distinction between intertextuality as a theory of the production of discourse—any discourse—and a mode of composition. As a theory, intertextuality is, in a restricted sense, a logical development of the axiom of language's autonomy. In a broader sense, it is also a ramification of views about the ludic nature of language, since language games must have their rules articulated in terms of other language games. And, in Derrida's view, the indefinite play of *différance* is such that, in their free play, the signifiers of all texts must eventually refer to all others.

In its largest extension intertextuality implies that every text reproduces the library of Babel. Theory becomes a prescription for practice, when, again like Roland Barthes, one begins to call for the practice of the "Text," or the creation of writing that self-consciously dramatizes the "infinite deferment of the signified.''[16] The writer finds that his task is to recognize that the infinity of meanings that the signifier can generate imposes upon him the necessity of playing through "a serial movement of disconnections, overlappings, variations" (p. 159). He must play with a tissue of quotations that he draws from the "innumerable centres of culture," since his only power is to mix writings, to counter one text with another, in a "multi-dimensional space" in which writings blend and clash (p. 146). In short, the theory of intertextuality obliges the writer to play with other writings within the closed field of the culture that language imposes. *Nombres* reads much like a textbook application of Barthes's formulations.

Barthes has given the sharpest formulations, prescriptive and descriptive, of intertextuality, but as a practice of fiction intertextuality is much more widely spread than those Parisian milieux that coined the term. It should be understood as a broad phenomenon that, as I shall show in a different context in the following chapter, has consequences for the practice of fiction written in all the major European languages. The theoretical bases for intertextuality are often formulated in different terms, though I think they are all homologous with the views about language we have been discussing here. When German critics write about the "desirableness of a theory of quoting"[17] or the practice of montage and quotation, they are also recognizing how the play of quotation and of intertextual reference has come to command a dominant role in much contemporary fiction written in German. Describing works by Helmut Heissenbuttel, Peter O. Chotjewitz, and Oswald Wiener, for example, the critic Manfred Durzak speaks of an ideological caesura that separates the work of these writers from an earlier generation of German-language writers. In the works of these later writers the practice of montage and quotation has resulted in texts in which all writing is citation. Writing has thus lost its referential function *(Verweisungscharackter)*.[18] Literature has become a kind of mechanical process—a writing machine, perhaps—as the author has liquidated himself. He has become a machine for reading other texts, which is, as Durzak sees it, a sign of the writer's ideological rejection of the traditional novel as a form of individual accomplishment. The abolition of the writer as the determination of the writing's meaning is, for these German writers, a means of demystifying literature and the bourgeois ideology that goes with it. Durzak's description of the "death of the author" is not unlike Roland Barthes's description of the same death that is found at the origins of the "text," but with a significant difference. It is with none of Barthes's elation that Durzak notes a break with modernism, modernism's practice of collage, and its belief that through collage it could represent the world and its complexity.[19]

Turning to American fiction, I call attention to the modernist practice of collage, since American readers may well wonder what is the difference between collage techniques, as practiced by, say, a Dos Passos, and the more recent practice of intertextual montage and quotation. One could argue that collage and intertextual montage share common roots, especially insofar as these techniques rely upon procedures of radical discontinuity. But the goal of most modernist collages is quite different from what the postmodern writer attempts to achieve through juxtaposing texts. To the degree that a Dos Passos or, later, the Sartre who imitated Dos Passos in *Les Chemins de la liberté* attempted to represent temporal simultaneity through juxtapositions, their collage techniques were modernist attempts to spatialize time. In this sense collage is little used by postmodern American writers who, like their French and German contemporaries, engage in ambivalent play with other discourses. Frequently these writers' use of intertextual reference and quotation is part of the pop play in which the writer assumes the role of an ironic relay in the transmission of the fallen discourse that invests the writer's world. Straight quotation—given as intertextual citation—is often sufficient to invest language with an ironic dimension, as witness the work of Barthelme or, in a comparable register, the work of writers publishing with the Fiction Collective. In Ronald Sukenick's *98.6,* for example, the first part of the novel is composed of a montage of journalistic quotations, dealing with the Manson family, pop persons, and stories of unmotivated murders, a montage that offers an intertextual web of citations constituting the world of Frankenstein. In a different vein Gilbert Sorrentino's *Splendide Hôtel* (1973) sets forth a lexical primer that is at once a pop exploration of the generating powers of the alphabet and an intertextual inhabitation in Rimbaud's *Illuminations.* Or, in a remarkable performance of ventriloquism, Sorrentino's more recent *Aberration of Starlight* (1980), is an attempt to speak the world of the thirties through a deadpan collation of its clichés, of its dead syntagms, in one long historical quotation of *das Man.* Robert Coover has done something of the same ventriloquism for the fifties, with allowance made for satiric pop distortions, in his *The Public Burning* (1976).

Quoting other texts inevitably brings up historical questions, for other texts necessarily bring some historical dimension to the fiction that quotes them. This shall concern us in the next chapter, but to conclude this chapter on a positive note, I should point out how American writers are perhaps unique in their use of intertextual play as a way of affirming the space of writing as the locus for their cultural identity. Two different kinds of fictions can hint at the scope of American intertextual explorations: Paul Medcalf's novel *Genoa, A Telling of Wonders* (1973) and Hugh Kenner's "historical comedy," *The Counterfeiters* (1968). These works will take us from intertextuality as play to the play of intertextuality in reference to history and its role in the constitution of what we take to be the order of the real.

Medcalf's novel is certainly one of the best to be published by the small-press circuit that continues to rival and perhaps surpass the official publishing circuit in making possible the appearance of significant American fiction. *Genoa* possesses an underlying narrative structure that, as in much American fiction, testifies to the continuance of a certain humanistic center to literature, for American writers appear far more reluctant to abandon humanistic ideology than their European counterparts. Medcalf's work is in part the musing of a narrator who, in his isolated study under the rafters of a house in Indiana, reflects upon history, upon his region, and upon his brother's death by capital punishment in Missouri. The book's quietly powerful mapping of the Middle West takes, moreover, the form of a series of textual encounters that unfold in the narrator's imagination— or in that imaginative space known as the book, a book that acts as a reflecting center for the larger space of those texts that make up our American culture and cultural identity. Columbus's journal, Melville's novels and letters, medical texts, and fictive newspaper articles are quoted and juxtaposed in a play of random associations that define culture as the play of multiple discourses, historical, archival, and literary, colliding with one another in the space of one man's reading. Medcalf's story of his Indiana narrator and the tale of the horrid life led by the narrator's brother originate in the present moment of narration; and that present moment is also the moment of actualization of all the past discourses that might enter into it. The library of American identity exists as the present moment of orchestrating texts, which is to say, the present moment during which, in an Indiana study, a writer transcribes those texts. Culture is an accretion of texts coming to form one synchronic moment, the moment of writing, taken as the culmination of a process that can begin with Homer and can culminate in a newspaper article recording a pointless death. And somehow the accretion contains within it, like Borges's library, the explanation of it all; or, in Wittgensteinian terms, that intertextual polyphony is perhaps *what* we mean today by a cultural or historical explanation.

If small-press writers in their search for America count among frequent intertextual players, so in many comparable ways do their counterparts in the academy who use university presses to publish their definitions of culture. Inventing critical fictions that purport to explore history, they often write intertextual montages that make of history a kind of aggiornamento of possible intertextual games. (No meta-criticism intended.) Hugh Kenner, for example, in *The Counterfeiters* recognizes a fictional status to his own "historical comedy," a work whose title proposes another name for intertextuality, to wit, counterfeiting. In *The Counterfeiters* Kenner claims that modernist collage came to an end with Joyce's *Ulysses* and that this practice has given way to the art of counterfeiting. After Joyce's parody and classicizing, modernism has seen the advent of a world of quotation and eclectic connoisseurship, in what Kenner calls a world that has become "one huge musée sans murs."[20] The museum without walls would be the space of culture, but of a culture that Kenner sees as existing only through incessant counterfeiting. Kenner's characterization of intertextuality as counterfeiting seems pejorative but, since in this book Kenner is a counterfeiter, one wonders where the irony lies. For *The Counterfeiters* delights in a kind of play that, as the work's introduction proclaims, bring into proximity Buster Keaton, bad poetry, Albrecht Dürer, Joyce, Swift, Pope, closed systems, Charles Babbage and his calculating engines, the late history of Latin abstract nouns, Andy Warhol, Gödel's proof, computers, games, etc., etc. All this is, it seems to me, a Borgesian intertextual game in which the writer would compete with the library in creating a different play-order that allows, as the reader can see in one of the book's drawings by fellow writer and academic Guy Davenport, the presentation of Mr. W. B. Yeats's aspiration toward mechanical birdhood as it collides with the present state of Vaucanson's duck.

Kenner's game has its agonistic side, for it seeks, by adroitly combining new tokens on the chessboard of textual permutations, to checkmate those who don't share his cultural presuppositions. This checkmating is of less interest, however, than the kind of expanded intertextuality in which Pope can converse with the contemporary pop artist Roy Lichtenstein, or Swift with Warhol. This form of intertextuality is not unlike Medcalf's when he allows Melville and Christopher Columbus to meet each other as interpenetrating texts, just as, according to *Genoa,* the ocean and the land meet each other. For the spaces of the world and the spaces of text interrelate as a play of *spacing,* and the following quote from *Genoa* shows other homologies with Derrida:

There is a law of excess, of abundance, whereby a people must explore the ocean, in order to be competent on land. . .

> *(Melville: "You must have plenty of sea-room to tell the Truth in. . ."*

Men must put out space, and nations ships . . .

> *Columbus, reported by a contemporary: ". . . the said Admiral always went beyond the bounds of truth in reporting his own affairs."*

and Typee, Melville's first book, was first rejected because "it was impossible that it could be true and therefore was without real value."[21]

There is also a law of excess and of abundance that *Genoa* and *The Counterfeiters* as well as *Hopscotch* and *Nombres* illustrate: for every point in a text there is an indefinite number of other texts that can maintain a relation with it—by association, by antithesis, as a replication or as a denial. This law of excess and abundance is perhaps the dominant rule of those textual games that seek a plurality of meanings by inscribing within themselves the possibility of intertextual play.

7. Reference

Considerations of intertextual play and the issues of cultural identity that this play engages bring one eventually to consider how language theory and fictions consider the way language can refer to the real. Reference is often thought of as the relation between words and things. I suspect that this naive view of reference derives from the metaphysics of the nomenclature theory of language that would like to fit out each object in the world with a name. *Thing* is, of course, the most undefined of categories, so undefined that I think it fairly useless for our discussion here. I propose in this chapter to discuss reference as the relationship between language and the real, or more precisely, that order of the real that, exclusive of nature, we traditionally have called history. Language theory has made suspect notions of representation and the metaphysics upon which theories of representation are based. The same suspicion holds for belief in reference, for many doubt that language or fiction can transcend its own order and connect with that order of events or things that we designate as the historical—that ordering of reality by which we understand the totality of what has been as well as what is.

History has depended for its existence upon an acceptance of an hypostatized order of the totality of what is. History has implied the existence of a transcendental narrative that allowed fictions from at least the time of Balzac to present themselves as variants on or specifications of that great historical narrative that united all other narratives, insofar as they were historical, in a common apprehension of the real. Though no one can produce this narrative in its totality, for that would mean narrating the totality of what is, the idea of this totalizing narrative has served as a court of final appeal for novelists from Dickens and Flaubert to Proust and Joyce. The realists accepted this relationship; many modernists sought at times to subvert it, though modernist attempts at subversion must appear as a form of recognition of the court's ultimate authority. As far as novelists were concerned, a certain Hegel remained triumphant until the 1930s, if not later, and even if history, at best, could be regarded as the totalization of the absurd.

The desire for new forms of historical totalization has given rise since the thirties to less narrative forms of history in the shape of quantitative studies, sociological monographs on daily life, and intertextual collages that seek to render history in the form of language-immanent archival patchworks. I suspect that much of this work is still animated by a zealous search for new access to the real—ultimately defined in terms of the same kind of earlier tautology that defined history as the totalizing narrative of what is and has been. The tautology, what has been is what has been, is a proposition that perhaps shows that history is a condition of grammar. In any case it is clear that the attitudes of contemporary writers toward history differ significantly from the attitudes held by nineteenth-century writers. In the New Novel, the postmodern text, absurdist fictions, and hyperrealist propositional dissections, most writers either ignore history as such or demonstrate such a suspicion toward it that one might be tempted to claim that history has been abolished in these works. I would dispute such a thorough-going claim. Were it so, some other subject would occupy this chapter. But the effects of such a suspicion with regard to fiction's relation to history are, to say the least, monumental. This suspicion, this radical doubting about the existence or nature of history can lead to radical changes in the way we believe that our collective identity has a dimension that transcends the immediate present. To the extent that we have such doubts, it can be argued that we have also lost a notion of the present: for a sense of the present depends on the existence of an otherness that allows for a sense that permits differentiation between the now and then.

Modern language-theory, as I shall show presently, has promoted in various ways and guises a rejection of our common understanding of history. In this regard theory has seemingly linked arms with postmodern fiction in order to bring about a considerable displacement in the way we think and, perhaps more important, write the past. Some would maintain that this generalized assault on history aims at a liberation from the tyranny of a constricting ideology or from a bogus metaphysical construct. Such views represent, probably, a majority opinion, for these views and analogous ones have presided over what we all recognize, in various ways, as the general loss of the historical sense or the sense of the tradition of Western culture, that great repository of texts that each era has selected in order to give itself a foundation of predecessors. Tradition has in the West been a matter of actively selecting an intertextual relationship with a past text or texts: Dante's to Virgil, Racine's to Euripides, Eliot's to Donne. I can think of no such intertextual foundations today. (Were one to invoke Beckett's relationship to Dante or Descartes, one might wish to speak of an entropic tradition.) And in terms of the transmission of the possibility of historical culture, antihistorical views have also had practical consequences in the virtual disappearance of the apprenticeship in the history of literature that, until recently, characterized all levels of education in most Western nations.

Despite unfortunate practical consequences, especially for American educa-tion, one should not exaggerate the importance of these views about the death of history. Before coming to any definitive conclusions one must attend to what are really redefinitions of history that have taken place in some of the most important fiction written in the past thirty years or so. In its anger with and fear of history (often understood as the events in a Hegelian process we call History), in its groping for new narrative modes that can express this anger and fear, postmodern fiction can be likened to a laboratory in which multiple experiments have brought about new insights into what history is and can be. These experiments have in turn displaced our views as to what relations history and fiction might entertain. For nothing seems less fixed to me than that relationship between the order of the real and the postmodern order of not always fictional fiction. This fiction often aims at probing how one can refer beyond language and appropriate an order of the real that may or may not be linguistic. Beneath the often chaotic surfaces of much contemporary fiction writers have, in addition, sought to make redefinitions of history that are assaults on older ways of viewing the relations between literature and history. In therapeutic terms these fictions often present attacks on the metaphysical underpinnings of traditional history, especially that vision of history bequeathed to us by the romantic and modernist writers, a history underwritten by metaphysical causality or necessity and for which Hegel is the emblematic thinker. In coming to grips with history/History, postmodern writing perhaps displays its most overtly ethical stance, for it is a dominant assumption of much contemporary fiction that only a proper understanding of history, a demystification of History, can allow us to gain the lucidity and freedom to deal with those confusions and atrocities that History, as we are still wont to say, thrusts upon us.

The view that all discourse is a form of intertextuality (or other analogous views) has been singularly instrumental in effecting the displacements I wish to discuss in this chapter. If language is essentially autonomous, and if history perforce can only be mediated by language, then history is a language game or a series of language games. From another standpoint it is only one form of discourse among others. The writing of history generates and is generated by intertextual play as in any other form of writing. The theory and practice of intertextuality leads, therefore, to an effacing of the ontological line that modernism, not to mention Aristotle, drew between literature and history. It is worth recalling that this line obliged modernists to admit the primacy of history; and that nearly every modernist work has a dimension of reference that makes history the final locus for determining the work's meaning. Proust's quest for essence was as much an attempt to transcend history as was Joyce's use of myth in *Ulysses*. But in the end the inexorable laws of time and temporal unfolding hold sway in Proust's novel, just as the irreducible space of history grounds *Ulysses* in one chronologically situated day in Dublin.

Intertextuality allows no such primacy of historical narrative, and in the intertextual games that constitute much contemporary fiction, history is often defined as a shifting locus in a space made up of multiple forms of writing. History is conceived of as one discourse among others, one language game whose rules may be different but in no way are prior to any others. Yet—and I wish to explore this central issue here—this loss of history's privileged status carries with it disarray, for it is not clear that we are certain about what we expect from writing. It is not certain that we really know what we want in proclaiming our liberation from History. How can we reconcile our desire to be freed from the tyranny of the logos of History with our need to bring forth history as a kind of testimony that grants identity as it validates our ethical concerns?

The theory of intertextuality comes in part as a response to these confusions. Understood in a broad sense, intertextuality is simply a de facto recognition that we live in a world constituted by multiple kinds of discourses that both interfere and obliterate each other as well as complete and complement each other. This proliferation of discourses began in the nineteenth century, the century during which the word "literature" came to acquire the meaning of a special realm of discourse that the term manages to retain today. This meaning of "literature" marks a shift in the Western typology of discourse; it corresponds to the emergence of a new intellectual economy, one whose final gasps may well be what we are calling postmodernism. Borrowing from Roland Barthes's *La Chambre claire,* I would propose that the most momentous of these nineteenth-century changes occurred when photography was invented at the same moment as history, history understood in the modern sense we are using. Niepce's recording the real on a light-sensitive plate is contemporary with Hegel's transcribing the absolute real on the pages of History. At the same time that modern history was conceived, technology made possible the creation of a new kind of discourse that had and has unlimited possibilities for the translation of the unmediated real.

A resolutely historical form of transcription, photography permits us to seize the absolute particular as a past being that persists in the present. Perhaps it is the advent of photography that explains, as much as anything, the demise of the search for visual essence or iconicity in literature. For photography, in its concrete specificity, stands in an antagonistic relation to modern history and to those discourses using history—such as realist and modernist fiction—that would offer themselves as the unfolding of the particular essence of the real. In this respect the influence of photography parallels that of much of modern language-theory in that it presents a discourse that stands, by its very nature, as a challenge to essentialist thought. I doubt, moreover, that we can yet grasp to what extent the invention of photographic discourses have, in their capacity for preserving and ratifying the past, destroyed our desire for historical discourse.[1]

Many so-called experimental American writers have tried to explore the uses of photography as an integral part of texts, such as Steve Katz in *The Exaggerations of Peter Prince* (1968) and *Moving Parts* (1977). Most of these American texts are not readily available, and the quality of what I have been able to see does not allow me to generalize as to what these experiments might represent.[2] Yet it seems clear that the combination of photography and writing offers possibilities for testing the relationship between the real and writing. One goal of this testing is to confirm or reject what our theories about what this relationship advance. A good comic example of this testing is provided by the German writer

Peter Chotjewitz and his laconically entitled *Roman* (1968), a "Novel" that also bears the subtitle *Einpassungsmuster*, a "Trial Model." This trial model combines photographs taken by Gaston Rambow with texts in an assemblage that expands the usual definition of the word "novel," though for many readers this work would seem less of a "novel" than works by Robbe-Grillet, Sarduy, or many of the works by the small-press writers in the United States. In Chotjewitz's self-proclaimed novel the reader confronts a discontinuous series of written passages that are often serially duplicated as if on carbon paper, these passages being mixed with verse-like texts, dealing obliquely with the past, and with a series of photographs. The latter mainly depict, in frontal poses, a naked young man or, in extreme close-up shots, views of old shoes. Wearing the narrow-frame glasses favored by hippies and young German intellectuals, the nude male is presumably the author.

The desire for self-revelation has rarely been taken so far. This outrageous and very funny series of nude frontal poses, alternating with the close-up shots of tattered shoes, poses more than a few questions about the nature of reading, history, the author as subject, and intertextuality. Conditioned to seek a higher level of integration, the reader-viewer tries to derive meaning from the images, and their smiling exhibitionism, and their relation to texts about fathers and fathers' fathers. The written passages make reference to the recent German past and would seem at times to be a meditation on that past. But the images, in their raw immediacy, work against the very idea of a past, for they present the image of very natural man, rid of all presence of history and culture. Chotjewitz is playing a comic game with the ontological properties of language and image to create a subversive reference system.

Language has a tense system that can seemingly recall "World War I, baker apprenticeship, cabbage-winter, a Revolution that wasn't one, a republic that couldn't become one, a peace that wasn't allowed to be possible, *Freicorps*, Spartacus, Noske the worker-killer was also a Social Democrat. . . . "[3] This past exists, however, only as the present instance of enunciation, an instance of writing that grows dimmer each time one turns the page and finds an increasingly tattered reproduction of it. The unfading photographic images present the smiling author in a tense that is apparently the present of our perception of the image. On reflection—when we question our perception—it is plain that the author and his shoe collection *are* a past, existing at the moment they were mechanically recorded on film (And language has, it seems, difficulty expressing this relationship with its tense system: the present-tense verb that refers to the piece of printed paper cannot really apply to the image printed on it.) Photographed images are a past that exists in or, perhaps better, toward the present.

Chotjewitz creates a kind of pop litany to the pastness of the image with the book's concluding twenty-two pictures. They all present rotting and torn shoes of various sorts, including a frogman flipper, with the caption, "Der ist jetz auch schon lange begraben" ("This one, too, has been buried for a long time"). The rottenness of the past is underlined by the language, but language itself, as a material signifier, is also tied to the past: the word *begraben* in the caption is called forth, as is the image of the shoe, by the memory of the shoes that the narrator's father threw at him when he would not *umgraben* ("dig") in the family garden. Verbal associations excavate a past that is the past of those fathers who once as *patres familias* reigned supreme in Germany. The photographs ask if this past can be dug up like a decaying piece of garbage.

Chotjewitz's play with the materials of a book shows that contemporary writing can mix photographs, personal verbal and graphic associations, the materiality of paper, and textbook discourses to produce an intertextual construct that we might call autobiography, a novel, history, or perhaps something else. Pushing language to ratify the absurd presence of images, *Roman* constructs parallel series that show history is one of a possible series of discourses, and perhaps an inferior one, for accounting for the past. Confronting the image, history seems in this montage to lose its nineteenth-century claim to being the arbiter of the real that it was when, with the great advance of the natural sciences, history seemed to be the only remaining area of knowledge in which the "human" could enjoy a protective autonomy.

I take Chotjewitz's play with image and word to be emblematic, if not of the death of history, of a postmodern displacement of historical discourse. To complete our perspective, and before turning to considerations of how modern language-theories have dealt with history, it is worth recalling that after Hegel and throughout the nineteenth century History replaced reason as the privileged judge of all discourses. This hegemony of History lasted into the work of such modernists as Croce, Malraux, and Collingswood. A text like Chotjewitz's, among many others, makes us see how unsatisfactory is the classical opposition between History and literature, with criticism serving as the mediator between the two. It is difficult to see how such an opposition, with its roots in classical metaphysics, could survive after the general economy organized by that metaphysics seems to have come apart. To be sure, one cannot deny the intellectual power of this opposition that was operative in the Western tradition from Aristotle through the modernists, with, during most of this time, literature as a form of essence judged to be superior to history, the merely contingent. The nineteenth century reversed this evaluation and proclaimed History, the quest for essence in the order of the real, to be the superior discourse. In their revolt against History, as the last defenders of Aristotelian aesthetics, modernists attempted to contest this evaluation. Heidegger's writing on poetry is, in this light, one of the later attempts to defend literature against Hegel's opinion that history had left literature behind: for the "modern" mind of the nineteenth century, poetry was a mere *Verganges*, superseded in the development of the history of Mind that in coming to know itself completed itself as absolute knowledge.

Chotjewitz's *Roman* might seem to be proof enough that contemporary writers are hardly intimidated by memories of Hegel and of the real as absolute. But memories of "father" Hegel, or at least of his version of history, still haunt the mind of many writers. Hegel remains present to writers not merely because the Hegelian system promises their writings an instantly archaic status as superannuated forms of knowledge, but primarily because Hegel remains the locus classicus of a totalizing historical discourse against which any historical system must be measured if it promises to deliver some aggregate sense of the real. The simple fact that many postmoderns are suspicious of Hegel would commend him to our attention in this inquiry into literature and language and their relation to the real. Postmodernism vents its main hostility, moreover, against the central feature of the *narrative* structure of Hegelian history, against its teleological unfolding. Hegel's system is the prototype for any type of closed historical discourse that sees in some telos a guide for finding the order of the supreme real. Hegel's vision of "reason in history" is based on an absolute narrative order for which all other discourses can be only constituent parts. This view that history/History provides an ultimate narrative structure still dominates much of our intellectual economy insofar as we continue to think in terms of "historical disciplines." Underlying history's superiority as the narrative of the real is a metaphysical vision that sees in historical discourse the unfolding of essence in accord with the necessary laws of its own potentiality. History becomes a necessary tautology.

By grafting history onto the tree of metaphysical thought, Hegel is our modern Aristotle. He introduced temporality into logos when he made the knowing mind a dynamic process that in coming to know itself realizes its essence in time. This self-realization is the telos of History; and, in reintroducing the notion of telos into historical discourse, Hegel made of historical writing a closed narration that has as its goal its own self-consciousness of itself as history. One might well ask what else could history be, except the coming to consciousness of history by the history-creating mind. Otherwise, history is merely an absurd chronicle of contingent events. For many postmodern writers, of course, history is precisely that, the annals of the incongruous. But postmodern absurdism should not cause one to underestimate the powerful rational circularity that unifies Hegel's writing of history as the history of mind.

For other postmodern writers it is the power of a historical system like Hegel's (or Marx's) that makes it most dangerous. And they would point out that it is one thing to conceive history as the necessary record of the progress of mind that constructs a narrative of the real, and quite another to make of History the realization of a preordained telos. Many would argue that the terrorisms with which the twentieth century has been forced to live have been unleashed by those who were convinced that they knew what that telos must be. Moreover, a Hegelian understanding of history is a kind of religious doctrine. History understood as the unfolding of absolute reason makes of History an absolute narrative, *the* Narrative. It displaces all others and becomes, as Hegel himself recognized, a theodicy.[4]

Hegel's example would therefore justify the suspicion that history, as a closed narration, must always function theologically in justification of some predestined telos. Other varieties of history may attempt to veil their theological telos by calling their goal Progress, the People, the Proletariat, Democracy, or "the triumph of Liberty."[5] This masking should not blind one to the way history as absolute narration demands an act of faith from all other discourses; for it proposes the scaffolding of a universal discourse that alone allows access to a revealed meaning of the real. Realist fiction presupposes this scaffolding and often tries to imitate the closed narration of teleological history, a practice, one recalls, that was parodied by Sartre in *Nausea*. It should also now be clear why I have claimed that those modernist texts that sought to contest history also depended on this scaffolding in order to challenge it. In addition, as regards their structure of meaning, one can see that both realist and modernist writings finally shared the essentialist goal of absolute History: they aimed at the revelation of a self-contained essence that might make sense of the otherwise absurd process of mere temporal flow. In spite of its nihilistic premises, as I suggested at the outset of this study, Flaubert's bleak realism is as theological in its essentialist functioning as is Hegel's gradiose historical pantheism. The Flaubertian quest for essence aims, while denying meaning to the contingent events of history, at the revelation of the Idea that can be gleaned from history.

With quite different tempos the development of photography and the elaboration of intertextual play have shaken the foundations of our belief in the closed narration of History. Equally, if not more, important in the undermining of this belief have been the onslaughts on essentialist thought undertaken by thinkers like Wittgenstein, Heidegger, and Saussure. Their critiques of the metaphysics of essence have by and large destroyed the intellectual foundations upon which traditional narrative history can be built, especially to the extent that this narration has almost always been the tale of the unfolding of some essence, some ultimate real, guided by a providential telos. Without essentialist foundations the question remains open as to whether history can be more than an arbitrary chronicle (even if defined statistically); or, more interesting to us, whether history is a form of intertextuality having a status little different from that of fiction. Modern language-theories, I must add, have done far more than implicitly challenge the essentialist foundations of historicism. In their various ways they have mounted a most explicit attack on the very idea of history. In the case of Heidegger and Derrida, this rejection of history is not self-evident. Yet I would maintain that their attack takes the rather perverse form of claiming to have a more fundamental view of history than the historians themselves. In short, the net effect of thought about language, in the twentieth century, with its rejection of essence and such founding principles of history as causality and sufficient reason, has been to evacuate history from discourse. And with this evacuation the very idea of reference becomes problematic.

My description of the effect of modern thought about language merits some elaboration. First, with regard to Wittgenstein, I would simply state that his legendary disdain for history is prototypical of the contempt for history that characterizes postmodern thought. This disdain informs his entire approach to language therapy, for rarely does he bother to confront specific historical examples of thought that have given rise to those confusions that he sees plaguing our language. Not unlike Heidegger and Derrida, Wittgenstein sees metaphysical errors as a mere repetition of the same misguided analogies and, hence, as having no historical dimension that could help us to understand them. This scorn for history accounts, I think, for the virtual loss of interest in the history of thought (one might say "mind") in universities in English-language countries and reinforces the influence of ahistorical positivism in other countries. Such a loss of interest in history is quite consonant with the way Wittgenstein views language games as unfolding in a synchronic space open to the immediate purview of the public eye. With regard to his dismissal of history there is substantial continuity in Wittgenstein's thought. The *Tractatus* initiates his work with an atemporal vision of language and logic, with no provision at all for how change might take place (necessarily through time) among elementary facts. In the later writings it is not atomic facts that exist in a radical present, but rather the criteria for language use. All criteria are present criteria. And in many cases involving the past (when I ask, for example, what are the criteria for the use of language about memory), there would often appear to be no criteria. Many language games that purport to deal with the past, such as certain games dealing with memory, are games for which there are no rules and hence no way of playing the game meaningfully. In often subtle ways Wittgenstein dislodges the past from language, depriving history of any ontological dimension, and reducing our statements about the past to questions about the (present) criteria for believing that such a statement can be meaningful.

Wittgenstein's hostility toward history as a form of explanation also takes more overt forms. He considered historical explanation to be a form of mystification in which the observable is explained by an hypothetical (and often mythic) unobservable. The epistemological consequences of his later thought undermine the possibility that history can offer any more than a tentative model of explanation. Wittgenstein's demystifying of history is analogous to his demythifying of science: history cannot, any more than science, suppose that it is ever coming closer to representing some problematic structure of reality. And as an explanation of phenomena, history often provides, according to Wittgenstein, the least interesting of all possible models. Explanation of many social phenomena can only consist in a kind of structural overview that lays bare the interrelating parts; and that is simply all we can mean by explanation.[6] Perhaps the most one can say for history in a Wittgensteinian perspective is that, once rid of its metaphysical ghosts, "history" will designate a certain number of language games; but even those games would, for Wittgenstein, not make very large claims on our interest.

Unlike Wittgenstein, Saussure was a man passionately taken with the study of the historical side of language. His own historical work notwithstanding, the primary result of the methodological priority he gave to the synchronic system over the past was to put an end to history's privileged role as the underpinnings of the study of language. As I shall suggest presently, linguistic thought can find a role for the diachronic within the synchronic, for history within language. But the net effect of Saussure's separation of language study into diachronic and synchronic fields of investigation has been the general apprehension that the present is essentially severed from the past. The present system owes the past nothing for a comprehension of how the system works. Equally important as this radical separation is Saussure's characterization of the diachronic realm as the area in which the irrational dominates. This characterization relegates historical explanation to a limbo where one finds only absurd, if regular, changes as the language systems of the past give way to their inherent instability. In methodological terms this inherent tendency toward change can have no significance for the linguistic system as it is studied: history must be placed aside if one is to understand how the differential relations between elements in the synchronous system generate meaning. And the role that the nineteenth century accorded organic models of development—often biological variants on metaphors for teleological thought—could not survive a methodology like Saussure's that made of language a series of disconnected present states.

Finally, to turn from Wittgenstein and Saussure to Heidegger, we encounter a mind that purports to think history more originally, and it must be conceded that many of his interpreters see in Heidegger's work an attempt to restore or create a new vision of history. I must demur and argue that, despite his placing of historicity in Dasein, Heidegger's attempt to overcome metaphysics is really an effort to overcome history. True descendents of Nietzsche in this respect, both Heidegger and Derrida would cure us of the malady known as historicism by abolishing the pastness of the past. A variant on Nietzsche's eternal recurrence of the same, Heidegger's reduction of history to a two-thousand-year reign of the undifferentiated dominance of metaphysics destroys any meaningful notion of historical differentiation. For all his talk about periods and eras (which Derrida seems logically to avoid), there is no historical alterity in Heidegger, and therefore no history in any normal or useful sense of the term. Even when he speaks of the era of modern technology, this seemingly historical discrimination reveals itself to be a repetition of the same fundamental event: technology is only another guise for metaphysics as it takes over the planet.

One may of course assent to an ahistorical vision of history, and many postmoderns do. But their assent could also be construed as a sign of a contemporary return to mythical thought, with its polarization of time between a recurring present moment and some mythic other moment that preceded the present. For Heidegger this mythic other is of course the time of the pre-Socratics, the prelapsarian time of grace. In the writings of Jacques Derrida, I hasten to add, this vision of historical repetition is extremely powerful, and one cannot deny that Derrida often makes a better case for the Heideggerian claim that the *Spielraum* of tradition is a two-thousand-year period of repression of all thought that would be other than metaphysics. In proposing his thought about the play of *différance* Derrida hopes to find a way of thinking around metaphysics, of thinking a possible closure of the reign of metaphysics. Derrida's thought of historical closure might be the first truly historical event in two thousand years of intellectual history, but it is not a way of thinking history in any conventional sense. Whether Heidegger or Derrida are correct or not cannot be the issue here; I cannot imagine for that matter what would be the criteria for truth in the case of such arguments that seek to redefine the criteria of truth. What concerns us is that their attack on the metaphysical foundations of essentialist historicism presents itself as a countertotalizing view of history. This revisionary schema dissolves the past (and Hegel) into an undifferentiated repetition in which Plato is forever our contemporary. In the realm of intertextual play that makes up Western culture, metaphysics speaks in many guises, but forever with the dominant voice.

These attitudes toward history find many correspondences in that thirties' novel that began our discussion of attacks on modernism and representation. Sartre's *Nausea* is also one of the most radical demonstrations that language and hence literature can never connect with the historical order of the real. With its attack on the modernist belief that literature might reveal the essence of the particular, that literature might recover the essential real that has been swallowed up by the past, *Nausea* is obliged to take up the old question as to the superiority of literature or history. In doing so, *Nausea* ridicules the idea that literature should rival history. For history is quite simply an impossibility.

It is no accident that Sartre's first-person narrator Roquentin is a historian who tries to do research. He soon despairs of the task of recreating the past by studying piles of old documents and letters, when he understands that any number of narratives he might construct, fictional or factual, could account for the contents of his dusty archives. If accounting for what other men have written, for so-called "evidence," is the only criterion for distinguishing fictional and factual narration, then there is no important difference between these two kinds of narration. Both are ideal constructs in language, and an indefinite number of such narratives could propose to make sense of the contradictory letters and reports that must be the basis for a historical text.

Roquentin discovers that both fiction and history share an essential trait: they formulate their function in terms of a pregiven telos. And if it seems permissible to arrange events in a novel for a desired ending, a mystification is involved when history orders events so that they form a significant arrangement. This teleological ordering in a history book has nothing to do with the uncertain way one lives the real events in one's life as an indefinite openness. Narrative teleology means that the narrative's final event is already contained in the writer's first sentence, as Roquentin ironically observed when he puts his life in order for a brief diary entry. As the first sentence is written, the end is already present, transforming the narrated events so that they appeared to be lived, in Roquentin's disgruntled words, as annunciations or promises.

The Sartre writing *Nausea* has the same sense of the historian's necessary bad faith as the Wittgenstein commenting on Frazer's *The Golden Bough,* though Sartre's antihistoricism is even more thoroughgoing. No narration could, in Roquentin's world, overcome the past's being evacuated from the present by nothingness; by a kind of progressive swallowing up that leaves the historical narrator confronting, on the one hand, his ideal order of words, and, on the other, the sheer present "thingness" of things in their total contingency. At the heart of Roquentin's nausea one finds an ontological divide between being and language that leaves no room for the past. All writing is an ideal construct existing in the present, and it is only out of naiveté that the historian believes he can cross that divide and, through his writing, use words to account for the contingency of what is. In *Nausea* Sartre comes down on the proliterature side of the debate between literature and history, between essence and the contingent, but he does so by abolishing history. All verbal constructs are literature.

Roquentin's abandonment of his research and his decision to write a novel signify that he wants to write a narration that consciously proposes nothing except an ideal order. This affirmation of a rather Platonic view of literature (though the "ideal" realm of words is never embodied in the world) is of less importance than Roquentin's renunciation of history. His rejection of history disallows the possibility of accounting, in language, for the historical order of the real or of any real to which language might refer. This rejection also cuts down the scope of fiction in extraordinary ways. Within this reduction room is left only for the following type of writing that reads like a primer for the hyperrealism of much contemporary German and French fiction or, with a slight shift in focus, for the schizoid absurdity of much recent American fiction:

> I looked anxiously around me: the present, nothing but the present. Furniture light and solid, rooted in its present, a table, a bed, a closet with a mirror—and me. The true nature of the present revealed itself: it was what exists, all that not present did not exist. The past did not exist. Not at all. Not in things, not even in my thoughts. It is true that I had realized a long time ago that mine had escaped. But until then I believed that it had simply gone out of range. For me the past was only a pensioning off: it was another way of existing, a state of vacation and inaction; each event, when it has played its part, put itself politely into a box and became an honorary event: we have so much difficulty imagining nothingness. Now I knew: things are entirely what they appear to be—and behind them . . . there is nothing.[7]

At this moment Roquentin resembles one of Beckett's disintegrating clowns, acting out the comedy of taking seriously his own intellectual premises. His past is nothingness, and he is in a state of anomie, a state of disorientation in which identity is impossible.

Sartre's own later thought about history is testimony to the past's refusal to consign itself easily to nothingness, but his radical expunging of the past from language, which marks *Nausea,* sets the stage for the doubts of a coming generation of writers, especially those of an existentialist bent (and most of those who began writing in the two or three decades after World War II have their existentialist bent). Existentialist writers have proceeded as if history were impossible; or, even worse, as if historical narratives were only so many neo-Hegelian attempts to rationalize a status quo responsible for the horrors to which the twentieth century has accustomed us. For writers from Albert Camus to Günter Grass official history is synonymous with the Hegelian theodicy that, in justifying the state's will to power, must inevitably justify the state's claim to divinity—by justifying some ultimate good that warrants the state's use of power. History is thus a justification of evil; which is to say that it is always an ideological narrative masquerading as an higher appreciation of the real. In this light, according to Jean-François Lyotard's analysis of postmodernism, a central aspect of postmodern consciousness is the recognition that the great historical systems of the past—those of Hegel, Michelet, Marx—were narrative codifications of a kind of knowledge whose only telos could be the legitimation of the state and society, be it the present state or the state to come.[8]

Many writers, especially those in Germany and in Latin American countries, find that a distrust of history/History cannot replace an understanding of the cultures and societies that, it would appear, History has produced—cultures and societies whose lamentable aspects demand some kind of explanation. Needing history to explain the destruction of history, the writer comes to the ambivalent awareness that the absence of history is as intolerable as a surfeit of it. I would suggest that these postmodern writers live the abolition of history as the same kind of oppression that the modernists felt when they saw themselves engulfed by History and its all-determining primacy. Nonetheless, these writers accept the basic postmodern tenets that history is only discourse, one text among others, and an arbitrary intertextual construct at that. They are obliged to recognize that history exists only as the present instance of enunciation that plays at retrieving a past. The criteria for this retrieval can exist only as a radically present form of rules. Within the limit of these game-rules history, if it is to exist, must be wrested from the proliferation of discourses that inundate the marketplace and risk obliterating any meaningful discriminations that the writer might be able to make. History in the marketplace is a commodity encoded, too, in the fallen logos of received discourse; it exists as the present opinion of *das Man.* Especially for German and the Latin American writers, writing takes the form of a struggle to endow otherwise senseless chronicles of defeat with a meaning that is responsive to the present. And this struggle ıs a supreme intertextual game seeking to go beyond the Sartrean anomie of the totally present text and to play new language games that might defy the obliteration of the past. This is not to say that the writers we shall now consider have won this game; but exemplary defeats are sometimes more rewarding than facile victories.

Günter Grass presents one of the most disconcerting as well as important examples of the postmodern search for a voice speaking history. Those critics who have seen in his work a simple affirmation of traditional humanism have shrunk before the task of measuring how monstrous his work often is, a monstrosity born of the tensions between Grass's desire to overcome a Hegelian version of History as destiny and his awareness that he can find no other source of explanation for the crimes of German history—except history. Grass's work aims at first overthrowing and then finding a replacement for the Hegelian kind of theodicy which, in his view, culminated in both Hitler and Stalin, in the creation of the Polish state in which socialist policemen shoot workers, in the metaphysical and hence humanist justification of the reign of terror. In spite of his contempt for Heidegger—and his overblown satire of Heidegger in *Dog Years* bears witness to the fascination Heidegger works on him—Grass has found partial solutions to his dilemmas about history through the creation of a series of Heideggerian-type texts in which all is repetition: history is the eternal recurrence of the same monstrous, evil text, the text of evil being the basis for the intertextual network that goes to make up what we call German history.

In contrast to a Colombian writer like Gabriel García Márquez, for whom forgetfulness is the defining trait of his nation's history, Grass confronts a culture that, after nearly having committed historical suicide, has freely chosen to forget as a way of dealing with its recent past. Germany has quite simply engaged in a project of collective *Vergessenheit* as its response to history. As a writer Grass finds himself "stuffed with history"; but his world-historical fatherland has had little difficulty in forging a chrome-plated refusal of the past as its response to its own monstrosity. This response has been a refusal to write the text of collective identity. What this refusal can mean in terms of a society's world view is difficult to say, but it seems to imply a kind of schizoid rupture with all that constitutes the past. In this vacuum in which silence about the past has been the rule, Grass sees his task to be that of finding a discourse that can overcome the collective repression of memory. His great difficulty, in the Federal Republic of self-satisfied economic miracles, is to find some criteria for the validity of the peculiar language games he would play. What can impose a discourse about the past upon a people who recognize their own success as the only criteria of truth?

Grass's multiple hesitations about the status of his novelistic discourse reflect his difficulties and uncertainties about how he might write a collective memory. In the *Danzig Trilogy* his most general game-plan is to present his narrations as texts generated by recurrent archetypes, archetypes understood here as the repetition of aberrant texts that official history cannot repress. *The Tin Drum* is a would-be novel for a three-year-old, a recapitulation of the effects of the nursery rhyme about the Black Witch. *Cat and Mouse* is also a play on a child's text, generated as it were by a game limerick that also gives the novel its title. And *Dog Years* is manufactured as a *Festschrift* in the underground factory that produces scarecrows that play historical roles in the pageant of our history. Each novel is doubled by other texts that are also the locus of the irrational that writes history in its various repetitions of the same texts. When Grass underwrites his fictions as doubles of imaginary texts, nursery rhymes, and games, he is motivated by a need to make them distortions of received history—the history of forgetting. Rooted in received history, like so many intertextual baffles, these novels mix archetype and the writing of the real in a play that relocates historical discourse in an intertextuality for which there can be no question of origins, causes, or telos. In his violent rejection of any rational structure to history Grass mocks the idea that there is any process intrinsic to historical development or that the mind mediating history can inscribe the process of its own growth in the text of history. History spins itself out in the grotesque proliferation of monstrous texts, though it is often not entirely clear how these texts can relate to those individual acts of terror that, written in the aggregate, we take to be the history of Germany in the first half of the twentieth century.

A comparable problem in understanding the concrete specificity of Western history troubles us with Heidegger and Derrida's version of history. In the case of Grass's often comic exuberance, one is perhaps more willing to be convinced that there must be connections: Oscar's refusal to grow up seems to be, in an appropriate, if teasingly obscure way, a response to the rise of National Socialism. Yet, when one asks what is the relation between the novel's nursery rhyme and German history, one finds only the very general response that the presence of the Black Witch (or, in German, the "Evil Cook") places the historical narration outside the bounds of the rationally explainable. Historical events—Hitler's occupation of Danzig, the organization of the Nazi regime there, the war—are incorporated into a fictional matrix that, as a repeating intertext, seems to divest them of any significance except that of exemplars of repetition. This repetition endows the novel with the status of a mythic text; and the criteria for the acceptance of myth are simply given by the myth's own statement that it is.

Grass does not allow the reader any certainty about where the center of his discourse might lie. Oscar, the narrator-drummer who at age three decides to grow no more, is perhaps a madman about whom it is not possible to decide if he is reliable, insane, or perhaps an emanation of the tempo of a nursery rhyme whose evil rhythms are captured in his drum and in his glass-breaking voice. In an analogous manner *Cat and Mouse* sends the reader in search of mythical repetitions, for this novel suggests that it is a double of that first text of crime, the myth of Cain and Abel. *Dog Years* also opens up mythical and parodistic possibilities of repetitions in the historical labyrinth. This derisive discourse is a genealogy of dogs, the final beast being Prinz, the descendant of wolves that becomes Hitler's favorite pet. This pseudo-genealogy, with its debt to biblical structure, enters into other intertextual relations such as, again, the myth of Cain and Abel, or, most noteworthy in the case of the Jewish protagonist Amsel and the gentile Aryan Matern, into an ambiguous relationship with Hegel's master and slave. And Amsel, in his identity as Brauxel, is a producer of history, a manufacturer of texts and historical scarecrows. Grass's decenterings, obliging the reader to make his way in multiple intertextual circuits, result in large ambiguities, but not necessarily of a fruitful sort. Is one to read the Hebraic tradition and its mythos as one of the founding partners in a history of history's atrocities? Or is the production of history a more recent refinement of the industrial state?

There is undoubtedly a modernist side to this use of myth in Grass's intertextual play, though his emphasis is exactly the opposite of that found in modernist writings. Grass writes in an attempt to reinstate some form of history. For all the gratuity of some of his capricious fabrications, Grass has perhaps the most acute sense of the ethical implications of the play of reference in fiction. Men act only on the basis of what they take to be the real, and for Grass this axiom means that writing bears a heavy burden of responsibility to the world and, to reenter the unbreakable circle, to history. One cannot deny the power of what is. This ethical sense is quite evident in the remarkable change in Grass's work that occurs in *The Flounder,* a comic history situated in the Pomeranian marshland where Grass was born. Hegel's world spirit never passed through this region on the confines of world history. Pomerania is therefore the ideal site for the parodistic tale of the development of Spirit, taking the form of the author's history of his mind's development through three thousand years of history. With satirical logic Grass uses his own version of the Hegelian phenomenology of the *Geist* to tell the tale of the stages in his own mind's history from prehistoric times to the present. Like the earlier trilogy, *The Flounder* is also the tale of the reign of texts, though in this case one privileged text, a Low German fairy tale found in the collection of the Grimm brothers. This tale has ruled over the development of History, at least Pomeranian and Prussian history, with all the tenacity of Heidegger's metaphysics. Moreover, this historical development of mind is a comic rendition of the coming to consciousness of "phallogocentrism" (the concatenation of the logocentric dominance of metaphysics with male dominance). Grass shows that the male principle emerged in Pomerania through the intervention of the *Butte,* the flatfish, who allowed the hapless prehistoric male, in the person of our Danzig-born narrator, to emancipate himself from the then dominant female.

History develops as the play of fairy tales, in this case "The Fisherman and His Wife." The insatiable wife Isebill is offered the realization of her wishes by the captured flounder. After a series of successful wishes she wants to be God, and, in wishing beyond the limits of the possible, she condemns herself to lose her wealth and return to her initial poverty. In Grass's novel the flounder becomes the source of knowledge that enables the rather stupid male narrator to liberate himself first from three-breasted Aura's matriarchate and then to maintain himself as the source of history throughout the ensuing ages. The male principle, represented by the flounder's power, might be understood as the complicity between men's use of metaphysics and their dominance in writing. In Grass's novel, however, the male principle and male writing of history are on trial. Quite literally on trial, since a women's liberation group has caught the fish and placed him on trial in Berlin. Grass's omnipresent male historian, with a narrating mind that belongs both to a neolithic brute and a defensive contemporary German writer, has followed the flounder's counsel until this world-historical moment when history is on trial. Again like metaphysics, the flounder has presided over the elaboration and appropriation of history as a male enterprise from which woman has been excluded: from the first smelting of metal through the development of technology and modern socialist organizing, the flounder has been at work, advising men, and only men, in the creation of history.

Like Hegel's version of desire, appetite has been the motivating force of this comic phenomenology. At each turning point in history the narrator's mind confronts his belly, for food provides the true infrastructure of history. All is built upon the culinary conditions of existence. Grass's portrayal of history is remarkable in the way he combines parody and a celebration of excess while at the same time proposing a reading of the real that at times appears to be motivated by a desire to correct simplistic readings of social history. At times Grass seems quite convinced that food is the determining locus of history and hence primordial in any discussion of social reality. The introduction of the potato into eighteenth-century Prussia brought about, for instance, the conditions that made possible the creation of the modern German state. To cooks, then, their due, those cooks who were usually women, maintaining the infrastructure while men warred and whored.

History can only be found in the present instance of writing. The narrator therefore speaks the past as the present "I" who was then, as he is now, the male principle of narration. History is the present telling of his past stories, stories centered to be sure on women, on his cooks, his matriarchs, his martyrs, and his bawds. Borrowing from Hegel, with comic intent, the structure of his discourse, Grass writes a past that is sublimated (*aufgehoben* would be the Hegelian term) into the present of the contemporary narrating mind. Grass is less interested in distinct Hegelian stages of development, however, than in presenting each historical moment as a repetition of the fundamental text of the flounder's dominance through history, or at least since that moment when the narrator emancipated himself. This history is on trial. (And I insist, with some surprise myself, on how this repetition is homologous with Heidegger's own response to Hegel: to deny the Hegelian theodicy by making each stage of development a repetition of the same text.)

To say that history is on trial is to question the dominance of those texts that repeat themselves, the eternal recurrence of the same irrational archetypes that would condemn one to the repetition of the same stories and the same history.

Such questioning imparts a pressing ethical sense to Grass's intertextual parodies; making all necessary allowances for the great differences that separate them, one can maintain that a similar ethical sense motivates the urgency of Derrida's attempt to deconstruct metaphysics. Perhaps this is the central ethical issue for the postmodern mind. Of course, Grass has a great comic sense of the questions involved in this demystification of the determining myths of Western culture. But his comedy is also problematic. It is difficult to say, for example, how seriously Grass takes this trial of the flounder and history by a women's liberation group. The Berlin judges are plainly portrayed as *ausgeflippt* (current slang for "flipped out"), and Grass's recourse to intertextual repetition has a tendency to transform everything into a comic repeating machine that no human agency could stop. Yet, the women's movement has clearly brought a new dimension to history: men can no longer keep women from claiming their place in creating/writing history. And Grass's repetition has more than one signification. Repetition is also a form of exorcism, and in Grass's case the repetition of the irrational can be construed finally as an attempt to demystify those demons of German history that do not allow themselves to be named except in negative parables.[9]

To turn from the best-known German writer to the best-known Latin American offers a study in inverse symmetry. Grass, the German, finds himself clogged on history, constipated, as he says, from the historical orgies and gluttony that have made up the diet of his nation. To pick up, after a work by Grass, a novel by a Latin American like Gabriel García Márquez, is to go from a repetition of surfeit to a repetition of poverty. For the Latin American, history also unfolds as the recurrent text of atrocities that, with mechanical repetition, are never transcribed, that cannot be inscribed into any history, because they are beyond meaning and thus beyond language. The Latin American is condemned to suffer a hunger for History, for some Hegelian odyssey whose tautologies would at least endow his misery with sense. This is the context that gives meaning to my claim that in *One Hundred Years of Solitude* history is the text of forgetting. The symmetry between Grass and Márquez completes itself when we realize that lands clogged with history and lands that the Hegelian epic never encountered find themselves today gripped by the same sense of a vacuous present, of *Vergessenheit* or *olvido,* that the writer wants to dispel. Latin American history, like any other, can only be discourses, but what can a discourse be that has no tense, no differential play with other discourses, and seemingly no telos? Within the paradoxical emptiness of this history without history today's Latin American writers have conceived some of the most powerful historical discourses about their anguished lack.

The Latin American suffers perhaps more acutely than others from the feeling that history cannot be written. Even worse, the postmodern abolition of history makes a mockery of his need for some discourse that can at least dignify this suffering, a suffering for his people's unspeakable plight. Like a Juan Rulfo in his *Pedro Paramo* (1953), he may react by scrambling the tenses of his fiction so that past and present coexist as the same recurrent fiction narrating the quest for the archetypical *caudillo* father. There is ultimately no temporality in the unfolding of this type of tale, narrating the search for a father. The father is a presence who would offer a sense of the past to the child, and who, as the center of the child's world, would offer a center to a discourse that narrates its attempts to find a foundation for time and meaning. Another option for the Latin American is to glorify the mythic qualities of his society, as if to declare that history has no meaning for those lands whose Indian cultures show how to live in some sense more authentically by living outside of time. This option directs the voyage of Carpentier's nameless protagonist takes in *The Lost Steps* (*Los Pasos Perdidos*, 1959). Carpentier's European hero is clearly deluded in his exaltation when he attempts to begin a new life in the jungle among primitive people. His failure to remain in this paradise is in effect a failure to be able to live outside of the tissue of that history that permeates Western life. After Carpentier's portrait of the intellectual's delusions, it is doubtful that any writer in Latin America could proclaim in good faith a belief in a more primordial ahistoricity. Finally, perhaps the best parable for the Latin American writers's dilemma is provided by Vargos Llosa's *La Casa Verde* (1965). The "green house," the recurrent brothel of our dreams, may disappear from history, but the Latin American writer is still obliged to narrate the nonexistence of that house—even if Wittgenstein's criteria for memory statements would validate the statement by the owner of the house that the house never existed. Nothing proves the house existed, except memory; nothing proves Latin America has a history, except need. This need for memory, for history, conjoined with the real exploitation and tyranny that engulfs their lands, explains why so many Latin American writers contradictorily declare themselves to be Marxists even as their fictions demonstrate the impossibility of History. Marx offers the illusion that memory might be a question of science.

One Hundred Years of Solitude is surely the most important novel of the postwar era to demonstrate the rueful coincidence of forgetting with the closure of history. The telos of history is, in this derisive sense, to be condemned to oblivion. Perceiving his national chronicle to be the recurrent pattern of absurd violence, patriarchal caudillos, and failed revolutions, the Latin American finds no way to make sense of this chronicle from within. His history can only be a Borgesian meta-text that narrates the attempt at narration of this meaningless chronicle, a text about a text filled with *One Hundred Years of Solitude*. History is a writing that, when deciphered, obliterates the reading of the chronicle in its self-annulling revelation (it is not for nothing that Márquez has said repeatedly that Kafka taught him what literature is). The novel *One Hundred Years of Solitude* destroys itself at the moment of closure when the bastard Aureliano finally decodes the "enigmatic literature" contained within the gypsy Malquíades's parchments. The last Buendía lives out the text of the prophecy that told that the Buendía family would come to an end when incest resulted in the birth of a child with a pig's tail. In the timeless world of recurrence a historical text reads forwards towards its own destruction as well as backwards toward the past. For *One Hundred Years of Solitude* and the prophecy reveal themselves as the same coinciding text in the moment of annihilation.

The gypsy prophecy and the parchments are the novelistic text of history before it is written in events that the novel in turn narrates. In a reverse perspective the occurrence of events are the writing of a text that already exists in the parchments. The events are the chronicle of eternal return, whereas the novel/ prophecy is a meta-text that can only predict or narrate (it is all the same) the fall of an entire people into oblivion. The two imagined historical texts, the novel and the parchments, reflect each other as doubles, in a relationship that is not unlike the text of History as it realizes itself in the mind of Hegel's *Geist:* Hegel's text of the progress of Reason is written in advance in its essence that comes to unfold in time as the retrospective text that History writes. In Márquez's novel the completion of its own telos is its own destruction. Nothing exists that cannot be written, but all that is written can only be a record of the condemnation to disappear, including the writing's own self-condemnation. *One Hundred Years of Solitude* dramatizes the defeat of Hegelian logos, the fall of logos, with an unsurpassed rage. The fall into silence at the end of the novel, the coming exile from the memory of men, is an anti-eschatology that undoes Western historiography from its biblical sources through Marx. In Márquez, as in Kafka's tales, there is no sign of the promised redemption. History is reduced to the paradoxical record of its own fall.

One Hundred Years of Solitude accepts the primacy of logos in order to undo it; the novel plays comic havoc with the autonomy of language. Language is the mediator of what is, but language is bound to fail, and the world then slips away. The capacity to refer to the world is bound up inextricably with the ability to master the way language articulates the world, as we see, for example, when the plague of insomnia strikes Macondo early in the town's existence. Insomnia is accompanied by forgetfulness. The town's citizens begin to forget their past, their identity, and what things are. Aureliano hits upon the idea of pasting on objects small pieces of paper that mark the object with its name. This literal application of the nomenclature theory of language is useless, since the inscriptions have no meaning if the people cannot remember the use of the marked object. In his struggle not to forget language—and therefore the world—Aureliano moves from Saint Augustine's theory of language to the later Wittgenstein. He discovers that the pieces of paper must contain, in addition to the name, an explanation of the use of the word-object if reality is to be maintained. The word "cow" pasted on an object with four legs means, among many other things, that the object must be milked every morning. This effort is finally useless, for such a "system" demands too much "vigilance" if reality is not to disappear. The complexity of language use reveals itself as too great, and people begin to forget the very meaning of the "values" of the written letters. Language, memory, and reality are easily defeated by forgetfulness.

One alternative to language-articulated reality is to institute a Borgesian play of chance. During the plague, people turn to Pilar Ternera who, having once read their future in the cards, now constructs the past by her card games. Prophecy and history are equivalent rolls of the dice. Or, in equally Borgesian terms, the real is always ready to give way to the imaginary, whether it be articulated by cards, fantastic books, or the English encyclopedia in which the last Aureliano learns the order of the world. The allure of a superior order or, in this case, of any order at all is sufficient to dictate what the real is. Like Borges, and like the Wittgenstein of *On Certainty*, Márquez in his ontology of language obliterates the easy distinction between the fictional and the real. Reference is subordinated to the play of articulation to convince, to provide order, to give a world view. Pilar Ternera is the only character to survive from the beginning until the end of the novel. She is the source of memory in the work, for she has the capacity, if only through the cards, to arrange some kind of order, an order that can impose itself as memory or prophecy.

For history, for a record of the real, the basic form of articulation should be writing, the trace that, if it could perdure, would be the foundation of the lasting memory. But books come apart, lose their pages, and disintegrate. Moreover, when Aureliano Secondo asks if there once really were marvelous happenings such as those he finds narrated in books, Ursula explains that books are actually bringing the world to its end. Pages are missing in the books, and things no longer are as they were when gypsies brought magic lamps and flying carpets to Macondo. As books come apart, there is less reality.

Books can reduce reality, for they can be transformed, and earlier narrations then vanish from memory. Crucial in this respect is the macabre episode in which José Arcadio Secundo is a witness to the massacre of some three thousand workers. Having been called to Macondo by the government, they are shot down in the town square and then carried away by train, to be dumped as so many rotten bananas. Even before José Arcadio Secundo can return to Macondo after his fortuitous escape from the train carrying the corpses, he discovers that this atrocity no longer exists. Official discourses consign this massacre, like all perturbing events, like history itself, to oblivion. Nothing ever has happened in Macondo. The history books say so.

The sotto-voce anguish of Wittgenstein's deliberations about the criteria for the status of memory statements illuminates the helplessness of someone who sees the language of official history ratify forgetting. For what can be the status of the statement that the massacre did take place when nothing speaks in its favor and when all writing speaks against it? The only writing that records this event is the novel itself, a meta-discourse that records in advance its own condemnation to disappear. Language is autonomous, but its autonomy can be manipulated to exclude anything from it and hence change what we take to be the order of the real. This extraordinary power of exclusion becomes apparent when the soldiers make a search of the Buendía house after the massacre: José

Arcadio Secundo is literally invisible to them when they enter his room. He is excluded from history, thrown out of time or, rather, isolated in a splintered fragment of time that has no relation to any other time. This sense of living outside time is exemplified in the room where José Arcadio Secundo devotes the rest of his life to deciphering the parchments. Here he initiates the bastard Aureliano into the hallucinated version of the history of Macondo, the isolated version of his own memory.

The bastard Aureliano is initiated into reality by means of the English encyclopedia, in which all is known. "All is known" resounds in this context as a comically derisive tautology that again ironically affirms the autonomy of language in its articulation of the real. Language is the taxonomy of what can be known, and the encyclopedia a compendium of that taxonomy in written form. Whatever is known must be written in some encyclopedia if it is to perdure and qualify as the known. In the novel's self-destructing perspective, this criterion means ironically that nothing is known. Within this same perspective, however, mastery of the encyclopedia gives the comic illusion of knowing, for to memorize the encyclopedia's language is to memorize an opinion about all that can be momentarily codified as the real.

One Hundred Years of Solitude places itself, by its very radicalness, on the other side of the modernist revolt against history that the Mexican poet Octavio Paz defines as the abolition of yesterday, today, and tomorrow in the conjoinings and couplings of language.[10] I would see, moreover, Márquez's novel as an acerbic critique of the modernist goal of transcendence. The novel demonstrates the modernist simultaneity of the text as a form of presence that abolishes time, in the mirroring between novel and parchments; but Márquez undertakes this demonstration only in order to show that this final realization of the presence of logos is self-obliteration. This is, as Vargos Llosa calls it, a form of deicide.[11] To destroy the unfolding of History, in the sense of the manifestation of Logos, is to destroy a god, the god who reveals what is through the essential revelation of his word in history. *One Hundred Years of Solitude* is in this sense a "textacide" that is at one with the antitheological gestures that characterize postmodern thought and fiction.

Márquez's novel also plays with an ambivalent intertextuality, especially in the way it incorporates, without distinction, allusions to what we conventionally take to be fictional and historical texts. It makes frequent reference to events of different logical orders—the life of Francis Drake, American imperialism, or the general outline of world chronology—that are taken from the canonical historical text that we accept as characterizing the order of the real. At the same time it refers to "real" fictional characters, such as Artemio Cruz or *Hopscotch's* Oliviera, as if they shared the same kind of linguistic space as that of received history or the parallel space invented for the novel *One Hundred Years of Solitude*. This refusal to demarcate different linguistic spaces stands in contrast to the realist and modernist practice of inserting the fictional within the general space of the historically real, often for purposes of marking a place within which a fictional transcendence might take place. As I have suggested, such a modernist and realist practice (and the two overlap in this respect) concedes in effect primacy to the historical text that the fiction relies upon. If Márquez places all texts on the same level, he does so precisely to reduce, perhaps sardonically, all to the same intertextual status. No discourse has any privileged ontological rank in the fall to oblivion.

At this point I would like to return to the question concerning photographic discourses and their power to ratify the real. For Marquez has not omitted them from consideration in the novel. When memory returns to Macondo after the insomnia plague, Melquíades comes back bearing with him a daguerreotype laboratory. Such a coincidence might suggest some relationship between the retention of the past and the photographic image; but the novel does not argue this connection. The novel gives a description of a family photo in which one supposedly sees on Aureliano's face the same clairvoyant look he would have years later when he faces a firing squad; but the description also notes that he had not yet received the premonition of his destiny. In Márquez's desire to demonstrate the equivalence of past and future, united in destiny, the photograph can only illustrate one end of the temporal pole. Márquez separates thereby the photographed past and destiny and, with a not altogether satisfactory turn of the hand, shoves photography aside. In his treatment of cinema Márquez also appears to want to disarm whimsically the power of photographic discourse. Márquez's attitude is perhaps the sign of a certain postmodern equivocation about the power of film to refer to something that might be beyond language, to an order of the real that might be articulated independently of the structures of language. The inhabitants of Macondo become indignant when cinema comes to their town. They are perturbed by the illusions it offers; it allows, for example, actors dead in one film to reappear in another, though transformed and wearing "the garb of an Arab." The mayor explains that such a machine for illusions is not worth violent outbursts. But the people's reaction makes one aware that Márquez is also aware that film might rival literature, literature being defined in the novel as the best way of making fun of people—"burlarse de la gente."

In their different ways, Grass and Márquez illustrate a generalized unhappy consciousness about the relations between language and the past or the capacity of language to be other than a record of forgetting. I should like now to turn to some writers who illustrate a somewhat different tendency in contemporary literature. Working more consciously within the confines of modern theory about language and writing, these writers investigate history as an integral dimension of language. The desire to find history within the fabric of language itself is consonant with Heideggerian views that language is the historical advent of being. This pursuit is also warranted by Wittgenstein's metaphor likening the multiple spaces of language to the development of a city. This metaphor argues that language games can be situated in a historical space. Moreover, later developments in structural linguistics have given greater weight to the diachronic side of language.[12] The Italian linguist Giulio C. Lepschy would characterize the relationship of the past, of diachrony, to the present linguistic system in very positive terms:

> Culture is characterized by continuity, tradition, the transmission of elements of preceding culture. This is true, naturally, even for culture without writing in which the tradition is oral. The linguistic part of that which is transmitted obviously consists in messages and not in codes. But whoever attempts to interpret these messages correctly must conform to the basic codes in which these were originally formulated. Semantic codes contain, superimposed as it were, codes from different eras. The universe of meaning of contemporary English includes the semantic systems of Shakespeare and Dickens. It is of little importance if individual speaking subjects have read these authors or not. The issue is that the semantic universes of contemporary English not only derive from other, preceding systems (such as happens for the phonological system), but must be sufficiently rich to allow the interpretation of messages of Shakespeare and Dickens (whereas, on the contrary, the phonological system of contemporary English derives from the phonological system of Shakespeare and Dickens but does not include it).[13]

The synchronous system carries within it, for any given language, the world view of preceding eras. Unless, of course, it does not; in which case the entry into those past world views must be afforded by some kind of archaeological inquiry.[14] Within these limits contemporary language theory offers a possible entry into the past through the substance of language itself. This view proposes that our history is an intertextual play among all the texts that a language disposes of through its history. And, replacing Hegelian mind with the linguistic system, linguistics says that the living history of any culture's successive systems of the real is the totality of meanings that are sublimated within the present state of the language.

This view of the relationship of history and language adds what I would call a dimension of semantic time to writing; this dimension takes on a great role in the elaboration of postmodern labyrinths. Intertextuality becomes a "polylogue" with the history of the play of meaning in a given language. Returning to American shores for examples, I would suggest that John Barth's critical formulations in his essay "The Literature of Exhaustion" make the most sense when read against this kind of desire for history. In quoting approvingly Borges's contention that all writers are more or less faithful amanuenses of the spirit, that they are translators and annotators of preexisting archetypes, Barth subscribes to the view that all writing is intertextual repetition of what are necessarily past texts. Barth implies that such an awareness is itself a historical phenomenon, since it comes at times, such as our own, that are periods of exhaustion. By exhaustion Barth does not mean to imply that we are living in a period of decadence (though the suggestion hardly seems avoidable). Rather, taking Borges's fictions and his critical fictions as the defining work of our era, Barth recognizes that literature is always an imitation, which is to say a repetition of literature and of language inscribed in literature. In its autonomy language gives rise to more language, in the historical play of intertextual recurrence.

Barth waffles a bit in his endorsement of Borges, since he also suggests that contemporary writers have the option of writing "proper novels." Proper novels are realistic works that do not acknowledge their intertextual relations. Amanuenses of the spirit write imitations of novels. This imitative task falls to writers who, living in periods of exhaustion, seek to write, as Barth puts it, in harmony with their times. One may cavil at Barth's Hegelian formulation that writers *should* attempt to write in harmony with the *Weltgeist*, though this echo of Hegel shows how difficult it is to think beyond Hegel in attempting to think the nature of history. One must also wonder why Barth feels the need to invoke the great American myth about works that offer an unmediated seizure of Life, which is the subject of "proper novels." Despite his hesitations, Barth's main point in this essay, one that has become the starting point for much critical discussion of contemporary American literature, is that in fiction today there is no originality in the romantic sense of the term. Novels are intertextual in their reproduction of other discourses; and except as parody they cannot pretend to be an imitation of life or nature in some neoclassical sense.

The novel is a historical act insofar as it sublimates into the present act of writing discourses that have preceded it. This intertextual genesis is evident in the first novel to which we usually give the name of the genre, in *Don Quijote* and the intertextual play it maintains with preceding romances. Whence Barth's (and our) fascination with Borges's Pierre Menard and his rewriting, word for word, the *Quijote* in the nineteenth century. A problem floats before our eyes, something like Wittgenstein's duck-rabbit illustration, that we have difficulty seizing. Depending on how we look at it, we see a different animal. Menard's text would be the seventeenth-century text that sits on our bookshelf. It would also be a curious example of archaic Spanish written in the nineteenth century. Cervantes's text written by Menard has three centuries of diachronic change added to it, so that in a certain sense it would be more complex than the original while remaining literally the same. Three centuries of different semantic systems accrue to the narration of the noble knight's adventures, a condition that changes, as Borges slyly remarks, the linguistic space in which they take place. Pierre Menard's *Quijote* represents a new language game occupying a different site in the city of language.

John Barth maintains that the artist who recreates Beethoven's Sixth Symphony in the twentieth century can do so only in an ironic mode. If he means by this re-creation a reproduction of Beethoven's harmonic schemes or themes, it seems to me that such quotation could function in a number of different ways. And even if he means by this a Pierre-Menard type of literal quotation, it does not appear inevitable that this "work" will be ironic, any more than the literal reproduction of a soup can is. Barth's claim brings up again the problem of postmodern irony, especially with regard to the intertextual game that consists in the Pierre-Menard practice of creative quotation of past texts. If history is embedded in language, then quotation becomes a form of direct access to history but, according to Barth, only in an ironic mode. Not all postmodern writers believe that quotation is an ironic act toward history, but those who like Barth do believe this, betray an ambivalence toward history, a kind of embarrassment before the traces of history in writing that they are not quite ready to accept. They are equivocal in their attitude; their irony betrays a belief that language is cut off from history, while their use of quotation signifies a belief that history invests every word one writes. They act, alternatively, as if they are prisoners of some closure of history and as if they wish to destroy history.

I shall return to this question with regard to John Barth, but for purposes of further illustration I ask the reader to interpret the following passage excerpted from a recent American novel by Frederick Tuten, bearing the ironically historical title *The Adventures of Mao on the Long March:*

But it is an awful thing, indeed, this endless endurance, this almost indestructibility, of a marble bust! Whether in our own case, or that of other men, it bids us sadly measure the little, little time during which our lineaments are likely to be of interest to any human being. It is especially singular that Americans should care about perpetuating themselves in this mode. The brief duration of our families, as a hereditary household, renders it next to a certainty that the great-grandchildren will not know their father's grandfather, and that half a century hence at furthest, the hammer of the auctioneer will thum its knock-down blow against his block-head, sold at so much for a pound of stone![15]

At a first reading the reader may have the impression that he is encountering a kind of ironic pastiche, lamenting the ephemeral nature of American social relations and, more generally, the American refusal of history in the form of enduring traditions. The prose is marked by all the syntactical features that historically mark the elevated style. In a twentieth-century context, however, this passage, with its reference to "our lineaments" and "hereditary house-holds," borders on the ludicrous. There is a disjuncture between language and referent, for such notions no longer have much function in our contemporary linguistic system. They refer to something belonging to a world view that, to be sure, is historically part of the history of English language and the world once articulated by the language. As such, they are connotatively marked by semantic time.

If the reader recognizes this passage as a direct quotation from Hawthorne's *The Marble Faun,* then he undoubtedly feels that, as with the *Quijote* wrtten by Pierre Menard, he is being asked to read two texts at once. As a nineteenth-century text this passage belongs to the history of the American concern with its own history or lack thereof. Framed within a pop history of Mao and the Chinese revolution, the Hawthorne passage generates ironic possibilities for reading that it cannot have as a nineteenth-century text. Like Menard's *Quijote,* the text is paradoxically richer than itself. Tuten would apparently agree that appropriation of the past can take place only as an ironic citation that affirms a disjuncture or rupture with the past. Yet, the pastness of the past is an intrinsic part of the language Tuten quotes, even if he does so without quotation marks, as if he wanted to show that this language continues to function as part of the ongoing linuistic system that defines our world. Tuten, like Barth, simultaneously takes his distance from history while exploiting its presence in writing.

Pop artist Roy Lichtenstein's cover image of Mao for Tuten's novel says much about how a contemporary American writer views history as a kind of pop assemblage. Pop irony serves to diffuse the weight of history, to work against a closure of history whose telos has been "greatness," "democratic progress," or some other illusory ideological pretensions that seem shallow or hollow today. Quoting without attribution from a range of writers that includes, in addition to Hawthorne, Melville, Pater, Faulkner, and Engels, Tuten uses these texts as a kind of ironic punctuation for the creation of an intertextual collage. His collage is comparable in many ways to the use of historical texts in Paul Medcalf's *Genoa:* in both cases history is a play of discourse, an interplay of multiple writings within a common space called a book.

Unlike Tuten, however, with his ironic deflation, Medcalf makes detailed attributions of quotations in a clear belief that past discourses enter the present space of the book and speak, without irony, of the land and the sea that was. The founding of America with its culture can be spoken through a combinatory order in which all texts speak in juxtaposition with other texts. In Medcalf's work, past texts, of Homer and Columbus, speak a harsh judgment when contrasted with narratives of our contemporary fallenness. Tuten's irony is perhaps more liberating than the kind of conservative evaluation of the present that emanates from *Genoa,* the kind of work in which the past speaks to condemn the present.

Medcalf's *The Middle Passage* (1976) seems to push to the limit this convention of granting privileges to past texts. Assembling quotations from various sources in this book—hardly a novel—Medcalf quotes descriptions of the Luddite rebellion against machines, graphic depictions of the transportation of slaves, and passages on whales and whaling. This "Triptych of Commodities," as Metcalf call its, has no narrative structure, but sets forth various writings that stand metonymically for the beginning of our civilization's fall. Medcalf's view of history and historicity is not unlike Heidegger's, especially his seeming belief that texts inaugurate, with no interpretation, the onset of historical moments; or rather, as Heidegger would say, they are historical moments. Medcalf's sense of historicity springs from the same revulsion before the present that characterizes

Heidegger's work, as well as the work of other conservative postmoderns. This judgment of the present often leads to a denial of historical alterity, as one sees in *Genoa* where Medcalf makes no differentiations as he juxtaposes a fragment from Homer with a quote from Columbus or Melville. Writing is history; it is the perduring trace that always speaks with the same fullness.

The kind of irony that Tuten and others practice finds an extraordinary development in John Barth's *The Sot-Weed Factor* (1960), though it is less certain if Barth is doing history or comic archaeology in his novel. This chronicle is made up of a series of quotations of late seventeenth-century syntagms or, better yet, language games. Barth's reading of Wittgenstein might have suggested to him that, if one is to restore the past, one must reconstitute the multiple language games that made up the past's world view. *The Sot-Weed Factor* is in this sense an archaeological compendium of seventeenth-century discourses, of science, philosophy, aesthetics, history, and daily lore as they are embedded in language. Through its comic bravura the entire reconstitution is set off with ironic quotation marks, leaving the reader to ask why Barth should expend so much energy in depicting, from within its language, the world view of a Restoration Englishman. As a work of linguistic archaeology, the novel enacts its proof that this language still speaks to us; at the same time the work parodies its own enterprises. Seen in this light, *The Sot-Weed Factor* would support the contention that any aspect of writing that aims at the past is a comic enterprise. But, to return to my earlier remarks, this language of the seventeenth century does speak to us, in its comic play, of a world that we recognize as belonging to the past, even as its alterity is present to us in our language.

The Sot-Weed Factor, with its tale of Maryland's poet laureate, is another postmodern case of self-allegorization. (Barth is a native of Maryland.) The self-awareness that a representation is predicated upon another—in this case the representation of the seventeenth-century world view—seems inevitably to lead to ironic and parodistic structures that one could characterize as the American postmodern reflex. In other literatures this is not necessarily the case, as, for example in the writings of the French novelist Claude Simon. Simon is also concerned with the appropriation of the past, through language, as it invests the present, in various ways. His work exemplifies a quite different sense of a possible linguistic archaeology. This archaeology does not so much note a rupture with the past as it strives to retrieve the past out of the presence of multiple forms of representation that compose our daily culture. It is this accomplishment that I propose to discuss as the conclusion of this chapter. Simon's work allows us to follow a clear change from an existential awareness of history to the more recent practice of intertextuality. His work offers in addition an exemplary response to the antihistorical points of view that have flooded the intellectual marketplace since the thirties. And his work is especially instructive for our purposes because it is characterized by an increasing awareness of the kinds of theoretical issues that have made problematic the once unquestioned acceptance of a natural relationship between language and literature. As a politically militant writer, Simon brings an overtly ethical concern to exploring history and making sense of it, a concern that is not plagued by the fear of forgetting that haunts Grass and Márquez. In the wake of Sartre, but also influenced by Proust, Conrad, and Faulkner, as well as Heidegger and structuralist writers, Simon has sought ways of overcoming what he sees as the separation of language and experience. This search finds its earliest full fruition in *Histoire* (1967), the novel that many would consider to be his major achievement. It is certainly one of the most important novels of the second part of the twentieth century, not least of all because it makes a subtle critique of existentialist views of history. I shall therefore devote some detailed analysis to this novel, before turning to a later work, *The Battle of Pharsalus*, in which Simon's self-conscious practice of intertextuality reaches its full development.

Histoire bears an ambiguous title, for the French word, in its double meaning, can designate either "story" or "history." Much as the latter term once had the double meaning that eighteenth-century English novelists put to such splendid use, so Simon's *Histoire* is a joining of history and stories. The stories are generated by reactions to the everyday objects that the book's narrator encounters as he goes about one day's business. Cumulatively, these stories might be taken to be the histories—or history—that impinge on one man's consciousness in the present moment. Composed of a series of fragmented discourses, *Histoire* proposes an existential rendering of how various histories might be orchestrated in a unified field of consciousness. The novel suggests in fact that no attempt at unity can succeed, since, for the individual, history always dissolves into stories, narrative fragments, memories, and projections. The novel asks what the meaning of history can be for the concrete individual. In *Histoire,* if history is to have any significance, one requirement appears to be that history be capable of accounting for all the quotidian objects and acts that go to make up what we call, perhaps for lack of a better term, daily life. History must be capable of endowing our daily environment with meaning.

Many sorts of objects, perhaps all objects, can pose historical questions. Simon's novel, for instance, tells many fragments that bear in large part on the postcards that the narrator sifts through as he prepares to settle a family inheritance and sell some furniture. The narrator's concern with his family and its past emerges from the reflections and questions inspired by the postcards, many of them sent to the narrator's mother when she was a girl at the turn of the century. He comes across many other images in going through the drawers. Family paintings, photos, stamps, engravings, and even figures on banknotes present images that seemingly demand a narration or *histoire* to account for their presence as various forms of the past. But especially postcards, representing as they do particular scenes from throughout the world at the time of Europe's greatest colonial expansion, seem to embody whatever history might be. Images of Arabia, Africa, Asia, as well as of European scenes, produce a textual web of references that establish one historical level: particularizations of the colonial world as it was, before the narrator's birth, when his father was courting his mother. European history and family stories intertwine in this past that the narrator can only indirectly know. In a psychoanalytic perspective this period is the past first defined through images as a family past from which the child is irremediably excluded. The family album of photographs presents a past seen as a present from which the child is longingly absent. His desire for the past is first motivated by his desire to overcome exile from a world beheld in nostalgia.

Many other historical levels and texts clash within *Histoire*. Memories of Latin translations and quotations from a history of the Russian revolution (unattributed, but from John Reed) are juxtaposed with what appear to be the narrator's memories of the Spanish Civil War. Images recall strikes from the days of violent working-class protest, while texts about the Flanders front are contrasted with remembered or imagined tales of the family. Many of these fragments are taken from situations in Simon's earlier works, such as the tale of French defeat in *The Flanders Road*, the Spanish Civil War in *The Palace*, or provincial life in a southwestern French city in *The Wind*. In these self-mirrorings Simon is not interested in creating some kind of *roman fleuve* as in Balzac or in early twentieth-century works like those of Jules Romain. One thinks rather of Faulkner's self-citation as a model for the intertextual practice of referring to one's own work as so many sources whose interplay can create a world. (Such as the reference in *Absalom, Absalom!* to *The Sound and the Fury*.)

Although *Histoire* is indebted to Proust and Faulkner in the formulation of its search for history, the practice of fragmentation in Simon's work is postmodern. This practice derives from the widely held view that there is no historical essence, no Idea, that can unify discourse or narrative. Moreover, if as a consequence there are only histories, and no History, there can be no unified subject that underwrites the narrative project. For the unified subject, as Hegel knew well, is both a presupposition for history as well as a product of history. In this practice of fragmentation the narrating "I" becomes a mobile token. It can, for example, be projected onto an image, which then endows the image with a grammatical subject that allows the image to "narrate" its history. The narrator finds a photograph of his fatherly uncle from a period when his uncle was an artist in Paris. The picture, depicting the uncle with a nude model, calls forth not only a third-person narrator who tells a hypothetical tale about the image, but also a first-person voice. Through this voice the uncle seems to speak directly in the text. As frozen fragments of the past these images become the enunciating center of discourse. This transformation permits the images, in a manner reminiscent of cinematic technique, to become animated, as the description of a static scene takes on active verbs and changes into a narration of events. In this sense the photographic image, a fragmented but present piece of the past, becomes another discourse circulating in the narrator's mind, itself a fragmented place trying to hold all these discourses together.

Histoire has its modernist roots; like Joyce, Simon attempts to exhaust the lines of temporal convergence from past events that can center upon a single day. But Simon's histories differ from those in Joyce's *Ulysses;* no mythic dimension grounds these fragments in some atemporal space that escapes from history. The various levels of history/stories that are imbricated in this work's wandering narrative project remained confined to a meandering within historical time, a time immanent to the objects to which the novel refers. Solidified as images, disappearing as memory, the past exists, however, only as hypotheses and speculations, hence, as discourse. The images described within the novel also exist, to be sure, but with all the fullness of a past presence existing enigmatically in the present. Finally, *Histoire* asks what can be said about these images—how their muteness can *speak* the past—unless they be animated from within by a narrative project, or a projection.

The past exists in this novel primarily as a narrative intentionality, which is that aspect of an existential exploration of history that led Sartre to declare history impossible because arbitrary. However, *Histoire* is deeply suspicious of its own mechanism for generating history and stories, even as the novel shows itself to be a discourse that springs from a nostalgic projection. In its ludicity *Histoire* performs a demystification of the kind of narrative that originates in a desire to make everything we encounter speak the past. The novel makes one suspect that, as in the case of the past given by the photograph, a past present to us but to which we are absent, it is finally only our present language that speaks to us. The past that the photograph mutely offers allows many discourses, for which nostalgia is one powerful motivation. Nostalgia is a powerful current in much popular contemporary film and fiction, and most of the recent French and American work I have read and seen represents an often pathetic desire to take refuge in nostalgic celebrations. Perhaps this is a sign of a certain cultural immaturity, that history has become for us a realm for evasion, for dreams of magic decades such as the thirties or fifties, shining with neon lights that illuminate our infantile fantasies.

I do not wish to say that images such as *Histoire*'s postcards might not be invested with semantic codes that can speak the past. Nostalgia has little to do with reading these pictorial codes. For nostalgia is a desire to recover the past, often a past desired as a paradise, and in this desire to overcome exile it projects back onto objects our present narratives about them. *Histoire* is a powerful demonstration of this desire to create an order there where we are not, in a past order of the real whose objective forms—photos, portraits, letters—seems to deny our subjective existence. To this extent *Histoire* is drama of the modulations of consciousness; it is also an indirect critique of the modernist dream to recover time past as some objective essence in language. Language can seemingly only speak in the present.

After dramatizing the desire to turn objects, images, and yearnings into discourse, Simon has partially broken with the type of drama of consciousness one finds in *Histoire*. After this novel Simon reversed his attitude toward writing, in a reversal brought about to a large extent by his change in attitude toward the nature of language. And in this case, as I have suggested, one can speak, in an interesting way, of a direct influence of theoretical concerns on a writer's practice. Simon's work after 1967 also represents an adjustment, if not an answer, to the kinds of suspicious questions that he put to history in his earlier works, including *Histoire*. Simon's later work brings together an attempt to reconcile history with the recognition of language's autonomy, while, at the same time, this work refuses, often in parody, any notion of history as a form of closure, teleology, or theodicy.

In *Orion aveugle* (1970), a volume produced by Skira for a well-known series that allows writers to discuss problems of art, Simon describes the act of writing as a kind of play undertaken within a closed space. Only discourse itself, Simon maintains, can produce a locus for history and creation, and not the interpretation of objects exterior to language. The paintings and other images that Simon selected for reproduction in *Orion aveugle*, a title of a work by Poussin, may serve as the point of departure for these fragmentary passages and their juxta-positions; but in the last analysis, according to Simon, writing must turn inward in a kind of self-exploration:

> And now this path opened by *Orion Aveugle* seems to me to need to be continued somewhere. Because it is quite different from the road that the novelist usually follows and which, starting from a "beginning," comes to an "end." My path turns and circles about itself, as might a voyager who is lost in a forest, coming back on his steps, setting out again, deceived (or guided?) by the resemblance of certain places that are, however, different and that he believes he recognizes, or, on the contrary, by the different appearances of the same place, his way crossing itself frequent-ly . . . and it can even happen that at the "end" one finds oneself again at the same place as at the "beginning."[16]

Using a labyrinthine doodle to illustrate his meaning, Simon implies that writing is the tracing of similarities and differences that give rise to meaning. The practice of writing is an indefinite series of semantic crossings, because the genesis of meaning is potentially infinite, a semiosis without end:

> Thus there can be no end except the exhaustion of the voyager who is exploring this inexhaustible countryside. At that moment will be completed what I call a novel (since, as is the case with all novels this is a fiction placing in scene characters who are involved in an action), a novel that, however, will not tell the exemplary *histoire* of some hero or heroine, but rather this quite different *histoire* that constitutes the singular adventure of the narrator who never ceases his exploration, discovering, as he gropes, the world in and through writing. (*Orion aveugle*, opening, unnumbered pages)

This view of writing entails, in practice, the destruction of any kind of narrative closure, of any end that might subordinate the workings of discourse to a pre-given telos. Refusing closure, the novel cannot make use of the realist plot whose usual teleological functioning suggests that writing is subordinated to some structure exterior to itself. And, with the theory of intertextuality in mind, one sees that in Simon's *The Battle of Pharsalus* (*La Bataille de Pharsale*, 1969) writing means the patching together of other discourses, of the multiple forms of writing that we variously call fiction and history.

In *The Battle of Pharsalus* fiction and history interpenetrate, and both are viewed as complementary forms of intertextuality. In this way the novel restores historical reference to fiction, but it does so by destroying the notion that fiction or history might recover some pure referential event that would be the origins of discourse. History functions here as a kind of *Weltbild,* to use Wittgenstein's expression, made up of the various histories that we take to function as definitions for the language games we play. An originating battle of Pharsalus in itself cannot be said to exist. It exists only as those texts such as Caesar's *Civil War,* that tell us that in 48 B. C. Caesar defeated Pompey in Thessaly. Comically emblematic of this quest for the originating event are the novel's fragments narrating the fruitless attempt of a tourist-narrator to find the plain in Greece where Caesar's legions might have withstood Pompey's cavalry. These plains have been the site of many wars. And for the contemporary Greek peasants who live there, the only important battles have been those against the Turks. They have never heard of Caesar.

Simon's novel accounts for its intertextual genesis by quoting a passage from a different writer at the onset of each of the book's three sections. Serving as points of departure for this textual mobile are the stanza from Valéry's "Graveyard by the Sea" that sets forth Zeno's paradox; a passage from Proust where the jealous narrator describes his feelings for Albertine; and a passage from Heidegger's *Being and Time* on the appearance of world. A riddle-like description of the contradictory nature of movement and time, Zeno's logical paradox about the arrow that flies and does not move is resolved by Simon's descriptions of paintings depicting ancient warfare: the flying arrows are fixed in the immobile representation of battles, the immobile battles of history. The Proustian text on jealousy seems to motivate a recurrent scene of copulation in Simon's novel; this text offers a narrative hypothesis for a jealous narrator-observer who witnesses the scene in which he is presumably made a cuckold. The Proustian text, concerned in general with the interpretation of signs and specifically with those signs that can confirm a jealous person's reading of the world, is the kind of "historical" narration that obsessively reconstructs the past in function of an emotional compulsion. The Proustian narrator's endless hypotheses about Albertine are so many interpretations of objects and signs that result in so many histories. This part of Simon's *Battle* continues the kind of deconstruction he undertakes in *Histoire.* It reduces the narrative hypothesis to a present instance of discourse, an obsessive text produced by an imagination that cannot stop dwelling on images of genital contact.

Simon's quotation from Heidegger bears directly on a concern with history insofar as it sets out a way for understanding how historical discourse can come to light. One recalls that *Dasein*'s world appears only when the realm of other directed reference becomes visible, as when for example a tool does not function:

> The tool turns out to be damaged or the material unsuitable. . . . When its unusability is thus discovered, equipment becomes conspicuous. . . . The context of equipment is illuminated, not as something never seen before, but as a totality constantly sighted beforehand in circumspection. With this totality, however, the world announces itself.[17]

The passage from Heidegger not only motivates the frequent descriptions of a broken-down harvester seen in a Greek field, but it also makes commentary on how the world, with its historical dimension, appears when discourse fails to function as we expect it to. Or, to use an analogy from Wittgenstein that parallels Heidegger's thought, our image of the world becomes evident to us, this constant backdrop for all our dealings becomes apparent to us, only when it becomes problematic. When our *Weltbild* can no longer be assumed without question, then we begin to see that it exists (much as Wittgenstein's scientist would see the breadth of his assumptions about his world when, confronting the people for whom the earth began to exist one hundred years ago, he should have to justify innumerable statements about what he takes for granted as reality).

In Heidegger's terms the world appears when the world of purpose-directed reference breaks down. We know that we inhabit a world, we sight it "beforehand in circumspection," but this world does not become fully present to our consciousness *as* a world until something goes awry that obliges to look at the full network of referential dealing for which the world is the total background. In ordinary life tools and their functions constitute a network of purposes in which *Dasein, man in* the world, is absorbed. Whereas a working tool "refers" to a realm of other-directed purposes that are unquestioned in daily life, a broken tool stops us and forces us to consider it against the horizon of our concerns—against the backdrop of the world. Like a broken tool, Simon's novel, with its fragmentation, its refusal of closure, its conscious intertextuality, lays bare the world in which historical reference takes place, without question, in normal circumstances of language use. Simon's text would force us to take cognizance of the world of reference—the world of unquestioned intertextual reference—that serves as the historical world that we in fact normally inhabit. One of an indefinite number of events that constitute our ordinary world of reference, the battle of Pharsalus exists through and as a multiplicity of overlapping and mutually dependent texts. Quite literally, these texts go to make up our world. We inhabit a world in which the statement that there was a battle at Pharsalus defines what we mean by the historical referential world.

Simon uses the machine metaphor as a bridge between the Heideggerian vision of world and his own notions of intertextual play. History is a realm of reference to which various texts contribute like so many parts in a functioning machine. When, in the *Battle of Pharsalus,* the narrative machine breaks down, the parts stand revealed against the background of the whole and we are obliged to interrogate how the parts make the whole, like the narrator who studies the harvester on the fields of history:

> As it stands, the machine is evidently incomplete; several of its parts are missing, either because it has been damaged in an accident or because, as is more likely, since the machine is useless anyway, these parts have been removed in order to replace corresponding ones in another machine, or quite simply in order to be utilized as they are, that is, as plates, planks or rods for fences or some other purpose. . . .

As the description of the machine continues, one begins to wonder if this is not also the ruins of Helegian logos:

> Still, though its present state makes any precise notion of its functioning impossible, it appears that when it was in running order the energy transmitted from the axle of the wheels to the various parts was then transformed into either rotating movements, like that of the axle itself, or, by the effect of the tie rods mounted on eccentric cams, alternating back-and-forth movements, the machine itself, when in operation, drawn by one or two (the shafts having disappeared, it is difficult to tell; however, given the size and the weight of the machine, it is more likely to have been two) horses, evidently capable, in a metal clatter of elytra, joints and mandibles, of a series of simultaneous operations. . . . (Pp. 102-3)

Simon's intertextual collage, resembling a broken-down machine when compared with the once powerful functioning of Hegelian narrative, exhibits its parts as parts. Not parts of a whole, but parts as parts, for there is no unified machine to produce historical discourse for us. The historical world emerges as the composite of all those bits and parts of language that go to make up history.

Every aspect of language use is called upon for the composition of a historical world. Simon's practice of intertextuality draws, for example, on associations making use of the linguistic signifier, of the material domain of language's shapes and sounds. (And in this respect, as one may already have noted, Simon's historical machine is less the product of an engineer than of Lévi-Strauss's *bricoleur.*) Metaphors, puns, and other figures often motivate the appearance of the themes, motifs, and events in the novel. This use of the material shape of words playfully demonstrates the multiple functions of language. Language can even play against its own smooth functioning. The multiple play-possibilities of language engender the multiple possibilities of writing history—the multiple battles of Pharsalus that we have in innumerable writings.

The historical world is revealed, then, in a proliferation of discourses that

give rise not to History but to histories; not to a closed theodicy, but to an open-
ended exploration of the world of reference; not to a refusal of history but to a
celebration of the multiple possibilities of the act of writing. Simon introduces
numerous forms of representation in the form of descriptions, often of images,
and of quotations. Paintings by Ucello, Caravaggio, Piero della Francesca, and
the Poussin of *Orion aveugle* give us multiple representations of battles. Comic
strips, mosaics, photographs, stained-glass images, theatrical scenes, statues,
films, and cartoons all enter into this assemblage of possible historical representations. Caesar, Lucan, Plutarch, Apuleius, Proust, earlier Simon texts, Elie
Faure, newspapers, among other texts, are quoted, usually without attribution,
as part of this textual matrix that plays at recreating that total realm of reference
we call history. This language and these representations are spoken by no one.
Language itself incorporates the historical world, and therefore it is language
that speaks. Any O (observer) can be a point in the world to which discourse
is ascribed. Taken as this plurality of received discourses, history is an autonomous linguistic domain that offers as many possibilities of reading as there are
possibilities of writing and speaking. And the plurality of readings of these
multiple discourses constitutes finally "the battle of Pharsalus." Held together
by the inner motivation of metaphors, metonymic associations, alliterative plays,
oxymorons, and puns, these textual tools, stripped of their unquestioned functioning, stand revealed, in Heideggerian terms, as language that is present at
hand; and with them is revealed the historical world-horizon contained in language.

One of the last images in *The Battle of Pharsalus,* before the novel returns
to describe the table on which it has been written, is an ancient, cracked bas-
relief or perhaps a decaying statue that, in representing an image of a couple in
the act of lovemaking, fixes the mobile image of the couple that has recurred
throughout the novel. This reduction of the novel to a final decaying plastic
image is not unlike Fellini's recomposition of history, especially at the end of
his version of *The Satyricon.* After narrating this fragmentary tale of Roman
decadence, Fellini shows us, as if the viewer now stood two thousand years later
on the site of an ancient city, the ruined statues of Ascyltus and Encolpius. In
their final disintegrating form as statues, they seem to embody the sedimentation
of those two thousand years that separate us from the Rome of *The Satyricon.*
Yet those statues "exist." As fragments of fragments they are generators of
histories. They are a ruined representation that can nonetheless enter into the
circuits of multiple discourses, discourses that can be read in a book or seen in
a film, or transformed into the historical museum of our infinite possibilities for
narration that language carries within itself. And after Simon's deconstructive
work, perhaps I can best conclude by recalling what once—historically—was
said about French kings, "l'histoire est morte, vive l'histoire!"

Afterword

To return to the beginning of this study, let us recall that the modernist belief in iconic revelation paralleled Plato's belief that helos, the sun, not only made things visible, but also brought them into existence. But this existence had no historical dimension, since true being, for both modernist and Plato, was conceived as eternal and everlasting. If semiosis has replaced helos as the reigning literary deity, it is not clear, as the last chapter has suggested, that we are always sure where time and history enter into the play of language, least of all where it is a question of understanding the history of literature itself.

Consider in this regard the way literature is taught today, especially the way that teaching is organized in the form of the literature textbook. One opens many literary textbooks today to find Hamlet nestling next to Mickey Spillane in a great ecumenical synchronicity. These anthologies usually celebrate rhetorical techniques—how the author speaks to you—or perhaps eternal human interests, such as classical tragedy and the human emotions. The linguistic system of seventeenth-century London and twentieth-century Paterson (New Jersey) cohabit that readerly space created for an equally bizarre space, the classroom, though perhaps this place is not unlike the reading space of every eclectic reader since printing began. In any case, reading is taught as a kind of spatialized potlatch of great texts and lesser texts, drawn into one timeless and, as it were, mythical realm known as Literature. It is as if *Finnegans Wake* has become a pedagogical model.

If a history of literature were to exist, and the university presses give some cause to believe that there is still some interest in the topic, what would this history look like? I admit to thinking most recently that this history would look like a series of superimposed geological strata that have few connections other than proximity. Undoubtedly my vision was affected by looking through the prism afforded by recent structuralist work, and above all by the brilliant work of Michel Foucault. His formulations of the historical epistemē or the synchronic systems that set the conditions of possibility for all conceptual activity at a given moment are insightful, daring, and solve a good many problems by eliminating them. Foucault's thought is structuralist in its emphasis on synchronic states. History is conceived less as a linear movement along a vertical axis and more as a series of static states to be investigated horizontally. The ruptures between synchronic systems eliminate causal relations in a vertical sense of development and make of them a kind of horizontal affair in which all is mutual conditioning. For biology, economics, and linguistic science this all seemed very convincing, though in my own area of interest—theories of language—there remained problems. Can one really deny Lockean influences on later linguistics? Are the ruptures really so seamless between the classical period and, say, modern thought on linguistics? The most difficult counterexample I found for a structuralist determination of history as rupture came, however, from another domain: mathematics. No domain of mathematical inquiry, since the beginning of mathematical thought, has ever been superannuated. No mathematics is ever out of date. And in this regard literature is more like mathematics than like, say, biology, medicine, and physics, sciences for which one may truly have to undertake an archaeology to find the epistemic grounds that once allowed a given body of concepts to make sense.

One has of course a certain choice in what one asks of history: do we want a history of literature to be a chronicle of works or an archaeology of the grounds of possibility for the creation of the works (perhaps something like the history of formal determinants that Valéry called for)? Or do we want something else, say, a history of the social classes to which texts were addressed, or a history of the semantic fields that are privileged by literature at given historical moments? Each of these prior determinations as to what one wants from history generates different expectations and different criteria for deciding if the history we write has been adequately or inadequately conceived and carried out. In this light it seems to me that Foucault's ideas, for example, work reasonably well, for certain types of investigation, but not for all. His work describes well that type of thought having a large derivative axiomatic component that needs to be elaborated in terms of large epistemic structures. But his work seems not to offer equal help in describing more self-contained intellectual and creative manifestations, such as mathematics or literature, manifestations moreover that derive explicitly from a tradition of preceding works.

If the notion of rupture has a certain dramatic and hence aesthetic appeal as a model for history, the converse belief in continuity has its own less dramatic but perhaps more powerful attraction. In its extreme form—and what can be said about an idea unless we work out and enjoy its extreme implications?—the idea of continuity telescopes all historical movement into one undifferentiated repetition. Postmodernism is a development of modernism, in turn a development of late romanticism, in turn begat by the Enlightenment or the Renaissance, that child of Antiquity, *und so weiter*. The argument for continuity often engenders genealogies that argue, as twentieth-century thought about language seems to show, for the eternal recurrence of the same. To be sure, sufficient numbers of neoclassicists, Nietzschean wagerers, and Zen Buddhists flourish to keep alive the claim that all is contained in all. Perhaps it is, but this argument makes for rather dull history; which is to say that the affirmation of the eternal return is not history, but the refutation of history.

This study has placed its major emphasis on historical change, though it has also pointed up some continuities. I hope that this use of both continuity and rupture has not been construed as a sign of trying to have my argument both ways at once. As a defense against a charge of waffling eclecticism, I should like to propose another image of history. This image has hovered over the elaboration of this study, and I think it might be useful at this point to examine it. I offer the reader a trope that proposes a useful way of looking at rupture and continuity without having recourse to Hegelian dialectic or other metaphysical notions that often accrue to these Ping-Pong opposites. The source of the trope is the sixty-seventh of the *Philosophical Investigations*. Here Wittgenstein uses a striking image of a twisted thread to counter his opponent's tactics to search for the "essence" of what Wittgenstein is calling "family resemblances," in this example, all the family resemblances that characterize what we call "number." Since numbers share many traits, Wittgenstein can characterize our use of the word by saying, "we extend our concept of number as in spinning a thread we twist fibre on fibre. And the strength of the thread does not reside in the fact that some one fibre runs through its whole length, but in the overlapping of many fibres."

This image of the thread seems to me especially apt for describing how the same phenomenon gives rise to two opposing views of essence and, finally, allows one to describe how we fit together the family resemblances that characterize the various things we commonly (and uncommonly) designate by the word "history." For those who find continuity to be the essence of history, the image of the thread gives them, as it does Wittgenstein's seeker for essence, the image of the continuous overlapping of fibres. They can point to the intertwining of events as an unbroken weave of threads. With this trope they can group everything under the rubric of history as a single strand. As Wittgenstein remarks, however, it is somewhat less than satisfactory to discover that the commonality one seeks consists in the overlapping of many different fibres of different lengths, some ending while others continue. On the other hand, the image of the thread gives those for whom the essence of history is rupture another feature to emphasize. They can point to the thread and claim that there is something common "to all constructions of this sort," namely, the constant disjuncture of their common properties. Wittgenstein's sarcasm in proposing disjuncture as an essence, one defined by a common absence, would seem to be a fit commentary on its adequacy as essence.

In a nonmetaphysical sense, however, the image of the thread proposes a concrete way of looking at the ruptures and continuities that go into the operations that we undertake in order to construct history. We can make the thread as large as we like, including within it as many of the totality of possible fibres as we find useful. For example, a rather thick historical rope is the history of Western culture. A minor strand of this rope would be the history of Western fiction, and within this a thread called the novel. And that thread could itself be separated into various fibres, some perhaps running the entire length of the thread, others intertwining for only short distances. In this book, then, I have used primarily two terms, modernism and postmodernism, to talk about fibres, or about defining characteristics, that seem to run mainly one after the other, with perforce some overlapping to tie them together. And one should not lose sight of other, longer fibres that traverse the entire length of the thread that we call the history of the novel.

The strength of Wittgenstein's metaphor is its potential to free us from the misguided search for those essences that are often supposed to be hiding behind words like "historical phenomena." The metaphor allows us to realize that we are, to a larger degree than we often think, in charge of these language games. Certainly we are free to pick which language games we want to play. And then redefining the rules may be perfectly permissible, though that will not necessarily make the game any more rewarding. For those language games that we call history, this metaphor puts rupture and continuity in their proper place. In this game they characterize all possible fibres that go into the series of family resemblances that allow us to construct a historical thread. In fact, rupture and continuity are versions of the more general notions of the other and the same that are involved in the play of all meaning.

Then, does postmodernism exist? If one means by this term some fixed essence unfolding itself in history, with a Hegelian necessity, as some recent discussions seem to suggest, then the answer is no. If one means by this term a series of discriminating traits—identifiable fibres of an approximate length—that allows us to see ruptures as well as continuities, then I think the term is reasonably useful, if not especially felicitous for its connotations: "Postmodernism" suggests at once living through something apocalyptic and existing with an identity that is forever subordinated to the past. The term must correspond to some felt need, however, for it has imposed itself on us in a remarkably short time; and even those who deny the existence of postmodernism can usually describe it with precision (though I suppose that this is also true of unicorns). The word has become a counter in our language games. The coining of such a word is in itself a historical fact that will be of no small interest to future historians. They may prefer of course to dismiss the notion and reorganize the entire semantic space known as twentieth-century culture or post-Enlightenment literature in terms of some new classifications, some new language games. As the nineteenth century invented that lovely notion, the Renaissance, so perhaps the twenty-second will find for us a more euphonic name, though we shall, alas, take little comfort in it. Meanwhile we should perhaps resign ourselves to being those uncomfortable creatures, postmodern men and women.

Notes

Chapter One

1. Ludwig Wittgenstein, *Tractatus Logico-Philosophicus* (Frankfurt: Suhrkamp Verlag, 1975), p. 7. My translation (though I have consulted the translation by D. F. Pears and B. F. McGuinness [New York: The Humanities Press, 1961]). In subsequent references to the *Tractatus* I shall use Wittgenstein's numbering system for the axioms and the subparagraphs and comments. There are seven basic axioms, each of which is followed by subnumbers indicating what Wittgenstein somewhat obscurely calls the "logical weight" of the proposition.

2. *Tractatus*, trans. by Pears and McGuinness, p. ix.

3. Some critics would point to 4.024 and claim that this shows Wittgenstein's agreement with the positivistic epistemology of the Vienna circle: "To understand a sentence *[Satz]* means to know what the case is when it is true.

"(One can also understand it, without knowing if it is true.)

"One understands it, when one understands its components." It seems to me that this comment is an elucidation of Wittgenstein's correspondence theory of truth as well as a recognition that, in Frege's terms, one can understand the *sense* of a proposition (through its simple parts) without knowing if it refers to anything that is the case (without understanding its *Bedeutung*).

4. *Wittgenstein's Vienna* (New York: Simon and Schuster, 1973). This is a key book for an understanding of the milieu in which Wittgenstein grew up.

5. Max Black may overstate his case in his *A Companion to Wittgenstein's Tractatus* (Cambridge: Cambridge University Press, 1964), p. 4, but he is surely right that it is the *Tractatus* that marks the beginning of the "linguistic turn" in modern philosophy.

6. Cf. Ludwig Wittgenstein, *Notebooks, 1914-1916*, trans. G. E. M. Anscombe (New York and Evanston: Harper and Row, 1969), p. 39:

"My *whole* task consists in explaining the nature of the proposition. That is to say, in giving the nature of all facts, whose picture the proposition *is*.

"In giving the nature of all being.

"(And here being does not stand for existence—in that case it would be nonsensical.)"

So much for the complaint that Wittgenstein gives no examples. Would it be misleading to see here an analogous concern with Heidegger's interest in Being, as opposed to mere existent beings? In this respect, see Arne Naess, *Four Modern Philosophers*, trans. Alastair Hannay (Chicago: University of Chicago Press, 1968), pp. 167-71.

7. Ludwig Wittgenstein, *Philosophical Investigations*, 3d ed., trans. G. E. M. Anscombe (New York: Macmillan 1958), no. 97. Note that the reference is to a specific

section of the *Tractatus* that Wittgenstein had in mind in writing the *Investigations*. All future references to the *Philosophical Investigations* will note the section or page.

8. *Notebooks, 1914-1916*, p. 85.

9. Jacques Bouveresse has, in the past decade, written three good works of commentary on Wittgenstein in French: *La Parole malheureuse* (1971), *Wittgenstein: La Rime et la raison* (1973), and *Le Mythe de l'intériorité, expérience, signification et langage privé chez Wittgenstein* (1976), all published in Paris by Les Editions de Minuit. And Jean-François Lyotard's *La Condition Postmoderne* (Paris: Les Editions de Minuit, 1979), a work whose very title is significant of a shift in French thinking, makes the notion of language games a central part of his analysis of the way in which societies legitimate themselves.

10. *The Blue and Brown Books, Preliminary Studies for the Philosophical Investigations*, were dictated to students in 1933-34 and 1934-35. To my mind *The Blue Book* is the best starting point for an introduction to Wittgenstein's later thought.

11. Fundamental studies in this respect are Johan Huizinga's *Homo Ludens* (Boston: Beacon Press, 1955), and Roger Caillois's *Les Jeux et les hommes* (Paris: Gallimard, 1958). A work inspired by Heidegger's thought, Eugen Fink's *Spiel als Weltsymbol* (Stuttgart: Kohlhammer, 1960), should also be noted.

12. Ludwig Wittgenstein, *Philosophische Grammatik* (Frankfurt: Suhrkamp Verlag, 1973), p. 63. My translation.

13. J. L. Austin, *Philosophical Papers*, ed. J. O. Urmson and G. J. Warnock (Oxford: The Clarendon Press, 1961), p. 221.

14. *Philosophische Grammatik*, p. 59.

15. Owen Wister, *The Virginian, A Horseman of the Plains* (New York: Grosset and Dunlap, 1911), p. 30. First published in 1902.

16. In his *Companion to the Philosophical Investigations* (Ithaca: Cornell University Press, 1977), Garth Hallet offers the following useful summary on this point: "Just as no mental equivalent of the whole [mathematical] series exists in the mind of one who understands a series . . . and no inner surrogate of the person meant occurs in the mind of one who means him, . . . so no logical shadow assures a target for the thought of one who asserts, commands, negates, expects, and so on. . . . The connection is . . . made in and by language . . . , not by a mere act of the mind" (p. 463).

17. Denying that Wittgenstein says that there can be no private language, Stanley Cavell explores the fear of solipsism in these terms: "So what is the point of 'trying' to 'imagine' a 'language' which 'another person' 'cannot' 'understand'? Evidentally, the effort is to illuminate something about the publicness of language, something about the *depth* to which language is agreed in. I would like to say: its point is to release the fantasy expressed in the denial that language is something essentially shared." And: "So the fantasy of a private language, underlying the wish to deny the publicness of language, turns out, so far, to be a fantasy, or fear, either of inexpressiveness, one in which I am not merely unknown, but in which I am powerless to make myself known; or one in which what I express is beyond my control"(In *The Claim of Reason* [New York: Oxford University Press, 1979], p. 344 and p. 351). As we shall see, these comments point to a possible typology of postmodern fiction.

18. This view, drawing increasingly on Wittgenstein, has been put forth, for example, in his most recent work by the philosopher and historian of science Thomas S. Kuhn. I have explicitly in mind a lecture that he gave at the University of Missouri in 1978; I

wish to thank him here for help he gave in subsequent correspondence on the question of the growth of knowledge.

19. Wittgenstein's views on the foundation of mathematics are hardly accepted by all today, though his argument for "conventionalism" is one of the most developed in contemporary thought. See "Foundations of Mathematics," *The Encyclopedia of Philosophy*, ed. Paul Edwards (New York: The Free Press, 1967), vol. 5. pp. 200-201. Also, Willard Von Orman Quine, *From a Logical Point of View*, 2nd ed. (Cambridge: Harvard University Press, 1980), pp. 13-19. Though not specifically on Wittgenstein, Quine's work offers a clear introduction to the problems characterizing modern thought about the foundations of mathematics.

20. Ludwig Wittgenstein, *On Certainty*, trans. Denis Paul and G. E. M. Anscombe (New York: Harper and Row, 1972), no. 4. The page numbers for subsequent citations from this work, and from the other works quoted here, after their first citation, will be found in the text.

21. *Philosophical Papers*, p. 130.

22. Ludwig Wittgenstein, "Bemerkungen über Frazers *The Golden Bough*," *Synthese* 17 (1967):234. My translation.

Chapter Two

1. Martin Heidegger, *The Question of Being*, trans. with an introduction by William Kluback and Jean T. Wilde (New Haven: College and University Press, 1958), p. 71. This is a translation of *Zur Seinsfrage*, an essay originally published as *Uber "Die Linie,"* in 1955.

2. Martin Heidegger, *Being and Time*, trans. John Macquarrie and Edward Robinson (New York: Harper and Row, 1962), p. 444. In *Sein und Zeit*, 12th, unchanged, ed. (Tubingen: Max Niemeyer Verlag, 1972), p. 391. All future references to *Being and Time* will be given in the text. Heidegger makes a distinction between the science of history and the more fundamental *Geschichte*. One of the best interpreters of this aspect of Heidegger's thought, David Hoy, asks the following questions about this distinction: "The question must also be raised whether it really makes sense to 'ground' historical science in historical existence, as Heidegger—following Dilthey and Yorck—attempts to do. Heidegger distinguishes between history as science *(Historie)* and history as what actually happens *(Geschichte)*. In *Being and Time* he introduces a new notion, that of human historicity *(Geschichtlichkeit)*. The idea that human existence is a temporal happening *(Geschehen)* that is aware of itself as happening and changing, as stretching along between birth and death, has the status of a condition for the possibility of *Geschichte* and *Historie*. Is this ontological grounding of history in historicity necessary, and will it actually have important consequences for historiography?" Hoy answers this question rather negatively. See "History, Historicity, and Historiography in *Being and Time*," in *Heidegger and Modern Philosophy*, ed. Michael Murray (New York: Yale University Press, 1978), p. 338.

3. Martin Heidegger, *Der Satz vom Grund* (Pfullingen: Verlag Günther Neske, 1957), p. 83. My translation.

4. See Hermann Schweppenhäuser, "Studien über die Heideggersche Sprachtheorie," *Archiv für Philosophie*, vols. 7 and 8 (1957 and 1958), pp. 279-324, and pp. 116-44.

5. Maurice Merleau-Ponty, *Signes* (Paris: Gallimard, 1960), pp. 105-6.

6. Heidegger plays on the possible meanings of *Lichtung*, literally a "clearing," as in the woods, in such formulations as: "Das Stehen in der Lichtung des Seins nenne ich die Eksistenz des Menschen." This gives in English: "Standing in the lighting/clearing of Being I call the existence of man." The French translator offers: "Se tenir dans l'éclaircie de l'Etre, c'est ce que j'appelle l'ek-sistence de l'homme." From the bilingual edition of Martin Heidegger, *Lettre sur l'humanisme*, trans. Roger Munier (Paris: Aubier, Montaigne, 1964), pp. 56-57.

7. *An Introduction to Metaphysics* is in many ways a companion piece to "The Origin of the Work of Art." It proposes the same notion that poetry is the primordial language that a people speaks. And it also sets forth the philological underpinnings of Heidegger's later thought. For example, here Heidegger maintains that "*Physis* and *logos* are the same. *Logos* characterizes being in a new and yet old respect: that which is, which stands straight and distinct in itself, is at the same time gathered togetherness in itself and by itself, and maintains itself in such togetherness." From *An Introduction to Metaphysics*, trans. Ralph Manheim (Garden City, N.Y.: Anchor Books, 1961), p. 110.

8. Philip Wheelwright, *Heraclitus* (New York: Atheneum, 1964), p. 22.

9. Martin Heidegger, *Der Ursprung des Kunstwerkes* (Stuttgart: Philipp Reclam, 1960), p. 18.

10. Martin Heidegger, "The Origin of the Work of Art," in *Poetry, Language, Thought*, trans. Albert Hofstadter (New York: Harper and Row, 1971), pp. 33–34. Translation slightly changed.

11. See the essays by Jacques Derrida in *Marges de la Philosophie* (Paris: Les Editions de Minuit, 1972), especially "La Différance" and "Ousia et grammé, note sur une note de Sein und Zeit."

12. Cf: Joseph N. Riddel, "From Heidegger to Derrida to Chance: Doubling and (Poetic) Language," in *Martin Heidegger and the Question of Literature*, ed. William V. Spanos (Bloomington: Indiana University Press, 1979), p. 241.

13. This lecture, "What Are Poets For?" was first given in 1946. It appears in *Poetry, Language, Thought*, p. 91. The earliest lecture in the *Erläuterungen zu Holderlins Dichtung*, "Hölderlin und Das Wesen der Dichtung," was given in Rome in 1936.

14. Martin Heidegger, *Erläuterungen zu Hölderlins Dichtung*, 4th, expanded, ed. (Frankfurt: Vittorio Klostermann, 1971), p. 76. My translation.

15. Martin Heidegger, "Holderlin and the Essence of Poetry," in *Existence and Being*, introduction by Werner Brock (Chicago: Henry Regnery, 1949), p. 271.

16. Martin Heidegger, *Unterwegs zur Sprache* (Pfullingen: Verlag Günter Neske, 1975), p. 181.

17. Ibid., p. 12.

18. *Erläuterungen zu Hölderlins Dichtung*, p. 69. My translation.

19. See *Was ist Metaphysik*, 11th, revised, ed. (Frankfurt: Vittorio Klostermann, 1975), p. 52.

20. *Erläuterungen zu Hölderlins Dichtung*, p. 76.

21. *Unterwegs zur Sprache*, p. 259.

22. Martin Heidegger, *On the Way to Language*, trans. Peter D. Hertz (New York: Harper and Row, 1971), p. 126.

23. Maurice Blanchot, *L'Entretien infini* (Paris: Gallimard, 1969), p. 169.

24. Wheelwright, *Heraclitus*, no. 27, p. 29.

25. *On the Way to Language*, p. 106. Translation somewhat changed.

26. George Steiner, *Martin Heidegger* (New York: Viking Press, 1978), p. 155.
27. Martin Heidegger, *What Is Called Thinking?*, trans. J. Glenn Gray (New York: Harper and Row, 1972), p. 119.
28. Ibid., p. 105.
29. G. S. Kirk, *Heraclitus, The Cosmic Fragments* (Cambridge: Cambridge University Press, 1954), pp. xiii and 5.
30. Martin Heidegger, *Der Satz vom Grund* (Pfullingen: Verlag Günter Neske, 1958), p. 188. My translation.

Chapter Three

1. Saussure called for the development of a science that he named semiology. This science would study the life of signs as they exist in the heart of social reality. Saussure's science of signs has developed, though it is often now called semiotics. Semiotics is an old term, one used by Locke and later by the American philosopher Pierce. In contemporary usage semiotics and semiology can usually be taken as synonyms for the science of signs that Saussure once called for.
2. Frederic Nietzsche, *Beyond Good and Evil*, trans. Helen Zimmern, in *The Philosophy of Nietzsche* (New York: The Modern Library, 1954), p. 402.
3. Saussure's Copernican laurelling comes from R. H. Robins, *A Short History of Linguistics*, 2nd ed. (London: Longmans, Green, 1969), p. 200; Chomsky is made a more recent laureate by, among others, Frederick J. Newmayer, *Linguistic Theory in America* (New York: Academic Press, 1981), p. 19.
4. Ferdinand de Saussure, *Cours de linguistique générale*, ed. Tullio de Mauro (Paris: Payot, 1978), p. 16. My translation.
5. See, for example, Louis-Jean Calvet, *Pour et contre Saussure* (Paris: Payot, 1975). Calvet sees the notion of value as the central concept from which the rest of the organization of Saussure's thought logically follows. He is especially harsh on the present edition of the *Cours*. In English one can consult Jonathan Culler's *Ferdinand de Saussure* (New York: Penguin Modern Masters, 1977). Culler stresses that the first principle of Saussure's theory of language is the arbitrary nature of the sign. To each his own Saussure.
6. Louis Hjelmslev, *Prolegomena to a Theory of Language*, trans. Francis J. Whitfield (Madison: University of Wisconsin Press, 1963), p. 9.
7. In the *Cours* Saussure distinguishes between other sciences and linguistics by noting that the linguist must create the very object of his science by the choice of his way of looking at it: "Bien loin que l'objet précède le point de vue, on dirait que c'est le point de vue qui crée l'objet" (p. 23). Of course, the contemporary physicist might say the same thing.
8. See Jacques Derrida, "La différance," *Marges de la Philosophie* (Paris: Les Editions de Minuit, 1972), pp. 16-17; or in a different vein, cf. the notion of self as trace or writing in his essay on Freud, "La scène de l'écriture," *L'Ecriture et la différence* (Paris: Editions du Seuil, 1967). The question of the metaphysical status of the subject occurs throughout Derrida's work.
9. I shall hide my antipathy for Chomsky in this note: he is a metaphysical thinker who often seems rather naïve when he offers philosophical speculations about the nature of language. The search for the secret essence of language—his universal grammar—is a kind of metaphysical project that strikes me as having no grounding in any kind of

scientific logic. See Noam Chomsky, *Reflections on Language* (New York: Pantheon, 1975).

10. See the introduction to the critical edition of the *Cours* by Tullio de Mauro; or his *Une Introduction à la sémantique*, trans. L.-J. Calvet (Paris: Payot, 1969), pp. 166-67.

11. Claude Lévi-Strauss, *Tristes Tropiques* (Paris: Collection 10/18, 1962), pp. 42-44.

12. Jacques Derrida, *De la grammatologie* (Paris: Les Editions de Minuit, 1967), pp. 24-25. Derrida is referring to Roman Jakobson, *Essais de linguistique générale*, trans. Nicolas Ruwet (Paris: Les Editions de Minuit, 1963), p. 162.

13. Guilio C. Lepschy, *Intorno a Saussure* (Turin: Stampatori Editore, 1979), p. 72.

14. Saussure, like Locke, has also been criticized by a major, later thinker. In his "Nature du signe linguistique" (in *Problèmes de linguistique générale* [Paris: Gallimard, 1966]), Emile Benveniste claims that Saussure should have defined the relation between the signified and the signifier as a necessary one, not an arbitrary one. It seems to me that there is something of a confusion on Benveniste's part. He is speaking of the way a speaker perceives the relationship. Benveniste is at best making a psychological statement or analysis. This critique is really at cross-purposes with linguistic analysis or with an ontological description of language. His critique might suggest, however, that the distinction of signifier and signified is not necessarily a very economical one. And some linguists and semioticians today prefer to speak, instead of a signifier and a signified, of a unitary sign function.

15. Frank Lentricchia, *After the New Criticism* (Chicago: University of Chicago Press, 1980), p. 119.

16. Saussure often appears to use "word" and "sign" as equivalent terms, though there is nothing within his system of differential meanings that would justify this. If later linguistics have come to correct this equivocation by speaking of "morphemes," or units of meaning that can be smaller than words, other critics of Saussure would claim that the measurable signifier is often larger than a single word.

17. Jonathan Culler, "Jacques Derrida," in *Structuralism and Since*, ed. John Sturrock (New York: Oxford University Press, 1979), p. 166.

18. Johan Huizinga, *Homo Ludens* (Boston: Beacon Press, 1955), p. 5.

19. Jacques Derrida, *Positions* (Paris: Les Editions de Minuit, 1972), p. 15. My translation.

20. My paraphrase of Derrida's lines on the artist Titus-Carmel: "je me serai contenté de me servir de quelques mots, d'en proposer l'utilité ou la formalité économique d'autres, les mots *cartouche*, par exemple, *paradigme, article, duction, contingent*, et pas mal d'autres, eux-mêmes aléatoires *et* inévitables, qui formeront à leur tour une série parallèle, la fatalité d'un nouvel idiome." In "Cartouches," *La Vérité en Peinture* (Paris: Flammarion, 1978), p. 230.

21. Derrida, *L'Ecriture et la différence*, p. 411. My translation.

22. Derrida, *De la grammatologie*, pp. 24-25.

23. Derrida, *Of Grammatology*, trans. Gayatri C. Spivak (Baltimore: The Johns Hopkins University Press, 1974), p. 73.

24. A bibliography of such a subject would of course be immense. But an especially revealing instance of such a privileging of a communication model is to be found in John Searle's critique of Chomsky. One of the leading philosophers of the ordinary-language persuasion, Searle condemns Chomsky precisely because the linguist's formal models do

not account for the essence of language—communication. See "Chomsky's Revolution in Linguistics," *The New York Review of Books,* 29 June 1972, pp. 16-24.
25. Derrida, *Marges,* p. 11. My translation.
26. Derrida, *L'Ecriture et la différence,* p. 21.
27. Ibid., p. 45.
28. Derrida, *De la grammatologie,* p. 63.
29. Derrida, *Of Grammatology,* p. 71. Translation slightly changed.
30. Derrida, *L'Ecriture et la différence,* p. 423. My translation.

Chapter Four

1. Dieter Wellershoff, *Ein Gedicht von der Freiheit* (Frankfurt: Fischer Taschenbuch Verlag, 1977), p. 7.
2. Though I have all of Robbe-Grillet's critical essays and discourses in mind, see in particular *Pour un nouveau roman* (Paris: Gallimard, Collection Idées, 1963), p. 51.
3. Roquentin's ideas obviously have their roots in Leibniz and perhaps even more in Kant's considerations about necessary truths. But I think I am correct in maintaining that in Kant thought, or the mind, is the locus where synthetic a priori statements are formed, not language. Mind supplies the a priori connections to things. Kant did not want language to muddle up his picture of how we represent reality.
4. Jean-Paul Sartre, *Situations I* (Paris: Gallimard, 1947), p. 58. My translation. This review was written in 1939.
5. Vladimir Nabokov, *Despair* (New York: Simon and Schuster, Pocket Books, 1968), p. 13. According to Nabokov's Introduction, in translating this work he revised it considerably.
6. Descartes, *The Philosophical Works of Descartes,* vol. I, trans. Elizabeth Haldane and G. R. T. Ross (New York: Dover Publications, 1955), p. 150.
7. Samuel Beckett, *Molloy,* trans. Patrick Bowles with the author, in *Three Novels by Samuel Beckett* (New York: Grove Press, 1965), p. 31.
8. Hugh Kenner, *Samuel Beckett,* new edition (Berkeley: University of California Press, 1968), p. 59.
9. This according to Linda Ben-Zvi, who has convincingly argued for the influence on Beckett of Fritz Mauthner and his *Beiträge zu einer Kritik der Sprache.* The Viennese thinker Mauthner was probably also a significant influence on Wittgenstein, or, perhaps more precisely, one might argue that Wittgenstein was influenced by the kinds of questions about language prevalent in the Viennese milieu that gave shape to Mauthner's thought. One aspect of this thought was that language cannot express the content of thought because the very act of verbalizing destroys the uniqueness of thought. See Ben-Zvi, "Samuel Beckett, Fritz Mauthner, and the Limits of Language," *PMLA* 95, no. 2 (March, 1980): pp. 183-200. Cf. William M. Johnston, *The Austrian Mind* (Berkeley: University of California Press, 1972).
10. Samuel Beckett, *Watt* (New York: Grove Press, 1959), p. 77.
11. Alain Robbe-Grillet, *Two Novels,* trans. Richard Howard (New York: Grove Press, 1965), p. 137.
12. One's historical perspective on self-representation can be as broad as the history of the novel or the history of Western literature. For example, Robert Alter would delineate a tradition that runs from Cervantes to Nabokov—with a noticeable lapse in the nineteenth

century. Or, in his structuralist study of the technique of *mise en abyme* Lucien Dällenbach offers examples that run the gamut from *The Golden Ass* through the German romantics and that culminate in the practices of nearly all the so-called *nouveaux romanciers* in France today. See Alter's *Partial Magic* (Berkeley: University of California Press, 1975); Dallenbach, *Le récit spéculaire* (Paris: Editions du Seuil, 1977).

13. William Gass, *Fiction and the Figures of Life* (New York: Alfred A. Knopf, 1970), p. 60.

14. Michel Foucault, *Les mots et les choses* (Paris: Gallimard, 1966), p. 9.

15. Roland Barthes, *S/Z* (Paris: Editions du seuil, 1970).

16. Peter Handke, *Das Gewicht der Welt, Ein Journal* (November 1975—March 1977) (Frankfurt: Suhrkamp Taschenbuch, 1979), p. 32.

17. Peter Handke, *Three by Peter Handke*, trans. Michael Roloff (New York: Avon Books, 1977), p. 49.

18. Gerhard Roth, *Der Wille zur Krankheit: Roman* (Frankfurt: Suhrkamp, 1973), p. 55. My translation.

19. Helmut Eisendle, *Jenseits der Vernuft oder Gespräche über den menschlichen Verstand* (Salzburg: Reisdenz Verlag, 1976), pp. 71-72. My translation.

Chapter Five

1. William Faulkner, *Absalom, Absalom!* (New York: Modern Library, 1951), p. 303.

2. Céline, *Death on the Installment Plan*, trans. Ralph Manheim (New York: New American Library, 1966), p. 39.

3. "There is nothing frightful in us and on earth and perhaps in heaven above except what has not yet been said. We shall never be at peace until everything has been said, once and for all time; then there will be silence and one will no longer be afraid of being silent. It will be all right then." Céline, *Journey to the End of Night*, trans. John H. P. Marks (New York: New Directions, 1960), p. 325.

4. Beckett, *Three Novels*, p. 335.

5. Ludwig Wittgenstein, *Zettel*, trans. G. E. M. Anscombe (Berkeley: University of California Press, 1970), no. 61, p. 13.

6. Emile Benveniste, *Problems in General Linguistics,* trans. Mary Elizabeth Meek (Coral Gables: University of Miami Press, 1971), p. 227.

7. Julio Cortazar, *Hopscotch*, trans. Gregory Rabassa (New York: Avon Books, 1975), p. 89.

8. Michel Butor, *A Change of Heart*, trans. Jean Stewart (New York: Simon and Schuster, 1959), p. 48.

9. Carlos Fuentes, *The Death of Artemio Cruz*, trans. Sam Hileman (New York: Farrar, Strauss, and Giroux, 1964), p. 234.

10. Robert Pinget, *Passacaglia*, trans. Barbara Wright (New York: Red Dust, Inc., 1978), p. 23.

11. Ronald Sukenick, *98.6* (New York: Fiction Collective, 1975), p. 135.

12. Dieter Kühn, *Ausflüge im Fesselballon, Neufassung* (Frankfurt: Surhkamp, 1977), pp. 132-33. My translation.

13. Since I have made frequent reference to this notion of fullness or plenitude, perhaps I might do well to recall through example what I mean by it. For a clear case of language that is not fallen logos or alienated otherness, I turn to the beginning of Joyce's *Ulysses*

(New York: The Modern Library, 1934) for the description given as Daedalus-Telemachus, thinking of his dead mother, looks out from the Martello tower upon the sea. A quotation from Yeats precedes this example of the music of language that aims to be, in itself, a fullness of presence:

> Woodshadows floated silently by through the morning peace from the stairhead seaward where he gazed. Inshore and farther out the mirror of water whitened, spurned by lightshod hurrying feet. White breast of the dim sea. The twining stresses, two by two. A hand plucking the harpstrings merging from their twining chords. Wavewhite webbed words shimmering on the dim tide. (p. 11)

Joyce refuses the temporal flow that normal syntax might impose upon the flow of language, as if a kind of eternal stasis could emerge from the fragments. "Wavewhite wedded words"—which Joyce allowed to be translated into French as "vagues couplées du verbe"—enter into hymen with being, and being is in turn coupled with language in an alliterative repetition that underscores their presence one to the other. In this early chapter of *Ulysses* Joyce presents a supreme example of the modernist confidence in language as a form of music beyond time, a static rhythm, caught as an iconic presence in the mirror of the sea, the mirror of being.

14. Obviously a good bit of this analysis is inspired by Roland Barthes, especially the Barthes of *Mythologies*.

15. Manuel Puig, *Betrayed by Rita Hayworth*, trans. Suzanne Jill Levin (New York: Avon Books, 1973), p. 120.

16. Thomas Pynchon, *Gravity's Rainbow* (New York: Viking Press, 1973), p. 760.

17. Thomas Bernhard, *Watten* (Frankfurt: Suhrkamp, 1969), p. 41. My translation.

Chapter Six

1. Such is the thesis of Michel Foucault in his *Histoire de la folie* (Paris: Plon, 1961). I bring this up because of the interesting contradiction it poses. Just as much of modern literature expends energy talking about silence—Joyce's "sonorous silence"—so does much of this literature invest itself in inventing voices spoken by those who cannot speak and leave no works. Cf. Jacques Derrida, "Cogito et histoire de la folie," in *L'Ecriture et la différence* pp. 51-98.

2. Samuel Beckett, *Three Novels*, p. 181.

3. For this idea I have drawn upon the work of Heidegger's student and collaborator Eugen Fink. See his "The Oasis of Happiness: Toward an Ontology of Play," in *Game, Play, Literature,* ed. Jacques Ehrmann (Boston: Beacon Press, 1971), pp. 19-30.

4. French theorists are especially useful in broadening this understanding of play. See Roger Caillois, *Les jeux et les hommes* (Paris: Gallimard, 1958). Or various works of George Bataille, such as *L'Expérience intérieure* in *Oeuvres*, vol. 5, (Paris: Gallimard, 1973).

5. A work I found very suggestive for using the mathematics of board games to explain a number of contemporary scientific models is that by Nobel laureate Manfred Eigen and Ruthild Winkler, *Das Spiel, Naturgesetze steuern den Zufall* (Munich: Piper, 1975). Also, Heinz R. Pagels, *The Cosmic Code, Quantum Physics as the Language of Nature* (New York: Simon and Schuster, 1982).

6. In his *Horizons of Assent, Modernism, Postmodernism, and the Ironic Imagination* (Baltimore: The Johns Hopkins University Press, 1981), Alan Wilde finds acceptance to be the dominant postmodern response. Arguing (wrongly, I think) that postmodernism is essentially an American affair, he finds irony to be the key to differentiating between modernist nostalgia and postmodern acceptance of the world: "Acceptance is the key word here. Modernist irony, absolute and equivocal, expresses a resolute consciousness of different and equal possibilities so ranged as to defy solution. Postmodern irony, by contrast, is suspensive: an indecision about the meanings or relations of things is matched by a willingness to live with uncertainty, to tolerate and, in some cases, to welcome a world seen as random and multiple, even, at times absurd. . . . postmodernism has managed to establish enclaves of occasionally odd and curious pleasures . . . while continuing to acknowledge, if only covertly, the confusion that attends and surrounds them" (p. 44).

7. Jacques Derrida, "Structure, Sign and Play," in *The Structuralist Controversy*, ed. Richard Macksey and Eugenio Donato (Baltimore: The Johns Hopkins University Press, 1972), p. 260.

8. Jorges Luis Borges, *Labyrinths, Selected Stories and Other Writings*, ed. Donald A. Yates and James E. Irby (New York: New Directions, 1964), p. 8.

9. Vladimir Nabokov, *The Defense*, trans. Michael Scammell in collaboration with the author (New York: G. P. Putnam, Perigee Books, 1980), p. 8.

10. Vladimir Nabokov, *Transparent Things* (New York: Fawcett Publications, 1974), p. 28.

11. With his *Cent mille milliards de poèmes* Raymond Queneau offered an aleatory text that has an upper mathematical limit for readings, and in some ways this is the most interesting conceptual experiment in giving the reader a chance to play actively with reading possibilities. Queneau wrote ten sonnets, each having fourteen lines that are complete units of meaning. He then placed the sonnets together sequentially, the lines apart so that each could be turned individually and the lines could thus be combined among themselves. This allows the reader to combine any lines from any of the ten sonnets, giving him the mathematical possibility of 10^{14} sonnets, or one hundred thousand billion poems. The mind must strain a bit when beholding this little book, with its strange format, to realize that one could read this book twenty-four hours a day for a lifetime and never exhaust it. Yet there is a finite number of possibilities for the combinatory system as determined by the binding that holds the lines in place on the left.

12. Cortazar, *Hopscotch*, p. 383.

13. Derrida, *L'Ecriture et la différence*, pp. 345-358.

14. Influenced by but independent of Heidegger, Hans-Georg Gadamer has been one of the major thinkers to use game models to describe the ontology of the art work. See his "Die Ontologie des Kunstwerks und ihre hermeneutische Bedeutung" in *Wahrheit und Methode* (Tubingen: J. C. B. Mohr (Paul Siebeck), 1972), pp. 97-161.

15. Philippe Sollers, *Drame* (Paris: Editions du Seuil, 1965), p. 14. My translation.

16. Roland Barthes, *Images-Music-Text*, trans. Stephen Heath (New York: Hill and Wang, 1977), p. 158. The complete quotation shows, I think, how much Barthes was influenced by Jacques Derrida for his views of intertextual play (thought the influence was reciprocal): "The Text . . . practices the infinite deferment of the signified, is dilatory; its field is that of the signifier and the signifier must not be conceived of as 'the first stage of meaning', its material vestibule, but, in complete opposition to this, as its

deferred action. Similarly, the *infinity* of the signifier refers not to some idea of the ineffable (the unnamable signified) but to that of *playing;* the generation of the perpetual signifier (after the fashion of a perpetual calendar) in the field of the text (better, of which the text is the field) is realized not according to an organic progress of maturation or a hermeneutic course of deepening investigation, but, rather, according to a serial movement of disconnections, overlappings, variations.''

17. Cf. Peter Horst Neumann, "Das Eigene und das Fremde. Uber die Wünschbarkeit einer Theorie des Zitierens," *Akzente,* 4 (August 1980): pp. 292-305.

18. Manfred Durzek, "Zitat and Montage im deutschen Roman der Gegenwart," *Die deutsche Literatur der Gegenwart,* ed. Manfred Durzek, 3d ed. (Stuttgart: Philippp Reclam, 1976), p. 233.

19. The varieties of intertextual play in contemporary German-language fiction are rich and obviously deserve a much greater development than space allows in this chapter. And of course the same can be said for Latin American fiction. I shall return to this question in the following chapter. In this context, however, I should like to call attention to one other novel and the type of intertextuality it proposes, the novel by the Austrian Helmut Eisendle, *Exil oder Der braune Salon, Ein Unterhaltungsroman* (Salzburg: Residenz Verlag, 1977). Eisendle ties together speech and play in this work in which four characters meet to play billiards and give vent to various discourses: Marxism, Freud, psychology, physiology, phrenology, Wittgenstein, among others. These discourses circulate like billiard balls in a novel in which one of the characters recalls that all this is like what takes place in a novel called *Exil oder Der braune Salon,* etc. Intertextuality logically becomes self-quotation in a fiction that recognizes that it mirrors itself and that its characters exist only as *Sprache und Spiel*—language and game—which is also the case for all representations of the real, such as Marxism, psychology, physiology, etc. Eisendle's works should be translated.

20. Hugh Kenner, *The Counterfeiters, An Historical Comedy* (Garden City, N.Y.: Anchor Books, 1973), p. xiii. I note that this self-proclaimed comedy was first published by Indiana University Press.

21. Paul Medcalf, *Genoa, A Telling of Wonders* (Penland, N.C.: The Jargon Society, 1973), p. 83.

Chapter Seven

1. Cf. Roland Barthes, *La Chambre claire* (Paris: Gallimard, 1980). I speak as one who, in his role as teacher, labors to help students acquire a historical sense. Perhaps this has always been a difficult acquisition, one fundamentally at odds with the naive world view that is probably mythic in its fundamental structure. Heidegger's writings, particularly *Being and Time,* should be of help here, since he attempts to show that historicity is constitutive of Dasein. Inauthentic Dasein can lose its historicity and, in addition, according to Heidegger, a people with no written tradition can keep a more profound openness to historicity than a people that produce great quantities of written history. Perhaps. But I think that, by historicity, Heidegger means, a preserving of the past in the present, the guarding of a tradition that has no historical alterity. This notion seems to me fundamentally ahistorical, in spite of Heidegger's intention. One does not get around Hegel very easily.

2. I recently read a book review by Guy Davenport in which he claims Joyce was,

in *Ulysses,* the first to describe a photograph in a novel. I do not know if this is true or not, but if it is even nearly true, then it must be said that fiction took a fairly long time to take cognizance of the existence of photographic discourses. It seems to me that this is an area for research, not only for the way literature has come to appropriate or defend itself against photography, but concerning the integration of the photograph physically into books as part of the total discourse. There has been a great deal of experimentation of late in this respect, but, as I said, it is very difficult to get hold of these experimental books. For a description of some of this work, see Richard Kostelanetz, "New Fiction in American," in *Surfiction,* ed. Raymond Federman (Chicago: Swallow Press, 1975), pp. 85-100.

3. Peter O. Chotjewitz, *Roman, Ein Einpassungsmuster,* with photographs by Gunter Rambow (Darmstadt: Melzer, 1968).

4. I stress the word "theodicy," for Hegel was quite aware, unlike many lesser historical thinkers, that he was setting out to justify creation: "Our mode of treating the subject is, in this aspect, a Theodicaea,—a justification of the ways of God—which Leibnitz attempted metaphysically, in his method, *i.e.* in indefinite abstract categories,— so that the ill that is found in the World may be comprehended, and the thinking Spirit reconciled with the fact of the existence of evil. Indeed, nowhere is such a harmonising view more pressingly demanded than in Universal History; and it can be attained only by recognizing the *positive* existence, in which that negative element is a subordinate, and vanquished nullity. On the one hand, the ultimate design of the World must be perceived; and, on the other hand, the fact that this design has been actually realised in it, and that evil has not been able permanently to assert a competing position." From *The Philosophy of History,* trans. J. Sibree, in *Hegel, Selections,* ed. Jacob Loewenberg (New York: Charles Scribners Sons, 1957), p. 357. The question one must then ask is, if every narrative history (and are there histories that do not contain some narrative element?) is constructed in function of some telos, can history be anything other than some form of theodicy? See Hayden White, "The Value of Narrativity in the Representation of Reality," *Critical Inquiry* 7, no. 1 (Autumn 1980):5-28.

5. For purposes of example, and for these purposes only, I take the expression "the triumph of Liberty" from Clinton Rossiter's *The First American Revolution,* part of *Seedtime of the Republic* (New York: Harcourt, Brace and World, 1953). I note the germination metaphor of the second part of the title, which parallels the Hegelian notion of the development of the potentiality contained within essence or logos. Professor Rossiter's book exemplifies a kind of history that is Hegelian in all but name, though written, as was frequently the case in the fifties, as a theodicy whose Spirit is the Republic and Liberty. Every element in colonial history—slavery, puritanical repression, abuse of women and Indians—finds its justification in the telos of that history, which is the triumph of the Liberty that the Republic now embodies. This history is a great symphony orchestrated in time, as it were, which one can fault only for its lack of self-consciousness, as when it portrays the American essence unfolding according to its potentiality in the following type of tautology: "The most powerful single force for freedom in early America was the devotion to liberty in the colonial mind" (p. 191). I invite the reader to look for the Hegelian scaffolding in the next work of history he or she reads (or writes).

6. Wittgenstein's thoughts on history can be gleaned from various places in his works, but they are best spelled out in "Bemerkungen über Frazers *The Golden Bough*" that Rush Rhees published in *Synthese,* no. 17 (1967):233-53.

7. Jean-Paul Sartre, *Nausea*, trans. Lloyd Alexander (New York: New Directions, 1964), pp. 95-96.

8. Jean-François Lyotard, *La Condition Postmoderne* (Paris: Les Editions de Minuit, 1979).

9. Grass's view of history as comic repetition takes a somewhat different twist in his later *Das Treffen in Telgte* (1979) in which a (fictitious) meeting of (real) seventeenth-century poets is described in terms of a contemporary writers' conference whose main subject is the political role of the writer in the Thirty Years-Cold War. This is a quite successful allegory that suggests Grass sees certain comic limitations to the ethical claims that mere writers can make in a world given over to rape and plunder as its first order of business.

10. Octavio Paz, *The Children of Mire*, trans. Rachel Phillips (Cambridge: Harvard University Press, 1974), p. 110.

11. Mario Vargas Llosa, *García Marquez: Historia de un deicidio* (Barcelona: Barral Editores, 1971).

12. In a different perspective, one that Derrida has pursued in *Of Grammatology*, one could consider how Lévi-Strauss sees history as a product of writing: there is no history without writing to consign it. For these thoughts and others concerning peoples with and without history, see George Charbonnier, *Entretiens avec Lévi-Strauss* (Paris: Editions 10/18, 1969; First published by Plon in 1961).

13. Lepschy, *Intorno a Saussure*, pp. 30-31. My translation.

14. This view opposes, I think, that of Foucault and other thinkers for whom their brand of structuralism means that all history is archaeology, a recovery of the lost strata of past synchronous systems. I shall address myself to this question in more detail in this book's Afterword.

15. Frederic Tuten, *The Adventures of Mao on The Long March* (New York: The Citadel Press, 1971), p. 12. There is something rather Borgesian about this note, I think.

16. Claude Simon, *Orion aveugle* (Geneva: Albert Skira, 1970). This quotation is from the opening handwritten, unnumbered pages, as is the next quotation. My translation.

17. Claude Simon, *The Battle of Pharsalus* trans. Richard Howard (New York: George Braziller, 1971), p. 128.

Index

Addison, Joseph, 1, 159
Aristotle, 12, 36, 39, 55, 58, 64, 71, 190, 193, 194
Augustine, 24, 52, 71, 207
Austin, J. L., 23, 34, 135

Balzac, Honoré de, 95, 188, 217
Barth, John, 107, 113, 176, 211-13, 214, 215; "The Literature of Exhaustion," 211; *The Sot-Weed Factor*, 113, 215
Barthelme, Donald, 119, 142, 185; *City Life*, 150; *Come Back, Dr. Caligari*, 149, 150; *The Dead Father*, 149
Barthes, Roland, 69, 92, 143, 183-84; *La Chambre claire*, 191; *Fragments of an Amorous Discourse*, 119; *S/Z*, 1, 113
Beckett, Samuel, 16, 110, 117, 118, 157, 171, 180, 189, 199; and the autonomy of language, 102-8, 112-13; and voice, 128-34, 138, 143, 145, 154. Works: *Malone Dies*, 106, 129, 156; *Mercier and Camier*, 106; *Molloy*, 102-3, 106-7, 129; *Murphy*, 106; *The Unnamable*, 106, 128-32, 153; *Waiting for Godot*, 62; *Watt*, 102, 103-5, 106, 107
Benveniste, Emile, 135-36, 142
Berkeley, George, 3, 4
Bernhard, Thomas, 114, 154
Borges, Jorge Luis, 164-65, 169, 170, 174, 186-87, 206, 211; and the autonomy of language, 83, 112, 208; and imaginary fictions, 85, 117, 172; and Nabokov, 98, 99; and the role of play, 167-68, 179. Works: *Death and the Compass*, 164; *El Aleph*, 162; *Ficciones*, 160; "The House of

Asterion," 162; "Library of Babel," 163-64; "The Lottery in Babylon," 163; "A New Refutation of Time," 141; "Pierre Menard, Author of the *Quijote*," 160-61, 212-14; "Tlön, Uqbar, Orbis Tertius," 161-62
Brautigan, Richard, 152
Burroughs, William, 171, 173
Butor, Michel, 140; *A Change of Heart*, 137-38, 142

Camus, Albert, 172, 200
Céline, Louis-Ferdinand, 147, 169; and voice, 121, 124-28, 133, 136, 140, 153; *Death on the Installment Plan*, 121, 125-26; *Journey to the End of Night*, 125
Cervantes, Miguel de: *Don Quijote*, 106, 160, 161, 212-14
Chomsky, Noam, 64, 66, 69, 70
Chotjewitz, Peter, 184, 192-93
Coover, Robert, 152; *The Public Burning*, 185; *The Universal Baseball Association*, 174-76
Cortázar, Julio, 107, 112, 117, 134; *Hopscotch*, 136, 168-73, 187, 209

Dante, 107, 113, 189
Derrida, Jacques, 6, 81-90, 91, 107, 114, 119, 126, 128, 143, 170, 178, 187, 205; and arche-writing, 85-87; and the doctrine of *différence*, 87-89, 101, 158, 172, 183; and Heidegger, 50, 61, 82, 85-90; and history, 82, 89-90, 195-96, 197-98, 202; and Nietzsche, 82, 85, 86; and Saussure, 63, 64, 67, 72, 76, 81-82, 83-86, 92; and Philippe

Sollers, 179, 181, 182; and *trace*, 88-90; and voice, 120, 122, 132, 135, 136, 140. Works: *L'Ecriture et la différence*, 84; *Of Grammatology*, 84, 85, 89, 182; *Positions*, 82
Descartes, René, 19, 27, 31, 80, 94, 189; and Heidegger, 38-39, 46, 58; and Nabokov, 100-101; and the self, 27, 102, 105, 116, 128
Duvert, Tony, 138

Eisendle, Helmut, 117-19
Eliot, T. S., 37, 189

Faulkner, William, 141, 214, 216; and voice, 121-25, 126-28, 133, 137, 140, 144; *Absalom, Absalom*, 121-24, 126, 217; *The Sound and the Fury*, 121, 217
Federman, Raymond, 117, 119, 170
Fellini, Federico, 148, 223
Fiction Collective, 146, 185
Flaubert, Gustave, 5, 110, 139, 188, 195; *Madame Bovary*, 3-4
Foucault, Michel, 64, 128, 161, 224-25
Frazer, Sir James George, 34, 199
Frege, Gottlob, 11, 110
Freud, Sigmund, 70, 82, 100, 115, 172
Fuentes, Carlos, 117, 134; *The Death of Artemio Cruz*, 139-43; *Terra Nostra*, 140, 143

García Márquez, Gabriel, 201, 205-10, 216
Gass, William, 107, 112
Goethe, Johann Wolfgang von, 2-3, 4, 5, 16, 46, 107
Goytisolo, Juan, 107, 134, 138, 140, 149
Grass, Günter, 200-205, 210, 216; *Cat and Mouse*, 201-2; *Danzig Trilogy*, 201; *Dog Years*, 201, 202; *The Flounder*, 203; *The Tin Drum*, 201

Handke, Peter, 147; *The Goalie's Anxiety at the Penalty Kick*, 115-16; *Short Letter, Long Farewell*, 138, 151

Hawthorne, Nathaniel, 213-14
Hegel, Georg Wilhelm Friedrich, 203, 211, 212, 226; and Heidegger, 36-38, 45-46, 49-50, 53, 54, 62, 204; and history, 188, 190-95, 198, 200, 201, 204, 205, 207, 217, 222, 227
Heidegger, Martin, 6, 8, 35-62, 91, 101, 107-8, 114, 135, 148, 149, 150, 152, 153, 154, 182; and the artwork, 45-52, 59-60; and Beckett, 62, 102, 104, 129-30, 131, 132-33; and Céline, 126, 127; and *Dasein*, 37, 39-44, 45, 46-48, 49, 51; and Derrida, 50, 61, 63, 82-83, 85-90; and Helmut Eisendle, 117-19; and Faulkner, 123, 126, 127, 128; and Günter Grass, 201-4; and Hegel, 36, 37, 38, 45-46, 49-50, 53, 54, 62; and history, 36-39, 46, 50, 53, 54, 62, 193, 195, 196, 197-98, 214-15, 221-22; and Hölderlin, 36, 45, 50, 52, 53, 55-56, 60, 128; and Husserl, 38, 41, 55; and Kant, 38, 40, 45-46; and language's relation to Being, 28, 35, 39-40, 42, 44, 45, 47, 51-58, 59, 74, 83, 92-93, 97, 108, 111, 127-28, 210, 223; and Nietzsche, 36, 38; and play, 21, 52, 54, 59-62, 79, 90, 157, 158-59, 167, 173, 179; and religious thought, 35-36, 39, 42-43, 44-45, 50, 51, 53-54, 55, 56, 59, 89; and Robbe-Grillet, 108, 109, 110, 178; and Sartre, 38, 93, 96; and Saussure, 64, 67, 71, 76, 77, 79, 81; and Claude Simon, 216, 221-22, 223; and Wittgenstein, 16, 28, 30-31, 33, 35, 36, 41, 44, 45, 47, 49, 51, 52, 55, 60, 61, 62. Works: *Being and Time*, 30-31, 35-62, 66, 92, 147, 154, 220; *Der Satz vom Grund*, 38, 61; *Identity and Difference*, 59; *An Introduction to Metaphysics*, 45; "The Nature of Language," 59; "On the Essence of Truth," 45; *On the Way to Language*, 56, 57; "The Origin of the Work of Art," 45-49, 52-53, 58, 59; *Poetry, Language, Thought*, 50-52, 55;

Ursprung, 50; "The Way to
Language," 57; "What Are Poets
For?" 52-53; *What Is Called
Thinking?*, 60-61; "Wie wenn am
Feiertage . . .," 55
Heissenbuttel, Helmut, 184
Heller, Joseph, 113, 152
Heraclitus, 38, 47, 50, 55, 58, 61, 62,
   157
Hjelmslev, Louis, 66, 85
Hölderlin, Friedrich, 36, 37, 45, 50, 52,
   53, 55, 60, 128
Homer, 58, 106, 107, 186, 214, 215
Huizinga, Johan, 21, 79
Husserl, Edmund, 31, 38, 41, 55, 93

Jakobson, Roman, 72, 84
James, Henry, 4, 5, 123
Janvier, Ludovic, 138
Johnson, Uwe, 114
Joyce, James, 4, 37, 51, 102, 107, 136,
   188; *Finnegans Wake*, 106, 172-73,
   224; *Ulysses*, 106, 186, 190, 218

Kafka, Franz, 10, 32-33, 93, 106, 113,
   115, 117, 179, 206, 207; *The Castle*,
   103; "The Penal Colony," 96, 108;
   The Trial, 172
Kant, Immanuel, 38, 40, 45-46, 80, 88,
   135, 159
Katz, Steve, 191
Kenner, Hugh, 103, 185-87
Kesey, Ken, 152
Kierkegaard, Sören, 48, 49
Kühn, Dieter, 114, 147-48

Leibniz, Gottfried von, 14, 72, 96
Lepschy, Giulio, 72, 211
Lévi-Strauss, Claude, 63, 66, 70, 82,
   172, 222
Lezama Lima, José, 172
Lichtenstein, Roy, 187, 214
Llosa, Vargos, 206, 209
Locke, John, 1, 15, 31, 64, 71, 72, 159,
   225
Luther, Martin, 39, 52, 59

Mallarmé, Stéphane, 11, 12, 37, 163,
   164, 168, 179
Marx, Karl, 70, 115, 194, 200, 206, 207
Mauro, Tullio de, 69-70, 71
Medcalf, Paul: *Genoa, A Telling of
Wonders*, 185-86, 187, 214, 215; *The
Middle Passage*, 214-15
Melville, Herman, 186, 214, 215; *Moby
Dick*, 113; *Typee*, 187
Moore, G. E., 28, 32
Musil, Robert, 115, 136

Nabokov, Vladimir, 98-101, 104, 115,
   165-68; *Ada*, 165; *Bend Sinister*, 97;
   The Defense, 165, 166; *Despair*, 98-
   101, 165; *Laughter in the Dark*, 165;
   Lolita, 97, 100, 165, 166; *Pale Fire*,
   97, 100, 101, 165, 166; *Transparent
   Things*, 97, 165, 167
New Grammarians, 63, 68
Newton, Sir Isaac, 13, 66, 114
Nietzsche, Friedrich Wilhelm, 9, 95,
   145, 158, 171-72, 225; and Derrida,
   82, 85, 86, 197; and Heidegger, 36,
   38, 197; and Saussure, 63-64, 66;
   Beyond Good and Evil, 63-64

Perec, Georges, 176
Pinget, Robert, 143-45, 173
Plato, 1, 12, 64, 85, 90, 198, 224; and
   the autonomy of the signified, 71, 72,
   75, 83, 84, 91, 199; and the
   metaphysical, 20, 36, 43, 55, 60, 159
Pope, Alexander, 186, 187
Pre-Socratics, 37, 39, 46-47, 50, 53, 87,
   197
Proust, Marcel, 6, 38, 123, 125, 136,
   188; and Beckett, 105, 106; and
   revealed essences, 5, 37, 190; and
   Sartre, 93, 96; and Claude Simon,
   216, 220, 223; *Remembrance of Things
   Past*, 106
Puig, Manuel, 151-52
Pynchon, Thomas, 113, 147, 176;
   Gravity's Rainbow, 152, 153

Queneau, Raymond, 101, 134, 176

Rilke, Rainer Maria, 36, 37, 45, 60, 106, 136
Robbe-Grillet, Alain, 93, 107, 112, 113, 149, 177, 192; and voice, 134, 138, 140, 143. Works: *For a New Novel*, 178; *In the Labyrinth*, 178-79; *Jealousy*, 108-11, 178; *Project for a Revolution in New York*, 178
Roth, Gerhard, 114-15, 116
Roth, Philip, 113, 146-47, 152
Rousseau, Jean-Jacques, 69, 82
Roussel, Raymond, 101, 176
Rulfo, Juan, 205
Russell, Bertrand, 10, 11, 13, 110

Saporta, Marc, 170-71, 173
Sarduy, Severo, 117, 192
Sarraute, Nathalie, 143
Sartre, Jean-Paul, 38, 104, 143, 172, 216, 218; *Les Chemins de la liberté*, 185; *Nausea*, 33, 93-98, 101, 124, 195, 198-200; *What Is Literature?* 97
Saussure, Ferdinand de, 6, 35, 63-90, 115, 148, 171, 182, 195; and the autonomy of language, 65-66, 70, 71, 72, 79; and Barthes, 69; and chess, 21, 78-80, 158, 165; and Chomsky, 64, 66, 69, 70; and Derrida, 63, 64, 67, 72, 76, 81-90; and diachronic linguistics, 65, 67, 68, 78, 158, 162, 197; and Hegel, 64; and Heidegger, 64, 67, 76, 77, 79, 81; and Lévi-Strauss, 63, 66, 70, 82; and Locke, 64, 71, 72; and the New Grammarians, 63; and Nietzsche, 63-64, 66; and play, 21, 77-80, 158, 159, 162, 165, 167; and representation, 70-71, 73, 83, 92; and Robbe-Grillet, 177, 179; and synchronic linguistics, 68, 78, 158, 197; and Tullio de Mauro, 69-70, 71; and voice, 126, 128, 135, 153; and Wittgenstein, 8, 15, 21, 31, 64, 69-70, 71, 76, 77, 78, 79; *Course of General Linguistics*, 64-90, 92
Schiller, Johann von, 3, 159
Schmidt, Arno, 173
Simon, Claude, 107, 117, 134, 215-23;

The Battle of Pharsalus, 216, 220-23; *The Flanders Road*, 217; *Histoire*, 216-20; *Orion aveugle*, 219; *The Palace*, 217; *The Wind*, 217
Sollers, Philippe, 117, 119, 134, 177; *Drame*, 179-82; *Nombres*, 179, 181-84, 187
Sorrentino, Gilbert, 117, 185
Sukenick, Ronald, 117, 119, 147, 149; *98.6*, 146, 185

Tuten, Frederick, 213-15

Valéry, Paul, 220, 225
Vonnegut, Kurt, 152

Wellershoff, Dieter, 93
Wiener, Oswald, 149, 184
Wittgenstein, Ludwig, 3, 6, 7, 8-34, 74, 93, 111, 113, 135, 139, 179, 182, 186; and Beckett, 16, 102, 103, 104, 105, 130-32, 133; and John Barth, 212, 215; and chess, 21, 158; and Derrida, 86, 87, 90; and Helmut Eisendle, 117, 118, 199; and essence, 11, 18-19, 20, 34, 76, 104, 195, 226-27; and García Márquez, 206, 207, 208, 210; and Heidegger, 8, 21, 30-31, 33, 35, 36, 39, 41, 44, 45, 47, 49, 51, 52, 55, 60, 61, 62, 76, 77, 79, 221; and history, 32, 34, 195, 196, 199, 215, 220; and Kafka, 32-33; and Locke, 15, 31; and logic, 10, 11-12, 13, 15, 25, 27, 35, 110, 133; and Nabokov, 100, 165, 167; and play, 19-24, 25-33, 60, 61, 77-79, 87, 131, 157, 158, 159, 161, 167-68, 174, 177, 196, 215, 220; and positivism, 8, 9, 10-11, 13, 17, 35, 126-27; and representation, 8, 9, 12, 14, 15-16, 17-18, 24, 34, 101, 112; and Bertrand Russell, 10, 11, 13; and Sartre, 96, 199; and Saussure, 8, 15, 21, 63, 64, 69-71, 76, 77-79, 197; and science, 11, 13, 18, 27, 30, 41, 66, 196; and silence, 10, 13, 16, 44, 55, 132, 153; and voice, 120, 126-27, 130, 132, 154. Works: *The Blue and the Brown*

Books, 18, 19; *Notebooks,* 15, 17; *On Certainty,* 18, 24, 28-33, 118, 161, 208; *Philosophical Grammar,* 18, 21, 24; *Philosophical Investigations,* 8, 12, 17-18, 21, 23-28, 33, 70, 92, 127, 226; *Remarks on Colour,* 18; *Tractatus,* 8-18, 19, 23, 26, 27, 32, 44, 49, 55, 63, 92, 97, 107, 114-15, 116, 126-27, 130, 131-32, 138, 147, 153, 154, 181, 196; *Zettel,* 18, 25

Woolf, Virginia, 95, 106; *To the Lighthouse,* 3-6, 9, 22

Yeats, William Butler, 37, 187